MULTILINGUALISM, LITERACY AND DYSLEXIA

This fully revised new edition provides advice on the assessment and support of bi/multilingual learners and assists practitioners in identifying the difference between literacy difficulties due to bi/multilingualism and dyslexia. An essential text for staff development, it includes innovative approaches in technology and teaching programmes beneficial to bi/multilingual learners and advice on learning additional languages. With contributions from experts from across the globe, this book will provide guidance on key themes, including:

- the assessment of bi/multilingual learners,
- the impact of dyslexia on bi/multilingualism,
- the literacy challenges facing learners from Indigenous cultures,
- the role of the SENCo in identifying children with English as an additional language and dyslexia,
- the emotional needs of learners with bi/multilingualism and dyslexia.

This book will provide guidance to anyone involved in literacy development and language learning. With the increase in international schools around the globe and the ever growing desire of parents to ensure that their children become proficient in English, this book will appeal to teachers, teaching assistants, specialists, and all other practitioners who work with bi/multilingual children.

Lindsay Peer, CBE, is an educational and chartered psychologist, international speaker, author and expert witness. Her previously published titles with Routledge include *Glue Ear*, *Dyslexia: Successful inclusion in secondary schools* and *Introduction to Dyslexia*.

Gavin Reid is an international consultant and psychologist. His previously published titles with Routledge include: *The Routledge Companion to Dyslexia*, *Assessing Children with Specific Learning Difficulties*, *Dyslexia and Inclusion*, *Addressing Difficulties in Literacy Development* and *Meeting Difficulties in Literacy Development*.

MULTILINGUALISM, LITERACY AND DYSLEXIA

Breaking down barriers for educators

Second edition

Edited by Lindsay Peer and Gavin Reid

Routledge
Taylor & Francis Group

LONDON AND NEW YORK

Second edition published 2016
by Routledge
2 Park Square, Milton Park, Abingdon, Oxon OX14 4RN

and by Routledge
711 Third Avenue, New York, NY 10017

Routledge is an imprint of the Taylor & Francis Group, an informa business

First edition published by David Fulton Publishers 2000

British Library Cataloguing in Publication Data
A catalogue record for this book is available from the British Library

Library of Congress Cataloging in Publication Data
Names: Peer, Lindsay. | Reid, Gavin, 1950- | British Dyslexia Association.
Title: Multilingualism, literacy and dyslexia : breaking down barriers for educators / edited by Lindsay Peer and Gavin Reid.
Description: Second edition. | Milton Park, Abingdon, Oxon ; New York, NY : Routledge, 2016.
Identifiers: LCCN 2015039809| ISBN 9781138898639 (hardback : alk. paper) | ISBN 9781138898646 (pbk. : alk. paper) | ISBN 9781315708478 (ebook)
Subjects: LCSH: Multilingualism in children--Congresses. | Dyslexic children--Education--Congresses. | Literacy--Congresses. | Dyslexia--Congresses.
Classification: LCC LC4708.5 .M85 2016 | DDC 371.91/44--dc23
LC record available at http://lccn.loc.gov/2015039809

ISBN: 978-1-138-89863-9 (hbk)
ISBN: 978-1-138-89864-6 (pbk)
ISBN: 978-1-315-70847-8 (ebk)

Typeset in Bembo
by Saxon Graphics Ltd, Derby
Printed by Ashford Colour Press Ltd.

CONTENTS

EDITORS

Lindsay Peer CBE is an educational and chartered psychologist, international speaker, author and expert witness; Lindsay is widely recognised as an expert in the range of specific learning difficulties, special educational needs and mainstream education. In 2002 she was appointed CBE for services to education and dyslexia. In 2011 she was awarded the Outstanding Lifetime Academic Achievement Award by the British Dyslexia Association (BDA). She is Patron of GroOops, a charity dedicated to creating an emotionally healthy dyslexia-aware world. She has lectured extensively as a keynote speaker internationally since the late 1980s and advises governments, trade unions, policy makers, lawyers, adults, schools, psychologists, therapists and parents. She is an Associate Fellow and Chartered Scientist of the British Psychological Society and a Fellow of both the International Academy of Research in Learning Disabilities and the Royal Society of Arts. She is a member of the Association of Child Psychologists in Private Practice and of the Association for Child and Adolescent Mental Health (ACAMH). She is registered to practise with the UK Health and Care Professions Council (HCPC). She has been a keynote speaker in the UK, the USA, India, Sweden, Belgium, Finland, Israel, Iceland, Norway, Italy, Spain, Majorca, Greece, South Africa, Botswana, Swaziland, Cyprus, the Czech Republic and the Netherlands. She held the posts of Education Director and Deputy CEO of the BDA until 2003. She has many years' experience as a teacher, teacher trainer and SENCo. She has published a considerable body of both theoretical and practical material, and published the first ground-breaking book linking 'Glue Ear' with dyslexia. She assesses children, students and adults facing challenges in learning. Her email is lindsay@peergordonassociates.co.uk and her website is www.peergordonassociates.co.uk.

Gavin Reid is an international consultant and psychologist with consultancies in Canada, the UK, Europe, the Middle East, Asia and Australasia. He was Visiting Professor at the University of British Columbia in Vancouver, Canada in the Department of Education and Counseling Psychology and Special Education in 2007 and 2010. He is Chair of the BDA accreditation board and an ambassador for the Helen Arkell Dyslexia Centre in the UK. He is also a consultant for the Child Enrichment Medical Centre in Dubai, the Centre for Child Evaluation and Teaching (CCET) in Kuwait and for the Institute of Child Education and

Psychology Europe (ICEPE). He is a director of the Red Rose School for children with specific learning difficulties in St Annes on Sea, Lancashire, UK, and is a visiting educational psychologist to organisations and schools in Switzerland, the UK, the Middle East, Egypt and Canada. He was Senior Lecturer in the Department of Educational Studies (formerly Department of Special Education), Moray House School of Education, University of Edinburgh from 1991 to 2007. He has written 30 books on learning, motivation and dyslexia and lectured to thousands of professionals and parents in 80 countries. He has also had books published in Polish, Italian, Arabic, Hebrew, French, Chinese and Slovak. He is an experienced teacher with over 10 years' experience in the classroom and has held external examiner appointments at 18 universities worldwide for PhD and master's courses.

His email is gavinreid66@gmail.com and his website is www.drgavinreid.com.

CONTRIBUTORS

Sheena Bell is a Senior Lecturer in special educational needs and inclusion at the University of Northampton, UK. She is a member of the CeSNER (Centre for Special Needs Education and Research) team and leads courses for specialist teachers and assessors of dyslexia/specific learning difficulties. She has taught in a range of settings in England and abroad, from further and higher education settings including prisons, to primary schools. She has had considerable experience with supporting and teaching learners with dyslexia from other cultures and language backgrounds.

Sarika Cherodath is a graduate student at the Laboratory for Language, Literacy and Music at the National Brain Research Centre in India. Her research is focused on understanding how reading networks in the brain are organized in children who receive simultaneous instruction in two languages written in two orthographies – Hindi and English. She investigates these processes by designing behavioural and functional neuroimaging experiments.

Te Hurinui Clarke affiliates to the Te Arawa confederation and Ngāi Tahu tribes in Aotearoa New Zealand. His research and publications focus on student retention in Māori language programmes in English-medium secondary schools. He has been a classroom teacher of Māori language in secondary schools and now lectures in undergraduate and postgraduate programmes at the University of Canterbury, New Zealand. Te Hurinui is currently Programme Co-ordinator and a Lecturer in a Postgraduate diploma in bilingual and immersion teaching (Hōaka Pounamu).

Kate Currawalla is President of the Maharashtra Dyslexia Association, India. She is a strong advocate for individuals with dyslexia and is actively associated with creating awareness of dyslexia in India and providing appropriate intervention.

Michael Dal is an Associate Professor and Head of the Centre for Research in Foreign and Second Language Learning at the School of Education at Iceland University. His primary research interests focus on foreign language acquisition, didactics in foreign languages and the use of new technology in foreign language learning. He has conducted and participated in several European research programmes on foreign language learning. His areas of expertise include inclusive education, literacy, and dyslexia and foreign language learning.

Gad Elbeheri is the Dean of the Australian College of Kuwait; a university providing internationally recognized and accredited tertiary education to the business and engineering sectors. He is also an expert providing consultancy to the Center for Child Evaluation and Teaching, Kuwait. An applied linguist who obtained his PhD from the University of Durham, UK, Dr Elbeheri has a keen interest in cross-linguistic studies of dyslexia and other specific learning difficulties and their manifestations in Arabic.

John Everatt is a Professor of Education at the University of Canterbury, New Zealand. He received a PhD from the University of Nottingham, UK, and has lectured on education and psychology programmes at universities in New Zealand and the UK. His research focuses on literacy acquisition and developmental learning difficulties. His current work is investigating the relationship between literacy and language by considering the characteristics of different scripts and how these might lead to variations in learning/acquisition.

Angela Fawcett is Emeritus Professor, Department of Psychology, Swansea University, UK. She was a mature student following experience of dyslexia in her family, with a BA and PhD in psychology. Her research with Professor Rod Nicolson at Sheffield University produced three major theories of dyslexia, and eight normed screening tests, which are best sellers worldwide. She is Vice President of the British Dyslexia Association, and former editor of *Dyslexia*, and continues to present ongoing research in keynote presentations internationally, consulting in Wales, Poland, with the Dyslexia Association of Singapore and in the rest of Asia.

Esther Geva is full Professor of Applied Psychology and Human Development at the University of Toronto, Canada. Her extensive research, publications, and graduate teaching focus on the development of language and literacy skills in students from diverse linguistic backgrounds, second language students with learning difficulties, and cultural perspectives on children's psychological problems. She has presented her work internationally, and served on numerous advisory, policy and review committees in the USA and Canada concerned with policy and research on literacy development in culturally and linguistically diverse children and adolescents.

Abigail Gray has spent over 20 years in special educational needs. Her career in education has taken her from the role of Learning Support Assistant in a London, UK, comprehensive to the headship of The Moat School in Fulham. After 12 years in leadership, Abigail launched a special educational needs consultancy service, Senworks, which provides training, advice and support to schools and families on improving provision and outcomes. She also volunteers for IPSEA (Independent Parental Special Education Advice) as part of their free Tribunal Support Service.

Jennie Guise is a practitioner psychologist with extensive experience of assessing working memory. She is highly qualified in the areas of psychology and education, and has worked in research, and now in applied practice as Director of Dysguise Ltd, UK. Dr Guise also has years of experience in teaching students of different ability levels, and of putting theory into practice. Her main interests are in identifying what will help individual learners, and working collaboratively with teachers and tutors to use that knowledge in the classroom.

Mim Hutchings specialized in social and educational inclusion within educational and childhood studies and master's programmes at Bath Spa University, UK. She was part of the Dyslexia and Multilingualism team mainly responsible for the qualitative elements of the research. Her previous lives have included teaching in mainstream and special schools, and universities, and working as an advisor for special educational needs and within minority ethnic support services.

Maya Jakubowicz is a trilingual TEFL teacher and a British Dyslexia Association qualified dyslexia specialist practitioner and PgCert Education Studies (Bangor University, UK). She has worked with those with severe learning difficulties. She has a personal interest in language development and dyslexia. She currently lives in Germany where she teaches dyslexic children. She is deeply interested in the emotional issues experienced by dyslexic learners, and alongside academic development, works on development of skills to raise self-esteem, confidence, resilience and a sense of hope and possibility.

Bhoomika Kar is Associate Professor at the Centre of Behavioural and Cognitive Sciences, University of Allahabad, India. She has a PhD in clinical psychology from the National Institute for Mental Health and Allied Sciences, Bangalore. Her research interests are normative development of attention and control, disorders including dyslexia and attention deficit hyperactivity disorder, cognitive–affective control, bilingualism and cognitive control using behavioural, electrophysiological (EEG/ERP) and neuroimaging methods.

Judit Kormos is a Professor of Second Language Acquisition at Lancaster University, UK. She was a key partner in the award-winning DysTEFL (Dyslexia for Teachers of English as a Foreign Language) project sponsored by the European Commission and a lead educator in the Dyslexia and Foreign Language Teaching massive open online learning course offered by Future Learn. She is the co-author of the book *Teaching Languages to Students with Specific Learning Differences* and has published widely on the effect of dyslexia on processes of second language learning.

Rozzel Kosera was a summer intern at the Laboratory for Language, Literacy and Music at the National Brain Research Centre in India and is interested in understanding behavioural assessments in biliterate children.

Colin Lannen is co-founder, Director and Principal of the Lancashire Centre for Specific Learning Difficulties (SpLD), UK, including the Red Rose School. He is an international speaker and teacher trainer on SpLD, including autism spectrum disorder and learning styles in Canada and Europe. He was Joint Project Co-ordinator of an EU Lifelong Learning Grundtvig Project: 'SpLD Roadmap for Teacher and Adult Learner Training', 2011–2013. He is currently Project Co-ordinator for the EU 'Erasmus Plus' project which aims to introduce SpLD teacher training in Europe. The project is of three years' duration and runs from 2014 to 2017.

Sionah Lannen is a chartered educational psychologist; co-founder, Director and Head Teacher of the Red Rose School (for Specific Learning Difficulties, SpLD); and involved in teacher training in educational psychology in Canada, the Middle East and Europe. She is Co-director of the EU 'Erasmus Plus' project which aims to introduce SpLD teacher training in Europe (2014–2017).

Angus Hikairo Macfarlane affiliates to the Te Arawa confederation of tribes in Aotearoa New Zealand. His research and publications focus on exploring Indigenous and sociocultural phenomena that influence education and psychology. He has received several prestigious awards including the University of Canterbury Research Medal, and the national (Ako Aotearoa) tertiary teaching award. Dr Macfarlane is the Kaihautū (Senior Māori Advisor) of the New Zealand Psychological Society, and the Professor of Māori Research at the University of Canterbury, New Zealand.

Sonja Macfarlane affiliates to the Ngāi Tahu tribe in Aotearoa New Zealand. Her research and publications focus on culturally responsive evidence-based practices in education, psychology and counselling. Her career pathway has seen her move from classroom teacher to itinerant teacher, to special education advisor, to the national Professional Practice Leader: Services to Māori (Pouhikiahurea) in the Ministry of Education, Special Education. Dr Macfarlane is an Associate Professor in the School of Human Development and Movement Studies at the University of Waikato, New Zealand.

Deirdre Martin is Professor of Disability and Multilingualism at Goldsmiths, University of London, UK. Her research interests are situated in disabilities affecting language, literacy and learning, particularly in multilingual contexts in education and health provision. She has held research grants from the Economic and Social Research Council, the Nuffield Trust and the Leverhulme Trust. Her publications include *Researching Dyslexia in Multilingual Settings* (2013), *Language Disabilities in Cultural and Linguistic Diversity* (2009) and with Professor Marilyn Martin-Jones, *Researching Multilingualism: Critical and Ethnographic Approaches* (2015).

Tilly Mortimore is a Senior Lecturer in Inclusion/Specific Learning Difficulties (SpLD)/ Dyslexia at Bath Spa University, UK. Tilly has worked in schools and individually with dyslexic students of all ages, lectured across Europe, Africa and India, established master's courses in SpLD/dyslexia, and provided consultancy and training in dyslexia, literacy, speech and language difficulties and learning styles in many educational and other settings. Her books include *Dyslexia and Learning Style: A Practitioner's Handbook* (2008) and with Jane Dupree *Dyslexia-Friendly Practice in the Secondary Classroom* (2008). Articles, chapters and research projects cover dyslexia, inclusion, approaches to learning and children with English as an additional language.

Elizabeth Nadler-Nir is a speech–language pathologist who qualified at the University of Cape Town, South Africa; she did her master's research on literacy intervention within a disadvantaged community. She is a clinician who teaches about language and literacy barriers and has developed teaching materials for second language learners and volunteers. In 2007 she opened The Reading Language Gym in Cape Town, a centre that provides language-based literacy intervention to school-aged students. She also developed The Virtual Reading Gym™, an online remedial reading intervention, to make structured literacy intervention more accessible.

Joanna Nijakowska is a Professor in Linguistics at Lodz University, Poland. She was an initiator and co-ordinator of the award-winning DysTEFL (Dyslexia for Teachers of English as a Foreign Language) project sponsored by the European Commission and an educator on the dyslexia and foreign language teaching massive open online learning course offered by Future Learn. She is the author of the book *Dyslexia in the Foreign Language Classroom* and has published on dyslexia and effective classroom practices as well as foreign language teachers' professional needs, concerns and beliefs about dyslexia.

Geet Oberoi is President of ORKIDS foundation in New Delhi, India. She has a doctoral degree in clinical psychology and provides special education for children with reading and language difficulties. Her main areas of work include assessment and remediation to children with special needs and professional development courses primarily for instructors. In recent years she has worked in research to enhance the concept of inclusion in the Indian education system. She is an active member of numerous national committees and forums under the National Council of Educational Research and Training and Central Institute of Educational Technology, to enhance inclusive education.

Gilda Palti is a Chartered Child and Educational Psychologist who specialises in assessments of individuals of all ages for a range of learning difficulties. She is registered as a member of the UK Health and Care Professions Council (HCPC); an Associate Fellow of the British Psychological Society (BPS); a member of the Division of Child and Educational Psychology of the BPS, and holds a certificate for family and child therapy. She completed her Doctor of Education Degree at the University of Bristol. Her research focused on the social and emotional aspects of dyslexia. For her research experience and publications see www.spld-matters.com.

Michelle Pascoe is a Senior Lecturer in the Department of Health and Rehabilitation Sciences at the University of Cape Town, South Africa. She is an experienced speech and language therapist who has worked with children with speech, language and literacy difficulties in mainstream and special schools locally and in the UK. Her research focuses on speech and literacy difficulties in mono- and multilingual children, and interventions that may be effective in supporting such children and their families.

Marie Rontou has worked as a teacher of Greek and a teaching assistant in the UK during her EdD studies. She has worked as an English as Foreign Language (EFL) teacher in primary, secondary and further education in Greece for the last 10 years. She is currently working on an e-learning training programme on dyslexia and foreign languages which she designed and wrote for the University of Athens. She has published articles on dyslexia and EFL, and on teaching and learning EFL.

Linda Siegel is the former Dorothy C. Lam Chair in Special Education and an Emeritus Professor in the Department of Educational and Counselling Psychology and Special Education at the University of British Columbia in Vancouver, Canada. She has over 200 publications on early identification and intervention to prevent reading problems, dyslexia, reading and language development, mathematical concept learning, mathematical learning disabilities, and children learning English as a second language. She has been the President of the Division of Learning Disabilities of the Council on Exceptional Children. In 2010, she was awarded the Gold Medal for Excellence in Psychological Research from the Canadian Psychological Association. In 2012 she was awarded the Eminent Researcher Award from the Learning Difficulties Association of Australia.

Nandini C. Singh is Professor and Head of the Laboratory of Language, Literacy and Music at the National Brain Research Centre in India. One of her primary interests is developing appropriate tools for assessment of dyslexia in Indian languages. She uses a combination of behavioural and neuroimaging methods to study literacy and music.

T.A. Sumathi is a Research Assistant at the Laboratory of Language, Literacy and Music at the National Brain Research Centre in India. Her research interests include signal processing methods and analysis of functional neuroimaging data. She is particularly interested in understanding circuits for picture naming in patients with frontal lobe tumours.

Richard Soppitt is a consultant child and family psychiatrist with 20 years' postgraduate experience working in child and adolescent mental health services in the UK, including working in early intervention in psychosis as well as with children and young people with mental health disorders who require consideration for inpatient admission. He has published in the field of attention deficit hyperactivity disorder, autism spectrum disorder, mental health, psychosis and depression. Dr Soppitt has been instructed in Special Educational Needs and Disability Tribunal proceedings since 1998 and also in other medicolegal areas such as acquired brain injury. He relaxes by running and engaging in watercolour painting.

Emma Tudhope currently works at the University of Sheffield, UK, as a Specific Learning Difficulties (SpLD) specialist tutor. She also has a wide range of experience supporting students with SpLD and English as an additional language issues in a further education setting. Additionally, Emma has taught a diverse range of students at various levels of study: from secondary school level to undergraduates at the University of Newcastle. She has a particular interest in ways that tutors can make their resources and teaching methods accessible for students with SpLD.

Yueming Xi is a doctoral student at the Ontario Institute for Studies in Education of the University of Toronto, Canada. She received her BA in Japanese from Dalian University of Foreign Languages in China and an MEd in curriculum and instruction from Boston College, USA. She is a former adjunct faculty member of Japanese language and literature at Simmons College and Northeastern University in Boston. Yueming specializes in literacy development among academically at-risk school-aged students, with a particular focus on linguistic minority populations.

FOREWORD 1

The beginning of the new millennium promised a continuing acceleration in global migration and multilingualism. In societies that had previously appeared largely monolingual that acceleration challenged social scientists and human services professionals to move beyond a vision that had traditionally been quite limited. As this century began there were a number of initiatives to address the issue, including an earlier collection of papers put together by the editors of this book. Researchers and teachers in the fields of dyslexia and bilingualism had previously worked quite separately but began to learn from each other. This new collection shows the progress of this fertile activity in a number of countries and in various aspects of the effort to understand learning difficulties in literacy and intervene to ameliorate them. A successful bilingual reader must co-ordinate sensory, intellectual, linguistic, emotional and cultural resources in a single smooth, automated process. The chapter authors show how the many elements of that process may be challenged, but sometimes also enhanced, by working across languages. If we fully understand and respond to multilingualism and dyslexia when they occur together, we may better respond to the challenges of each in themselves.

5 October 2015
Tony Cline
Educational Psychology Group, University College London, UK

FOREWORD 2

This new edition of *Multilingualism, Literacy and Dyslexia: Breaking Down Barriers for Educators* provides a timely and welcome update on editors Peer and Reid's 2000 offering on this same topic. Major geopolitical and demographic shifts are shaping the cultural and linguistic landscape of countries globally. For example, within the United States, census trends indicate that by the mid 21st century, speakers of first languages or dialects other than English will comprise the majority of citizens. Population changes such as these challenge educators to provide effective identification and intervention for literacy difficulties in multilingual learners.

This edition, with contributions from respected authors in different corners of the world provides helpful guidance through chapters dealing with: current theoretical questions in literacy learning; central issues related to test development; and perspectives on such important topics as foreign language learning, inclusion and public policy. In addition, readers will find meaningful explorations of multilingual identity formation and of mental health factors in immigrant populations. A linguistic sampling of the book's multilingual contexts includes but is not limited to Chinese, Arabic, German, Māori, English and Scandinavian languages. Practitioners and researchers alike should find this new edition's inspired contributions to be both useful and engaging.

29 September 2015
Charles W. Haynes, EdD
Senior Advisor, Global Partners Committee, International Dyslexia Association
Professor, Communications Sciences and Disorders Department
at the MGH Institute of Health Professions, Boston, Massachusetts, USA

PART I

Multilingualism, literacy and dyslexia

The context

1

INTRODUCTION

Lindsay Peer and Gavin Reid

This chapter will:

1. Identify some of the key issues in multilingualism and dyslexia
2. Provide an overview of the book
3. Highlight some issues that are critical in order that all people irrespective of culture are fully included in the education system (see also the Postscript)

The context

It is now over 15 years since we edited the first edition of this book. At that time it was very much a landmark book and we attempted to incorporate contributions from a diverse range of cultures and languages. The book followed the first international conference on multilingualism which was held at UMIST in Manchester in England in 1999 and organized by the British Dyslexia Association (BDA). It was by all accounts a well-attended and very successful event. Lindsay Peer, the education director of the BDA at that time, liaised with the International Dyslexia Association CEO – J. Thomas Viall – who secured the board's support for the event.

A follow-up conference was held in Washington DC in the USA several years later, organized by the International Dyslexia Association (IDA) and arranged through the efforts of one of the board members, Dr Charles Haynes.

The European Dyslexia Association (EDA) ran the third in the series of three conferences as was originally agreed. Since then the EDA have arranged a series of European conferences which – by the very nature of a larger and diverse Europe – have focused on issues relating to multilingualism and this has contributed to taking the debate forward. Additionally there have been a number of high-profile European projects through Erasmus and Socrates European funding that have witnessed many European countries entering this area for the first time.

The European collaboration is a significant step in preparing and implementing diagnostic and intervention strategies to cater for the diverse needs of students who are utilizing more than one language within the family, education and community context. The area of teacher training has also been highlighted and there is currently a high-profile three-year 'Erasmus

Plus' project underway which is commented on by authors from the lead institution of this project (see chapter 6). Despite these initiatives there is still much to be accomplished and further constructive government initiatives and support are needed at local, national and international level.

It is however recognized that dealing with dyslexia and issues relating to bi/multilingualism is a significant concern, particularly in the current climate, for example of free movement within Europe and the migration of large populations to western Europe, but also the ongoing migration taking place on the world stage in Asia, Australasia and North America. For that reason we have contributions for this book from these areas: Angela Fawcett from Singapore, Sonja MacFarlane and colleagues from New Zealand and Linda Siegel from Canada. These very positive contributions add to the debate and present messages that can be taken on board by all countries.

The key issues are therefore identification of dyslexia, accessing culturally and linguistically appropriate resources, and acknowledging the educational and social needs of all children who are operating in more than one language and culture. It is important to ensure that they are able to fully access the curriculum and that they feel included within the school community.

Overview of the book

It is appropriate to start this book with the chapter by Professor Angela Fawcett on the link between theory and practice in relation to the learning process for young people with dyslexia. Angela relates the research studies carried out by her and colleagues looking at procedural learning and the crucial point that children with dyslexia need specialized teaching to achieve mastery. Of particular interest is the debate which centres round the benefits of bilingualism and that bilingual speakers may have advantages when learning to read. Angela also refers to the Strand Report (Strand *et al.*, 2015) which identifies Special Educational Needs (SEN) as the major risk factor for English as an Additional Language (EAL) pupils. Although not all these SEN pupils will have dyslexia, it is acknowledged that dyslexia is the most frequently reported area of need. As Angela points out despite the importance of this topic, there have been relatively few publications on EAL and dyslexia.

Professor Fawcett points out that the success of intervention depends to a certain extent on the transparency of the language and she goes on to discuss that point in her chapter. The nature of the language can therefore be a barrier to success. The issue of barriers to learning is taken further by Lindsay Peer in her chapter on otitis media (glue ear). As Dr Peer indicates, little has been done to investigate the impact of otitis media on educational success although this affects so many children in the early years and in all countries. Dr Peer goes on to discuss appropriate interventions and relates these very much to dyslexia and multilingualism.

In chapter 4 Dr Deirdre Martin provides a critical perspective on multilingualism and dyslexia and introduces the complex phenomenon of dyslexia in 'superdiversity'. She refers to the work of Vertoveç (2007) that describes new patterns of migration as 'superdiversity'. She describes this as a recent phenomenon in Europe, the USA, Canada and Australia, characterized by a change in the linguistic landscape and that in some areas, the sum-population of linguistic minority speakers is larger than speakers of the majority language. She relates this new context to literacy development and in particular to the dyslexia debate and the sad omission in that debate (Elliot and Grigorenko 2014) of multilingualism. Dr Martin includes an informative and thought-provoking section on the construction of dyslexia in multilingualism. She also indicates that drawing on critical pedagogy in professional development can offer a methodology that can raise awareness in primary and secondary schools, and challenge assumptions about multilingualism in relation to classroom/curriculum learning.

This is followed by the chapter by Dr Gad Elbeheri and Professor John Everatt who discuss principles and guidelines in test construction for multilingual children. This is a crucial chapter as it is important that appropriate assessment tools are used to ensure that bilingual children are fairly represented in the population of children who are identified as dyslexic. At present this is not always the case. As the authors concede, multilingualism has been a problem in psycho-educational assessment for quite some time and there is a lack of diagnostic tools that allow practitioners to distinguish between 'language differences related to the environmental context of growing up as a multilingual immigrant and language impairments of a neuro-linguistic origin'.

In their chapter they also refer to the importance of assessing the child in their first language in order to distinguish between an underlying cognitive deficit, as opposed to a lack of second language acquisition leading to poor vocabulary that may be improved simply by increased practice.

They refer to the Arabic context as an example of the importance of robust test construction and particularly the importance of assessing phonological processing skills. They indicate that dyslexia assessment is a dynamic process but, as they suggest, it is important that linguistic, cultural and other background elements of the individual should collectively form a framework for a dyslexia assessment.

This is followed up in chapter 6 by Dr Jennie Guise and colleagues who show how culturally and linguistically appropriate material can be accessed for an accurate assessment. They emphasize the importance of culture-fair assessment but also mention the underrepresentation of dyslexia among the multilingual school population. They also raise the issue of self-esteem – crucial for effective learning – and the importance of information gathering to ensure the assessment hits the right mark. The importance of assessing non-verbal skills is also raised as well as a range of intervention strategies. In addition, there is reference to a European-wide project spearheaded by Lannen and Lannen on Specific Learning Difficulties (SpLD) teacher training in order to create an EU SpLD website for information and long-distance interactive training.

In chapter 7 we travel to the other side of the world to New Zealand where Dr Sonja Macfarlane, Te Hurinui Clarke and Professor Angus Macfarlane reflect on the contemporary literacy challenges facing Indigenous cultures that draw from oral language traditions. They suggest that the way forward is to engage in a culturally responsive and holistic approach to literacy. They refer particularly to Māori and Pacific learners but their chapter has wider implications and the message is relevant to all countries.

This is followed by a chapter by Elizabeth Nadler-Nir and Dr Michelle Pascoe on language-based literacy interventions in South Africa. They focus on innovative practice and their chapter introduces 'The Virtual Reading Gym™' and the opportunities it presents for developing links between language and literacy and supportive feedback. They also refer to adult literacy and provide a very comprehensive and well-researched overview of the situation in South Africa.

In the following chapter Joanna Nijakowska and Judit Kormos look at foreign language teacher training on dyslexia. They emphasize the importance of a shared understanding of foreign language teaching and learning that constructively responds to the diversity of individual learners, including those foreign language learners with dyslexia. They suggest that marginalization and exclusion from foreign language education frequently results from poor awareness of teachers of inclusive practices, and that teacher knowledge, teacher classroom practices and student achievement are tightly linked. They refer to the pedagogical principles of the DysTEFL (Dyslexia for Teachers of English as a Foreign Language) teacher training resources which take a task-based approach to teacher development and employ tasks to enhance learning and reflection. They comment that this requires accepting difference as an asset rather than an obstacle to the learning progress of the child. This is a message that is very relevant to dyslexia.

In chapter 10 Abigail Gray discusses the variety of new demands placed on the SENCo (Special Educational Needs Co-ordinator) in light of the 2014 reforms in the UK. Abigail makes a case for inclusive and holistic assessment of pupils' language and literacy needs in order to prevent failure. She supports a proactive position as opposed to a reactive one. This is a current and cutting edge chapter which highlights the key issues in both teaching and learning with messages for teachers and management.

In chapter 11 Drs Mim Hutchings and Tilly Mortimore present findings from a multilingualism project. Their chapter endorses the role of research in providing evidence-based practice to inform choices about planning and implementation of interventions for multilingual children. This is an important chapter with key messages for researchers and practitioners.

Professor Linda Siegel in the following chapter, using her extensive international research experience, argues strongly for the inclusion of EAL students in foreign language programmes. There is an important curricular and pedagogical message here and one that has implications for children with dyslexia.

Perspectives from the higher education sector are discussed next in the chapter by Dr Sheena Bell and Emma Tudhope. They show how EAL students can be supported in the context of further and higher education. They also discuss the key issue of transition into employment for EAL students. They raise the important question of how institutions need to adapt in order to enable people with dyslexia from diverse cultural and language backgrounds to access the knowledge and skills they need to take their place in a skilled workforce. In addition, they discuss the crucial environmental factors that can impact on a successful outcome for EAL students. This very comprehensive chapter examines a number of aspects of further and higher education that can impinge on the educational and social development of EAL students as well as what we mean by effective support.

In chapter 14 Maya Jakubowicz presents a practical chapter from the classroom perspective. The chapter discusses key issues in the classroom as well as looking at the emotional needs of bi/multilingual children. Maya reviews key factors in German orthography and presents case studies which highlight the challenges and strategies that can be used through the formation of a comprehensive intervention plan. Maya also discusses the need for teachers to be aware of the potential negative impact the classroom can have on a bilingual child and the need to engage sensitively in helping to meet their needs.

This is followed by the chapter by Marie Rontou who discusses the dilemmas and contradictions around differentiation of homework for those with dyslexia studying English as a foreign language. The context for this chapter is Greece and she highlights key issues in orthography, government policy, accommodations made and social–cultural influences, all of which impact on the EAL student with dyslexia. The chapter also reports on the findings of Marie's research study in Greece, including methodological issues.

Chapter 16 is by Dr Gilda Palti who, through referring to research studies, highlights key issues including the cognitive advantages of bilingualism. She also details the principles of multisensory education provision for EAL students. In addition, Gilda refers to the need for provision to account for the variation within bilingual populations including those who use one language at home (a minority language), and another language at school or in the outside world (the majority language) which can be further complicated by different dialects or pronunciation of words used at home and in school.

In chapter 17 Professor Nandini Singh (National Brain Research Centre) and co-authors in India look at the development of reading skills in children provided simultaneous instruction in two distinct writing systems. They present a comprehensive literature review of the area and detail the findings from a study of their own. They suggest their findings have important implications for biliterate education and they argue that in the light of cross-linguistic phonological transfer, language teachers should focus on building strong language skills in the native language and recognize that strong native language skills can be transferred to the second language.

This chapter is followed by Dr Richard Soppitt, a consultant child and family psychiatrist, who addresses the emotional and mental health aspects of migration for children and adolescents and also discusses the challenges of cultural integration for young people's mental health. He suggests that migration has been viewed as both a source of crisis and of opportunity for individuals and societies and it is important to make this process a positive, rather than a negative one. He discusses the important aspect of acculturation – the process of cultural and psychological change that follows intercultural contact. He asserts that the foundational principle of multiculturalism is the emphasis on cultural diversity. But he contends that the value of this is often perceived differently by majority and minority group members reflecting their competing interests. In this insightful chapter Richard Soppitt also discusses some of the issues around multilingualism and cognitive and language development as well as the mental health implications of immigration and multiculturalism.

Professor Esther Geva and Yueming Xi in the next chapter discuss policy considerations in addressing the needs of second language learners who have dyslexia. They provide a critical review of diagnostic assessment of dyslexia among students who speak more than one language and give an overview of dyslexia-related policies in five countries – the USA, Canada, Mainland China, Taiwan and Hong Kong. They make the important point that early identification and intervention targeting deficits in phonological processing skills, orthographic processes and morphological skills are the most effective means of preventing severe subsequent reading failure in first language and English language/second language learners. They argue that 'wait and see' policies should be replaced with evidence-based policies. This is an important message for all those who deal in any way with students with dyslexia – both monolingual and bilingual.

In chapter 20 Michael Dal from Iceland looks at issues in Scandinavia and discusses the necessity of developing a communicative, context-related and content-based pedagogy for learning neighbour languages in Scandinavia. He discusses the findings from a research project in Scandinavia. He asserts that in this globalized and multilingual world it is important to conserve the ability for individuals to be able to understand and speak to each other in their own mother tongue. There is certainly an important social and educational message here, and it is fitting to end the book with this chapter.

In this volume we have accessed information from around the world, and from contributors who are all dedicated professionals. We are indeed delighted by their response, and the direction they provide to help forge a path to make education and society a more positive and successful experience for all children, young people and families.

References

Elliott, J. and Grigorenko, A. (2014) *The Dyslexia Debate*, Cambridge: Cambridge University Press.

Strand, S., Malmberg, L. and Hall J. (2015) *English as an Additional Language (EAL) and educational achievement in England: An analysis of the National Pupil Database.* https://educationendowment foundation.org.uk/uploads/pdf/EAL_and_educational_achievement2.pdf

Vertoveç, S. (2007) Super-diversity and its implications, *Ethnic and Racial Studies* 30, 6, 1024–1054.

2

DYSLEXIA AND LEARNING

Theory into practice

Angela Fawcett

This chapter will:

1. Consider the costs and benefits of bilingualism
2. Summarise theories of dyslexia and their impact on bilingualism
3. Present case studies of screening and intervention with bilingual children

Introduction

In this chapter I shall introduce some of the emerging factors in educational research that have highlighted the performance of bilingual or multilingual children (English as an Additional Language – EAL) in comparison with English peers. Interestingly, these children will include those who are fluent in English but where another language is spoken in the home, as well as those who come into school with virtually no English.

Dyslexia is found in all languages including Asian languages such as Chinese and Japanese. The difficulty that children experience in learning is directly related to the structure of the language they are learning, with languages such as Italian being transparent (every sound is pronounced) by contrast with English, one of the most difficult in terms of the complexity of the links between phonemes and graphemes. However, a recent study by Caravolas and colleagues (2012a) found a similar pattern in English, Spanish, Slovak and Czech in terms of phoneme awareness, letter–sound knowledge, and memory span as a predictor of progress in early schooling. Furthermore, Duncan *et al.* (2013) identified a similar impact for phonological skills in six different alphabetic scripts (English, French, Greek, Icelandic, Spanish and Portuguese), relating to rhythm of the language. Recently, the importance of visual attention span has also been established for all languages, regardless of their orthography (Lallier *et al.*, 2014). In summary, to simplify, it seems that in transparent languages, fluency is the key, whereas in English, progress for dyslexic children is likely to be both slow and inaccurate.

Research background

In order to better understand the issues involved in learning, I shall first summarise the theoretical research conducted in Sheffield by Rod Nicolson and myself on dyslexia, and why we did not simply examine reading. Then I shall consider practical implications, how this impacts on multilingual learners, and more specifically the impact of multilingualism when combined with dyslexia, across the world.

The issue of multilingualism according to a recent report (Strand *et al.*, 2015) is becoming of increasingly higher relevance in the UK, with growing numbers of EAL children in our schools, just over 1 million in the 2013 census, with percentages of 56% in schools in inner London and 43% in outer London. It has always been argued that ethnic minorities are at a disadvantage within the UK education system, but this report indicates that disadvantaged white children with poor language skills are now showing the greatest difficulty in achievement, indexed by their results at GCSE.

Dyslexia: the theory

What is dyslexia? I think most people are agreed that there is a problem in reading, but of course this is only the tip of the iceberg. Dyslexia is a problem that is evident before children try (and fail) to learn to read, and impacts across the lifespan. Dyslexia has been plagued by controversy, not least by recent work from Joe Elliott on the 'Dyslexia myth' (Elliott and Grigorenko, 2014) which seems to claim that dyslexia does not exist, and there is no difference in the provision for children with dyslexia and those with more generalised difficulties, so why bother with the cost and the legislation? It is rare that a consensus is reached on dyslexia, but this may simply reflect the different perspectives of the individuals involved in dyslexia. The worried parent simply wants their child to be happy or successful, the teacher would like their class to be more manageable, the politicians would like to cut back further on resources, and the researcher may be trying to help children with dyslexia improve their reading, or to identify the underlying cause. For me, the most important aspect has been to consider dyslexia as a difference in learning, rather than simply a reading deficit. Living with dyslexia, with my young son Matthew, I was aware of a number of surprising difficulties in an intellectually able boy with strong language skills. This led me to consider whether the phonological deficit might not be the whole story, and to work with my colleague Rod Nicolson towards an explanatory theory that could cover all aspects of dyslexia. We knew there were problems in reading, so we decided to consider learning in all its aspects to establish whereabouts these problems originated.

In our early research we considered automaticity, first identifying a problem in automaticity in one of our most over-learned skills, balance (Nicolson and Fawcett, 1990) and then in a range of primitive skills (Nicolson and Fawcett, 1994). We argued that children and adults with dyslexia had to work harder in a process of conscious compensation, to achieve what others achieved without apparent difficulty, and that tiredness could account for much of the day-to-day variability in their skills. We trained up two simple reaction times, which we had found were not impaired in dyslexia, blending them into a choice reaction time. Fourteen-year-old dyslexics started more slowly, learned more slowly, made more errors and were slower after 2,500 trials than the matched control group (Nicolson and Fawcett, 2000). We then started to consider which area of the brain might be involved in learning, and showed with behavioural data from our panel of dyslexics (Fawcett *et al.*, 1996) and PET scans from adults (Nicolson *et al.*, 1999a) that the cerebellum was impaired in dyslexia. Strikingly, our study of motor learning in adults showed only 10% of the activation of the controls, and heightened activation in the frontal lobes, suggesting that even learned skills were still effortful. Moreover, data from the cell count of the dyslexic brains showed a difference in structure for dyslexic adults, with more large cells in the cerebellum (Finch *et al.*, 2002). The cerebellum has traditionally been overlooked when considering the brain, but it is known to be critically involved in learning and has now been identified as linked to reading and phonology, through the links with Broca's area. In terms of theory, most recently, we argued that procedural learning (learning how to do things) was impaired in dyslexia, while declarative learning was spared or over-achieving, in a neural systems approach that bridges brain and behaviour (Nicolson and Fawcett, 2007, 2011). We also showed that dyslexic adults do not consolidate their skills in the same way as controls, showing that after sleep, controls improve their performance on a simple motor task pre-learned the day before, whereas dyslexic students fall back in both speed and accuracy (Nicolson *et al.*, 2010).

Implications for practice

Our studies of automaticity and primitive skills clarified that there are problems in phonology, motor skills and speed, in line with the major theories of dyslexia, but that no one theory was a complete solution. This helps us to understand that all these theories contribute to the jigsaw of dyslexia, and that these are all different aspects of learning. Our study of learning helped us to understand why it is so difficult to teach dyslexic children, because it takes them the 'square root' longer to learn a task than a non-dyslexic child, even on this simple button press task, where skills must be blended together. This means that where a task would take 2 hours it will take 4 and where it would take 10 hours it would take 100. This is dynamite if generally true, and explains the difficulties even the most competent teachers have in bringing dyslexic children up to scratch, given that it takes over 1,000 hours for non-dyslexics to become expert in a task. Our study of consolidation means that one of the most basic involuntary learning mechanisms is impaired in dyslexia, and explains why dyslexic children's skills are so fragile and can fall back after a break, such as the summer holidays. This suggests that even the best teaching will not be enough, and that dyslexic children need specialised teaching to achieve mastery. Our framework for the development of the procedural learning deficit can explain the overlaps with other learning difficulties, based on two procedural learning systems, which are differentially affected in different developmental disorders. We argue that dyslexia is specific to the language-based procedural learning system, but dyspraxia is linked to the motor-based learning system, with some overlap between the two conditions.

In terms of identifying dyslexia and providing support, our work with screening and early intervention, in common with research from across the world has shown that support is best provided in the early years, in order to prevent failure and the negative effects of stress. Torgesen *et al.* (2001) for example have shown that 67.5 hours of individual intervention is needed to bring children up to the level of their peers, and that this is most effective and cost-effective when delivered in 1st grade or before. We ourselves have shown (Nicolson *et al.*, 1999b; Fawcett *et al.*, 2001) that screening for dyslexia at the ages of 5–7 can identify those children at risk, and that 10 weeks of small group support, for 1 hour a week can significantly improve both reading and spelling with lasting impact.

In terms of the early development of dyslexia, we have recently identified 'delayed neural commitment' as key to dyslexia (Nicolson and Fawcett, submitted 2015). This means that dyslexic children do not have the necessary skills in place between the ages of 4 and 7 to benefit from formal schooling. Executive skills such as attention, memory and inhibition need to be ready in order to learn, in addition to the underlying language skills. Evidence for deficits in executive skills has come from a study that examined a broad range of executive functions such as verbal phonological and categorical fluency, spoonerism abilities, visual–spatial and auditory attention, verbal, visual and spatial short-term memory, verbal working memory, and visual shifting. Deficits were found in 8–17-year-old dyslexics in comparison with controls in all tasks but visual shifting non-verbal errors (Varvara et al., 2014), and spoonerisms and both auditory and visual spatial attention are related to reading. This confirms the role of executive attention in reading, regardless of the sensory modality involved.

We therefore propose that early schooling should concentrate on training up these areas instead of introducing formal literacy when a child is destined to fail.

Benefits of multilingualism

Let us turn here to consider the possible costs and benefits of multilingualism or bilingualism. For many years, there has been controversy on this very topic, because it has been clear that children who are learning more than one language are initially delayed in their acquisition of both language and literacy. There have been suggestions that children become confused when more than one language is spoken in the home and that this can affect their school performance. Research has shown (Kuhl, 2004) that in the first months infants can discriminate a wide range of sounds, but over time, just by listening to their native language, their receptive language becomes tuned to their native language. The process involved is called 'statistical learning' that tunes up the infants' neural networks between 6 and 12 months to commit to their native language. Children who are multilingual have an extended period where they are able to benefit from receiving this broader range of sounds. This means that their neural commitment is naturally delayed, which brings both costs and benefits. This more complex linguistic environment means that they will be delayed in the production of language (Garcia-Sierra et al., 2011) but over time they will be able to build up their abilities in both languages with an accompanying enriched neural network. This may mean that when they start school their language baseline is lower in English, if this is the language in which they will be taught. Nevertheless, their executive skills, memory and attention will have been trained up by this switch between languages, so their strengths in terms of school readiness may well offset their limitations in language. Research shows that at age 2 their executive skills will be better than in monolingual children, and their memory at age 8 will be superior. The benefits of multilingualism may well outweigh the costs for normally developing children. Interestingly, recent research has shown that statistical learning is implicated in successful literacy acquisition of a novel second language including Hebrew and Chinese (Frost et al., 2013), and the extended statistical learning period for language in bilingual speakers may therefore confer advantages when learning to read.

In terms of education, by the end of reception the chances of showing a good level of development in EAL children is 10% lower than in their peers, but this gap decreases with age, with greater progress between the ages of 7 and 16. The recent report (Strand et al., 2015) suggests that poor white pupils are now the lowest achieving, with only 32% achieving good GCSE results (defined as five A★–C grades, including English and Maths), whereas the

Chinese, Indian and Bangladeshi groups were amongst the highest achieving of those receiving free school meals. Different patterns emerge for EAL for different languages at 16, with Portuguese, Somali, Lingala and Lithuanian speakers the lowest achieving, and Russian and Spanish speakers achieving particularly well (Murphy and Unthiah, 2015). In this review of interventions targeted at EAL, the authors identified only 29 that met their criteria for controlled interventions, most of these were conducted in the USA and 27 out of the 29 targeted vocabulary. Those who were struggling with literacy were also given phonological skill training, with particularly strong results when listening comprehension was targeted. Within these results, what pattern emerges for those who are both dyslexic and multilingual, given that dyslexia is not specifically addressed?

Multilingualism and dyslexia

So how does multilingualism impact on the dyslexic child? Naturally, it is more difficult to diagnose dyslexia in a child who does not have English as their native language, because most screening and diagnostic tests use English as their medium. These children may suffer from a double whammy, in the American terminology, where they have a natural delay in neural commitment linked to their multilingualism, coupled with delayed neural commitment that can be traced back to their dyslexia. Although delays in tuning up their language system will be minor based on their dyslexia, these may well be compounded by inconsistencies in their language environment. Strand *et al.*'s 2015 report identifies Special Educational Needs (SEN) as the major risk factor for EAL pupils, with impact broadly similar to that in FLE (First Language English) pupils, but of course not all these SEN pupils will be dyslexic, although this is the most frequently reported need. Despite the importance of this topic, there have been relatively few publications on EAL and dyslexia. A notable exception is the work of Dr Kath Kelly from Manchester Metropolitan University, whose 2002 study identified that 95% of a group of 200 Bengali-speaking children showed automaticity deficits in balance that have been linked to dyslexia. Moreover, Kelly (2002) also found that in a class of Punjabi-speaking 7–8-year-olds followed over a 4-year period, these automaticity deficits were linked with phonology.

Dyslexia in practice: the case studies

Screening internationally

Since the publication of our suite of screening tests by Psychological Corporation, later Pearson Education, there has been considerable interest in them and they are now in their second editions and are best sellers. *The Dyslexia Early Screening Test* (DEST – Nicolson and Fawcett, 2003) is designed for ages 4.5–6.5, and *The Dyslexia Screening Test – Junior* (DST-J – Fawcett and Nicolson, 2005) for ages 6.6–11.5. They were designed to tap the broad range of skills we had identified as problematic in our study of primitive skills outlined above, and to cover all the major theories of dyslexia at that time. We wanted the tests to be suitable for teachers or teaching assistants to deliver in a simple paper and pencil format, taking around 30 minutes per child. The tests include tests of readiness for the younger children, including memory, receptive vocabulary, speed of auditory processing and naming, letter knowledge, and simple tests of phonology including rhyming and discrimination, as well as motor skills such as copying, bead threading and balance. For the DST-J we include tests of fluency in literacy, such as single word reading, nonsense word reading, naming, copying, verbal and semantic fluency segmentation, receptive vocabulary, as well as bead threading and balance. Individual results can be compared with the norms for the age group, with different norms for every 6 months for the DEST, and every year for the DST-J.

In terms of multilingualism, a recent study showed that the DEST had great potential in identifying Singaporean children at risk for dyslexia, in this case tested in English, the language of instruction for Singapore, and compared with UK norms (See and Koay, 2014). Although the Singaporean children showed strengths in memory, motor skills and knowledge, they showed significant problems with phonology, particularly rhyming. In a country where a child is expected to read the word 'neighbourhood' when they start school in both English and Mandarin, dyslexia is a particular problem and still carries a stigma, despite the dyslexia revealed by the former Prime Minister, Lee Kwan Yew. These screening tests have also been translated and norms collected for children in a number of different languages, including Hebrew, Spanish and Dutch amongst others. The DST-J was recently launched for India where children have committed suicide in their early teens on discovering they are dyslexic. The DEST is to be translated into Bahasa Malay prior to developing norms for Malaysia with support from the National Early Childhood Intervention Council (NECIC), and the norm collection for the Malaysian DST-J is underway. The DEST has inspired an Indonesian computerised screening test currently under development.

The difficulty that dyslexic children experience is directly related to the transparency of the language, and in many countries dyslexia will first show up as a speed rather than an accuracy issue. It is possible to decode the sounds accurately but performance remains slow. In an interesting study of Dutch children, in comparison with immigrant children in the Netherlands (Verpelan and van der Vijer, 2015), the authors use the DST-NL as a tool to examine relative difficulties for these different groups of children in 3rd and 5th grades, predicting that these differences will lessen as the children grow older and more competent linguistically. A total of 125 children in 3rd grade aged 6–7 (33% Dutch, 67% immigrant), and 149 children in 5th grade aged 8–9 (47% Dutch, 53% immigrant) took part in the study. The immigrant children were drawn from largely Turkish or Moroccan backgrounds, with some Asian and Eastern European, with significantly more of their parents having a low educational level (54% immigrant, 2% Dutch). Interestingly, although the authors had predicted that greater differences would be found in 3rd than 5th grade, contrary to their expectations, the differences between dyslexic and non-dyslexic children increased with grade equally for both Dutch and immigrant children. There were only very small effects of the differences in culture.

Screening and intervention with Somali children

One of the largest groups of EAL children in the UK is Somali and their progress is dictated by the age at which they arrived in the country. In earlier research (Lynch *et al.*, 2000) we adopted an intervention technique used successfully with younger children to screen and intervene with two Somali children recently arrived in the UK (4 years and 2 years ago respectively) and in the first year of comprehensive school in Sheffield. This was part of a larger study of computer assisted learning with dyslexic secondary school children. Bilingual children with mild language problems may soon catch up with their peers, but where exposure to English is delayed or they show signs of dyslexia the prognosis is likely to be significantly worse. Firstly, we screened the children, one male and one female, on the dyslexia screening test to identify risk level and accompanied this with tests of receptive language (BPVS) and reading (Neale analysis). These children had not even achieved complete mastery of grapheme–phoneme conversion skills. Over the 10-week period of intervention, delivered by a customised computer program, RITA, the girl made over 9 months' progress, and we concluded that her problems were largely attributed to EAL and some attention problems (she preferred to chat to her friends) rather than to dyslexia. Despite the fact that their starting levels were very similar, the boy made very little progress, apart from a 6-month improvement in comprehension. His profile showed strong indications of dyslexia as well as EAL, and his problems were likely to be more entrenched.

Scores for the Somali boy are given in Table 2.1.

This boy was fiercely competitive and proud and rather embarrassed by his difficulties, so although he was clearly bright and committed he would rush through his work making wild guesses in his reading. The program we designed for him emphasised sound differentiation and sight vocabulary. His strengths lay in writing, which if anything was too fast and error prone. He had problems with the sounds 'b' 'p' 'v' and 'd' that are not differentiated in Somali and therefore seemed irrelevant to him. He was extremely keen and motivated to work with the computer and one of the programs we used asked him to differentiate a bus and a van, a cloze procedure where pictures are provided and the child completes the word by dragging the appropriate letter in response to the computer spoken word. He had initially noted that tasks were given a level of difficulty from 1 to 4, and demanded to work at level 4. By careful choice of tasks we were able to give him this task that incorporated basic skills, without compromising his dignity. As a bright but impatient boy, he found it hard to slow down to listen to the teacher or the computer. We found that our best approach was to repeat the word ourselves after the computer, and encourage the children to repeat the words afterwards, in order to break down the sounds and identify the first and last sounds, so that they could choose the appropriate word from the four provided under the picture. This maintained the children's interest in the program, they found the task quite challenging and needed to concentrate hard to follow the instructions. This modification to the basic program allowed the children to be successful in both speed and accuracy, and our records showed that they achieved 100% correct results. This program was a particular favourite and although

TABLE 2.1 Scores for a Somali boy learning English as second language

Gender	*Male*
Chronological age	11.8
Dyslexia Screening Test risk	1.1 (0.9 = risk)
Reading age	6.6
Spelling age	7.3
British Picture Vocabulary Score centile	52
Reading standard score	64
Reading centile	1
Spelling standard score	69
Spelling centile	2

originally designed for young children, allowed this boy to achieve success without any feelings of humiliation in response to failure. Although his reading age did not improve significantly, his score on the Neale analysis improved by 6 months in terms of comprehension, because we had encouraged him to slow down slightly to allow himself to understand the passage. This change in his learning style impressed the staff, and the boy himself was encouraged by these results. The differences between the outcomes for the boy and the girl make it very clear that an Individual Education Plan is vital for children such as these, even when superficially their problems may seem very similar. This boy's family had become concerned because despite 4 years' exposure to English, he was failing to progress, and clearly their concern was justified.

Developing the Welsh dyslexia test – DST-W

Wales, although part of the UK has an increasingly divergent educational system from the one that operates in England. The Welsh language and the English language have equal status in the country and in many Welsh homes the first language is in fact Welsh. Consequently many primary schools, especially but not exclusively in the more rural counties, operate through the medium of Welsh throughout Key Stage 1, introducing English in year 3 at the beginning of Key Stage 2 in English lessons, and often using it for science lessons, with the remainder of the curriculum being delivered through the medium of Welsh. Around a quarter of children are educated in the medium of Welsh in primary school, falling to 20% by secondary school. It is therefore inappropriate to screen for dyslexic-type difficulties in English and important that we develop a Welsh version of the screening test. Recent reports to the Welsh assembly government highlighted the lack of resources then available for screening or testing in the Welsh language (Kirby *et al.*, 2012; Caravolas *et al.*, 2012b).

Dyslexia in Wales – the literature

There are a limited number of studies on the Welsh language and in particular on dyslexia among Welsh speakers. However, research suggests that reading acquisition may be quicker and easier in Welsh than in English (Ellis and Hooper, 2001; Spencer and Hanley, 2003, 2004). Ellis and Hooper (2001) investigated reading in typical Welsh and English 6–7-year-olds. Children reading in Welsh read more accurately than those reading in English, but they do not read more quickly. Welsh children also used a different strategy, tending to blend whereas English children tended to guess words they could not read. This may be due to the transparency of the Welsh language.

Spencer and Hanley (2003) considered reading development in younger children aged 5–6 and found that children reading in Welsh were more skilled in both real and nonsense words, and in phoneme awareness. In terms of the lowest achievers, English readers had a greater gap between their age and their achievement, again suggesting the regular orthography of Welsh as a protective factor. However, Hanley *et al.*, 2004 showed that this advantage had diminished by age 10, with the groups equivalent for regular words, the English readers slightly behind in irregular word reading, but the lowest 25% significantly behind the Welsh-speaking children. Surprisingly, comprehension skills in Welsh were lower, showing that accuracy and phonological skills are not enough. Similar results have been found for spelling (Mayer *et al.*, 2007).

In the only study we found on dyslexia in Welsh, Thomas and Lloyd (2008) found that Welsh-speaking dyslexic children performed worse than their peers on reading, spelling and text copying tasks. Overall, any advantages in literacy in Welsh would be lost by age 10 and problems in speed and phonological awareness are likely to be found in both English- and Welsh-speaking dyslexics.

Translating the DST for Welsh use

In translating the test into Welsh we were very aware of the need to capture the spirit of the test, rather than simply translating word for word. We therefore consulted with experts in the Welsh language, and the translation was made with a great deal of diligence to ensure that the spirit of the test was maintained and subtleties in the Welsh language addressed. We considered differences in usage between North and South Wales, and decided to opt for South Wales usage as the version utilised, because this was where we had access to the greatest number of schools.

The DST-J was originally designed for children aged 6.5–11.5. However, in collecting these norms we have been mindful of the Welsh Foundation stage that emphasises the development of pre-literacy skills through play up to age 7. In view of this difference between England and Wales in terms of their curriculum it was decided that it was most appropriate to concentrate on Key Stage 2, thus limiting our testing to the junior school age range. The difficulties are compounded for some children learning in Welsh because they come from an English-speaking background and may be short of Welsh spoken vocabulary. We therefore collected data on family background for these norms. We then used this to produce two sets of norms, one for the group overall, and secondly for children from a Welsh-language background.

The approach adopted here in translating screening tests for dyslexia has also been used in Bridgend in a project led by Nichola Jones and the inclusion team. English-speaking children in reception have been screened for risk, using the DEST, and a 12-week intervention 'Hands on literacy' developed with a team led by Debbie Avington, and a post test used to evaluate progress. This approach has proved very useful, and is now in use in 75 schools in the South Wales and Pembrokeshire areas, with records maintained to age 10, with plans for the Welsh cluster schools joining in autumn 2015 working with year 1 children, using the DEST translated by Robat Powell, formerly from the National Foundation for Educational Research. Results have shown that around 75% of the children improve in their pre-reading skills, and that this transfers into a similar percentage reading up to their chronological age by age 8 (Jones and Fawcett, 2013).

The DST-J W was normed on over 400 children and data was collected on the home language. Across most of the age groups, apart from 9.6–10.5, the majority of parents spoke English rather than Welsh. It is interesting to note that this impacts on the naming speed, the speed of which is significantly slower at the lowest level than for the English norms. This is possibly because some of the children from English-speaking homes are less fluent in their speed of access to the Welsh language because they do not practise the language at home.

A total of 267 of the children tested were from English-speaking backgrounds, 180 from Welsh-speaking backgrounds, including 34 mixed Welsh–English, plus 2 English/ Polish Home language.

TABLE 2.2 Children at risk on the dyslexia screening test – Welsh

Home language	Mild risk	Strong risk
English	34	65
Mixed Welsh/English	5	6
Welsh	17	9
English/Polish	0	2

The results (Table 2.2) give us 29% risk level overall, with 14.4% risk in the children from Welsh-speaking backgrounds attending Welsh-speaking schools, 3% of this was strong risk. By the age of 9.6 differences between the groups have evened out.

Comparison with original DST-J norms

In comparison with the original English norms for the DST-J there was a clear effect of the length of Welsh words on the speed of rapid naming (RAN). This meant between 30 and 40 seconds longer to retrieve the names of the Welsh pictures than for the English pictures, across the age group for the overall sample. One-minute reading, by contrast was more fluent at the top end (up to 26 words extra in the minute) with this advantage based on the greater regularity of the Welsh language evening out by age 9.6. There was also a slight advantage in spelling up to and including age 9.6, and a slight advantage in nonsense word reading for the sample overall. By contrast, the one-minute writing was much slower, up to 10 words less at age 6.6 in the most fluent writers and again this persisted to age 8.6. All of these findings might be predicted from the literature (e.g. Hanley *et al.*, 2004; Ellis and Hooper, 2001).

In order to check for the importance of having a strong role model in usage of the Welsh language at home, separate norms were calculated for those children from Welsh-speaking families. It was notable that the range of reading skills was much wider in the younger age groups, with higher scores at both the bottom and the top end, and that the RAN speed was faster for this group up to the age of 8.6. It is likely that this reflects greater familiarity and fluency in the Welsh language. In the remainder of the tests, there was a slight advantage for the children from a Welsh-speaking background. The vocabulary scores for children at 6.6 from a Welsh-speaking background for example, were similar to those at 9.6 for the overall group.

These results suggest that extra support in language and vocabulary may be necessary for children attending a Welsh-speaking school, if there is no Welsh in their home background. However, there will also be individual differences in exposure to Welsh, depending on the area and the peer group exposure.

Conclusions: The way forward

It may be seen from the literature and the case studies provided in this chapter that children who are multilingual have an enriched language environment that allows their intellectual development to flourish, despite some initial delays in language learning. These advantages persist throughout life and protect them from the potential depredations of dementia. Nevertheless, the outlook for children with dyslexia working within a multilingual system may be impaired and further research is needed in the area to ensure that early support is provided to ensure the best possible outcomes for these children.

References

Caravolas, M., Lervag, A., Mousikou, P. *et al.* (2012a) Common patterns of prediction of literacy development in different alphabetic orthographies. *Psychological Science*, 23, 678–686.

Caravolas, M., Kirby, A., Fawcett, A.J. and Glendenning, K. (2012b) *Literature review on the state of research for children with dyslexia.* A report commissioned by the Welsh Government: Research document no: 058/2012. http://wales.gov.uk/docs/dcells/publications/120906researchen.pdf

Duncan, L.G., Castro, S.L., Defior, S., Seymour, P.H.K., Baillie, S., Leybaert, J. and Serrano, F. (2013) Phonological development in relation to native language and literacy: variations on a theme in six alphabetic orthographies. *Cognition*, 127, 398–419. http://dx.doi.org/10.1016/j.cognition.2013.02.009

Elliott, J.G. and Grigorenko, K.L. (2014) *The Dyslexia Debate.* Cambridge: Cambridge University Press.

Ellis, N.C. and Hooper, A.M. (2001) Why learning to read is easier in Welsh than in English: orthographic transparency effects evinced with frequency-matched tests. *Applied Psycholinguistics*, 22, 571–599.

Fawcett, A.J. and Nicolson, R.I. (2005) *The Dyslexia Screening Test – Junior.* London: The Psychological Corporation.

Fawcett, A.J., Nicolson, R.I. and Dean, P. (1996) Impaired performance of children with dyslexia on a range of cerebellar tasks. *Annals of Dyslexia*, 46, 259–283.

Fawcett, A.J., Nicolson, R.I., Moss, H., Nicolson, M.K. and Reason, R. (2001) Effectiveness of reading intervention in junior school. *Educational Psychology*, 21, 3, 299–312.

Finch, A.J., Nicolson, R.I. and Fawcett, A.J. (2002) Evidence for an anatomical difference within the cerebella of dyslexic brains. *Cortex*, 38, 529–539.

Frost, R., Siegelman, N., Narkiss, A. and Afek, L. (2013) What predicts successful literacy acquisition in a second language? *Psychological Science*, 24, 1243–1252.

Garcia-Sierra, A., Rivera-Gaxiola, M., Percaccio, C.R. *et al.* (2011) Bilingual language learning: an ERP study relating early brain responses to speech, language input, and later word production. *Journal of Phonetics*, 39, 4, 546–557.

Hanley, J.R., Masterson, J., Spencer, L.H. and Evans, D. (2004) How long do the advantages of learning to read a transparent orthography last? An investigation of the reading skills and reading impairment of Welsh children at 10 years of age. *The Quarterly Journal of Experimental Psychology Section A*, 57, 1393–1410.

Jones, N. and Fawcett, A.J. (2013) Screening children with dyslexia in South Wales. In *Dyslexia Handbook*. Reading: BDA.

Kelly, K. (2002*) The early detection of dyslexia in bi-lingual pupils.* Unpublished PhD thesis. Manchester Metropolitan University.

Kirby, A., Caravolas, M., Fawcett, A.J. and Glendenning, K. (2012*) Current literacy and dyslexia provision in Wales.* www.cymru.gov.uk

Kuhl, P.K. (2004) Early language acquisition: cracking the speech code. *Nature Reviews Neuroscience*, 5, 11, 831–843.

Lallier, M., Valdois, S., Lassus-Sangosse, D., Prado, C. and Kandel, S. (2014) Impact of orthographic transparency on typical and atypical reading development: evidence in French–Spanish bilingual children. *Research in Developmental Disabilities*, 35, 1177–1190.

Lynch, L., Fawcett, A.J. and Nicolson, R.I. (2000) Computer-assisted reading intervention in a secondary school: an evaluation study. *British Journal of Educational Technology*, 31, 333–348.

Mayer, P., Crowley, K. and Kaminska, Z. (2007) Reading and spelling processes in Welsh–English bilinguals: differential effects of concurrent vocalisation tasks. *Reading and Writing: An Interdisciplinary Journal*, 20, 671–690.

Murphy, V. and Unthiah, A. (2015) *A systematic review of intervention research examining English language and literacy development in children with English as an Additional Language (EAL)* www.bell-foundation. org.uk/assets/Documents/EALachievementMurphy.pdf?1422548394

Nicolson, R.I. and Fawcett, A.J. (1990) Automaticity: a new framework for dyslexia research. *Cognition*, 30, 159–182.

Nicolson, R.I. and Fawcett, A.J. (1994) Comparison of deficits in cognitive and motor skills in children with dyslexia. *Annals of Dyslexia*, 44, 147–164.

Nicolson, R.I. and Fawcett, A.J. (2000) Long-term learning in dyslexic children. *European Journal of Cognitive Psychology*, 12, 357–393.

Nicolson, R.I. and Fawcett, A.J. (2003) *The Dyslexia Early Screening Test*. 2nd edition. London: The Psychological Corporation.

Nicolson, R. I. and Fawcett, A.J. (2007). Procedural learning difficulties: reuniting the developmental disorders? *Trends in Neurosciences*, 30, 4, 135–141.

Nicolson, R.I. and Fawcett, A.J. (2011) Invited article, special issue on dyslexia, dysgraphia and procedural learning. *Cortex*, 47, 117–127.

Nicolson, R.I. and Fawcett, A.J. (submitted 2015) Development of dyslexia: the delayed neural commitment framework. *Annals of Dyslexia*.

Nicolson, R.I., Fawcett, A.J., Berry, E.L., Jenkins, I.H., Dean, P. and Brooks, D.J. (1999a) Association of abnormal cerebellar activation with motor learning difficulties in dyslexic adults. *The Lancet*, 353, 1662–1667.

Nicolson, R.I., Fawcett, A.J., Moss, H., Nicolson, M.K. and Reason, R. (1999b) An early reading intervention study: evaluation and implications. *British Journal of Educational Psychology*, 69, 47–62.

Nicolson, R.I., Fawcett, A.J, Brookes, R.L. and Needle J. (2010) Procedural learning and dyslexia. *Dyslexia*, 16, 194–212.

See, S.J. and Koay, P.S. (2014) The identification of dyslexia in preschool children in a multilingual society. *Asia Pacific journal of developmental differences*, 1, 43–61.

Spencer, L.H. and Hanley, J.R. (2003) Effects of orthographic transparency on reading and phoneme awareness in children learning to read in Wales. *British Journal of Psychology*, 94, 1–28.

Spencer, L.H. and Hanley, J.R. (2004) Learning a transparent orthography at five years old: reading development of children during their first year of formal reading instruction in Wales. *Journal of Research Reading*, 27, 1–14.

Strand, S., Malmberg, L. and Hall, J. (2015) *English as an Additional Language (EAL) and educational achievement in England: An analysis of the National Pupil Database*. https://educationendowment foundation.org.uk/uploads/pdf/EAL_and_educational_achievement2.pdf

Thomas, E.M. and Lloyd, S.W. (2008) Developing language appropriate tasks for identifying literacy difficulties in Welsh-speaking children. *Dyslexia Review*, 20, 1–9.

Torgesen, J.K., Alexander, A.W., Wagner, R.K., Rashotte, C.A., Voeller. K.K. and Conway, T. (2001) Intensive remedial instruction for children with severe reading disabilities: immediate and long-term outcomes from two instructional approaches. *Journal of Learning Disabilities*, 34, 1, 33–58, 78.

Varvara, P., Varuzza, C., Sorrentino, A.C.P., Vicari, S. and Menghini, D. (2014) Executive functions in developmental dyslexia. *Frontiers in Human Neuroscience*, 8, 1–8.

Verpalen, J.M.P. and van de Vijver, F.J.R. (2015) Differences in neurocognitive aspects of dyslexia in Dutch and immigrant 6–7- and 8–9-years old children. *SpringerPlus*, 4, 105. DOI: 10.1186/s40064-015-0874-1

3

DYSLEXIA, BI/MULTILINGUALISM AND OTITIS MEDIA (GLUE EAR)

A sticky educational problem!

Lindsay Peer

This chapter will:

1. Address dyslexia and highlight its complexities within a bi/multilingual context
2. Help in understanding the medical condition otitis media (glue ear) and its impact upon dyslexic learners
3. Raise the hypothesis of otitis media as an additional possible cause of dyslexia

The phone call came:

> Muhammed [name changed] has been in the country for eight years. He is about to take his GCSEs. We thought that his difficulties were due to speaking another language and it was taking him time to learn English … but now we wonder whether this is the case.

A SENCo telephoned me, the then Education Director of the British Dyslexia Association. A teacher of English as a foreign language had been employed to support Muhammed and his teachers, but progress was minimal and teaching eventually ceased. Chat language had developed, but academic language faltered. Staff and family felt that that he was not listening, was disinterested or incapable; however, this did not fit the profile of the hard-working learner. It later transpired that he was dyslexic and had needed specialist dyslexia teaching and support. He significantly underachieved; self-esteem and confidence dropped along with his hopes for the future.

Dyslexia

The following UK description of dyslexia was used in the Rose report (2009):

- Dyslexia is a learning difficulty that primarily affects the skills involved in accurate and fluent word reading and spelling.
- Characteristic features of dyslexia are difficulties in phonological awareness, verbal memory and verbal processing speed.
- Dyslexia occurs across the range of intellectual abilities.

- It is best thought of as a continuum, not a distinct category, and there are no clear cut-off points.
- Co-occurring difficulties may be seen in aspects of language, motor co-ordination, mental calculation, concentration and personal organisation, but these are not, by themselves, markers of dyslexia.
- A good indication of the severity and persistence of dyslexic difficulties can be gained by examining how the individual responds or has responded to well-founded intervention.

The British Dyslexia Association adds the following characteristics to this:

- The visual and auditory processing difficulties that some individuals with dyslexia can experience.
- Dyslexic readers can show a combination of abilities and difficulties that affect the learning process.
- Some also have strengths in other areas, such as design, problem solving, creative skills, interactive skills and oral skills.

Dyslexia and bi/multilingualism

Dyslexia occurs in at least one in ten people, putting more than 700 million children and adults worldwide at risk of life-long illiteracy and social exclusion (Dyslexia International, 2015). In the UK, there has been a move towards cultural awareness and fairness. Documents such as The British Psychological Society Working Party report 'Dyslexia, Literacy and Psychological Assessment' (British Psychological Society, 1999) and the Ofsted report 'Overcoming Barriers: Ensuring that Roma children are fully engaged and achieving in education' (2014) are contributing to change. However, there is still relatively little skilled knowledge of assessment and intervention for bi/multilingual dyslexic learners. A further critical need is the recognition and prevention of the emotional fall-out of struggling monolingual dyslexic learners (Alexander-Passe, 2006) and bi/multilingual dyslexic learners. See also the chapter by Dr Richard Soppitt in this book (chapter 18). For the interest of the reader, a charity by the name of GroOops in the UK focuses upon the emotional aspects of dyslexia (www.grooops.com); it is not short of work!

Peer (1999) and Peer and Reid (2000a) noted:

> Teachers and psychologists have tended to ignore the difficulties in learning experienced by these (multilingual) students, because of the multiplicity of factors which are apparently relevant: a non-supportive home background resulting in different or impoverished language skills; unusual learning profile; apparently low intelligence (which sometimes arises out of insensitive testing); unbalanced speech development; and restricted vocabulary in one or more languages. These are assumed to be the relevant factors; that there might be a biological basis for children's reading, writing and spelling retardation is sometimes overlooked, with disastrous consequences.

Another problem, so often unlinked to literacy acquisition and access to the curriculum, is the historical and/or current presence of otitis media. My research on a cohort of 1,000 dyslexic individuals found that over 70% had experienced this medical condition, to the extent that grommets were surgically inserted.

What is otitis media?

Otitis Media (OM) is a term that covers a continuum of similar diseases. Inflammation of the ear is very common in children; it sometimes manifests as ear infections and sometimes as fluid in the ear. In healthy children the space in the middle ear is filled with air, allowing the flow of sound to the inner ear. In cases of OM, the space in the middle ear is either partially or totally filled with fluid which reduces the transmission of sound. Most children will have either an ear infection or an episode of OM; most resolve, yet for some the problems persist and may lead to ongoing difficulties. As yet, it is not known why some children suffer more persistent problems.

Medical research continues in this field. Richard M. Rosenfeld, MD, President of the International Society for Otitis Media reported (2015) that

> A review of 21 World Health Organization regional areas estimated 709 million annual episodes of acute otitis media and 31 million of chronic suppurative otitis media. Moreover, otitis-related hearing loss affects 31 per 10,000 people and 21,000 die every year from complications of otitis media. Put simply, otitis media is a major global concern, with disproportionate impact in Oceania, South Asia, and Sub-Saharan Africa.

He observed that 'Given the ubiquity of otitis media, it should be no surprise that organized symposia have existed for almost four decades'.

The Fourth Research Conference on Recent Advances in Otitis Media addressed the issue of terminology. The Panel on Definition and Classification used clinical criteria to define the following terms:

- *Otitis Media*: An inflammation of the middle ear. This general term encompasses all the diseases of the OM continuum.
- *Acute Suppurative Otitis Media*: Clinically identifiable infection of the middle ear of sudden onset and short duration. Synonyms include acute otitis media and acute purulent otitis media.
- *Secretory Otitis Media:* Presence of middle ear effusion behind an intact tympanic membrane without acute signs or symptoms. This category includes the clinically non-infectious forms of OM. Common symptoms are chronic otitis media with effusion, otitis media with effusion, nonsuppurative otitis media, serous otitis media, mucoid otitis media, catarrh, serotympanum and mucotympanum.
- *Chronic Suppurative Otitis Media*, or *Chronic Otitis Media*: Chronic otorrhea through a tympanic membrane perforation.

As OM is treated by medical practitioners and/or speech and language therapists working at an early stage; educators mostly remain uninformed about it. Common problems may include: language delay, weak phonological skills and working memory, poor auditory processing and distractibility, problems in following conversation in background noise and in the learning of additional languages. Little has been done to investigate the impact of OM on educational success which affects so many in the early years. In some countries, this is due to the funding regime which separates the areas of speech and language from education.

For the purposes of this chapter, I will use the definition of OM as given in the first bullet point above. In different countries and even within the same country there has been no standard use of one definition (Daly, 1997); likewise with definitions of recurrent OM. International statistical comparisons therefore are challenging. What is clear is that this is a significant problem that results in a huge financial cost to society as well as problems to the individual. The Wellcome Trust (2013) notes that:

> If the loss of hearing is persistent, however, it can lead to impairments in later life, even after normal hearing has returned. These impairments include 'lazy ear', or amblyaudia, which leaves people struggling to locate sounds or pick out sounds in noisy environments such as classrooms or restaurants.

Galaburda (1994) suggested that 'there may be a familial tendency to have autoimmune and allergic disorders, which may lead to subtle brain damage during the second half of gestation'. Personal experience of numerous cases has led me to believe that the links to family history and allergies, especially to milk, are common in high numbers of dyslexic profiles.

Intervention/treatment

Treatment for the condition varies, some children take antibiotics; others eventually undergo surgery. Doctors often employ a period of 'watchful waiting'. Significance in educational terms is the considerable time children experience hearing loss during the management process. For some, hearing returns to normal within a month, for others hearing loss can continue for three months or longer. For large numbers of children, significant hearing loss is experienced as well as extreme discomfort/pain in the ears. In cases of recurrent episodes, weeks if not months of the early years are affected.

OM may well lead to lack of concentration as well as an inability to process the fine sounds that are necessary for auditory perception and speed of processing – keys to language learning. Tallal (1999) states that:

> Timing cues present in the acoustic waveform of speech provide critical information for the recognition and segmentation of the ongoing speech signal.

In its Response to the Department for Education Consultation on the Year 1 Screening Check (NDCS, 2011), the National Deaf Children's Society noted that many deaf children, including those with 'glue ear' may take longer than their hearing peers to acquire phonic knowledge. Amongst other recommendations, they noted that such children should be given additional time to process information.

Goswami *et al.* (2011) note that studies in sensory neuroscience reveal the critical importance of accurate sensory perception for cognitive development, especially 'the possible sensory correlates of *phonological processing*, the primary cognitive risk factor for developmental dyslexia'. Across languages, children with dyslexia have a specific difficulty with the neural representation of the phonological structure of speech. Goswami *et al.* note that 'Speech rhythm is used across languages by infants to segment the speech stream into words and syllables. Early difficulties in perceiving auditory sensory cues to speech rhythm and prosody could lead developmentally to impairments in phonology'. Looking at three very different spoken and written languages, English, Spanish and Chinese in both dyslexic and non-dyslexic learners, they found that the key sensory cue measured was rate of onset of the amplitude envelope (rise time), known to be critical for the rhythmic timing of speech. Despite the phonological and orthographic differences of each language, rise time sensitivity was a significant predictor of phonological awareness, and rise time was the only consistent predictor of reading acquisition. The data supports a language-universal theory of the neural basis of developmental dyslexia on the basis of rhythmic perception and syllable segmentation. Goswami *et al.* also suggest that novel remediation strategies on the basis of rhythm and music may offer benefits for phonological and linguistic development.

Friel-Palti and Finitzo (1990) suggest that hearing loss during the first two years of life may result in a delay in the emergence of receptive or expressive language or both. Gravel and Wallace (1995) maintain that although communication skills may appear normal for this group of children on entry to school, other auditory-based deficits may emerge in the classroom situation. They and others suggest that there are weaknesses associated with listening comprehension, academic achievement, attention and behavioural difficulties.

There is a potentially large group of dyslexic learners who may not suffer from abnormal brain function at birth, but rather suffer from a phonological and speech disorder that is acquired as babies or in early childhood through the presence of OM. Early development of language is crucial to academic success.

The overlap between dyslexia and otitis media

Dyslexic learners demonstrate differing clusters of difficulties, but the overlap with OM is notable. The overlaps are indicated by ★ in the list below (adapted from Peer, 2005):

* Speed of processing: spoken and/or written language slow★
* Poor concentration★
* Difficulty following instructions★
* Forgetful of words★
* Poor standard of written work compared with oral ability
* Messy work with many crossings out and words tried several times, e.g. 'wippe', 'wype', 'wiep', 'wipe'
* Persistently confused by letters which look similar, particularly 'b'/'d', 'p'/'g', 'p'/'q', 'n'/'u', 'm'/'w'
* Poor handwriting with many 'reversals' and badly formed letters
* Spells a word several different ways in one piece of writing
* Makes anagrams of words, e.g. 'tired' for 'tried', 'breaded' for 'bearded'
* Produces badly set-out written work; doesn't stay close to the margin
* Poor pencil grip
* Produces phonetic and bizarre spelling: not age/ability appropriate★
* Uses unusual sequencing of letters or words
* Makes poor reading progress, especially using 'look and say' methods
* Finds it difficult to blend letters together★
* Has difficulty in establishing syllable division or knowing the beginnings and endings of words★
* Pronunciation of words unusual★

- Lacks expression when reading
- Comprehension poor*
- Is hesitant and laboured in reading, especially when reading aloud*
- Misses out words when reading, or adds extra words
- Fails to recognise familiar words
- Loses point of story – read or written*
- Difficulty in picking out the most important points from a passage*
- Confusion with number order, e.g. units, tens, hundreds
- Confused by symbols such as + and × signs
- Difficulty remembering anything in a sequential order, e.g. tables, days of the week, the alphabet
- Difficulty in learning to tell the time
- Poor time keeping and general awareness
- Poor personal organisation
- Difficulty remembering what day of the week it is, birthdays, order of seasons/months of the year
- Difficulty with concepts – yesterday, today, tomorrow
- Poor motor skills, leading to weaknesses in speed, control and accuracy of the pencil
- Limited understanding of nonverbal communication*
- Confusion of left/right, up/down, east/west
- Possible indeterminate hand preference
- Performs unevenly day to day
- Work avoidance tactics
- Seems to 'dream', does not seem to listen*
- Easily distracted*
- Is the class clown, disruptive, withdrawn (often cries for help)*
- Excessively tired due to the amount of concentration and effort required.*

Theories of dyslexia

The major theories of dyslexia research have very much focused within the following causal areas:

1. Phonological Deficit Hypothesis
2. Magnocellular Deficit Hypothesis
3. Double Deficit Hypothesis
4. Dyslexic Automisation Deficit Hypothesis
5. Cerebellar Deficit Hypothesis.

It is my view that there is a further hypothesis – one that links to the others and relates to the presence of OM. There are many children who experience subtle difficulties in hearing, such as high-frequency hearing loss (e.g. 's') or low frequency-loss with difficulty in recognising vowel sounds/consonants (e.g. 'b'). Auditory perception does not refer to hearing or acuity problems, but to levels of auditory discrimination and coding. Auditory discrimination difficulties can be due to developmental lags in speech perception, and are partly dependent upon auditory acuity. Typically, such a child might have difficulty discriminating between 'pin' and 'pen' or struggle to hear the correct sound of three soft vowels: 'a', 'e', 'u'. Is therefore incorrect encoding a problem of learning disability, auditory perception or linguistic confusion?

Linguists have long appreciated the importance of the relationship between spoken and written language. In spoken language the primary skill is one of face to face communication, in which the child develops individual, sometimes idiosyncratic knowledge of structure, rule systems and vocabulary which enable the construction of meaning from the sample of language available in their background. Parameters leading to the establishment of a phonological structure are essential. A central aspect of phonological awareness is the link between the speech children hear and the utterances they produce (Snowling, 1996) – and consequently with the written representation of words. Recurrent bouts of OM will interfere with this. There is a vast body of research focusing upon the phonological processes involved in the acquisition of literacy and the development of language skills. Stanovich (1988) suggested that a major key to the failure in the development of the reading process for some learners is a weakness in the phonological processing system in the learning of grapheme–phoneme correspondences. Receptive and expressive language skills are predictors of reading comprehension and phonological awareness; rapid naming skills are better predictors of word recognition.

Bishop and Adams (1990) proposed a 'critical age hypothesis' suggesting that if there has been a resolution of speech difficulties by approximately five years of age, there is a likelihood that reading and spelling will progress normally – notwithstanding other learning difficulties or other language interference.

Stackhouse (1996) maintains that although there are some visual deficits that may affect performance in reading, verbal skills have by far the greatest influence in development of literacy. Whilst maintaining that spoken language skills have the greatest effect on written language abilities, she recognises that the relationship is complex:

> Language problems affect comprehension and semantic development and are likely to restrict the use the child can make of contextual clues to develop reading skills. Speech difficulties affect spelling development in particular

and:

> phonological processing skills play a major role in the development of reading and spelling. Without intact input phonology a child cannot discriminate and sequence what he or she hears. This auditory processing problem will have a knock-on effect to how words are stored in the child's lexicon. Fuzzy lexical representations will be problematic when the child needs to name or spell. Output phonology is particularly important for rehearsing verbal material in memory and for reflecting on the structure in preparation for speech and spelling. Problems with rehearsal affect the child's ability to develop phonological awareness – a necessary skill for literacy to develop satisfactorily. Literacy success is dependent on coupling these phonological processing skills at the input, representation and output levels with alphabetic knowledge gained through orthographic experience.

When considering the implications of Stackhouse's views for those with dyslexia and who speak more than one language, there are major implications for identification, assessment and remediation at a young age; for those with a history of OM, this is even more critical.

Literacy, language and phonological awareness

Programmes have been developed which include the training of phonological skills, demonstrating that progress made by learners with difficulties in the acquisition of reading skills can be substantially enhanced (Hatcher *et al.*, 1994). However, most such programmes address difficulties experienced by monolingual dyslexic learners. We should ask:

* What is the effect of a different set(s) of phonological structures?
* Is the number of languages spoken an influence on functioning across the curriculum?
* Is spoken language different for this group?
* Is the ability to access literacy in bi/multilinguals different from that of monolingual dyslexics?
* What is the effect of excess stress caused by the need to study in more than one language on learning?
* What are the cultural implications?

The knowledge of structure, rule systems and vocabulary enables the learner to listen to, and process increasingly complex utterances. Knowledge and skills in the reception of ideas communicated to the learner by others through speech are greatly increased over time. With improved abilities in phonology, construction of expressive language becomes more precise. These skills provide the essential linguistic base required for success in the reading process. The knowledge of vocabulary, structure and rule systems derived from receptive and expressive speech usage is critical in the development of reading and becomes essential at a later point in the use of written language to express ideas and think coherently across the curriculum. Even though early speech has been described as basic communication/chat, it is of great importance in the development of thinking. Cline and Fredrickson (1991) analyse these matters in great detail in their consideration of what constitutes language proficiency. They indicate that the ability of the learner to use language can be considered from five different perspectives:

* Competence in phonology and syntax
* Competence in semantics
* Pragmatic competence
* Conversational competence
* Socio-linguistic competence.

They consider that the proficiency of a bilingual speaker is best understood if all five of these factors are taken into account. A speaker's proficiency is not comprised solely of knowledge of language and skill in listening and speaking. Additional essential factors are the speaker's attitudes and feelings about the situations in which each language is used. They firmly state that a proficient bilingual speaker requires not just competence, but also confidence across a wide range of situations. Cline and Fredrickson's key points are derived from the views of Cummins (1984) who distinguished between Basic Interpersonal Communicative Skills (BICS) and Cognitive Academic Language Proficiency (CALP).

Cummins hypothesised that it is the CALP aspects of language which are vital for educational success. BICS, whilst important, is insufficient. Learners need to use language for analysis, synthesis and evaluation of ideas. Cummins (1984) estimated that ethnic minority learners require two years to develop peer-appropriate communicative language, but need between five and seven years to fully develop language proficiency. I have not found equivalent figures for dyslexic learners.

Cummins assumes that this pattern is the norm for bilingual learners. He asserts that there could be unexpected difficulties for learners who evidence a different pattern of language acquisition. For example, one who is relatively fluent in English but experiences academic difficulties in his curriculum studies (CALP) may be assumed to have learning difficulties; he considers this an incorrect assumption. How then is it possible to differentiate between those with and those without learning difficulties, having analysed the underlying assumptions supporting the view that monolingualism is the norm, and that bilingualism is a possibly risky deviation?

Grosjean (1985) reflects upon a more holistic perspective. He suggests that bilingual speakers are advantaged in being able to maintain a flexible communicative competence through different situations and in the face of changing demands from their two languages. Whilst code switching can be a feature of monolingual speakers from two social backgrounds, it can also be seen as a useful example of bilingual language proficiency which indicates the complexity of the learner's representation and expression of ideas. Code switching occurs when two languages are mixed in a single sentence or conversation; this is often regarded as evidence of confusion, but is really a stage that bilingual learners go through. Switching languages may be used to signal a change in intimacy, as an 'in-group' reference or sentiment; to give meaningful emphasis to important language, such as the punch line in a joke; or to compensate for the lack of a precisely suitable word in one of the languages. It is common for very young bilingual children to code switch at syntactically inappropriate points in a sentence. However, more mature speakers will select the boundary of a relative clause or the beginning of a verb phrase for the change. This practice can be a rich variant in the representational repertoire of the bilingual speaker, which is much too frequently disparaged by those accepting the monolingual stance as the prestige viewpoint.

Bilingualism and bilinguality

Bilingualism was defined by Hamers and Blanc (1989) as:

> The state of an individual or community characterised by the simultaneous presence of two languages.

However, I believe that this is an overly simplistic definition as it is more accurate to assert that a range of bilingual conditions exist. For example, in *Diglossic Bilingualism*, a state of bilingualism is observed, in which two languages, each with separate and distinct ranges of social functions co-occur. In contrast, in *Territorial Bilingualism*, two or more languages co-occur which have official status within a designated geographic area. Another example is the coexistence of two or more unilingual areas within a single political structure as in the unilingual regions within a multilingual state.

Bilinguality is a more important concept which Hamers and Blanc (1989) define as:

> The psychological state of the individual who has access to more than one linguistic code as a means of social communication. This access is highly individual and will vary along a number of dimensions.

This gives additional dimensions of bilinguality:

*   *Additive Bilinguality* is defined as a situation in which the learner derives maximum benefit for his cognitive development from the bilingual experience. This is often the case where the two languages are highly valued in the learner's environment.
*   *Balanced Bilinguality* is a state of skills development in which an equivalent competence is reached in both languages. It should be noted, however, that whatever the level of competence, the balance is not equally distributed for all domains and functions of language.
*   *Compound Bilinguality* is a state of language development where two sets of linguistic signs are associated with the same set of meanings. This type of bilinguality is usually linked to a common context of acquisition.
*   *Consecutive Early Bilinguality* is a form of childhood bilinguality in which the second language is acquired before the age of five–six years, but after the acquisition of basic skills in the mother tongue.
*   *Dominant Bilinguality* is a state of bilinguality in which competencies in one language are superior to competencies in the other. The dominance is not equally distributed for all domains and functions of language.
*   *Subtractive Bilinguality* is a situation where the bilingual learner's cognitive development is delayed in comparison with his monolingual peers. This sometimes occurs when the mother tongue is devalued in the environment.

Influences of bi/multilingualism and cultural background upon learning

Bi/multilinguals must subconsciously be aware of their expressions, expletives, movements, gestures, pitch and tone, when communicating in different languages. This is also evident in written language contexts. Cline and Fredrickson (1991) point out that the various elements that create the context in which the child grows up, i.e. the 'background variables', are of considerable significance in determining the efficiency of learning. In their analysis, they specify three major background variables:

*   Society
*   The learner's own community
*   The learner's family.

The learner beginning school brings a set of competencies and attitudes derived from the interaction between capabilities stemming from innate potential, temperament and individual background variables. Cline and Fredrickson describe this set of competencies and attitudes as 'child input variables'.

The learner in school will be greatly influenced by what they categorise as 'educational treatment variables'. They postulate that the key points are:

*   The languages policy of the school
*   The patterns of language usage in the classroom and elsewhere in the school
*   The attitudes and expectations of peers and, of crucial importance, teachers.

The background variables, child input variables and educational treatment variables combine to influence both the learner's further acquisition of Language 1 and Language 2, and ultimate educational performance.

The bi/multilingual child is born into a home where the parents choose consistently to use particular language options, which may include one, two or more languages, as appropriate for them. Differences are evident between the child who has access to two or more languages from birth, compared with the child who initially learns only one language, and has the other superimposed at a later stage. Within the home the pre-school child learns the phonological structure from the available speech sample. In homes where early literacy is considered a high priority, children will have been introduced to the written word at nursery age, before the commencement of school. The shapes of the letters are learned, as are their sequence within the language structure, the direction in which books are opened and the text processed. The child may even have been introduced to the written form or forms of language through copying.

When the child is enrolled in school he or she is expected to use a sophisticated language code to convey ideas. Almost certainly this will be different from the language code used in the home. He or she will then be introduced by the teacher to the shapes of words in reading and will be expected to decipher a form of language, which is unfamiliar to them. In certain forms of bilinguality such as Arabic–English, there will be a clear conflict between direction of processing for the two scripts. Motor movements of the musculature of the throat, tongue and lips, giving rise to the organised sound patterns will also be different. Even such basic factors as the procedures for expulsion of air are different.

The differences described give rise to challenges in the use of language to represent ideas. This may be further complicated in some cases by the introduction of a third or more languages. This may well lead to an overload on working memory, causing academic failure. Dyslexic learners who experience weaknesses in working memory, processing and sequencing are particularly vulnerable.

Many working in the field of literacy would agree with Peer and Reid (2000b) who suggest that before children can begin the process of reading acquisition they have to learn spoken English to a minimal level. They note that due to the lack of research, it is difficult to determine whether any literacy difficulties experienced by these children are the result of:

a)   specific learning difficulty, e.g. dyslexia,
b)   developmental delay caused by lack of English language, or
c)   difference caused by diverse patterns of literacy development in ethnic minority children and their monolingual peers.

Where a learner has dyslexic-type difficulties, the ability to reach fluency in the second (or more languages) will be key to effective functioning, achievement and self-esteem. A learner needs to be competent at various levels of functioning in a range of languages in which they are required to perform – 'chat'/'academic' proficiency. Learners will also need to be proficient in written language, as well as in reading in relation to speed, accuracy and comprehension. These skills will determine achievement at school, success in further/higher education and in the appropriate workplace.

In countries where there is a requirement to function in more than one language, it is often found that there are a significant number of adults who are unable to cope with the academic rigours and employment expectations demanded of them, despite giving the impression that they are intellectually able. It is often due to diminished functioning that someone will begin an investigation leading to the identification of dyslexia.

Dyslexia in different linguistic systems

Grigorenko (2001) notes that the concept of dyslexia was initially developed and verified in studies of English-speaking populations. English is a language that is particularly difficult due to its irregularities in the area of phoneme–grapheme relationships, unlike languages which are highly regular. Also, definitional differences or educational practices cause different understanding, e.g. there are no characters in Chinese or Japanese whose meaning is equivalent to the term 'reading disability'.

Tarnopol and Tarnopol (1981) conducted a survey of data collected in 26 countries in an attempt to try to ascertain the percentage of school children who are dyslexic. The results ranged from a low 1% in China and Japan to a high 33% in Venezuela.

Glezerman (1983) noted that children with reading difficulties in English-speaking countries registered at about 20%, whilst those in Scandinavia were 10% and those in Germany 5%.

Wolf's Double Deficit theory (Wolf and Bowers, 1999) suggested that phonological deficits and processes underlying naming-speed deficits represent two separable sources of reading dysfunction, and that developmental dyslexia is characterised by both phonological and naming speed 'core' deficits. This is of clear importance when referring to dyslexia in a range of linguistic systems.

Grigorenko (2001) noted that the varying incidence of dyslexia in different languages is as follows:

> it appears that the mechanism leading to difficulties associated with the mastery of reading is universal in all languages and is related to the metalinguistic ability to decompose words into sounds, link phonemes to graphemes and to automize these skills. The manifestation of reading problems, however, will be different in different languages, depending on the phonological demands imposed by a given linguistic system.
>
> (p. 96)

This thinking clearly explains why the incidence of dyslexia in different countries and among different languages is so diverse. Not only is it highly likely that definitions are different, but the identification of dyslexia may well be carried out earlier and more easily in one place than in another. In the UK we recognise that dyslexia relates to far more than a reading problem; this is not the case internationally.

There are many thousands of children and adults who have not been identified as dyslexic and who live with unexplained failure and low self-esteem. The number of under-employed and unemployed in this group can only be speculated. The number of those caught up in penal systems internationally, whose lack of functional numeracy and literacy have prevented them from working has been variously estimated at between 50% and 70%. Temptations and/or frustrations may lead some into antisocial routes in a world where manual labour is fast on the decline and they have been prepared for little else.

When bi/multilingual dyslexic children do not appear to be functioning effectively in school, investigation should take place. All too often there are preconceived notions about the ability (or lack of ability) of specific cultural groups; or decisions are made about individuals without an attempt to understand the effects of the specific linguistic background. Furthermore, when these children are affected by a history of recurrent episodes of OM it would appear that even more strain is placed upon the processing system and more children fail. Effective packages of training need to be used in cross-disciplinary ways.

References

Alexander-Passe, N. (2006) How dyslexic teenagers cope: an investigation of self-esteem, coping and depression. *Dyslexia*, 12: 256–275. DOI: 10.1002/dys.318

Bishop, D.V.M. and Adams, C. (1990) A prospective study of the relationship between specific language impairment, phonological disorders and reading retardation. *Journal of Child Psychology and Psychiatry*, 31, 1027–1050.

British Psychological Society (1999) *Dyslexia, literacy and psychological assessment.* Report of a working party of the Division of Educational and Child Psychology. Cline, T. and Fredrickson, N. (1991) *Bilingual Pupils and the National Curriculum: Overcoming Difficulties in Teaching and Learning.* London: University College.

Cummins, J. (1984) *Construct of Learning Disability – Bilingualism and Special Education: Issues in Assessment and Pedagogy.* Clevedon: Multilingual Matters.

Daly, K.A. (1997) Definition and epidemiology of otitis media, in Roberts, J.E., Wallace, I.F. and Henderson, F.W. (Eds) *Otitis Media in Young Children: Medical, Developmental and Educational Implications*, pp. 14–15. Baltimore, MD: Paul Brookes Publishing.

Dyslexia International (2015) www.dyslexia-international.org/wp-content/uploads/2014/10/DIReport-final-4-29-14.pdf

Friel-Patti, S. and Finitzo, T. (1990) Language learning in a prospective study of otitis media with effusion in the first two years of life. *Journal of Speech and Hearing Research*, 33, 188–194.

Galaburda, A.M. (1994) Neuroanatomic basis of developmental dyslexia. *Neurologic Clinics*, 11, 1, 161–173.

Glezerman, T.B. (1983) Minimal brain dysfunction in children, in Grigorenko, E.L. (Ed.) Developmental dyslexia: an update on genes, brains and environments. *Journal of Child Psychiatry*, 42, 1, 95–96.

Goswami, H.-L., Wang, S., Cruz, A., Fosker, T., Mead, N. and Huss, M. (2011) Language-universal sensory deficits in developmental dyslexia: English, Spanish, and Chinese. *Journal of Cognitive Neuroscience*, 23, 2, 325–337. DOI:10.1162/jocn.2010.21453.

Gravel, J.S. and Wallace, I.F. (1995) Early otitis media, auditory abilities and educational risk. *American Journal of Speech–Language Pathology*, 4, 89–94.

Grigorenko, E.L. (2001) Developmental dyslexia: an update on genes, brains and environments. *Journal of Child Psychiatry*, 42, 1, 91–125.

Grosjean, F. (1985) The bilingual as a competent but specific speaker–hearer. *The Journal of Multilingual and Multicultural Development*, 6, 467–477.

Hamers, J.F. and Blanc, M.H.A. (1989) *Bilinguality and Bilingualism.* Cambridge: Cambridge University Press.

Hatcher, P., Hulme, C. and Ellis, A.W. (1994) Ameliorating early reading failure by integrating the teaching of reading and phonological skills: the phonological link hypothesis. *Child Development*, 65, 41–57.

NDCS (National Deaf Children's Society) (2011) Response to the Department for Education Consultation on the Year 1 Screening Check. www.ndcs.org.uk/document.rm?id=5606

Ofsted (2014) 'Overcoming barriers: Ensuring that Roma children are fully engaged and achieving in education'. www.gov.uk/government/uploads/system/uploads/attachment_data/file/430866/

Overcoming_barriers_-_ensuring_that_Roma_children_are_fully_engaged_and_achieving_in_education.pdf

Peer, L. (1999) Dyslexia and multilingualism. *Dyslexia: An International Journal of Research and Practice*, 5, 1, 53–55.

Peer, L. (2005) *Glue Ear*, pp. 28–29. London: David Fulton.

Peer, L. and Reid, G. (2000a) Multilingualism, literacy and dyslexia: a challenge for educators, in Peer, L. and Reid, G. (Eds) *Multilingualism, Literacy and Dyslexia: A Challenge for Educators*. London: David Fulton.

Peer, L. and Reid, G. (2000b) Literacy development in emergent bilingual children, in Peer, L. and Reid, G. (Eds) *Multilingualism, Literacy and Dyslexia: A Challenge for Educators*. London: David Fulton.

Rose, J. (2009, June) 'Identifying and Teaching Children and Young People with Dyslexia and Literacy Difficulties'. An independent report from Sir Jim Rose to the Secretary of State for Children, Schools and Families.

Rosenfeld, R.M. (2015) www.otitismediasociety.org/about.html

Snowling, M. (1996) Developmental dyslexia: an introduction and theoretical overview, in Snowling, M. and Stackhouse J. (Eds) *Dyslexia, Speech and Language: A Practitioner's Handbook*, p. 5. London: Whurr Publishers.

Stackhouse, J. (1996) Speech, spelling and reading: who is at risk and why? in Snowling, M. and Stackhouse, J. (Eds) *Dyslexia Speech and Language: A Practitioner's Handbook*. pp. 29–30. London: Whurr Publishers.

Tallal, P. (1999) Lecture entitled 'Language Impairments and Their Remediation' at the Center for Molecular and Behavioral Neuroscience, Rutgers University–JHU.

Tarnopol, L. and Tarnopol, M. (1981) *Comparative Reading and Learning Difficulties*. Lexington, MA: Lexington Books.

Wellcome Trust (2013) www.wellcome.ac.uk/News/Media-office/Press-releases/2013/WTP053037.htm

Wolf, M. and Bowers, P.G. (1999) The double-deficit hypothesis for the developmental dyslexias. *Journal of Educational Psychology*, 91, 415–438.

4

MULTILINGUALISM AND DYSLEXIA

A critical perspective

Deirdre Martin

This chapter will:

1. Show that there is an immense challenge to education brought by the social, political and geographical phenomenon of multiple diversities, known as superdiversity (Vertoveç, 2007) which has brought multilingualism to many countries that are ideologically monolingual, at a pace and diversity of change not previously experienced
2. Argue that the development of digitalised communication to meet the needs of globalisation, both socially and in the work force, is driving the progress of e-communication that could bring benefits as well as exclusion to multilingual users with literacy difficulties
3. Discuss how the significant turn in multilingual literacy studies affords the potential of critical sociolinguistics methodology to offer new perspectives on the complex phenomenon of dyslexia in superdiversity

Introduction

In this chapter I address some realities that compel change for academics and educationists involved with multilingual students who have difficulties with print.

New and changing contexts of multi-diversities of language and literacies afford an impetus to explore new approaches to researching difficulties with print and literacy. The social sciences, particularly studies of race, ethnicity, gender, disability and language, research through a critical lens. A critical view focuses on the nature and effects of relationships around power, reflexivity, positioning and identity. Critical research has rarely, or to a limited extent, embraced dyslexia in multilingual educational contexts. Teaching the curriculum for language, literacies and literacy skills through English to multilingual learners, and identifying substantial learning needs (such as dyslexia) is not a niche skill. It is a demand on the profession that many educators experience daily. I present a critical sociolinguistic approach to multilingualism and multilingual literacy practices. I discuss implications of this approach for multilingual learners with literacy difficulties and dyslexia in ideological monolingual educational settings such as the UK.

Multilingualism in 'superdiversity'

Many countries have historically been accustomed to diversity of languages, cultures and ethnicities which are both indigenous (e.g. Welsh and Gaelic in the UK) as well as languages of migration from previous colonisation (e.g. the languages of the Indian subcontinent in the UK). However, at the end of the twentieth century and in the early twenty-first century, major demographic changes have resulted from transnational migration, post-migration, and fresh population flows. These new patterns of migration have been termed 'superdiversity' (Vertoveç, 2007). Referring to these population movements in the UK, Vertoveç noted that they are characterised by:

> a dynamic interplay of variables among an increased number of new, small and scattered multiple origin transnationally connected, socio-economically differentiated and legally stratified immigrants who have arrived over the last decade.
>
> (Vertoveç, 2007: 1024)

Superdiversity is a recent phenomenon experienced in Europe, the USA, Canada and Australia, where these areas have bilingual histories described as majority language speakers and minority language speakers. Superdiversity has changed this linguistic landscape so that in some places, the sum-population of linguistic minority speakers is larger than the number of speakers of the majority language (Kalantzis and Cope, 1999), with implications for education.

Ideological discourses

While multilingual speakers have diverse linguistic resources relative to monolinguals, some resources are more 'equal' than others. Heller (2007, 2012) argues, after Hobsbawm (1990), that multilingualism comes out of the ideological complex of the nation-state with its focus on homogeneity. The hierarchical discourses of language and languaging in schooling are ideologically driven: the organisation of schooling is one of the arms of the political processes of the country (Blommaert, 2010). In most countries hierarchies of languages are evident in educational policies and implemented in pedagogic practices of language and literacies of schooling. Official discourses of language inclusion and exclusion frame language hierarchies that shape the contexts of pedagogy and narrow the access to students' linguistic resources. Hornberger and colleagues have conceptualised continua of hierarchies of perceived power differentials across a range of contexts of bilingualities and biliteracies, evident in ranking from more to less ideologically preferred (e.g. Hornberger and Skilton-Sylvester, 2000).

Enduring monolingual ideologies

Despite phenomena such as globalisation through population movements, multi-diversity of languages and cultures, and digitalised communication, there is much evidence of the persistence of monolingual ideologies of the 'one language–one state' kind. Bailey (2012: 504) notes that being a monolingual English speaker in countries such as the UK, the USA and Australia:

> [is] an ideological default position against which difference or distinctiveness is constructed. For example, in the USA, there are aspects of legislation that seek to

criminalise use of languages other than English in official contexts such as school, government, and workplaces. This position portrays language alternation as undermining US unity, citizenship and decency.

In England, the education curriculum requires that primary, secondary and special school education is conducted in English, including Early Years education for 2–5-year-olds. The secondary school modern foreign languages curriculum differentiates between two main groups of languages: selected European and Chinese languages (e.g. French, German, Spanish and Mandarin) and other world languages spoken by post-colonial migrant communities (e.g. Punjabi, Urdu and Arabic). In the UK the linguistic capital of these two sets of modern foreign languages differs: only the former is recognised as a qualification for university entrance.

Modalities

Language and languaging

Many sociolinguistic studies continue to construct multilingualism in terms of

> language as whole bounded systems, lined up as neatly as possible with political, cultural and territorial boundaries.
>
> (Heller, 2012: 24)

Structural approaches understand languages and literacy orthographies/logographies as whole, bounded, unique systems that retain a distinct integrity across social, political, historical and geographical contexts. Psycholinguistic and cognitive-orientated studies also understand language in a similar bounded way, and by extension, multilingualism as a multiple of bounded language systems. From this perspective, multilingualism has been construed as a complicating factor in researching, and assessment of performance within each language and literacy system across multiple languages and literacy skills.

Critical sociolinguistics offers a contrasting view that:

> [language is] a set of resources which circulate in unequal ways in social networks and discursive spaces, and whose meaning and values are socially constructed within the constraints of social organizational processes, under specific historical conditions.
>
> (Heller, 2007: 2)

Here Heller presents languages as fluid, drawn upon as communicative resources to meet the meaning-making demands of the social, historical and political needs of the speakers. Thinking of languages in this way suggests that language can be construed less as a 'count noun' and more as a verb (Pérez–Milans, 2015). In the same way, fluidity across languages in multilingualism has prompted terms such as 'translanguaging' (e.g. García, 2009). This description of multilingualism affords a positive understanding of networking linguistic resources across languages and communicative resources that supports rather than 'interferes' with communication, learning and the learner.

Multimodality

There has been an increasing shift away from monomodality, that is using each language and communicative resource alone, and towards multimodality to communicate interwoven and complex meanings (Kress and Van Leeuwen, 2001). Monolinguals and multilinguals share a range of multimodal resources and semiotic signs, other than language codes; such as gesture, artistic performance, music, dance, graphics and digital resources. Furthermore, this shift is clearly evidenced in the growing distance between the largely monomodality of schooling, through written texts, and the multimodality of students' out-of-school lives. For example, studies of literacies at home using drawings, artefacts and text (Volk, 2013; Gregory *et al.*, 2013; Pahl, 2007, 2012); college students using English–Welsh in shared online activities (Martin-Jones, 2011); and 'unofficial' multimodality in complementary school classes, such as using mobile phones (e.g. Lytra, 2012) illustrate the richness of multimodal meaning-making available to multilingual learners. There is an imperative to consider multimodality in literacy work in monolingual and multilingual classrooms.

Criticality as method

A critical perspective is one that questions the way things are and interrogates the status quo, the accepted mainstream view, the dominant voice, the more powerful discourse about the subject being studied in order to understand and change inequalities. Following Kress and Van Leeuwen:

> Discourses are socially constructed knowledges of (some aspect of) reality. By 'socially constructed' we mean that they have been developed in specific social contexts and in ways which are appropriate to the interests of social actors in these contexts.
>
> (Kress and Van Leeuwen, 2001: 4)

Criticality is a method of understanding the construction (e.g. discursively, culturally, legally) of the realities of others in order to notice difference. Rather than being blind to differences between dominant voices and 'silent' voices, criticality notices, analyses and confronts these differences (Pothier and Devlin, 2006). Critical methods are not so much a set of technical skills, but rather:

> practices of enquiry, shaped by the questions we ask, and by what we experience … methods evolving as questions emerge, and … wanting to account for things … not noticed before, or which may not have been around before.
>
> (Heller, 2012: 24)

Developing awareness of how embedded privileges and inequalities orientate the nature and outcome of research and educational practice is fundamental in critical approaches. I discuss three characteristics of a critical approach to research practice, assessment and pedagogy: reflexivity, positionings and identities, and their role in constructing (in)competence in multilingual learners.

Reflexivity

Reflexivity is the capacity for sympathetic self-critical introspection about the work in hand, involving self-conscious scrutiny of the conduct of interactions and tasks. This quality of reflection brings deeper understandings, insights and new discoveries about the nature of work and research. Reflexivity affords researcher–participant relationships to develop a dialogic and collaborative partnership towards scrutiny and interpretation of research findings. Both these aspects of reflexivity carry the potential to enrich practitioners' work in both assessment and pedagogy with multilingual students with difficulties with print. Developing reflexive practices in research and pedagogic settings affords the researcher/practitioner and students/participants, spaces to develop awareness of the assumptions underpinning the distribution of power and knowledge in the enactment of assessment/testing and performance and pedagogy.

Positionings

Critical reflexivity brings an awareness of positionings between research/teacher–students and student–student of perceived power differentials and how (unequal) distributions of power shape identities of those involved. The status that languages are awarded in a society may also be awarded to the speakers and writers, that is language/languaging positions the speaker and writer. Gal (2006) gives an example of the way English and Spanish in the USA are positioned as having higher and lower status respectively, and speakers know who can say what to whom in which language. Research involves outsider–insider positionings of researcher and participants, where the 'outsider' researcher/teacher is usually more privileged and empowered than the 'insider' participants/students. A further example is the positioning of students' literacy work through comparative appraisals of the language and literacy skills with which they accomplish their work and consequently are positioned in terms of 'normativity' and 'normalcy', as well as non-normativity and abnormalcy.

Identities

Identity is the way(s) in which we make sense of ourselves: we make an account of ourselves according to whom or what we are. We describe ourselves by categories that we place ourselves either in or out of and we identify ourselves by characteristics and set boundaries that distinguish us as much by being like the people in those categories as by being different from 'the other' (Martin, 2009: 135). Identities for multilingual learners developing reading and writing skills in the school language are likely to be complex and multiple, and 'imposed, contested and negotiated' (Pavlenko and Blackledge, 2004). At any one time a student's race, ethnicity, culture and languages can attract one or several identities. For example, assessments/ tests and other performances of classroom learning can impose an identity of failure on multilingual/EAL (English as an Additional Language) pupils learning to read and to write for schooling. Students or parents may contest this identity, seeking recognition of capacities and capabilities, and opportunities to negotiate an alternative new identity of becoming a more successful reader/writer. This example is evidenced in the continuing conflation of EAL and SEN (Special Educational Needs) in UK schooling (Arnot *et al.*, 2014) which is further discussed later in this chapter.

Putting criticality to work in dyslexia assessment and intervention

Assessment and intervention are important sites for constructing identities of success or failure of learning literacy skills for multilingual learners. Assessment primarily concerns the appraisal of (in)competence (Kovarsky *et al.*, 1999). From a critical perspective, the testers can also be appraised. Maynard and Marlaire (1999) challenge the assumptions and protocols that

> presume that examiners are neutral conduits of pre-specified items to which examinees respond with correct or incorrect answers reflecting individual level of ability.
>
> (p. 171)

Competence in testing lies in a set of skills that accomplish official testing activities, such as through a protocol of specific question and response. Tester 'mistakes' such as breaking the protocol to give the student additional support, are often a competence call judgement by the tester, e.g. opting to repeat the question when the student may not have orientated to the task. In such a scenario, identities are being *negotiated*. An example of mutually assumed failure is offered by Meek (1983: 225) in a study of literacy learning in white English-monolingual primary schools. Identities of failure are *assumed* by both teachers and pupils for pupils with difficulties learning reading skills, evidenced in the 'inescapable challenge' of these learners to their teachers: 'You think I'm thick, don't you'.

However, in contexts of multilingualism and dyslexia, students' (in)competence in language and literacy skills is usually assessed only in the language of education. Thus students learning through English as an additional language are more likely than others to have *imposed* an identity of poor language skills. For example, discursive construction of (in)competence may appear in the wording of a report indicating a student's incompetence by making a case for additional support/changing class group; or by contrast a report emphasising progress and low need, suggests competence and can put the case for less support (Maynard and Marlaire, 1999).

A further example illustrates constructing (in)competence in a multilingual education setting in a Chinese complementary school[1] in the UK, and then *negotiating* an identity of achievement. The researcher set up a three-way discussion between a Chinese pupil, his Chinese teacher and the tester/researcher, about the pupil's logographic 'mis-spellings' in a test (Hancock, online January 2016). The post-test discussion challenged the *imposed* identity of failing the assessment. The pupil drew on 'think alouds' (Wade, 1990) to explain his reasoning for his 'mistakes' thus negotiating an alternative 'competence' identity through his analysis of his writing 'mistakes'. Understanding the student's emic perspective of his performance enabled both teacher and student to engage more effectively in logographic pedagogy. The important issue here is that a capacity for criticality through reflexivity was created which enabled re-positionings and new identities for teacher and student.

While this approach combining formal testing with ethnographic method 'ruins' formal assessment, it is eminently justified as more likely to identify features of the student's learning potential and indicate ways forward for dynamic assessment and pedagogic methods. This approach also affords a further critical turn to inform classroom assessment, by including language and literacy skills and practices available to students in their homes, and complementary schools. A combined school–home–community approach to assessment of literacy skills learning builds on socialisation studies by linguistic anthropologists and educationists to identify and document the abilities, resources and 'funds of knowledge' that multilingual families and communities have, rather than the abilities, resources or proficiencies that they do not have (Warriner, 2012: 511; Bayley and Schecter, 2003; Moll and Gonzalez, 2005; Gregory *et al.*, 2013; Pahl, 2007, 2012; Zentella, 2005). We also need to bear in mind a further critical perspective: that while a community may engage in a particular set of practices, the literacy practices of each family and each family member are unique.

Literacy skills and literacy practices

An important critical turn in research in the field of literacy studies is Street's anthropological ethnographic studies (1984, 1993) of the social uses of written language. Street conceptualised *literacy being put to use* through macro processes of ideological uses of literacy, such as literacy for schooling, and through micro processes involved in day to day literacy practices, such as magazines and texting. He also distinguished literacy practices from *literacy skills* of reading and writing orthographies taught in schooling. Teaching and learning literacy skills are the main 'stuff' of primary schooling, in settings that focus on teaching/learning these skills for use across curriculum contexts. That is, literacy skills are autonomous, without the need for a meaningful context, which can be applied across curriculum contexts. In contrast, the macro processes underpinning language and literacy curricula reflect the ideologies of particular education systems and are contextualised by curriculum subject areas which orientate to different pedagogies. Street described these macro and micro processes of literacy played out and evidenced in two relationships, respectively: *ideological* and *autonomous literacies*. Most countries have signed up to universal enfranchisement and rights of inclusion, through education, for autonomous literacy skills for everyone, especially in schooling for children and young people, to enable wider literacy practices, as an important feature of the development of an educated citizenship.

Discourses of autonomous literacy skills at home and in schooling

What are the implications for multilingual learners who fail to learn literacy skills? Kalantzis and Cope (1999: 262) identify the importance of schooling for social access:

> schooling is a critical site for social mobility, and part of this process is successful induction into the culture of schooling, such as schooled literacy (reading and writing) and the linguistic and cognitive capacities that come with it. These are educational tools for social access.

They note that traditional approaches in education and curriculum that assume a universal cultural approach will achieve 'predictable patterns of failure'. They argue that if one of the objectives of education is to increase social access then those for whom the cultures and discourses of power do not come 'naturally', need to have the ways and means of these cultures and discourses spelt out explicitly (Kalantzis and Cope, 1999: 263). By using the term 'naturally', Kalantzis and Cope refer to the socialisation and enculturalisation that privileged families and social groups experience.

In some ways this debate reflects what Street identified as literacy skills and literacy practices, and which is reflected in the tension between prescribed literacy skills and practices of schooling and the everyday language of literacy practices. This dichotomy is reflected in school pedagogies.

On the one hand, there is the pedagogy of 'cracking the code' of linguistic knowledge through expert teaching, and on the other hand, there are pedagogies drawing on literacies as 'a communicative practice' through dialogue between teacher and learners. Multilingual home literacies are an important resource in this respect, although not always drawn upon.

Home literacies

An important body of research on literacy learning provides an alternative to schooled literacy learning, and offers salient insights into the development of multilingual literacies, literacy practices, and literacy skills in homes and complementary schools. Multilingual ethnographic studies in the UK and USA of young and older learners show the pedagogic importance of relationships between grandchildren and grandparents in the development of literacy skills and demonstrate the wealth of multilingual literacy practices that are generated in multilingual homes (Volk, 2013; Gregory *et al.*, 2013; Pahl, 2007, 2012). The families in these studies were not the privileged families from dominant socio-cultural groups in US or UK society to whom Kalantzis and Cope (1999) refer. Yet, approaches relevant to schooled literacy practices and skills were evident in multilingual homes.

Research studies of literacies and literacy practices and literacy skills in complementary schools across a range of home languages in the UK (Creese and Blackledge, 2010: 92) show that new multilingual literacies are emerging where young people

> use a vast array of linguistic resources which constantly change and develop, and which derive their linguistic features from many sources.

Wider dissemination to mainstream teachers of the findings of multilingual literacy practices at home and in complementary schools is developing awareness of the literacies and literacy skills as well as methods of engagement with literacies that multilingual students are learning, to afford more inclusive practices in school literacy/ies education to all educationists. However, there still remains a gap in the research literature concerning multilingual learners in these contexts who have additional literacy needs.

Dyslexia and multilingualism

In an important text, *The Dyslexia Debate* (2014), the authors, Elliott and Grigorenko, present their view based on a rigorous review of the neuro-biological–cognitive research literature that seeks to explain developmental dyslexia. They conclude that difficulty learning literacy skills has a biological–cognitive base which is amenable to appropriate assessment and pedagogy. They concur with a currently favoured approach that emphasises individual minds through assessment approaches and more prescriptive pedagogical models of programmes across a range of literacy difficulties and ages.

Elliott and Grigorenko also note there is a small body of literature which holds that 'dyslexia' and 'reading disability' are synonymous (e.g. Siegel and Mazabel, 2013), and that reading difficulties are better understood through sociocultural perspectives without recourse to biological explanations (e.g. Riddick, 2001; Soler, 2010; Anastasia and Kauffman, 2011). They concur with Fletcher *et al.* (2007) and the literature on the negative impact on literacy skills of socio-economic disadvantage such that:

> it is impossible to distinguish between neurobiological and environmental etiologies when considering the needs of individual children who have scored poorly on reading-related measures.
>
> (Elliott and Grigorenko, 2014: 11)

Indeed, the negative effect of social, environmental deprivation on learning to read is noted in the important historic Bullock Report: *A Language for Life* (1975). Persisting literacy difficulties were associated with children from 'areas of social deprivation', as well as high absence rates from school, and ineffective pedagogy (Bullock, 1975). More recently, concern for learning literacy skills among EAL pupils has been included. Yet, describing multilingual school students who are learning literacy skills, using terms such as 'social exclusion' may be more accurate than 'social deprivation', as 'social exclusion' refers to the drivers of the absence of material well-being among many EAL students. That is, key aspects of identity, which are bound up with access to material resources, include race, ethnicity, class, citizenship, and linguistic identities and proficiencies, and where linguistic aspects of identities are least researched in this regard (Piller, 2012: 281).

There are three important issues here. First, there is no mention of multilingual learners in Elliott and Grigorenko's book. Second, the emergence of a shift of focus from the biological–diagnostic axis of dyslexia towards a sociocultural–intervention axis cannot be underestimated in the context of multilingual learners, whether newly arrived or established, yet this group is not discussed in the text. The third issue concerns a renewed emphasis on the centrality of a sociocultural approach to assessment and pedagogy. Sociocultural approaches to learning, such as the work of Vygotsky, Bruner, and in second-language pedagogy, Lantolf and Poehner (2008), van Lier (2000), Thorne (2000) among others, are based on the premise that whatever the biological predisposition of the learner, *appropriate* pedagogic intervention brings about development and learning for literacy difficulties.

There is a gradual re-positioning of the fields of research and practice towards the broader conceptualisation of 'difficulties with print' which re-orientates education less towards diagnostic purposes and more towards a focus on assessment-for-intervention. Assessment aims to identify indicators of learning potential which could inform teaching–learning intervention approaches for literacy skills. That is, the emphasis moves to identifying and constructing competence rather than incompetence.

Construction of dyslexia in multilingualism

It is difficult to over-estimate the challenge that superdiverse multilingualism presents to classroom pedagogy in educational systems orientated to monolingualism, such as English-only policies and curricula. Critical perspectives focus on the spaces where race, colour, ethnicity, language and disability, intersect to ensure failure through the creation of hierarchies. Critical race theory, and critical whiteness theory overlap to racialise learning failure as learning disability in the conflation of EAL and SEN in schooling multilingual multi-ethnic learners. Gillborn's (2010) research indicates specifically that the educational dice are loaded in favour of white students ensuring their access is maintained to better resources and opportunities. It is a noticeable lack that language, EAL, is not identified in these studies as a racialising feature. This section discusses the construction of racialising disability through the particular lens of assessment practices of dyslexia in multilingual contexts. Despite the best efforts of cognitive and psycholinguistic psychology, learning and its assessment are profoundly social activities.

Intersectionality and conflation of EAL/SEN

Intersectionality has recently been applied to contexts where educational failure has been interpreted through a conceptualisation of race, ethnicity, language, literacy skills, and a conceptualisation of learning disability. Thus, in contexts of race, ethnicity and multilingualism, intersectionality could explain failure in school achievement for non-biological reasons, such as racialising educational disability.

Special educational needs in the UK are defined not only by assessment/test scores but by a relational approach between the learner's needs and the contextual capability to meet those needs:

> Thus the teaching and education offered in any particular school may have a crucial impact on whether a child is identified as being in need of special [educational] provision. The same child might be a candidate for special education in one school but not in another.
>
> (Evans, 1995: 203)

Government documents additionally note that a student must not be regarded as having a learning difficulty solely because the language or form of language of the home is different from the language in which he/she will be taught:

> Lack of competence in English must not be equated with learning difficulties as understood in this Code.
>
> (DfE, 1994: 2.18; DfEE, 2001: 6.3)

Nevertheless, there is a body of evidence in the UK that indicates that educational practice equates presumed or actual lack of competence in English with learning difficulties. Gillborn and Youdell (2000: 74–75) report:

> Concentrating EAL pupils in certain of the 'left-over' mixed ability classes immediately has the effect of barring them from any of the 'fast groups'. This is vitally important because it conflates EAL with lower 'ability' in practice if not in principle. What we see here is a confirmation of the concerns raised in previous research that suggested that white teachers might sometimes misread Asian pupils' *language* problems as symptomatic of deeper-seated *learning* difficulties.
>
> (CRE, 1992; Gillborn and Gipps, 1996: 56–57;
> Troyna, 1991; Troyna and Siraj-Blatchford, 1993)

Additional evidence is provided in a review of literature (Cline and Shamsi, 2000) and in an interim research report of practices in UK schooling of EAL students (Arnot *et al.*, 2014) which evidence continuing conflation of language and learning needs.

Between Troyna's work (1991) and the interim report by Arnot *et al.* (2014) there is nearly a quarter of a century of research that reveals practices that racialise language and learning needs in the English education system. Long overdue questions are: Why does the confusion persist? How can practitioners and researchers approach assessment with multilingual learners to distinguish capabilities and difficulties in language and/or learning?

Professional development

Throughout this chapter there have been references to professional development. Like all learning it needs to be performative as well as informative. The following example is a view of critical pedagogy in professional development for teachers of English as a Foreign Language (EFL) in Brazil (Andreotti, 2005).

Drawing on critical pedagogy in professional development offers a methodology that could raise awareness in primary and secondary teachers of their views and assumptions about multilingualism as a competence for classroom/curriculum learning; for example, re-considering the premise for teaching through English-only and English-only pedagogy, and considering the opportunities for working with students through translanguaging practices as a pedagogic tool for students to achieve English-only literacy skills. Achieving this quality of self-realisation is an important goal, which is constrained by powerful legislative discourses enshrining monolingualism in curriculum content and pedagogic practices.

In a funded project for professional development for EFL teachers in Brazil, Andreotti (2005) describes the effect of a critical pedagogic approach on teachers as they moved to a critical turn in their own pedagogy and purpose. Through three phases of professional development courses/seminars involving up to 200 EFL teachers, participants' awareness was raised concerning 'the elitism generated by the hierarchies created around levels of English proficiency and teaching competence' (p. 84). The first phase produced an outcome where 'developing their professional practices and pedagogical lives suggested that there was a growth of elitism and a growth of fragmentation' (p. 84). The second phase challenged these conceptualisations and the contradictions in their views, such as that teaching English as a commodity for upward social mobility implied that poverty was due to a deficit of knowledge. In the third phase, participants created a 'safe' space where they openly addressed difficult and complex questions. The participants chose to engage in 'unlearning' (Spivak, 1988; Landry and MacLean, 1996), that is, they re-evaluated their past experience in order to better understand the present and their potential for the future. It was an exercise that the teachers had not engaged in before, and drew on learning processes similar to those in post-colonial pedagogy (e.g. Janks, 1995).

This example of professional development, in line with the orientation of the chapter, presents a critical alternative approach that offers sociocultural conceptualisations of language and literacy learning in contexts of complexity.

New research lenses

Recent global population movements have brought multiple diversities to many ideologically monolingual countries, at a rate and range of change not previously experienced. Critical sociolinguistic study has presented important reconceptualisations concerning 'culture', 'identity' and 'language' (Eisenhart, 2001). Recent social, cultural and linguistic changes have had far-reaching effects on research and there are calls in the fields of sociolinguistic and sociocultural research for new research lenses. Studies of multilingual literacy practices in families and complementary schools have potential to inform pedagogies for literacy skills required for curriculum literacy practices in mainstream schools. An important focus of future research is the interplay between multilingual literacies and monolingual literacy skills for curriculum purposes.

For dyslexia studies this perspective means developing new ways of researching with families, teachers, and students with educational needs, whose lives and education are experienced through migration flows. It means working and researching collaboratively in multilingual teams within and beyond schooling, to broaden perspectives and knowledge of multilingual literacies, develop insights, and extend relationships with families and communities around literacy practices. It means using multimodal resources across languages and literacies in assessment and intervention practices in curriculum work. It means, rather than focusing exclusively on individual students with difficulties, to reconceptualise assessment practices and pedagogies of literacy skills for a range of multilingual students. It means equipping and empowering multilingual learners who have complex literacy needs to negotiate their learning identities through the different phases of their schooling and education.

Note

1   Complementary schools in the UK are additional to, and support, the national education system and offer teaching in the home/heritage languages, literacy and literacies to children and adolescents with minority languages spoken by their families.

References

Anastasia, G. and Kauffman, J. (2011) A social constructivist approach to disability: Implications for special education. *Exceptional Children* 77, 367–384.

Andreotti, V, (2005) Reclaiming the right to question: language teachers in Brazil, in Osler, A. and Starkey, H. (Eds) *Citizenship and Language Learning: International Perspectives*. Stoke: Trentham Books Ltd, with the British Council.

Arnot, M. *et al.* (2014) *School approaches to the education of EAL students: Language development, social integration and achievement*, Interim Report, April 2014. Funded by the Bell Foundation (2013–2015). www.educ.cam.ac.uk/research/projects/ealead/Fullreport.pdf

Bailey, B. (2012) Heteroglossia, in Martin-Jones, M., Blackledge, A. and Creese, A. (Eds) *The Routledge Handbook of Multilingualism*. London: Routledge (pp. 499–507).

Bayley, R. and Schecter, S. (2003) *Language Socialization in Bilingual and Multilingual Societies*. Clevedon: Multilingual Matters.

Blommaert, J. (2010) *The Sociolingusitics of Globalisation*. Cambridge: Cambridge University Press.

Bullock, A. (1975) *A Language for Life*. Report of the Committee of Enquiry appointed by the Secretary of State for Education and Science. London: HMSO.

Cline, T. and Shamsi, T. (2000) *Language needs or special needs? The assessment of learning difficulties in literacy among children learning English as an additional language: A literature review*. Research Report 184. London: Department for Education and Employment.

CRE (Commission for Racial Equality) (1992) *Ethnic Monitoring in Education*. London: CRE.

Creese, A. and Blackledge, A. (2010) *Multilingualism: A Critical Perspective*. London: Continuum.

DfE (Department for Education) (1994) *Code of Practice on the Identification and Assessment of Special Educational Needs*. London: HMSO.

DfEE (Department for Education and Employment) (2001) *Code of Practice on the Identification and Assessment of Special Educational Needs, and SEN Thresholds: Good Practice Guidance on Identification and Provision for Pupils with Special Educational Needs*. London: HMSO.

Eisenhart, M. (2001) Educational ethnography, past, present and future: Ideas to think with. *Educational Researcher* 30, 8, 16–27.

Elliott, J. and Grigorenko, A. (2014) *The Dyslexia Debate*. Cambridge: Cambridge University Press.

Evans, P. (1995) *Integrating Students with Special Needs into Mainstream Schools*. Paris: OECD.

Fletcher, J., Lyon, G., Fuchs, L. and Barnes, M. (2007) *Learning Disabilities*. New York: Guilford.

Gall, S. (2006) Migration, minorities and multilingualism: Language ideologies in Europe, in Mar-Molinero, C. and Stevenson, P. (Eds) *Language Ideologies, Policies and Practices: Language and the Future of Europe*. Basingstoke: Palgrave Macmillan

García, O. (2009) *Bilingual Education in the 21st Century: A Global Perspective*. Oxford: Wiley-Blackwell.

Gillborn, D. (2010) The colour of numbers: Surveys, statistics and deficit-thinking about race and class. *Journal of Education Policy* 25, 2, 253–276.

Gillborn, D. and Gipps, C. (1996) *Recent Research on the Achievements of Ethnic Minority Pupils*. London: Ofsted.

Gillborn, D. and Youdell, D. (2000) *Education: Policy, Practice Reform and Equity*. Buckingham: Open University Press.

Gregory, E., Lytra, V., Choudhury, H., Ilankuberan, U., Kwapong, A. and Woodham, M. (2013) Syncretism as a creative act of mind: The narratives of children from four faith communities in London. *Journal of Early Childhood Literacy* 13, 3, 322–347.

Hancock, A. (online January 2016) Creating a dialogic space for research: A reading conference in a Chinese Complementary school. *Language and Education* Special Issue 'Researching language-in-education in diverse, twenty-first century settings'.

Heller, M. (Ed.) (2007) *Bilingualism: A Social Approach*. Basingstoke: Palgrave Macmillan.

Heller, M. (2012) Rethinking sociolinguistic ethnography: From community and identity to process and practice, in Gardner, S. and Martin-Jones, M. (Eds) *Multilingualism, Discourse and Ethnography*. London, Routledge (pp. 24–33).

Hobsbawm, E. (1990) *Nations and Nationalism since 1780: Programme, Myth, Reality*. Cambridge: Cambridge University Press.

Hornberger, N.H. and Skilton-Sylvester, E. (2000) Revisiting the continua of biliteracy: International and critical perspectives. *Language and Education* 14, 2, 96–122.

Janks, H. (1995) *Language, Literacy and Education*. Critical language awareness books/teaching materials developed reproduced in McKinney, 2003: 193.

Kalantzis, M. and Cope, B. (1999) Multicultural education: Transforming the mainstream, in May, S. (Ed.) *Critical Multilingualism: Re thinking Multicultural and Antiracist Education*. London: Falmer Press (pp. 245–276).

Kovarsky, D., Duchan, J. and Maxwell, M. (Eds) (1999) *Constructing (In)Competence: Disabling Evaluations in Clinical and Social Interactions*. Mahwah, NJ: Lawrence Erlbaum.

Kress, G. and Van Leeuwen, T. (2001) *Multimodal Discourse: The modes and Media of Contemporary Communication*. London: Arnold.

Landry, D. and MacLean, G. (Eds) (1996) *The Spivak Reader: Selected Works by Gayatri Chakrovarty Spivak*. Routledge: London.

Lantolf, J. and Poehner, M. (2008) *Sociocultural Theory and the Teaching of Second Languages*. London: Equinox.

Lytra, V. (2012) Multilingualism and multimodality, in Martin-Jones, M., Blackledge, A. and Creese, A. (Eds) *The Routledge Handbook of Multilingualism*. London: Routledge (pp. 521–537).

Martin, D. (2009) *Language Disabilities in Cultural and Linguistic Diversity*. Bristol: Multilingual Matters.

Martin-Jones, M. (2011) Languages, texts and literacy practices: An ethnographic lens on bilingual vocational education in Wales, in McCarty, T.L. (Ed.) *Ethnography and Language Policy*. New York: Routledge (pp. 231–253).

Maynard, D. and Marlaire, C. (1999) Good reasons for bad testing performance: The interactional substrate of educational testing, in Kovarsky, D., Duchan, J. and Maxwell, M. (Eds) *Constructing (In) Competence: Disabling Evaluations in Clinical and Social Interactions*. Mahwah, NJ: Lawrence Erlbaum (pp. 171–196).

McKinney, C.W. (2003) Developing critical literacy in a changing context: Challenges of 'critique' in South Africa, in McKinney, C.W., Goodman, S., Mercer, N., Maybin, J. and Lillis, T. *Language and Literacy in a Changing World: A Reader*. Human Sciences Research Council, South Africa.

Meek, M. (1983) *Achieving Literacy: Longitudinal Studies of Adolescents Learning to Read*. London: Routledge and Kegan Paul.

Moll, L. and Gonzalez, N. (2005) *Fund of Knowledge: Theorising Practices in Households, Communities and Classrooms*. Mahwah, NJ: Erlbaum.

Pahl, K. (2007) Timescales and ethnography: Understanding a child's meaning-making across three sites, a home, a classroom and a family literacy class. *Ethnography and Education* 2, 2, 175–190.

Pahl, K. (2012) Every object tells a story: Intergenerational stories and objects in the homes of Pakistani heritage families in South Yorkshire, UK. *Home Cultures* 9, 3, 303–328.

Pavlenko, A. and Blackledge, A. (2004) Introduction: New theoretical approaches to the study of negotiation of identities in multilingual contexts, in Pavlenko, A. and Blackledge, A. (Eds) *Negotiation of Identities in Multilingual Contexts*. Clevedon: Multilingual Matters (pp. 1–33).

Pérez-Milans, M. (2015) Language education policy in late modernity: (Socio) linguistic ethnographies in the European Union. *Language Policy* 14, 2, 99–107.

Piller, I. (2012) Multilingualism and social exclusion, in Martin-Jones, M., Blackledge, A. and Creese, A. (Eds) *The Routledge Handbook of Multilingualism*. London: Routledge (pp. 281–296).

Pothier, D. and Devlin, R. (2006) *Critical Disability Theory: Essays in Philosophy*. Vancouver: UBC Press.

Riddick, B. (2001) Dyslexia and inclusion: Time for a social model of disability. *International Studies in Sociology of Education* 11, 223–236.

Siegel, L.S. and Mazabel, S. (2013) Basic cognitive processes and reading disabilities, in Swanson, H.L., Harris, K.R. and Graham, S. (Eds) *Handbook of Learning Disabilities*. New York: Guilford Press (pp. 186–213).

Soler, J. (2010) Dyslexia lessons: The politics of dyslexia and reading problems, in Hall, K., Goswami, U., Harrison,C., Ellis, S. and Soler, J. (Eds) *Interdisciplinary Perspectives on Learning to Read*. London: Routledge (pp. 179–192).

Spivak, G.C. (1988) Can the subaltern speak? in Nelson, C. and Grossberg, L. (Eds) *Marxism and the Interpretation of Culture*. Chicago: University of Illinois Press (pp. 271–313).

Street, B. (1984) *Literacy in Theory and Practice*. Cambridge: Cambridge University Press.

Street, B. (1993) *Cross-cultural Approaches to Literacy*. Cambridge: Cambridge University Press.

Thorne, S. (2000) Second language acquisition theory and the truth(s) and the truth(s) about relativity, in Lantolf, J. (Ed.) *Sociocultural Theory and Second Language Learning*. Oxford: Oxford University Press (pp. 245–259).

Troyna, B. (1991) Underachievers or underrated? The experiences of students of South Asian origin in a secondary school. *British Educational Research Journal* 17, 4, 361–376.

Troyna, B. and Siraj-Blatchford, I. (1993) Providing support or denying access? The experiences of students designated as 'ESL' and 'SN' in a multi-ethnic secondary school. *Educational Review* 45, 1, 3–11.

van Lier, L. (2000) From input to affordance: Social-interactive learning from an ecological perspective, in Lantolf, J. (Ed.) *Sociocultural Theory and Second Language Learning*. Oxford: Oxford University Press (pp. 245–259).

Vertoveç, S. (2007) Super-diversity and its implications. *Ethnic and Racial Studies* 30, 6, 1024–1054.

Volk, D. (2013) 'Contradictions, clashes, cominglings': The syncretic literacy projects of young bilinguals. *Anthropology & Education Quarterly* 44, 3, 234–252.

Wade, S. (1990) Using think alouds to assess comprehension. *The Reading Teacher*, 43, 442–451.

Warriner, D.S. (2012) Multilingual literacies, in Martin-Jones, M., Blackledge, A. and Creese, A. (Eds) *The Routledge Handbook of Multilingualism*. London: Routledge (pp. 508–520).

Zentella, A.C. (Ed.) (2005) *Building on Strength: Language and Literacy in Latino Families and Communities*. New York: Teachers College Press; California Association for Bilingual Education (CABE).

5

PRINCIPLES AND GUIDELINES IN TEST CONSTRUCTION FOR MULTILINGUAL CHILDREN

Gad Elbeheri and John Everatt

This chapter will:

1. Provide the reader with a background to understanding issues in the assessment of individuals within a second or multilingual context
2. Identify some of the issues that need to be considered when conducting such an assessment and when developing tools to support these assessment practices
3. Suggest some possible solutions to the challenges that assessments within a second or multilingual context can pose

Introduction

Progress on methods of dyslexia assessment has been hampered by ongoing debate concerning diverse issues such as the role and validity of IQ in the assessment process, labelling and definitions (Miles, 1994; Stanovich, 1991, 1992). The situation is further complicated by the emergence of cross-linguistic studies of dyslexia. Although such studies have paved the way for the important realization that the manifestation of dyslexia is different in different languages (Goulandris, 2003; Smythe, Everatt & Salter, 2004), they have also highlighted the critical need for culture-fair assessment and called for this to be considered when assessing bilingual and multilingual individuals with dyslexia. (For a review of the situation in Arabic, refer to Elbeheri, Everatt, Reid & Al-Mannai, 2006.)

An ever-changing geopolitical situation coupled with the need for sustainable development in hot spots around the world has led to international migrations and increasing numbers of children growing up with immigrant origins and speaking several languages (Organization for Economic Co-operation and Development, 2009). This is further compounded, at least in the Middle East region, by the over-reliance on expatriate teachers and professional psychologists who do not speak the same vernacular (even if they speak the same language) as the majority of the children they are testing. This results in assessment tools being neither culturally fair nor linguistically appropriate. It also gives rise to subtle linguistic differences in the spoken vernacular between professional psychologists conducting psycho-educational evaluations and the individuals undergoing such evaluations, which negatively affects test administration, test results and subsequently test interpretation. Such complications may lead to false positives or false negatives with eventual loss of resources, or critical chances of educational support being missed.

Given the perceived importance of dyslexia assessment, intervention, support and policy throughout the world, Smythe and Everatt (2000) highlight the need for systematic research in order to identify the similarities and differences across countries and language contexts. Smythe and Everatt conclude that this would ultimately help in the development of culture- and language-appropriate diagnostic strategies. Reid and Fawcett (2004) observe that one of the areas which has gained momentum in recent years has been the acknowledgement of the need to 'promote appropriate and effective practices both in the assessment and in the intervention for students whose first language is not English' (Reid & Fawcett, 2004: 13). The practice of cross-linguistic and cross-orthographic studies of dyslexia is important in explaining the nature of the condition and how it is manifested in different orthographies, which in turn assists in furthering an understanding of the relevant and subsequent areas of interventions, policies and practices. An appreciation of language-specific factors is critical because 'in many countries there are as yet few test instruments available to assess and identify children with specific learning difficulties' (Goulandris, 2003: 13). Standardized tests are generally biased in favour of individuals from the majority culture for whom the test language is native.

Multilingualism has been a problem in psycho-educational assessment for quite some time (Lang, Chew, Crownover & Wilkerson, 2011). Studies have repeatedly described and identified difficulties in using standardized instruments whose norms are based and developed for British or American individuals and applying those for other ethnically, culturally and linguistically different individuals (refer to Figueroa, 1983, and Valencia & Rankin, 1985, both as cited in Lang *et al.*, 2011). Simply translating from one language to another may not produce construct measures that are similar enough to be psychometrically acceptable. Currently, there is a lack of diagnostic tools that allow practitioners to distinguish between language differences related to the environmental context of growing up as a multilingual immigrant and language impairments of a neuro-linguistic origin (de Abreu, Baldassi, Puglisi & Befi-Lopes, 2013).

Cross-linguistic studies of dyslexia

Cross-linguistic research on developmental dyslexia highlights factors such as the consistency between the written form and spoken language as an important aspect in the acquisition of an alphabetic writing system. Goulandris (2003) presents a cross-linguistic comparison that involves a consideration of the nature of the language and the range of skills required for reading in different languages. She argues that in order to identify and appreciate the signs of dyslexia in a particular language, it is necessary to understand the relevant linguistic features of that language. Evidence in support of a linguistic basis of reading difficulties (Catts & Kamhi, 1999) has come from empirical research showing the importance of phonological (e.g., Goswami, 2002; Goswami & Bryant, 1990; Shankweiler & Liberman, 1989; Snowling, 2000; Vellutino, 1987) and orthographic (e.g., Breznitz, 2003; Hultquist, 1997; Miller Guron & Lundberg, 2004) processing for literacy learning. Snowling (2000) argues that writing systems differ in the inherent difficulty they pose to young readers, since they differ in the 'regularity or transparency of their orthographies' (p. 206). Transparency here refers to the association between written symbols and language sounds. A transparent script has a simple one-to-one relationship, whereas less transparent scripts, such as English, have a much more complex relationship between letters and sounds. Consistent with Snowling's position, cross-orthographic studies have found that readers of English make more errors on single word reading and non-word reading tasks than readers of shallower orthographies (e.g., Goswami, 2002; Landerl, 2003; Nikolopoulos, Goulandris & Snowling, 2003; Share 2003). Wimmer (1993) argues that transparent orthographies such as Italian, Spanish and Greek will pose fewer problems to beginning readers than inconsistent, opaque orthographies such as English and French. The Arabic script is fairly unusual in its transparency. The use of diacritical markers in beginning readers' texts makes the script highly transparent. However, these short vowel markers are absent in the majority of more advanced written works (i.e., non-vowelized texts), which produces a highly opaque script with a large number of homographs that can only be pronounced correctly through an appreciation of the context within which they are written.

Van der Leij (2004) argued that since reading is basically a mapping process between phonemes and graphemes, it is essential that, in order to understand the origins of dyslexia and develop instruments and methods for identification and treatment, we determine the processes and systems necessary for this learnt mapping process. For the present discussion, the question which emerges is whether the cognitive prerequisites of learning how to read and spell are universal; i.e., independent of environmental factors such as language, writing system, orthography, school and home factors. Van der Leij (2004) argues that although the view that the cognitive prerequisites of learning how to read and spell are universal has been assumed to be the case for a long time, cross-linguistic evidence to support this assumption has been found only recently. For example, Paulesu *et al.* (2001) conducted a cross-linguistic study of dyslexia and compared the brain activity of Italian-, French- and English-speaking individuals with dyslexia while they were reading. Their study has two major findings. First, the reading and phonological skills of all dyslexic groups were impaired compared to control groups. Second, when they employed Positron Emission Tomography (PET) scan technology, they found reduced activity in the same brain region for all three dyslexic groups. However, differences in the reading performance of the three groups were reported, with the Italians with dyslexia attaining, on average, higher levels of accuracy on single word reading and non-word reading than the French and English individuals with dyslexia. The researchers concluded that although a similar neurocognitive basis underlies dyslexia in all three groups, differences in the orthographies of the languages involved in the study influence the severity of the reading, spelling and phonological deficits. Hence, even if it is concluded that the same underlying factor is responsible for dyslexia across all languages, the way the learning difficulty manifests at a behavioural level (i.e., the level at which assessment practices operate) seems to vary across languages. As Miles and Miles (1999) put it 'in this new situation it is beginning to be appreciated that the ways in which dyslexia manifests itself are different in different languages' (p. 44).

Dyslexia assessment

Dyslexia assessment should be seen as a dynamic process that operates according to scientific principles embedded in clinical practice. Relevant information is gathered concerning the performance and/or behaviour of individuals on a selected number of tests. These tests are different in what elements of abilities and/or skills they aim to assess, but generally tend to include representations of the individuals' cognitive abilities and their educational achievements as well as some of the skills that are related to the underlying deficits in dyslexia as supported by relevant empirical research in the field. Reid (2003) notes that although there are a number of tests that contain the word dyslexia in their title, there is no single dyslexia test because the identification of dyslexia is a process and that process includes 'more than the administration of a solitary test' (p. 89).

Dyslexia assessment tests are diagnostic tests in nature which aim to ascertain whether the individual is actually failing and, if so, to what degree. Common to most is the establishment of the individual's current level of performance in attainments by identifying the individual's level of educational achievements and, in particular, their reading, writing and spelling skills. Beyond this, views about the purpose of an assessment may vary. Miles and Miles (1999), for example, maintain that the primary aim of dyslexia assessment should be 'that of clarification of the person's strengths and weaknesses' (p. 108). Farmer, Riddick and Sterling (2002) argue that one of the key functions which a dyslexia assessment should perform is the 'profiling of the individual student's strengths, weaknesses and learning style' (p. 117), while Stackhouse and Wells (1997) claim that the purpose of collecting assessment information regarding dyslexia is to arrive at a greater understanding of an individual's needs. Reid (2003) on the other hand, views dyslexia assessment as a tool to identify the individual's learning styles and establish various aspects of the curriculum and curriculum activities that motivate or de-motivate them.

Issues and guidelines

There are a number of issues that the dyslexia practitioner, whether a practising psychologist or an intervention specialist, should consider when assessing individuals who speak more than one language. These are presented below with a brief description and potential solutions in order to consider ways forward.

Vocabulary and language skills

Most studies comparing vocabulary performance of bilinguals and monolinguals conclude that bilinguals know fewer words in one of their languages compared to monolingual speakers (Bialystok, Luk, Peets & Yang, 2010; see also de Abreu et al., 2013). Therefore, when assessing children in their second or additional language, it needs to be noted that a test score that relies on vocabulary knowledge may be depressed when considered against scores (norms) produced by first language/monolingual speakers. Obviously, this will impact on tests of vocabulary that are typical of most IQ batteries and virtually all assessments of language skills. However, this can have additional impacts on other measures. Any measure that relies on language understanding will be influenced by vocabulary levels; even measures of non-verbal ability may be impacted by vocabulary weaknesses if instructions use complex vocabulary. Therefore, choosing tests carefully for the multilingual learner is vital. Where possible, the assessor should avoid measures that have standardized instructions that use complex language. Language assessments that use items that vary in vocabulary levels can be useful to specify weaknesses: if performance is fine with simpler vocabulary than more complex vocabulary, for example. However, this can be difficult as increases in language complexity needed to assess level of language performance often involve the use of less-frequent vocabulary. A specific measure of vocabulary, though, can be useful as much to determine potential impacts on other measures as to assess vocabulary levels themselves.

Experience will support the assessor in determining such impacts, and in the future fully researched bilingual assessment methods may provide specific criteria which take account of such weaknesses across measures, but for now awareness of the need to take poor vocabulary into account when interpreting test scores is essential.

One way of interpreting second language understanding problems is to assess the individual's first language (see discussions in Everatt *et al.*, 2013). Measuring first language skills can be useful to distinguish between an underlying cognitive deficit (which may require specific intervention/support and changes to the way learning is occurring) versus a lack of second language acquisition leading to poor vocabulary that may be improved simply by increased practice. If the language problem is evident in both first and second language measures, then an underlying deficit is most likely. On the other hand, if there is no evidence of difficulties with first language measures, then the second language weaknesses may be more to do with lower than optimum levels of learning experiences. Clearly, further work will be needed to specify the likely cause in the latter case, but first language assessments should support this process of identifying cause.

The main problem with using first language measures is their lack of availability (though see suggestions below). However, an additional major obstacle in conducting first language assessments may be the lack of a trained assessor in the first language. This can be a particular problem for language assessments that require the tester to be able to speak to the child in a native tongue and to be able to follow precisely the verbal responses of the child in the child's first language. There are no simple answers here. Some computerized tools (see discussion below on phonological processing) may allow formal assessments by a non-native speaker as long as the assessor is aware of any language differences between the child and the computer set-up. However, few such tools can assess verbal responses of a child, particularly when speech problems form part of the assessment profile. Another alternative is that the assessment is supported by a native speaker who may not be a trained assessor but has the skills to support identification of specific difficulties that the assessor is looking for. (The need for teams of individuals with different backgrounds and expertise is not new in special needs work and assessing multilingual learners is an area where such collective knowledge is vital.) Based on the assessment tools used, this pairing of assessor and native speaker could be accomplished in person, via recordings of an assessment or virtually over the internet (see discussions in Smythe, 2010).

Pronunciation and phonological processing

Another important issue is the vernacular of the individual being assessed. This is a world-wide issue, but there are certain contexts where its influence on test performance may be even more apparent. For example, there are more than 20 countries in the Middle East region where Arabic is the official language. Although Modern Standard Arabic is the unifying Pan-Arabic language spoken by more than 300 million native Arabic speakers, regional variations exist between native speakers, and such differences lead to a decrease in mutual intelligibility once geographical distance between native speakers increases. A Kuwaiti speaking in a Kuwaiti vernacular may have challenges in comprehending a Moroccan speaking in his local dialect, although both use the same language; i.e., Arabic. Furthermore, Modern Standard Arabic differs from the spoken vernacular of Arabic in terms of lexical items, phonology, morphology and syntax, and is not used by most Arabic children until they start school. Hence, assessments cannot simply rely on there being a unifying version of Arabic. Local dialects will need to be considered in test construction and by assessment practitioners when dealing with individuals from different Arabic-speaking countries.

Although Arabic provides a special case in which to consider (and study) vernaculars and pronunciation differences, many other contexts face similar challenges. China is another example where disparities in the spoken language experienced by children exist across regions. Differences between Mandarin and Cantonese are the most reported internationally, but there are also differences in the spoken forms of each of these versions of Chinese. Furthermore, in many places in China, a child may grow up with a local language that has more in common with non-Chinese languages (e.g., Indian, Persian, Russian), leading to Chinese being a high-importance additional language for the individual.

Similar differences may exist for speakers of English in the British Isles where English, Irish, Welsh and Scottish accents will lead to differences in the pronunciation of certain words; and the same will apply to other English-dominant countries such as New Zealand, Australia, South Africa and in North America. Often differences relate to the pronunciation of vowel sounds, which can lead to potentially large numbers of words being pronounced with varying degrees of disparity: the way simple words such as 'book' or 'pen' are pronounced can vary widely across regions and lead to misunderstandings, particularly when said out of a constraining context. For many around the world, English is also an important additional language, and this too can lead to differences in spoken forms that can reduce common intelligibility: a second language English speaker from one part of the world may have difficulty understanding a second language English speaker from another, even though both individuals can be clearly understood by compatriots.

Given that test measures will typically involve one individual verbally presenting information to another, then differences in spoken forms of a language need to be considered. This is particularly vital when assessments involve the need for precise articulation and the recognition of articulation, as is the case in most measures of phonological awareness, which are typical of most dyslexia assessment procedures. An awareness of basic sounds within the language (e.g., recognizing that /dog/ begins with a /d/ sound) has the potential to support the individual's recognition of the association between the written and spoken form. This can aid in the identification (decoding) of familiar and unfamiliar words: accessing a reasonable approximation to the correct pronunciation of a word will allow language systems to support processing. There is also a large body of research indicating that phonological awareness and decoding are related to effective literacy learning and that phonological deficits in these areas are associated with the literacy problems faced by children with dyslexia (see reviews in Gillon, 2004, and Snowling, 2000). This link between phonological awareness/decoding and literacy has mainly been derived from English-language data. However, similar findings have been evident in a number of cross-language comparisons (Smythe et al., 2008; Ziegler et al., 2010) and research on non-Latin-based scripts, such as Arabic (Elbeheri & Everatt, 2007) and Chinese (Ho & Bryant, 1997). The potential usefulness of such commonalities in skills across languages can be seen in research by Everatt, Smythe, Ocampo and Veii (2002). In this work, assessments of underlying phonological skills provided a distinction between individuals with dyslexia and non-dyslexic second language learners, despite both groups showing equally poor literacy levels. As such, the decoding difficulties often associated with dyslexia may be identifiable through appropriate assessment of phonological skills (see also Everatt et al., 2010).

Given the potential usefulness of measures of phonological processing, accurate and reliable procedures for such measures are vital. Accents with which the child is unfamiliar may seriously impair the accuracy and reliability of such measures. Hence, local dialects and pronunciations are a factor that needs to be taken into account by the practitioner working within a multi-language context. Choosing tests that have been designed with a local spoken form in mind is clearly useful, but using a local pronunciation to present materials will also be vital when incorporating aspects of phonological processing into dyslexia assessments. As discussed in the previous sub-section, a native speaker would be a useful member of a special needs team working within a multilingual context. In addition, some computerized tools have been developed to allow assessments in a particular accent that can be used by a non-native speaker. For example, Carson, Boustead and Gillon (2014) show how a well-designed computerized phonological awareness measure can be as predictive of phonological weaknesses as the version from which it was developed that relied on the assessor verbalizing test items precisely. This computer-based assessment has a local-accent voice recorded and materials that require the child to make a touch-screen response. It can, therefore, be administered by an assessor with a completely different accent to that of the individual tested. Other carefully designed tools should reduce the problems of precise pronunciation of phonological forms in an accent recognized by the person being assessed.

Literacy and orthography

Depending on the nature of the language and orthography of the individual being assessed, different emphasis might be placed on different sub-components of the reading process. Whereas, in English an assessment of reading accuracy may be a simple and reliable indicator of reading levels, in an orthography that is more transparent than English, an individual's rate of reading (i.e., the number of words read correctly per unit of time; sometimes also referred to as reading fluency) might be a more important indicator of reading ability (see Elbeheri *et al.*, 2006). Therefore, it is good practice for those conducting and interpreting assessments to understand the sub-components of the reading process and how the nature of the language/orthography used by the individual might influence the manifestations of dyslexia in that individual. This need to understand the components that lead to good reading was the main impetus for work undertaken in Arabic to develop assessment tools to support dyslexia assessments. The initial part of this development work involved basic research to understand the predictors of reading levels in typical children within the language/educational context of the work. The development of a basic model of reading for this context was part of this process. This was followed by the development of measures to assess literacy as well as these predictors of literacy levels. Hence, the development work by Elbeheri and colleagues focused on measures of phonological skills and reading and writing ability common to many dyslexia-assessment contexts. However, it also included measures of orthographic and morphology processing (see Elbeheri *et al.*, 2011; Mahfoudhi, Elbeheri, Al-Rashidi & Everatt, 2010), as well as working memory, in order to take account of the specific features of the language/orthography identified in the preceding research phases of the work. Similar research and development work across a range of language contexts should provide tools that can be used to support assessment practices in a multilingual setting.

The assessment of phonological processing skills, discussed in the previous sub-section and last paragraph, are based on the idea that an awareness of sounds within words will support the recognition of the association between letters and sounds, which will lead to better development of decoding skills that will lead to better sight word processing. The ability to decode strings of letters (often referred to as non-word, or pseudo-word, reading), therefore, has been another feature of many dyslexia-related assessment tools. However, although such measures can be useful in identifying dyslexia-related problems, they can be biased in the case of second language learners. Experience with an orthography leads to better processing of the elements of the orthography. Hence, those with higher levels of experience (usually first language individuals) typically score higher than those with lower levels of experience (i.e., second/additional language individuals) on measures of non-word reading. Thus, comparing a second language child against norms for a non-word reading task that have been obtained from first language cohorts can over-estimate weaknesses. Therefore, assessments need to control for experience of an orthography. If there are good records of the student's literacy learning background, this may be possible; however, assessing such experience can be difficult in many cases of children from differing school backgrounds. One alternative that is worth considering has been developed by Elbro, Daugaard and Gellert (2012) and involves more of a dynamic assessment of decoding skills. In this task, individuals are given a set of orthographic patterns (letters) that they are unlikely to have experienced before and are asked to learn the sound associated with these new letters. The level of learning of these associations between letters and sounds is an indication of the level of phonological decoding skills possessed by the individual. Given that neither first nor second/additional language learners were likely to have experienced these new associations, the range of scores should be consistent across groups – and norms for the test can be derived from mixed monolingual/bilingual cohorts.

Although word-level skills, particularly those related to decoding, may be the focus of assessments for children with literacy weaknesses associated with dyslexia, additional measures of the reading process may also be worthwhile to determine the level of difficulties experienced by the individual. This will be particularly important to distinguish those with word-level difficulties, consistent with our current understanding of dyslexia, versus those with specific deficits in reading comprehension; this is particularly important given that the latter group may require different intervention procedures from those with dyslexia (see examples in Bowyer-Crane *et al.*, 2008; Clarke, Snowling, Truelove & Hulme, 2010). Hence measures of reading comprehension will be worth considering in assessment packages; and this will certainly be vital when working with adults (see Fidler & Everatt, 2012). However, such assessments of second language or multilingual children may suffer from the same problems of language understanding as measures of language skills (see sub-section above). Linguistic comprehension is an important aspect of reading comprehension and will be predictive of literacy among second language and multilingual individuals, as well as monolinguals. Indeed, there may be comparatively greater influence of language-related rather than decoding-related factors for second language versus first language learners (e.g., Lervag & Aukrust, 2010). However, differences between monolingual and bilingual groups may be more an aspect of vocabulary level (see Sadeghi, Everatt, McNeill & Rezaei, 2014), suggesting that specific comprehension problems not associated with decoding deficits may be identified through careful interpretation of an individual's performance in an appropriate listening comprehension task. Similarly, skills more associated with specific reading comprehension levels, such as inferential skills, may develop somewhat independent of language. Again, development of measures of inferential skills may support the identification of literacy difficulties that stem from language processes not involved in decoding. Furthermore, both 'lower level' (e.g., vocabulary ability, syntactic ability) and 'higher level' (e.g., inferencing, comprehension monitoring) language skills support comprehension (Hogan, Bridges, Justice & Cain, 2011) and it is likely that exploration of the development of such constituent skills, rather than the unitary construct of language comprehension, may facilitate reading comprehension assessment and intervention in additional language learners. In the case of vocabulary, work in the second language is necessary. However, higher level skills (such as inferencing and monitoring) may have the potential to be supported through work in both languages.

Using standardized tests

In order to compare the performance of the individual being assessed against his/her peers, standardized psychometric tests use norms that have been developed from a representative sample. A representative sample takes into account cultural and linguistic aspects of the community against which the ability, or the achievement, of the individual is contrasted. However, there are many situations in which norms have not been developed for a certain community within which an assessment is to take place. As such, persons conducting the assessment, and psychologists interpreting the test results, might refer to norm tables that are not based on a representative sample: for example, a New Zealand psychologist might utilize a test of phonemic awareness that is normed on British children. Although this may be the only way forward in certain situations where representative norms do not exist, it is not optimal and may jeopardize the test interpretation.

In Malta, both Maltese and English are official languages, and important for both social and educational purposes. Although Maltese is the more widely spoken language and, for many, is the preferred language of communication, the lack of Maltese assessment tools means that English standardized tests have been typically used in assessments of literacy difficulties. Whether the content of such English-background assessment tools is suitable for most children for whom Maltese is the dominant language is questionable. For example, the Neale Analysis of Reading Ability (NARA; Neale, 1989) has often been used as an assessment tool to determine literacy levels of Maltese children (Firman, 1994). When Grech (2011) investigated the performance of Maltese-language-dominant children on this test, she found that the majority of these children would have reading comprehension scores approximately two years below what would be expected based on the test's norms. The English language data on which the test norms were derived were not appropriate for comparison with these Maltese children. In the context of Malta, experienced assessors are aware of this sort of problem and attempt to take this into account in their conclusions (C. Firman, personal communication). However, this can lead to difficulties in assessments, particularly for less-experienced assessors – and perceived differences between assessors that can bring assessment practices into question.

Clearly, the way forward is the development of standardized measures for use across different language contexts; though this will involve time and investment. For the present, given that second language assessment can be informative of problems within that language (see discussions in Everatt *et al.*, 2010), measures in the second language may be essential, but interpretations may need to be confirmed/supplemented by measures of first language abilities. One way forward is to search for measures that have been used across languages and have some evidence for their reliability across those languages: for example, the cross-language research literature can provide the basis for such a search and may provide a measure that can supplement a mainly second language assessment. The growing use of international assessments to produce league tables of countries, such as the Progress in International Reading and Literacy Study (PIRLS – see www.iea.nl/pirls_2016.html), may also provide the basis on which to search for a measure in another language. Given the number of countries/languages involved, PIRLS will potentially have a reading comprehension measure that may be used to look for reading weaknesses in a child's first language – given that use of the measure is allowed. A final way to support the assessment of different language skills is via links with colleagues working in different educational systems around the world who may provide access to a range of, most likely, curriculum-based assessment tools. Although there may be a lack of research evidence for the reliability of such first language measures, they may be useful in supporting the findings of a second language assessment.

Conclusion

This chapter confirms that linguistic and cognitive assessments for minority language children require careful choice among measures to ensure valid results (de Abreu *et al.*, 2013). Dyslexia assessment is a dynamic process which is ultimately intended to help the person with dyslexia. It is only following an appropriate assessment that an individual with dyslexia can obtain the help and support to which they are rightly entitled and, therefore, those conducting the assessment must do their best to 'get it right'. In order to assess someone for dyslexia, the assessor must know the likelihood of dyslexia manifestations in the context of the individual being assessed. Fairness and good practice in dyslexia assessment requires a basic knowledge of the specific linguistic features of the language of the individual being assessed. Fairness is also best served if assessment tools used are relevant to the context and culture of the individual being assessed. Such awareness of the linguistic, cultural and other background elements of the individual being assessed should collectively form a framework of dyslexia assessment.

References

Bialystok, E., Luk, G., Peets, K.F. & Yang, S. (2010). Receptive vocabulary differences in monolingual and bilingual children. *Bilingualism: Language and Cognition*, 13, 525–531.

Bowyer-Crane, C., Snowling, M.J., Duff, F.J., Fieldsend, E., Carroll, J.M., Miles, J., Götz, K. & Hulme, C. (2008). Improving early language and literacy skills: Differential effects of an oral language versus a phonology with reading intervention. *Journal of Child Psychology and Psychiatry*, 49, 422–432.

Breznitz, Z. (2003). Speed of processing of the visual–orthographic and auditory–phonological systems in adult dyslexics: The contribution of 'asynchrony' to word recognition deficits. *Brain and Language*, 85, 486–502.

Carson, K., Boustead, T. & Gillon, G. (2014). Predicting reading outcomes in the classroom using a computer-based phonological awareness screening and monitoring assessment. *International Journal of Speech–Language Pathology*, 16, 552–561.

Catts, H. & Kamhi, A. (1999). *Language and reading disabilities*. Boston, MA: Allyn & Bacon.

Clarke, P.J., Snowling, M.J., Truelove, E. & Hulme, C. (2010). Ameliorating children's reading-comprehension difficulties: A randomized controlled trial. *Psychological Science*, 21, 1106–1116.

de Abreu, P.E., Baldassi, M., Puglisi, M.L. & Befi-Lopes, D.M. (2013). Cross-linguistic and cross-cultural effects on verbal working memory and vocabulary: Testing language-minority children with an immigrant background. *Journal of Speech, Language and Hearing Research*, 56, 630–642.

Elbeheri, G. & Everatt, J. (2007). Literacy ability and phonological processing skills amongst dyslexic and non-dyslexic speakers of Arabic. *Reading and Writing*, 20, 273–294.

Elbeheri, G., Everatt, J., Mahfoudhi, A., Al-Diyar, M.A. & Taibah, N. (2011). Orthographic processing and reading comprehension among Arabic speaking mainstream and LD children. *Dyslexia*, 17, 123–142.

Elbeheri, G., Everatt, J., Reid, G. & Al-Mannai, H. (2006). Dyslexia assessment in Arabic. *Journal of Research in Special Educational Needs*, 6, 143–152.

Elbro, C., Daugaard, H. & Gellert, A.S. (2012). Dyslexia in a second language? A dynamic test of reading acquisition may provide a fair answer. *Annals of Dyslexia*, 62, 172–185.

Everatt, J., Ocampo D., Veii, K., Nenopoulou, S., Smythe I., Al-Mannai, H. & Elbeheri, G. (2010). Dyslexia in biscriptal readers. In N. Brunswick, S. McDougall & P. de Mornay Davies (Eds), *Reading and dyslexia in different orthographies* (pp. 221–245). Hove: Psychology Press.

Everatt, J., Sadeghi, A., Grech, L., Elshikh, M., Abdel-Sabour, S., Al-Menaye, N., McNeill, B. & Elbeheri, G. (2013). Assessment of literacy difficulties in second language and bilingual learners. In D. Tsagari & G. Spanoudis (Eds), *Assessing L2 students with learning and other disabilities* (pp. 27–43). Newcastle upon Tyne: Cambridge Scholars Publishing.

Everatt, J., Smythe, I., Ocampo, D. & Veii, K. (2002). Dyslexia assessment of the bi-scriptal reader. *Topics in Language Disorders*, 22, 32–45.

Farmer, M., Riddick, B. & Sterling, C. (2002). *Dyslexia and inclusion: Assessment and support in higher education*. London: Whurr.

Fidler, R. & Everatt, J. (2012). Reading comprehension in adult students with dyslexia: Areas of weakness and strategies for support. In N. Brunswick (Ed.), *Supporting dyslexic adults in higher education and the workplace* (pp. 91–100). Chichester: Wiley-Blackwell.

Firman, C. (1994). Dyslexia in Malta. In R. Salter & I. Smythe (Eds), *The international book of dyslexia*. London: World Dyslexia Network Foundation.

Gillon, G.T. (2004). *Phonological awareness: From research to practice*. New York: Guilford Press.

Goswami, U. (2002). Phonology, reading development and dyslexia: A cross-linguistic perspective. *Annals of Dyslexia*, 52, 141–163.

Goswami, U. & Bryant, P. (1990). *Phonological skills and learning to read*. Hove: Psychology Press.

Goulandris, N. (Ed.) (2003). *Dyslexia in different languages: Cross linguistic comparisons*. London: Whurr.

Grech, L. (2011). *Reading comprehension in Maltese–English bilinguals*. PhD thesis, University of Surrey, UK.

Ho, C.S.-H. & Bryant, P. (1997). Phonological skills are important in learning to read Chinese. *Developmental Psychology*, 33, 946–951.

Hogan, T.P., Bridges, M.S., Justice, L.M. & Cain, K. (2011). Increasing higher level language skills to improve reading comprehension. *Focus on Exceptional Children*, 44, 1–19.

Hultquist, A. (1997). Orthographic processing abilities of adolescents with dyslexia. *Annals of Dyslexia*, 47, 89–107.

Landerl, K. (2003). Dyslexia in German speaking children. In N. Goulandris (Ed.), *Dyslexia in different languages: Cross linguistic comparisons* (pp. 15–32). London: Whurr.

Lang, W.S., Chew, A.L., Crownover, C. & Wilkerson, J.R. (2011). Using the Rasch model to determine form equivalence in the trilingual Lollipop Readiness Test. *The International Journal of Educational and Psychological Assessment*, 8, 23–44.

Lervag, A. & Aukrust, V. (2010). Vocabulary knowledge is a critical determinant of the difference in reading comprehension growth between first and second language learners. *Journal of Child Psychology and Psychiatry*, 51, 612–620.

Mahfoudhi, A., Elbeheri, G., Al-Rashidi, M. & Everatt, J. (2010). The role of morphological awareness in reading comprehension among typical and learning disabled native Arabic speakers. *Journal of Learning Disabilities*, 43, 500–514.

Miles, T. (1994). Towards a rationale for diagnosis. In G. Hales (Ed.), *Dyslexia matters* (pp. 101–108). London: Whurr.

Miles, E. & Miles, T. (1999). *Dyslexia: A hundred years on*. Buckingham: Open University Press.

Miller Guron, L. & Lundberg, I. (2004). Error patterns in word reading among primary school children: A cross-orthographic study. *Dyslexia*, 10, 44–60.

Neale, M.D. (1989). *Neale Analysis of Reading Ability*. London: NFER-Nelson.

Nikolopoulos, D., Goulandris, N. & Snowling, M. (2003). Developmental dyslexia in Greek. In N. Goulandris (Ed.), *Dyslexia in different languages: Cross linguistic comparisons* (pp. 53–67). London: Whurr.

Organization for Economic Co-operation and Development (2009). PISA 2006: Technical report. Paris, France.

Paulesu, E., Demonet, J-F., Fazio, F., McCrory, E., Chanoine, V., Brunswick, N., Cappa, S.F., Cossu, G., Habib, M., Frith, C.D. & Frith, U. (2001). Dyslexia: Cultural diversity and biological unity. *Science*, 291, 2165–2167.

Reid, G. (2003). *Dyslexia: A practitioner's handbook* (3rd edition). Chichester: Wiley & Sons.

Reid, G. & Fawcett, A. (Eds), (2004). *Dyslexia in context*. London: Whurr.

Sadeghi, A., Everatt, J., McNeill, B. & Rezaei, A. (2014). Text processing in English–Persian bilingual children: A bilingual view on the Simple Model of Reading. *Educational and Child Psychology*, 31, 45–56.

Shankweiler, D. & Liberman, I. (Eds), (1989). *Phonology and reading disability: Solving the reading puzzle*. Research Monograph Series. Ann Arbor: University of Michigan Press.

Share, D. (2003). Dyslexia in Hebrew. In N. Goulandris (Ed.), *Dyslexia in different languages: Cross linguistic comparisons* (pp. 208–234). London: Whurr.

Smythe, I. (2010). *Dyslexia in the digital age*. London: Continuum.

Smythe, I. & Everatt, J. (2000). Dyslexia diagnosis in different languages. In L. Peer & G. Reid (Eds), *Multilingualism, literacy and dyslexia* (pp. 12–21). London: David Fulton Publishers.

Smythe, I., Everatt, J., Al-Menaye, N., He, X., Capellini, S., Gyarmathy, E. & Siegel, L. (2008). Predictors of word level literacy amongst Grade 3 children in five diverse languages. *Dyslexia*, 14, 170–187.

Smythe, I., Everatt, J. & Salter, R. (Eds), (2004). *The international book of dyslexia*. London: Wiley.

Snowling, M.J. (2000). *Dyslexia* (2nd edition). Oxford: Blackwell.

Stackhouse, J. & Wells, B. (1997). *Children's speech and literacy difficulties: A psycholinguistic framework*. London: Whurr.

Stanovich, K. (1991). Discrepancy definitions of reading disability: Has intelligence led us astray? *Reading Research Quarterly*, 36, 7–29.

Stanovich, K. (1992). The theoretical and practical consequences of discrepancy definitions of dyslexia. In M. Snowling & M. Thomson (Eds), *Dyslexia: Integrating theory and practice* (pp. 125–143). London: Whurr.

Van Der Leij, A. (2004). Developing flexible mapping in an inflexible system? In G. Reid & A. Fawcett (Eds), *Dyslexia in context: Research, policy and practice* (pp. 48–75). London: Whurr.

Vellutino, F.R. (1987). Dyslexia. *Scientific American*, 256, 20–27.

Wimmer, H. (1993). Characteristics of developmental dyslexia in a regular writing system. *Applied Psycholinguistics*, 14, 1–33.

Ziegler, J., Bertrand, D., Tóth, D., Csépe, V., Reis, A., Faísca, L., Saine, N., Lyytinen, H., Vaessen, A. & Blomert, L. (2010). Orthographic depth and its impact on universal predictors of reading: A cross-language investigation. *Psychological Science*, 21, 551–559.

6

DYSLEXIA AND SPECIFIC LEARNING DIFFICULTIES

Assessment and intervention in a multilingual setting

Jennie Guise, Gavin Reid, Sionah Lannen and Colin Lannen

This chapter will:

1. Highlight key issues relating to dyslexia and bi/multilingualism
2. Indicate how culturally and linguistically appropriate material can be accessed for an accurate assessment
3. Discuss processes and strategies relating to assessment and intervention/teaching strategies

Introduction: The context and issues

Multilingualism is an area that can present a challenge to those involved in assessment and teaching of children and adults with dyslexia and other Specific Learning Difficulties (SpLDs). It also presents a challenge to trainers, as there is a considerable need for specialised training courses on dyslexia and SpLD.

Although there is increasing interest in this area, there are still many issues to be resolved. The aim of this chapter is to highlight some of these issues, and to suggest pointers for the way forward. These include: the need to access culturally and linguistically appropriate materials, communication with parents, identifying the precise nature of the problem, mislabelling or inappropriate labelling, linguistic effects such as vocabulary, accent, grammar and syntax, the need to access appropriate curriculum materials, pace of learning, catering for diversity, study patterns and learning preferences. It is also important to consider social and emotional factors, to help the learner establish an appropriate self-image, and to handle social norms, values and culture in general very sensitively.

Culture-fair

This term (culture-fair) was used by The British Psychological Society (BPS) in their Working Party Report (BPS, 1999). The report emphasised the importance of culturally relevant materials for children with dyslexia and, particularly, culture-fair assessment. Dyslexia, the report suggests, may be 'masked by limited mastery of the language of tuition' (p. 60). It was also acknowledged in the report that dyslexia can occur across languages, cultures, socio-economic status, race and gender.

The MacPherson Report in the UK (MacPherson of Cluny, 1999) draws attention to the unconscious norms that continue to operate within our society, which can exclude and certainly disadvantage people from different ethnic groups. The Report comments on institutional racism, and suggests that this can be detected in processes, attitudes and behaviours that amount to discrimination through unwitting prejudice and ignorance. This can certainly apply to the identification of dyslexia, as the knowledge of how to assess children from varied ethnic backgrounds is not widely available, and the prevalent use of tests that are standardised on monolingual populations illustrates this.

There are, therefore, a number of key issues that need to be addressed in terms of policy and practice before teachers can feel adequately prepared to meet the varied needs of diverse groups of children who may have 'masked' dyslexic difficulties. There is also a responsibility to prevent a child being misdiagnosed (false positive) by describing the child as having a learning difficulty when one is not present (Peer and Reid, 2000). It is important therefore for teachers and professionals to engage in professional development in this area (Lannen and Lannen, 2015) in order to appreciate the dual role and the overlap between dyslexia and multilingualism.

Cultural factors

It is important for teachers and professionals to be culturally aware. Kelly (2002) suggests that teachers need to consult and collaborate with people who have a sound knowledge of the cultural background of the students, as this can avoid confusing common second-language errors of bilingual students with indicators of dyslexia. She suggests that these can sometimes overlap: as in the case of left–right confusion in Urdu, which is written from right to left; and with auditory discrimination with Punjabi speakers, who may have difficulty distinguishing 'p' from 'b'.

Additionally, it is important to consider information from parents as they will have a more complete picture of their child in a range of settings, including those not involving language skills. Teachers should therefore be alerted if the child has a lack of interest in books, a discrepancy between listening comprehension and reading skills, difficulties in acquiring automaticity or difficulties with balance, as well as persistent problems in phonological awareness despite adequate exposure to English.

Identification factors

One of the key challenges facing educators in relation to bilingualism and dyslexia is that of identification, and this is highlighted in some detail later in this chapter. It is important to flag up this issue, as it is one of the crucial elements in relation to linking assessment with support, as well as appropriate labelling. This is a challenge because syndromes such as dyslexia do not occur for only one reason, and usually there are a number of factors that contribute to the presence of this type of literacy difficulty, and if a child is also bi/multilingual then this will be an added factor that needs to be taken into account throughout the assessment. Many of the tests used do not explicitly take this into account (Everatt et al., 2000), and these tests can have an adverse outcome for the child whose first language is not English.

Landon (2001) addresses this by asking, 'what factors appear to lead to low rates of detection of dyslexia amongst bilingual learners, and could the same factors also explain the poor standards of literacy amongst many learners of English as an Additional Language (EAL learners)?' The importance of these questions is that they actually investigate the issues and provide a good example of the types of question teachers need to ask when assessing children who are bilingual. To answer the questions presented by Landon, one must consider the range of factors that contribute to dyslexia. It is important to acknowledge that culture-fair assessment utilises assessment materials in the language being taught and should make those materials culture-fair; but also there is a need to develop assessment materials in the first language of the child to assess whether dyslexia is present and affecting the development of skills in literacy in that first language.

Pace of learning and study skills

This is an important aspect for all children with dyslexia (Reid, 2016) and it is crucially important for children who are bilingual. It is important to consolidate learning before moving on to new information. It is only through this process of overlearning that the child can acquire automaticity. It is important that there is scope and opportunity for overlearning and that this is integrated into the teaching programme. Monitoring and reviews are therefore also an important element of this.

Study skills and the identification of the child's learning preferences are also crucial. Bell and Tudhope (chapter 13, this volume), in a study involving higher education students, found that the high level of independent work required and an emphasis on self-direction in the UK system, was unfamiliar to students from other cultures, and this has to be addressed in some way.

Equality issues

The Salamanca Statement (UNESCO, 1994) paved a powerful path on the road to educational equality and inclusive policies. The statement indicated that

> schools should accommodate to all children regardless of their physical, intellectual, social, emotional, linguistic or other conditions ... Many children experience learning difficulties and thus have special educational needs at some time during their schooling ... Schools have to find ways of successfully educating all children, including those who have serious disadvantages and disabilities ... [there is an] emerging consensus that children with special educational needs should be included in the educational arrangements made for the majority of children. This has led to the concept of the inclusive school.
>
> (UNESCO, 1994)

In the USA, the Federal Special Education Law – the Individuals with Disabilities Education Act (IDEA) – includes a clear definition of learning disabilities and states that every school in every city in every state must provide 'free and *appropriate*' special education programmes for all children with special needs. This means that groups whose first language is not English need recognition and appropriate instruction.

In the USA, Spanish is spoken by approximately 10–13% of the population and is the second most frequently used language in that country (Shin and Bruno, 2003). Additionally, in US schools, children learning English as an additional language – the vast majority of whom are Spanish-speaking English-language learners – lag behind their monolingual English-speaking peers in reading performance (US Department of Education, 2005, 2007).

In Canada, the Canadian Charter of Rights and Freedoms has been quoted as support for parental rights, and similarly in the UK, the government has created The Equality and Human Rights Commission which includes a series of written guides to explain people's rights and responsibilities under the Equality Act, 2010, which came into effect in October 2010. The Act brings together different pieces of legislation to make equality law simpler and easier to understand.

Self-advocacy

There is a growing trend towards self-advocacy in education and in society. This means that children, young adults and parents need to be aware of their rights and to be able to speak up for these rights. But it also means that schools should help to equip children with the ability to articulate their needs. This is a skill that will benefit them in later life, and particularly in the workplace. Parents also have a role to play in assisting their child in self-advocacy skills. Perhaps one of the best pieces of advice parents can give their child is to communicate with the school. It is too easy for children who are experiencing any type of difficulty in school to keep it to themselves or 'bottle it up' to such an extent that it manifests in the form of unacceptable, inappropriate and sometimes explosive behaviour.

The problem for parents is that often the child finds it difficult to identify exactly what is going wrong and why. Even at the best of times, parenting can be a challenge. Parents have to be both disciplinarians and counsellors. It is a question of balance, but there is no doubt that very often children with dyslexia will respond more to the counselling approach. Suggestions for parents on counselling children with dyslexia include the need to develop self-esteem.

It is more likely that the child with positive self-esteem will open up and be more likely to discuss problems than a child with a negative self-esteem. It is important therefore to make the child feel good, and that can clear the way for the discussion of any difficulties.

Identifying need: Points to consider in assessment for multilingual students

The key question is, how can we distinguish between English language difficulties and SpLDs? When we are working with a student who speaks English as an additional language, this question informs every aspect of the assessment – from the gathering of background information, to the administration of assessment tests and then the scoring and analysis of the student's performance. Each of these areas will be discussed below.

Pre-assessment

We can start assessments by collecting relevant information about the student's educational background and experiences. This can come from teachers/tutors, parents or guardians, and the student him- or herself. When it is known that English is an additional language, we should request extra information that can inform us about the student's competence in English, and in his or her first, and other languages. Specifically, we need to find out:

- What is the student's first language?
- How long has the student been speaking English?
- What other languages does the student speak?
- How much, and what level of education has been in English?
- What language is spoken by the parents or guardians?
- What language is spoken at home, with siblings, and with friends?

It is crucial to establish at this stage that the student has sufficient skills in English to be able to understand and carry out test instructions. Some guidance on the possible effects of the student's exposure to English is provided by the SpLD Working Group (2005) in the UK:

> Where the student's overall experience of English has been less than seven years, some impact on syntax, vocabulary and comprehension is generally to be expected. Where first exposure to English was after the age of seven, some impact on phonology and pronunciation is generally to be expected. However, much will depend on the quality and quantity of English experience during formative years.
>
> (SpLD Working Group 2005: 12)

In gathering background information, we should aim to find out about the student's areas of strength and weakness, and language use. For the bilingual or multilingual student, we particularly need to know about the student's experience of reading, writing and spelling in first *and* additional languages.

Linguistic characteristics

Some account has to be taken here of linguistic characteristics. For example, some languages are more 'transparent' than others (see Miles, 2000). That is, the spelling can be guessed more readily from the sounds. English is acknowledged to be one of the less transparent languages. This can be seen in the number of irregular words we have, and the number of different ways that we can write the same sound. Some languages (such as Chinese) are pictorial and not based on phoneme–grapheme correspondences. This means that the student might not previously have had to learn direct associations between sounds (phonemes) and how they are written (graphemes). Some languages (such as Arabic) use a different alphabet (Elbeheri *et al.*, 2006), and some (such as Russian) use an alphabet where letters used in English have a different associated sound.

Implications

There are two important implications of these differences that are relevant to the assessor who is trying to find out whether or not a bilingual or multilingual student has a specific learning difficulty. First, they are likely to make the learning of English spelling particularly challenging. So, it is understandable that a Spanish student (whose first language is more transparent) might find it harder to spell in English than in Spanish. Second, the research suggests that the language that we first learn to read and spell has an impact on *how* we learn to do these things (Ellis and Hooper, 2001; Spencer and Hanley, 2003). In a transparent language, learners may be less likely than English learners to use whole word recognition. These learners might therefore find irregular words a particular challenge. Those whose language is pictorial are likely to depend more on their visual processing skills than their auditory skills (Hu *et al.*, 2010). These learners might, for example, find spelling rules more difficult to remember.

We also need to take account of any similarities that might exist between languages. For example, English has common roots with Romance (Romanic) languages such as French and Italian. We also share some vocabulary with Germanic languages such as Dutch and German. This can help with reading and understanding English.

There are wider implications about the nature of specific learning difficulties, and how they present in people speaking different languages. According to Mahfoudhi and Haynes (2009), the development or delay of reading in English differs from the development of reading in other languages mainly because of the nature of writing systems (scripts). English has an alphabetic system that is rather opaque, or deep. Other languages that share the alphabetic system – like German or Spanish – are more transparent, or shallow than English (see Frost *et al.*, 1987). Transparent orthographies like Spanish, Finnish or Serbo-Croatian have a one-to-one relationship between sounds/phonemes and letters. Other languages such as French are less transparent. Of the languages with opaque orthographies, English perhaps provides the most extreme example of opacity: for example, a given sound can be represented by many different letters or letter combinations (/s/ = *ce* in cent, *ci* as in pencil, *s* as in sip, *ss* as in brass, *sc* as in scent) or an individual letter may represent many different sounds (*a* = /eI/ in baby, /'uh'/ in sofa, /a/ in father, /ae/ in dad).

The opacity of English comes at a cost to the rate of learning basic reading skills. In a study that examined development of word reading accuracy and decoding pseudo-words in the first grade in 14 European languages, English learners lagged at least one year behind children who were learning languages with highly transparent orthographies such as Greek, Finnish, German, Italian and Spanish (Seymour *et al.*, 2003).

Reading difficulties in German, a highly transparent orthography, are most evident at the decoding fluency level, and are best predicted with tests of phonological retrieval speed such as rapid serial naming (Wimmer, 1993). In contrast, reading deficits in English first appear in word-level decoding inaccuracies, and are best predicted by measures of phonological awareness, specifically segmentation tasks. These findings suggest that the nature of reading difficulties varies in relationship to the degree of transparency of the orthography

Learning environment

The student's learning environment is also relevant, and it is important to ask the student about any differences that he or she has found in teaching style and expectations. The nature and extent of screening, support and exam accommodations also varies in different countries and types of institution.

Assessment measures

When it comes to the assessment itself, we need to consider possible linguistic and cultural effects that might influence the student's performance in each sub-test. For example, it is possible that a vocabulary test in English will be more of a challenge for the non-native speaker. So, for example, the student might know the meaning of a word if it were given in his or her first language. Or, the student might know the answer, but might not know any synonyms, or might find it harder to form a response in English. There might be some delay in the student's repetition of numbers and letters that could affect performance in working memory sub-tests. Fortunately, perceptual reasoning and processing speed tests are less likely to be affected, so these can be used to give us some indication of the cognitive profile. In addition, some assessments allow for the pro-rating of scores when there is doubt about the validity of a sub-test.

Linguistic background

The assessor should make notes during the assessment about aspects of the student's performance or approach that might be linked to his or her linguistic background. These provide a valuable resource at the time of writing up. They might include information, for example, on the type of mistakes made when reading. In word or text reading, certain types of accent error (that is, placing the accent on the wrong syllable of the word) could be related to the student's first language. Hesitancy in speech may be related to the difficulties that most of us have when trying to pronounce words that are not in our first language. There is no doubt that people with different linguistic backgrounds will have varying levels of difficulty in pronouncing English words. In written expression tests, we are also likely to find mistakes that are associated with the different grammatical structures that are found across languages. For example, some languages make far less use of the definite and indefinite articles ('the' and 'a' or 'an'), or they use it where we do not in English. When we are reading work, we can sometimes 'hear' a foreign accent in unusual grammatical formulations.

We can see, then, that a number of issues have to be taken into account when we are assessing students who speak English as an additional language.

Information gathering

Essentially we need to do more information-gathering, and particularly when we have limited knowledge of the student's first language. We need to be sensitive to the kinds of issues that might affect performance, and scores, in the assessment tests.

Presenting results

It is important to be aware of possible linguistic effects when we are analysing the overall assessment results. This can be highlighted in the introduction to the report but it must be highlighted particularly if the student is assessed in an additional language.

One of the authors (S. Lannen) states that in her experience of assessing bilingual students in Canada, using the English Wechsler Intelligence Scale (WISC), she was able to use the French translation of the WISC to assist her assessment in asking questions and getting answers in French. She was therefore quite confident that she was obtaining an accurate assessment of the students. By contrast, she describes her work in the Middle East (specifically Saudi Arabia, where she was assessing students from other nationalities in addition to Saudis, such as Dutch and Swedish). In these cases, she supplemented the assessment information by talking to parents about early language environment (and developmental milestones in general), and also to teachers about the students' abilities in their own language. She found that with reference to students with specific learning difficulties, talking to their teachers was very important as they were able to indicate if the student was experiencing difficulties, in terms of their acquisition of phonics and reading in their native language. Reading and spelling tests carried out in their own language were of course also very useful.

Lannen states that it is important to explicitly display the factors that can adversely influence the bilingual student's performance. She indicates that performances in the learning situation can be adversely affected by an interaction between the following:

- a significant weakness in the area of short-term memory processing,
- difficulties with tasks requiring fine motor, visual tracking and speed of information processing,
- mixed laterality,
- light sensitivity.

She argues that it is important to recognise that these factors are 'language free', and therefore any challenges with these are not due to a second language situation. Additionally she believes it is also important to appreciate that the acquisition of literacy skills will be compounded by the bilingual student very likely being weaker in English language skills.

Assessing non-verbal intelligence

There are several tests that can yield information on non-verbal intelligence, and this is an important element in assessing bilingual children and adults. The Comprehensive Test of Nonverbal Intelligence (CTONI-2) (Hammill *et al.*, 2009) is an individually administered measure of non-verbal reasoning, and the age range is from 6 years to 89 years 11 months.

The CTONI-2 measures analogical reasoning, categorical classification, and sequential reasoning, using six sub-tests in two different contexts: pictures of familiar objects (e.g. people, toys, animals) and geometric designs (unfamiliar sketches and drawings). The six sub-tests are: (1) Pictorial Analogies, (2) Geometric Analogies, (3) Pictorial Categories, (4) Geometric Categories, (5) Pictorial Sequences and (6) Geometric Sequences.

The Wechsler Nonverbal Scale of Ability (WNV) (Wechsler and Naglieri, 2006) is a non-verbal measure of ability for culturally and linguistically diverse groups. The age range is from 4 years to 21 years 11 months. The full battery includes sub-tests on Matrices, Object Assembly (visual organisation), Coding (speed), Recognition, Spatial Span and Picture Arrangement (visual sequencing).

These tests are language- and culture-free tests of intelligence, and therefore it is possible for the bilingual learner to score above average in these tests, but below average in the linguistic tests. It is therefore extremely important to utilise non-verbal intelligence tests with bilingual students.

Intervention/teaching strategies

Language development

It is important that in every area of the curriculum students are given frequent opportunities for exploratory talk and small group discussion. This can help them put new information and ideas 'into their own words' and link the subject matter to what they already know. This procedure helps to develop new schemas, and this aids comprehension and the transfer of learning. These opportunities for discussion therefore allow them to manipulate language informally and develop more confidence in the language.

Strategies that can be used to facilitate this include:

- exploratory talk in small groups,
- oral reports following group discussion,
- problem-solving conducted orally,
- explanations of how something is made, or how and why things happen,
- announcements read by students,
- dramatisation and role-playing,
- simulation games,
- interviews (live or taped).

Language processing difficulties

- Cause–effect cards – the student is shown two cards, or alternatively just one card. If the first card is given, then the student must predict what will happen next. If the second card is given, s/he must work out what has just happened.
- Group guessing games – one student describes a picture for the others in the group to identify. The student describing must give good clues (informative but not too easy), and the others must make use of the combined information in the clues to help them guess what is being described.

  The group members can also ask questions to help them guess. They may need to be helped to ask useful, relevant questions, and to bear previous clues in mind when seeking further information. This activity, therefore, involves making use of adequate, appropriate and relevant information, and encourages the student to monitor the effectiveness of his/her communication by the response it brings about.
- Verbal sequencing – retelling. This can be challenging for bilingual children, and therefore sequencing stories are useful for assessing or helping the students to deduce information. By omitting pictures from the sequence, e.g. one from the middle, or the last one, the student has to use the information in the remaining pictures to work out the content of the missing picture.
- Composite pictures – it is useful to look at composite pictures and encourage students to think beyond the obvious information (adverts from magazines often provide suitable pictures for this). It may be necessary initially to ask lots of questions in order to get the students thinking, and to encourage them to make associations and inferences. Discourage them from getting distracted by irrelevant details. See if they can provide a suitable title for the picture – this is a good way of seeing whether they have processed all the essential information, or just part of it. Each student in a group is given a picture. Each picture

has an exact match within the group, although some of the pictures will be very similar. The students must discover who has the picture matching his/her own by asking questions and making use of other students' questions and answers.

- Working in pairs (with a screen in between), give each student an identical picture to colour – with several examples of pairs of similar objects. One student must instruct the other student to colour parts of the picture, taking care to give enough information so that the other student knows exactly what to colour, e.g. which car to colour when the picture contains two or more different cars. This can also be carried out using miniature toys/objects, i.e. one student must instruct another student to set up the toys/objects in the same way as s/he has set them up in front of her/him.
- Story telling with random pictures – one student turns over a picture and starts a story. Each student then takes a picture in turn and continues the development of the story – the last one bringing it to a logical conclusion. This activity can also be done without the use of pictures.
- Working in pairs, the students have to find out as much information as possible from their partners (e.g. about their house, holiday, etc.) by asking questions. Each then reports back to the group what s/he has discovered. Initial discussion about the sorts of questions to ask is essential.
- Students in a group are each given a picture that is part of a sequence. They have to discover the order the pictures should be in, by asking each other questions and not showing each other the pictures. This activity also requires the students to make inferences, thereby using pragmatic skills.

Listening skills

Listening skills development will help to develop language skills and auditory processing skills. Strategies which help to develop listening skills include:

- Ensure directions are clear and concise.
- Simplify complex directions; avoid multiple commands.
- Make sure the child comprehends before beginning the task.
- Repeat in a calm, positive manner, if needed.
- Help the child to feel comfortable with seeking assistance.
- Sit the child with other children who are good listeners.
- Tell the child to get ready to listen or say his/her name first.
- Ask the child to repeat the instructions given to him/her.
- Use music at the beginning of a lesson to help children 'switch on' their 'listening ears'.
- Read stories and ask related questions.
- Listening bingo (such as phonic bingo).
- Sound tracks (e.g. door creaking, animal noises, a baby crying).
- Digitally recorded books.

(See the appendix at the end of this chapter for suggested curriculum-based assessments.)

The context for specific learning difficulties

Lannen and Lannen (2015), who are spearheading a major European initiative in teacher training in SpLD, acknowledge that we need to see dyslexia within the wider context of SpLD. Within this context, SpLD can be identified as distinctive patterns of difficulties, relating to the processing of information, within a continuum from very mild to severe, which may result in restrictions in literacy, language, number, motor function, short-term memory and organisational skills. They also argue that a high priority should be given to providing a learning environment that caters for the diversity of cultural, emotional and learning needs.

It is important to recognise the practical experiences of emotional and social difficulties that can be associated with SpLD. Additionally, it is important to appreciate the overlap with dyslexia and the other SpLDs (dyspraxia, dyscalculia, high-functioning autistic spectrum disorder, speech and language impairment and attention deficit). Kaplan *et al.* (2001) indicated that in developmental disorders, co-morbidity is the rule, not the exception. Lannen and Lannen argue that this has great relevance to the 28 nations in the European Community. In the majority of these nations, co-existence of SpLD is neither accepted nor diagnosed and, as in the case of bilingual students, many learners are mislabelled or unidentified and, as a consequence, unsupported.

Lannen and Lannen's project aims to provide policy and practical recommendations on SpLD teacher training and create an EU SpLD website for information and long-distance interactive training, and the project publications and website will, in the future, be translated into a number of languages in order to disseminate the outcomes of the project.

Conclusion

It is important to ensure that culture-fair assessment and teaching are undertaken. It is considered that there is a high incidence of unidentified or mislabelled children among the bilingual student population at school and at college.

As indicated in this chapter, it is important to consider access to culturally and linguistically appropriate materials, as well as engaging in constructive communication with parents, and fostering good home/school/community links. Linguistic effects such as vocabulary, accent, grammar and syntax are also important and have been discussed in this chapter.

Accessing appropriate curriculum materials is crucial, as is ensuring that the pace of learning matches the bilingual student's current level of learning in relation to his/her second language skills. It is therefore important to cater for the diversity which will be evident in a bilingual population, and this includes study and learning patterns as well as linguistic factors. The chapter has also referred to teacher training and, very importantly, to social and emotional factors. Developing self-esteem and self-belief can be a crucial element of success.

References

BPS (1999) *Dyslexia, Literacy and Psychological Assessment*. Leicester: British Psychological Society.

Elbeheri, G., Everatt, J., Reid, G. and al Mannai, H. (2006) Dyslexia assessment in Arabic. *Journal of Research in Special Educational Needs*, 6, 3, 143–152.

Ellis, N.C. and Hooper, A.M. (2001) Why learning to read is easier in Welsh than in English: Orthographic transparency effects evinced with frequency-matched tests. *Applied Linguistics*, 22, 571–599.

Everatt, J., Adams, E. and Smythe, I. (2000) Bilingual children's profiles on dyslexia screening measures. In L. Peer and G. Reid (Eds), *Multilingualism, Literacy and Dyslexia. A Challenge for Educators*. London: David Fulton.

Frost, R., Katz, L. and Bentin, S. (1987) Strategies for visual word recognition and orthographical depth: A multilingual comparison. *Journal of Experimental Psychology: Human Perception and Performance*, 13, 159–180.

Hammill, D., Pearson, N. and Wiederholt, J. (2009) *The Comprehensive Test of Nonverbal Intelligence (CTONI-2)*. Harlow: Pearson.

Hu, W., Lee, H.L., Zhang, O., Liu, T., Geng, L.B., Seghier, M.L., Shakeshaft, C., Twomey, T., Green, D.W., Yang, Y.M. and Price, C.J. (2010) Developmental dyslexia in Chinese and English populations: Dissociating the effect of dyslexia from language differences. *Brain*, 133, 6, 1694–1706.

Kaplan, B.J., Dewey, D.M., Crawford, S.G. and Wilson, B.N. (2001) The term comorbidity is of questionable value in reference to developmental disorders: Data and theory. *Journal of Learning Disabilities*, 34, 6, 555–565.

Kelly, K. (2002) Paper presented at Multilingual Conference, IDA, Washington, DC, June.

Landon, J. (2001) Inclusion and dyslexia – The exclusion of bilingual learners? In L. Peer and G. Reid (Eds), *Dyslexia and Successful Inclusion in the Secondary School*. London: David Fulton.

Lannen, C. and Lannen, S. (2015) Erasmus Plus, September 2014 to August 2017. *Key Action 2 – Cross Sectoral Strategic Partnerships*, European Community Erasmus Plus.

MacPherson of Cluny, Sir William (1999) The Stephen Lawrence Inquiry (The MacPherson Report). London: Her Majesty's Stationery Office.

Mahfoudhi, A. and Haynes, C. (2009) Phonological awareness in reading disabilities remediation: Some general issues. In G. Reid (Ed.) (associate Eds Elbeheri, G., Everatt, J., Wearmouth, J.), *The Routledge Companion on Dyslexia*. London: Routledge.

Miles, E. (2000) Dyslexics may show a different face in different languages. *Dyslexia*, 6, 192–201.

Peer, L. and Reid, G. (Eds) (2000) *Multilingualism, Literacy and Dyslexia. A Challenge for Educators*. London: David Fulton.

Reid, G. (2016) *Dyslexia: A Practitioners Handbook* (5th edition) Oxford: Wiley/Blackwell.

Seymour, P., Aro, M. and Erskine, J.M. (2003) Foundation literacy acquisition in European languages. *British Journal of Psychology*, 94, 143–174.

Shin, H. and Bruno, R. (2003) *Language use and English-speaking ability: 2000* (Census 2000 Brief, Series C2KBR-29). Washington, DC: US Census Bureau.

Spencer, L.H. and Hanley, J.R. (2003) Effects of orthographic transparency on reading and phoneme awareness in children learning to read in Wales. *British Journal of Psychology*, 94, 1, 1–28.

SpLD Working Group (2005) *DfES Guidelines for Assessment of SpLDs in Higher Education*, available at: www.sasc.org.uk/%28S%282j2fuq45af3c3qafusymmw45%29%29/SASCDocuments/SpLD_Working_Group_2005-DfES_Guidelines

UNESCO (1994) *The Salamanca Statement and Framework for Action on Special Needs Education*. Paris: UNESCO.

US Department of Education (2005) *National Assessment of Educational Progress (NAEP): The Nation's Report Card: Reading 2005*, Institute of Education Sciences, National Center for Education Statistics, http://nces.ed.gov/nationsreportcard/pubs/main2005/2006451.asp

US Department of Education (2007) *National Assessment of Educational Progress (NAEP): The Nation's Report Card: Reading 2007*, Trends in Achievement Levels by Race/Ethnicity, http://nationsreportcard.gov/reading_2007/data.asp

Wechsler, D. and Naglieri, J.A. (2006) *The Wechsler Nonverbal Scale of Ability (WNV)*. New York: Pearson.

Wimmer, H. (1993) Characteristics of developmental dyslexia in a regular writing system. *Applied Psycholinguistics*, 14, 1–34.

Appendix

Examples of curriculum-based assessment (source: Red Rose School for Children with Specific Learning Difficulties (www.redroseschool.co.uk) adapted from the National Curriculum Attainment Targets).

Spoken Language – Years 1 to 6

- Can listen and respond appropriately to adults and their peers
- Asks relevant questions to extend understanding and knowledge
- Uses relevant strategies to build their vocabulary
- Articulates and justifies answers, arguments and opinions
- Gives well-structured descriptions, explanations and narratives for different purposes, including for expressing feelings
- Maintains attention and participates actively in collaborative conversations, staying on topic and initiating and responding to comments
- Uses spoken language to develop understanding through speculating, hypothesising, imagining and exploring ideas
- Speaks audibly and fluently with an increasing command of Standard English
- Participates in discussions, presentations, performances, role play/improvisations and debates
- Gains, maintains and monitors the interest of the listener(s)
- Considers and evaluates different viewpoints, attending to and building on the contributions of others
- Selects and uses appropriate registers for effective communication

Key Stage 1 – Year 1

- Applies phonic knowledge and skills as the route to decode words
- Responds speedily with the correct sound to graphemes (letters or groups of letters) for all 40+ phonemes, including, where applicable, alternative sounds for graphemes
- Reads accurately by blending sounds in unfamiliar words containing GPCs (Grapheme–Phoneme Correspondences) that have been taught
- Reads common exception words, noting unusual correspondences between spelling and sound and where these occur in the word
- Reads words containing taught GPCs and -s, -es, -ing, -ed, -er and -est endings
- Reads other words of more than one syllable that contain taught GPCs
- Reads words with contractions (for example, I'm, I'll, we'll), and understands that the apostrophe represents the omitted letter(s)
- Reads books aloud, accurately, that are consistent with developing phonic knowledge and that do not require them to use other strategies to work out words
- Rereads these books to build up fluency and confidence in word reading

7

LANGUAGE, LITERACY, IDENTITY AND CULTURE

Challenges and responses for Indigenous Māori learners

Sonja Macfarlane, Te Hurinui Clarke and Angus Macfarlane

This chapter will:

1. *Reflect* on the contemporary literacy challenges facing Indigenous cultures that draw from oral language traditions
2. *Reassure* educators that there are ethnically linked pathways of promise towards literacy success for Indigenous learners
3. *Reposition* the emphasis to one that views language, identity and culture as intertwined by proposing a culturally responsive and holistic approach to literacy

Introduction

Within the global education reform movement, literacy continues to be positioned as one of the core subjects, with basic skills within this specified curriculum area often taken to be a chief educational goal. In many countries this sustained focus on basic literacy skills is linked to drivers such as national standards, national curricula and sets of key competencies. Aotearoa New Zealand is also driven by educational initiatives of this kind, however a key debate that continues to be raised is the place of biculturalism within a contemporary education system that is purported to be serving a multicultural demography. Indigenous Māori theorists, scholars and proponents of equity and culturally responsive approaches continue to emphasise the significance of the bicultural imperative that is unique to Aotearoa New Zealand, specifically in regards to educational policies and practices. This bicultural imperative is one that emanates out of the obligations that are inherent within the three principles of a foundational accord, *Te Tiriti o Waitangi* (The Treaty of Waitangi); those of *Partnership*, *Protection*, and *Participation*. Many commentators view the Treaty as an unwavering contractual agreement that must continue to formally recognise the unique rights of *both* Treaty party signatories (Māori tribal leaders and representatives of the Crown) across all governmental organisations. For Māori as *tangata whenua* (the first people of the land) these Treaty obligations extend to the protection of, and access to, things that are regarded as *taonga* (treasures). These taonga include land rights, waterways, Māori knowledge, cultural customs and practices, and language (Durie, 1998; Penetito, 2006; Smith, 1991; Smith, 1992; Walker, 1973).

How then might a bicultural education system successfully optimise language, literacy, identity and cultural outcomes for Māori learners whose ancestors' educational system was characterised by the fact that an oral tradition prevailed right up to the time the new settlers arrived in Aotearoa New Zealand? How might culturally-lived Māori-preferred pedagogies assume integral and integrated status within Aotearoa New Zealand's education settings to support Māori learners' success? This chapter argues that a proactive commitment to biculturalism needs to be reflected within all educational policies and practice initiatives. It is also asserted that by adopting a proactive bicultural approach, a strong impetus for Māori learners to experience educational success – as Māori – in these critical domains will ensue, thereby predicating a platform for responsive multicultural education to naturally emerge. A culturally responsive Treaty-based framework will ultimately be presented to guide educators who are working with culturally and linguistically diverse learners who are presenting with challenges in their learning experiences.

Culturally informed policy development

Māori educational aspirations – and the revitalisation of Māori language and culture – have been progressed in earnest by way of a range of targeted initiatives for over 30 years. The retention of *te reo Māori* (the Māori language) and the notion of a bicultural (and an increasingly bilingual) society have been supported through the recognition of te reo Māori as an official language in Aotearoa New Zealand – a thrust which gained some traction with the Māori Language Act, 1987. Full-immersion early childhood language settings, *Kohanga Reo* (Māori language nests), were spear-headed in the early 1980s, followed soon after by language immersion learning contexts in the primary, secondary and tertiary education sectors. The Māori language and literacy education pathway that is available to Māori learners by way of Māori-medium contexts from birth through to adulthood continues to provide hope for the sustainability of Māori aspirations into the future. However, big questions remain with regards to English-medium settings that cater for Māori learners' language, literacy identity and cultural needs that span a bilingual continuum. How do Māori learners fare in these settings? What are the expectations of teachers and their pedagogical approaches? These important questions are to be addressed in subsequent sections of this chapter.

In response to the disparities that continue to exist for Māori learners across a range of social indicators, in 2001 at the *Hui Taumata Mātauranga* (Māori Education Summit), Sir (Professor) Mason Durie outlined a framework for educational achievement for Māori which includes three specific goals: *To live as Māori*; *To actively participate as citizens of the world*; and *To enjoy good health and a high standard of living* (Durie, 2001). Within seven years of these aspirational goals being delivered, the national Māori Education Strategy released in 2008 (*Ka Hikitia: Managing for Success*, Ministry of Education, 2008a), and later refreshed and renamed in 2013 (*Ka Hikitia: Accelerating Success*, Ministry of Education, 2013), continues to promote an integrated approach to facilitating educational success for every Māori learner. The *Ka Hikitia* strategy prioritises actions and resources that are targeted towards optimising Durie's three education goals for Māori learners by growing the evidence base that will support them to succeed in the areas of language, literature, identity and culture; to realise their full potential and to achieve enhanced educational and social outcomes. Māori learners have been identified by the Aotearoa New Zealand Ministry of Education as one of the four groups described as being 'priority learners'. According to the Education Review Office (2012, p. 4):

Priority learners are groups of students who have been identified as historically not experiencing success in the New Zealand schooling system. These include Māori and Pacific learners, those from low socio-economic backgrounds, and students with special education needs.

Culturally diverse literacy patterns

It has long been established that the development of literacy skills in children closely correlates to levels of academic enjoyment and success (Cowie & Moreland, 2015; Washington, 2001). This notion is explored further by Chu and Wu (2010), who highlight the fact that children's literacy development is heavily influenced by a range of factors that are reflective of ecological and sociocultural perspectives about learning. Vygotsky's (1978) sociocultural theory and Bronfenbrenner's (1986) ecological theory give weight to the influence that interactions *between people*, and *between people and their environments*, have on learning. These theories contend that literacy skill acquisition, language, and concept development happen within relationships between people and places – specifically, the education setting and the home context. Further, many other scholars argue that acknowledging the home context (the culturally lived reality of the learner) is crucial if the education context is to be more congruent and responsive to supporting language, identity and literacy development, and the specific learning needs of culturally and linguistically diverse learners (Gillon, Moran, Hamilton, Zens, Bayne & Smith, 2007; Gutierrea-Cellen, 2001; Hamilton & Gillon, 2006; Hammer & Miccio, 2004; Martinez-Rodan & Malave, 2004).

Given the significance of the home context, it needs to be recognised that many Māori learners are exposed to particular (and dual) language patterns and events that contribute to supporting their literacy trajectory at school. Many Māori learners are raised in bilingual homes, where te reo Māori is their first language; others are exposed to te reo Māori and English in equal amounts; and others are raised hearing predominantly English, with some te reo Māori. These varying amounts of exposure to two languages require educators to consider the grounded and growing body of research evidence that identifies the inextricable links between language, literacy, culture and identity (Brown, 1994; Clarke, 2011; Klippel, 1994; A. Macfarlane, 2007; Ministry of Education, 2008a, 2013; Saluveer, 2004, Thanasoulas, 2001). In her 2001 book entitled *Growing up with Two Languages*, Cunningham refers to the significance of identity, by declaring that: 'The language that people choose to use can be an expression of where they stand' (Cunningham, 2011, p. 128). This statement is noteworthy within the context of the aforementioned 'inextricable links' as (by implication), it conjectures that, should an identifiable language not be available or accessible 'by choice' within the learning context, then where might the learner feel safe to stand, to participate, and to learn?

Thanasoulas (2001, p. 4) raises the importance of teachers: '*teaching culture*' in literacy activities, arguing that language does not exist as a separate entity from a child's culture, and that a greater understanding of their culture is the key to understanding their language, and thereby supporting them to develop their literacy. Five reasons in support of this contention are offered by Thanasoulas (2001, pp. 4–5):

1. Language acquisition does not follow a universal sequence, but differs across cultures;
2. The process of becoming a competent member of society is realised through exchanges of language in particular social situations;

3. Every society orchestrates the ways in which children participate in particular situations, and this, in turn, affects the form, function and content of children's utterances;
4. Caregivers' primary concern is not with grammatical input, but with the transmission of sociocultural knowledge;
5. The native learner, in addition to language, acquires also paralinguistic patterns of the kinesics of his or her culture.

The reasonings offered by Thanasoulas (2001) highlight the significance of the notion of 'teaching culture' as a means of supporting language, literacy, identity and culture for Māori learners who emerge from homes where bilingualism spans a broad continuum.

Specific learning difficulties: In recognition of dyslexia

The Aotearoa New Zealand Ministry of Education officially acknowledges dyslexia as being a genuine specific learning difficulty (Ministry of Education, 2008b), defining it as follows:

> Dyslexia is a spectrum of specific learning difficulties and is evident when accurate and/ or fluent reading and writing skills, particularly phonological awareness, develop incompletely or with great difficulty. This may include difficulties with one or more of reading, writing, spelling, numeracy, or musical notation.
>
> (p. 3)

Persistent research-related messages of this order reiterate to educators the significance of learner and *whānau* (family) participation in responding not only to the learning challenges, but also in supporting self-concept and identity. Supplementary pages for caregivers in this teaching resource, entitled *Dyslexia: Breaking down the Barriers*, outline the importance of teachers and whānau working together to ensure that dyslexia is not a barrier to learners' success in life. One particular pull-quote (Ministry of Education, 2008b, p. 2) states that: 'A difficulty only becomes a problem if it doesn't get better with good teaching'. In relation to Māori learners, this statement is profound, and is in tandem with the seminal work of many Māori scholars in Aotearoa New Zealand who promote the notion of culturally responsive teaching as a means of responding to the needs of Māori learners (S. Macfarlane, 2009; A. Macfarlane, 2012; Macfarlane, Glynn, Grace, Penetito & Bateman, 2008; Macfarlane, Macfarlane & Gillon, 2014; Macfarlane, Macfarlane, Savage & Glynn, 2012; Macfarlane, Webber, Cookson-Cox & McRae, 2014; S. Macfarlane & A. Macfarlane, 2014; Margrain & Dharan, 2011). In consideration therefore, of the notions of working in partnership, self-concept, identity and teaching pedagogy, the construct of culturally responsive teaching pedagogy is now explored.

Culturally responsive approaches

It is important to note that according to White, Zion and Kozleski (2005), everyone has a culture, and this helps us to see how people are connected. Shaped by their own socialisation patterns, teachers bring their life experiences and cultural beliefs into the learning context (Phinney & Rotheram, 1987). They bring in their own assumptions and beliefs about what is of value, how people should interact, what is right and wrong, and what is deemed to be success or failure. It is critical that teachers who are working with culturally and linguistically diverse learners acknowledge and understand how their own cultural mores impact on their teaching practices, and on their learners' experiences.

For many Māori learners, discontinuities between the culture of the home and the school are (in large part) able to be ameliorated by teachers utilising culturally responsive teaching pedagogies. Gay (2000) discusses a range of strategies that can be instantiated by teachers, namely: connecting the home and the school by drawing on the cultural knowledge and prior experiences of learners in order to inform curriculum content. This extends to utilising particular and preferred learning styles (i.e. peer and cooperative learning strategies, known to Māori as the concept of '*ako*'), and embedding cultural values and practices within the culture of the learning context. A further strategy specific to literacy that is proposed by Gay (2000) is the notion of culturally responsive literacy instruction. Seven elements (summarised below) are suggested:

1. Establishing the learner's ownership of literacy, by teachers acknowledging and valuing the legitimacy of the learner's cultural heritage;
2. Engaging and valuing the role and contributions of the home, by teachers incorporating the cultural language of the home in the teaching and learning;
3. Including cultural knowledge, stories and literature, by teachers incorporating this in the curriculum;
4. Recognising the collective nature of Indigenous learners' culture, by teachers utilising preferred/reciprocal learning styles;
5. Connecting to the cultural community of the learner, by teachers integrating cultural values, language and experiences into the curriculum;
6. Providing authentic learning opportunities, by teachers enabling learners to use new learning and share knowledge in non-threatening settings;
7. Utilising culturally congruent (not culturally biased) assessment approaches, by teachers drawing on strengths-based, holistic and ecological information.

The above seven elements are in tandem with the work of Clarke (2011), Durie (1994) and Pere (1982, 1994), who collectively promote the notion that literacy improvement is a major contributing factor in the advancement of Māori learners' aspirations in Aotearoa New Zealand. Clarke (2011, p. 19) contends that: 'Good teaching and learning practices are the essential components to actively engaging students'. Clarke also discusses the impact of the classroom community (including the relevance of the curriculum, and teacher pedagogy), the significance of the wider school environment, and the importance of teachers paying attention to two key factors that acknowledge and affirm the identity of the learner; that is, their culture and language. All of these issues are encapsulated in a succinct statement made by Peer and Reid (2000, p. 1):

> It is necessary that culture-fair principles and practices are considered in the identification and assessment processes, in classroom practices and provision, the curriculum, in the training of teachers, support assistants and psychologists, in the selection and allocation of resources, in policy and in liaison with parents and the wider community.

Specific teaching and learning strategies

Many of the preferred teaching approaches promoted as being effective for use with learners with specific learning difficulties (dyslexia) (Reid, 1998), are in tandem with a range of Indigenous learning styles that are shared globally, as highlighted by Metge (1984). Several of these specific strategies are listed below (see Macfarlane, Glynn, Presland & Greening, 2000, p. 126):

- Adopting a holistic perspective when working with a child who may be diagnosed as dyslexic. This would include knowing about and accommodating the child's preferred learning style.
- Implementing assisted learning techniques, which can include programmes involving peer or adult support and incorporate the important principles of modelling.
- Overlearning or rote learning (e.g. chants) are important aspects of a multisensory approach (oral, visual, auditory, tactile and kinaesthetic) to learning, in particular the opportunity to be exposed to a wide variety of oral literature.
- Use of rhymes, alliterations and patterning, which are important components for children acquiring knowledge and skills about sounds. This then lays the foundations for confident transmission of oral language. Such oral knowledge acquired through rote learning strategies is not superficial learning but rather learning that is as complex as it is deep (Glynn & Bishop, 1995).
- Strong family links where every member of the whānau has a contribution to make in the belief that people learn from each other and that learning is an ongoing, lifelong process.
- Taped assisted reading, which is a highly structured and sequential step method of teaching reading where the student moves to the next level once mastery (or criteria) have been reached.
- Paired reading structures where children of similar reading abilities read to each other in turn. One child reads and the other listens. Topping (1996) suggests the strategy of paired reading can reduce the anxieties of reading for dyslexic children, reduce their all-consuming fear of failure and encourage reading practice.

It needs to be reiterated that each Māori learner who has a specific learning difficulty (dyslexia) is unique, and will therefore bring with them their own distinctive challenge. Each Māori learner also possesses inherent strengths and potential, and it is these factors that need to guide the teaching and learning strategies that promote their inclusion, participation, learning and success. To that end, a culturally grounded framework is now presented to guide educators in their approaches to working with Māori learners with specific learning difficulties (dyslexia).

A culturally grounded framework: Raising possibilities for Māori learners

Te Pikinga ki Runga (S. Macfarlane, 2009, 2012) literally means 'raising possibilities', and is a framework that is intended to guide educators who are working with Māori learners and their whānau. Originally developed for educators working with Māori learners exhibiting challenging behaviours in education settings, this framework has also been adapted for counselling, psychology, communication, learning, and educational governance. Te Pikinga ki Runga is not a recipe for 'treating' a particular situation or individual. Rather, it has at its foreground an intention to raise the aspirations of whānau, and unlock the potential of Māori learners as they grapple with learning, socialisation, peer interactions and – in some cases

– the very essence of their own cultural identity. Te Pikinga ki Runga (see Figure 7.1) is premised on three fundamental human rights principles; those which sit at the very heart of Te Tiriti o Waitangi:

> **Principle 1 – Partnership**: The whānau is at the core of this principle. A range of features that support effective partnerships with whānau and the home environment are suggested.

> **Principle 2 – Protection**: The learner is at the core of this principle. A holistic strengths-based response that supports enhancing self-concept and cultural identity is offered.

> **Principle 3 – Participation**: The learning ecology is at the core of this principle. An approach to curriculum, assessment and the classroom context is advanced.

Under Principle 2 (Protection), holistic frameworks promoted by Durie (1994, 1999), Irwin (1984) and Pere (1991) were drawn on to bring together four key domains deemed necessary to supporting wholeness and wellbeing for the learner. Three of these domains – relational (*hononga*), psychological (*hinengaro*) and physical (*tinana*) – comprise the core configuration, with a pervading and emanating fourth domain – self-concept and identity (*mana motuhake*) – completing the formation, as this is integral to, and an outcome of, all of the four domains working effectively together.

To further support the central section of Protection (specific to the holistic wellbeing of the Māori learner), each of the four holistic domains has been broken down further into three dimensions, resulting in 12 dimensions in total. This is depicted in a grid affectionately known as *Te Huia* (see Figure 7.2); a name that was gifted to this part of the framework by a

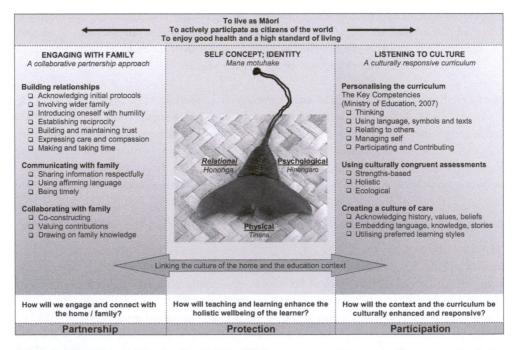

FIGURE 7.1 Te Pikinga ki Runga: Raising possibilities
Adapted from S. Macfarlane (2012)

	Domains			
	Relational aspects *Hononga*	**Psychological aspects** *Hinengaro*	Physical aspects *Tinana*	Self-concept; Identity *Mana motuhake*
Dimensions	Family (Whānau): *Interdependence and connectedness*	**Motivation:** *Inspiration and drive*	Demeanour: *Appearance and body language*	Cultural identity: *Pride and security*
	Land (Whenua): *Kinship and belonging*	**Emotions:** *Thoughts and feelings*	Energy levels: *Alertness and zeal*	Attitude / spirit: *Manner and disposition*
	Friendships: *Cooperation and empathy*	**Cognition:** *Learning, language and literacy*	Physical safety: *Respect for self and others*	Resilience: *Courage and confidence*

FIGURE 7.2 Te Huia: Protecting the wellbeing of the learner
Adapted from S. Macfarlane (2012)

respected Māori woman elder (*kuia*) in 2009. For her, the 12 dimensions of this grid metaphorically represent the 12 prized tail feathers of the now extinct native huia bird. She explained the importance of protecting or caring for these feathers (her metaphor for Māori learners), so that we do not risk their unnecessary demise.

Conclusion

When working with Māori learners in Aotearoa New Zealand who are presenting with specific learning difficulties (dyslexia), it is important that educators do not dismiss learners' culture, but recognise the gifts, uniqueness and potential that come with the culture to which they belong. It is argued in this chapter that a bicultural approach to responding to the specific needs of Māori learners should be premised on a form of cultural consciousness that promotes *Partnership*, *Protection* and *Participation*: the three fundamental tenets that provide meaningfulness and direction within the country's founding agreement, Te Tiriti o Waitangi. When premised on these tenets there is more likelihood that the espoused education goals for Māori development (Durie, 2001) will be attained – being Māori, being global citizens and being healthy. Be that as it may, thoughtful and reasoned frameworks are often required in order to provide meaningfulness and direction to these espoused goals. Te Pikinga ki Runga is such a framework. It is appreciative of the impact of engaging and collaborating with whānau and the home environment; responsive to the holistic wellbeing of the Māori learner; and cognisant of the need for culturally inclusive contexts, strengths-based pedagogies, and a differentiated curriculum. Te Pikinga ki Runga has the potential to appeal to educators because, in the final analysis, it offers a balanced focus on literacy skills, interpersonal skills, and cultural awareness.

To conclude this chapter it would be fitting to turn to one of Aotearoa New Zealand's most illustrious leaders, Sir Apirana Ngata (1874–1950). Ngata was earnestly involved in the protection and advancement of Māori language and culture, giving particular attention to promoting the performing arts and education. He made famous an axiom (*whakatauki*) (see the first line below) that encouraged Māori to become adept at new ways of meaning-making, while never relinquishing their cultural inheritance. This message resonates with the title of this chapter – language, literacy, identity and culture: challenges and responses for Indigenous Māori learners.

> *E tipu, e rea, mō ngā rā o tō ao*
> *Ko tō ringaringa ki ngā rākau a te Pākehā hei oranga mō tō tinana.*
> Grow tender child in the days of your world
> Seek bicultural tools as a means to support and sustain you.

Glossary

Aotearoa	the original Māori name for New Zealand (Aotearoa literally means 'land of the long white cloud')
ako	to learn as well as teach; the reciprocity of learning and teaching
hinengaro	the psychological domain
hononga	the relational/social domain
hui	meeting
Hui Taumata	summit meeting; conference
huia	a black bird, now extinct, which had prized white-tipped feathers and orange wattles
Ka Hikitia	Māori Education Strategy ('ka hikitia' literally means 'to step up')
Kohanga Reo	early childhood setting (literally means 'language nest')
kuia	a respected senior Māori woman
mana motuhake	self-concept; identity; potential
Māori	the generic term for the Indigenous people of Aotearoa New Zealand
o	of
pikinga	ascent
reo	language
tangata	person; people
tangata whenua	(first) people of the land
taonga	treasure(s)
taumata	summit
te	the
Te Pikinga ki Runga	a Treaty-based framework for advancing Māori educational aspirations (literally means 'raising possibilities')
te reo	the language
te reo Māori	the Māori language
Te Tiriti o Waitangi	The Treaty of Waitangi
tinana	the physical domain
tiriti	treaty
Waitangi	the place in Aotearoa New Zealand where the Treaty of Waitangi was first signed
whakatauki	proverb; saying; axiom
whānau	family; a connected group of people
whenua	land

References

Bronfenbrenner, U. (1986). Ecology of the family as a context for human development: Research perspectives. *Developmental Psychology, 22*(6), 723–742.

Brown, H.D. (1994). *Principles of language, learning and teaching* (3rd ed.). Englewood Cliffs, NJ: Prentice-Hall.

Chu, S. & Wu, H. (2010). Understanding literacy practices in culturally and linguistically diverse children's homes. *New Horizons for Learning, 8*(2). Retrieved from: http://education.jhu.edu/PD/newhorizons/Journals/Fall2010/Chu-Wu

Clarke, T. (2011). *He konohi kainūkere: An exploration into the factors that encourage retention in senior te reo Māori programmes in English medium secondary schools in Waitaha Canterbury.* Master's thesis, University of Canterbury, Christchurch, NZ.

Cowie, B. & Moreland, J. (2015). Leveraging disciplinary practices to support students' active participation in formative assessment. *Assessment in Education: Principles, Policy & Practice, 22*(2), 247–264.

Cunningham, U. (2011). *Growing up with two languages: A practical guide for the bilingual family* (3rd ed.). Abingdon, Oxon: Routledge.

Durie, M. (1994). *Whaiora: Māori health development.* Wellington, NZ: Oxford University Press.

Durie, M. (1998). *Mana tupuna*: Identity and heritage. In M. Durie (Ed.), *Te mana, te kawanatanga: The politics of Māori self-determination* (pp. 52–84). Auckland, NZ: Oxford University Press.

Durie, M. (1999, December). *Te Pae Māhutonga*: A model for Māori health promotion. *Health Promotion Forum of New Zealand Newsletter, 49*, 2–5.

Durie, M. (2001). *A framework for considering Māori educational advancement.* Opening Keynote Address at the Hui Taumata Mātauranga, Turangi, NZ.

Education Review Office (2012). *Evaluation at a glance: Priority learners in New Zealand schools.* Wellington, NZ: Education Review Office.

Gay, G. (2000). *Culturally responsive teaching: Theory, research, and practice.* New York: Teachers College Press.

Gillon, G.T., Moran, C.A., Hamilton, E., Zens, N., Bayne, G. & Smith, D. (2007). Phonological awareness treatment effects for children from low socioeconomic backgrounds. *Asia Pacific Journal of Speech Language and Hearing, 10*(2): 123–140.

Glynn, T. & Bishop, R. (1995). Cultural issues in educational research: A New Zealand perspective. *He Pūkenga Kōrero, 1*, 37–43.

Gutierrez-Clellen, V.F. (2001). Mediating literacy skills in Spanish-speaking children with special needs. *Language, Speech, and Hearing Services in Schools, 30*, 285–292.

Hamilton, E. & Gillon, G. (2006). The phonological awareness skills of school-aged children who are bilingual in Samoan and English. *Advances in Speech–Language Pathology, 8*(2): 57–68. http://dx.doi.org/10.1080/14417040600632529

Hammer, C.S. & Miccio, A.W. (2004). Home literacy experiences of Latino families. In B.H. Wasik (Ed.), *Handbook of family literacy* (pp. 305–328). Mahwah, NJ: Lawrence Erlbaum Associates.

Irwin, J. (1984). *An introduction to Māori religion.* Adelaide: Australian Association for the Study of Religions.

Klippel, F. (1994). Cultural aspects in foreign language teaching. *Journal for the Study of British Cultures, 1*(1), 49–62.

Macfarlane, A. (2007). *Discipline, democracy and diversity: Working with students with behavioural difficulties.* Wellington, NZ: NZCER Press.

Macfarlane, A.H. (2012). 'Other' education down-under: Indigenising the discipline for psychologists and specialist educators. *Other Education: The Journal of Educational Alternatives, 1*(1), 205–225.

Macfarlane, A., Glynn, T., Grace, W., Penetito, W. & Bateman, S. (2008). Indigenous epistemology in a national curriculum framework? *Ethnicities, 8*(1), 102–127.

Macfarlane, A., Glynn, T., Presland, I. & Greening, S. (2000). Māori culture and literacy learning: A bicultural approach. In L. Peer & G. Reid (Eds), *Multilingualism, literacy and dyslexia: A challenge for educators* (pp. 120–128). London: David Fulton Publishers.

Macfarlane, A., Macfarlane, S. & Gillon, G. (2014). Inclusion, disability and culture: The nexus of potential and opportunity for policy development. In M. Morton (Ed.), *Tales from school: Learning disability and state education after administrative reform* (pp. 255–270). Rotterdam: Sense Publishers.

Macfarlane, A., Macfarlane, S., Savage, C. & Glynn, T. (2012). Inclusive education and Māori communities in Aotearoa New Zealand: Introducing a paradigm of cultural affirmation. In S. Carrington & J. MacArthur (Eds), *Teaching in inclusive school communities* (pp. 163–186). Brisbane: John Wiley & Sons.

Macfarlane, A., Webber, M., Cookson-Cox, C. & McRae, H. (2014). *Ka Awatea: An iwi case study of Māori success.* Christchurch, NZ: University of Canterbury.

Macfarlane, S. (2009). *Te pikinga ki runga*: Raising possibilities. *SET: Research Information for Teachers, No. 2,* 42–50. Wellington, NZ: New Zealand Council for Educational Research (NZCER) Press.

Macfarlane, S. (2012). *In pursuit of culturally responsive evidence based special education pathways in Aotearoa New Zealand: Whaia ki te ara tika.* PhD Thesis. University of Canterbury, Christchurch, NZ.

Macfarlane, S. & Macfarlane, A. (2014). Culturally responsive evidence based special education practice: Whaia ki te ara tika. *Waikato Journal of Education, Special Edition,* 10–18.

Margrain, V. & Dharan, V. (2011). Connecting curriculum: Responsive pedagogy for teachers engaging with challenging behaviour. In V. Margrain & A. Macfarlane (Eds), *Responsive pedagogy for engaging restoratively with challenging behaviour.* Wellington, NZ: NZCER Press.

Martinez-Rodan, C.M. & Malave, G. (2004). Language ideologies mediating literacy and identify in bilingual contexts. *Journal of Early Childhood Literacy, 4*(2), 155–180.

Metge, J. (1984). *Learning and teaching: He tikanga Māori.* Wellington, NZ: Māori & Islands Division, Department of Education.

Ministry of Education (2007). *The New Zealand curriculum.* Wellington, NZ: Ministry of Education.

Ministry of Education (2008a). *Ka Hikitia: Managing for success. The Māori education strategy 2008–2012.* Wellington, NZ: Ministry of Education.

Ministry of Education (2008b). *Teacher resource: About dyslexia.* Wellington, NZ: Ministry of Education.

Ministry of Education (2013). *Ka Hikitia: Accelerating success. The Māori education strategy 2013–2017.* Wellington, NZ: Ministry of Education.

Peer, L. & Reid. G. (Eds) (2000). *Multilingualism, literacy and dyslexia: A challenge for educators.* London: David Fulton Publishers.

Penetito, W. (2006). *Ka Hikitia: A step in system performance for Māori education.* Unpublished paper prepared for the Ministry of Education, Wellington, NZ.

Pere, R.R. (1982). *Ako: Concepts and learning in the Māori tradition.* Hamilton, NZ: Department of Sociology, University of Waikato.

Pere, R.R. (1991). *Te Wheke: A celebration of ultimate wisdom.* Gisborne, NZ: Ao Ako.

Pere, R.R. (1994). *Ako: Concepts of learning in the Māori tradition.* Wellington, NZ: Te Kohanga Reo National Trust Board.

Phinney, J.S. & Rotheram, M.J. (Eds) (1987). *Children's ethnic socialization: Pluralism and development.* Beverly Hills, CA: Sage Publications.

Reid, G. (1998). *Dyslexia: A practitioner's handbook.* Chichester, UK: John Wiley & Sons.

Saluveer, E. (2004). *Teaching culture in English classes.* Unpublished thesis. University of Tartu, Estonia.

Smith, G.H. (1991). In absentia: Māori education policy and reform. In *Research Unit for Māori Education Monograph, 4.* Auckland, NZ: University of Auckland.

Smith, L.T. (1992). Engaging in history: Kura Kaupapa Māori and the implications for curriculum. In G. McCulloch (Ed.), *The school curriculum in New Zealand: History, theory, policy and practice* (2nd ed.) (pp. 219–231). Palmerston North, NZ: Dunmore Press.

Thanasoulas, D. (2001). The importance of teaching culture in the foreign language classroom. *Radical pedagogy, 3*(7), 1–25.

Topping, K. (1996). Parents and peers as tutors for dyslexic children. In G. Reid (Ed.), *Dimensions of dyslexia, Vol. 2, Language, Literacy and Learning.* Edinburgh: Moray House Publications.

Vygotsky, L.S. (1978). *Mind in society: The development of higher psychological processes.* Cambridge, MA: Harvard University Press.

Walker, R. (1973). Biculturalism in education. In D. Bray & C. Hill (Eds), *Polynesian and Pūkenga in New Zealand education: The sharing of cultures (Vol. 1)* (pp. 110–125). Auckland, NZ: Heinemann.

Washington, J.A. (2001). Early literacy skills in African-American children: Research considerations. *Learning Disabilities Research & Practice, 16*(4), 213–221.

White, K., Zion, S. & Kozleski, E. (2005). *Culture, identity and teaching: On point series 1.* National Institute for Urban School Improvement, Arizona University.

PART II

Planning and implementing intervention and addressing key issues

8

LANGUAGE-BASED LITERACY INTERVENTIONS

Innovative practice in South Africa

Elizabeth Nadler-Nir and Michelle Pascoe

This chapter will

1. Describe challenges associated with language, learning and literacy in South Africa
2. Discuss what is meant by language-based literacy intervention
3. Provide examples of innovative practice in our context

When Grade 1 children at a Cape Town school were asked to write a story, Nicky (aged 7 years, 9 months[1]) created a book about a beautiful butterfly. Figure 8.1 shows the cover page of this ambitiously embarked-on project. While Nicky still needs to learn the rules of English spelling – she writes 'ritin' for *written*; 'elestrata' for *illustrated*, 'Chapta' for *chapter* – she is a typically developing child who has benefited from her first year of formal schooling with a skilled teacher in a well-resourced school.

Not all children are as fortunate as Nicky. Although literacy is a basic human right, many children will struggle with the development of reading and writing. For some this will be because of specific language and literacy impairments. For others it may be linked to lack of opportunity, limited or poor teaching, ill health and social circumstances. The link between early language and later literacy development is widely acknowledged (Nation, Cocksey, Taylor & Bishop, 2010; Snowling & Hulme, 2012; Wolf, 2008), so for many children arriving at school with language development that is less than optimal, means they are already at risk for difficulties with formal literacy instruction. When a child is learning in a language that is not their home language, and is exposed to few or poor language models, the situation may be further complicated.

You will meet two other children in this chapter: Roni and Athule. Roni, like Nicky is a typically developing child, creative and eager to learn. Although she experienced difficulties due to her educational context, these were identified early and she responded well to intervention. In contrast, Athule is a young man with specific language and literacy difficulties that remained unidentified throughout his school career. Placed in a less than optimal educational environment, he 'slipped through the cracks'. The consequences for him were profound, and highlight the weaknesses of our education system, and the need for early, language-based interventions, especially for those with specific language and literacy difficulties.

FIGURE 8.1 Nicky (aged 7 years, 9 months) is a typically developing Grade 1 child who enjoys using her developing writing and spelling skills to create imaginative 'books'

This chapter focuses on language-based literacy interventions in the South African context. There is a literacy crisis in South Africa (Jordaan, 2011). Results from the Annual National Assessment (Department of Basic Education, 2011) suggest that fewer than 30% of learners in Grades 2–7 achieve appropriate levels of performance. We set out to describe the current challenges of our education system, best understood by adopting a historical perspective. As Speech and Language Therapists (SLTs) working in this situation, we describe the profession in relation to the education sector. In the second section of the chapter, we consider the relationship between language and literacy. What exactly do we mean by language-based literacy interventions? The third section focuses on examples of innovative practice in our context as we struggle to alleviate the crisis. The interventions described differ in their origins, age of individuals targeted and delivery models. What they share is a focus on serving a large population with literacy difficulties through the most cost-effective and efficient means possible, with a view to ensuring that every child can experience the same delight that Nicky felt when making her story. They also emphasise the close relationship between language and literacy, and are designed following theoretical principles related to learning, language acquisition and literacy.

The South African context

South Africa is a large country with a linguistically and culturally diverse population. The country's progressive constitution makes provision for 11 official languages, and most South Africans are multilingual. IsiZulu, isiXhosa and Afrikaans are the most widely spoken languages (Statistics South Africa, 2011). English is the fourth most spoken language, but is understood by most people living in the cities and is the language mostly used in the media and government. South Africa emerged as a democracy in 1994, and a new constitution with a strong emphasis on human rights was implemented in 1997. Part of this includes a drive to eradicate illiteracy and develop education (Fleisch, 2008). One of the main priorities of the new government was to strengthen Basic Education, with a number of policies created to facilitate this and ensure equality for all learners. However, there is evidence from a range of studies that the education system is still not serving all our learners well (Walton, Bekker & Thompson, 2015; Fleisch, 2008).

Many of the current problems in the education system derive from the country's history of colonialism and apartheid (Fleisch, 2008). The apartheid era (1961–1994), defined by racial segregation, inequality and injustice, saw segregation also occurring in the education system, which was divided into two tiers: one for those who were 'white' and another for black or 'mixed race' learners (Fleisch, 2008; Navsaria, Pascoe & Kathard, 2011). More finances were allocated to the white education system, so that this relatively small group of learners enjoyed a world-class education. In contrast, the Bantu Education Act of 1953 set out to provide inferior education to black students. Poorly resourced schools, overcrowded classrooms and inadequate training of teachers meant a substandard education for the majority of the population (Fleisch, 2008; Kathard *et al.*, 2011). Large numbers of learners with special needs were excluded from mainstream schooling, dividing the education system further.

Although the education system is now more integrated, difficulties remain. Teachers who were (poorly) trained for apartheid education continue to teach without the necessary support. Fleisch (2008) describes a government initiative in the Western Cape where all Grade 6 learners were assessed to determine competency levels in literacy and numeracy. Only 35% were performing at grade-appropriate levels. A significant achievement gap between learners from former 'white schools' and those from former 'schools of colour' was noted. Approximately four out of five learners attending the former 'white schools' were at a grade-appropriate level; while only one in four children from former 'schools of colour' achieved this standard.

Language of learning and teaching is another complex, contributing factor. In South Africa the majority of learners are taught in English, which is not their first language. Many researchers agree that learning in a second language is one of the main reasons why learners fail (Alexander, 2005; Brock-Utne & Skattum, 2009; Heugh, 2009; Webb, Lafon & Pare, 2010). Reddy (2006) describes results of the 2003 Trends in International Mathematics and Science Studies (TIMSS), which evaluated Grade 8 learners. South African children had the lowest scores of the 40 participating countries. Fluency in English was a significant factor linked to success in these subjects (Howie, 2001, 2004; Reddy, 2006). Fleisch (2008) cites a study carried out in the Western Cape with Grade 6 children which showed that first-language English speakers consistently outperformed first-language isiXhosa speakers. These studies show that although speaking English as a first language does not guarantee success at school, it is a strong predictor for it.

Broom (2004) investigated the language and performance of Grade 3 learners in the Gauteng province of South Africa. A cross-section of 20 schools – some advantaged, 'former white' and some previously disadvantaged – participated in this study. In typical urban schools – whether advantaged or disadvantaged – a range of three to seven languages were spoken in the classrooms, highlighting the multilingualism typical of classrooms in the region. There was, however, considerable variation in language practices and resources at these schools. Children performed better in their first language, and children attending advantaged schools performed better in their second language compared to those from the disadvantaged schools.

Some factors that contributed to the improved performance of advantaged learners were exposure to English in their environments; being taught by first-language English speakers; and greater access to English reading materials. In disadvantaged schools, where the language of learning and teaching was initially isiZulu, Setswana or Sesotho (for Grades R–3) the shift to English was made before or during Grade 4. Therefore, not only were these children not immersed in English in their environments, they were also only instructed and assessed in English at a later stage of their schooling.

SLTs in South Africa are well-trained and committed to working with school-age children. However, the profession is currently under-represented in the public education system. In a paper entitled 'How can speech–language therapists and audiologists enhance language and literacy outcomes in South Africa? (And why we urgently need to)', Kathard *et al.* (2011) contend that SLTs should play a key role in education since our expertise lies in language – the medium of classroom teaching and learning. They emphasise the need for collaborative practice with teachers, and provide suggestions for the type of involvement that is needed based on international literature regarding the SLT's role in the classroom and their potential impact. While there is no doubt that SLTs have an important role to play in schools and should be a strong presence in the education system, at present there are few SLTs employed by the education sector (Wium & Louw, 2013). Therapists employed in education, for the most part work in schools for learners with special educational needs (e.g. cerebral palsy, autistic spectrum disorder) rather than in mainstream schools. Private practitioners work in selected mainstream schools; however, since their services must be paid for directly by parents, they cater for a very small minority who either have medical aid or who can afford their fees. These SLTs typically use a 'pull-out' model, in which a child is removed from the classroom and receives 1:1 therapy. Such children are fortunate and unusual – like Nicky, the little girl introduced at the start of the chapter.

This section has introduced some of the complexities and challenges of the education system in South Africa, and the SLTs' struggle to make an impact on the crisis within it. Readers are referred to Jordaan (2015) and Walton *et al.* (2015) for further discussion. Our focus in this chapter is on some of the innovative hands-on work that is being done by SLTs, despite the current constraints and challenges of the system. In order to understand this work, the following section details what is meant by language-based literacy interventions and gives a theoretical framework for understanding the interventions.

Language-based literacy intervention

Stackhouse and Wells' (1997, 2001) psycholinguistic framework is an example of a theoretical framework that can be used to understand the relationship between language and literacy, and related cognitive activities such as learning and memory. Figure 8.2 shows an adapted version of a model from the framework which explicitly relates spoken language to literacy, and helps underline the message that language and literacy are closely bound together, although different.

Typically developing children start to develop spoken language (arrow 1) from birth. It usually develops without formal instruction through everyday exposure to language in the environment. In contrast, literacy development (arrow 3) requires formal instruction. Evolutionary theory suggests that the human brain is designed to process and produce spoken language, but has not yet fully evolved for reading and writing so that explicit instruction is

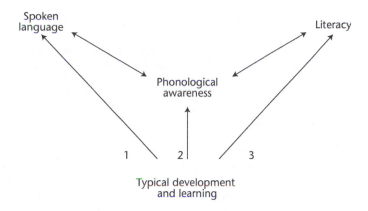

FIGURE 8.2 The typical development of language, phonological awareness and literacy
Adapted from Stackhouse and Wells (2001)

needed or an individual will remain illiterate (Liberman, Shankweiler & Liberman, 1989). Children who have a solid foundation of language (or languages) will typically respond well to being taught to read and write in that language (or those languages). They already know what to expect to find on the page in terms of vocabulary, sentence structure and the sound structure of their language. Many authors conceptualise awareness of the sound structure of a language – phonological awareness (arrow 2) – as a bridge linking language and literacy (Stackhouse & Wells, 2001; Gillon, 2004).

Children with English as their second or third language will find a mismatch between the phonology, vocabulary and grammatical systems of their first language and the language in which they are being taught to read. These children will need a longer time to become literate and a great deal of direct teaching of English vocabulary. For other students, there may be an inherited, neurobiological base to their reading difficulties overlaid on the challenges of learning to read in a second language. Roni, aged 8 years and 5 months, is in Grade 3 at an English-medium school in Cape Town. She speaks three languages (isiXhosa, seSotho and English). She is least proficient in English although this is the language in which she is taught at school. Assessment at the start of her Grade 3 year showed that she was in the lowest quartile for literacy, and this fitted with the struggles she had experienced with her schoolwork throughout Grades 1 and 2. She received additional volunteer-based support through the Shine Programme linked to her school. This programme is an excellent example of language-based literacy intervention and is discussed in more detail in the next section. Roni struggled to formulate sentences and was helped through the use of scaffolds (lines representing words) to write an English sentence (Figure 8.3).

Athule, a young man aged 20, was referred to an SLT by his line manager. Although his mother tongue was isiXhosa, Athule's job required the use of English. He had been managing well with spoken English but filling out a written form had proved too challenging for him. The SLT discovered that Athule had completed Grade 9. He had found exams extremely difficult and had spent many of them simply copying out the questions for the duration of the exam. He had never spoken about his inability to read or write, not even to his fiancée. Athule was functionally illiterate at the time of the assessment, only able to write his name and the alphabet in capital letters. He was a very talented performer and artist, who had compensated for his literacy difficulties in a variety of creative ways.

a   car Is   stop Its

FIGURE 8.3 Example of a scaffolded sentence (A car stopped at the robots) written by Roni (aged 8 years 5 months). She had fallen behind with her literacy at the end of Grade 2, and wrote this example with support

Spoken language development

Typically developing children acquire their speech and language/s in a way that appears effortless, whether it is one language or several. On entering Grade 1 a child's spoken language will closely resemble an adult's. As they progress through the school system, children continue to learn new vocabulary and finesse their use of language in social situations. While severe language difficulties are typically identified early, more subtle language problems often only become evident in the higher grades as linguistic and academic demands increase. In South Africa SLTs not only have to identify the presence of a language delay or disorder, but must also consider that many children are communicating and learning in languages that are not their home language. A typical situation is for children to acquire competency in a home language, e.g. isiXhosa or isiZulu, and on starting school to begin to acquire English. From Grade 4 (or earlier) English becomes the medium of instruction, leaving many children to struggle – not only with the new language – but with the learning that must now take place using that language as a tool. Jordaan (2015) describes the language policies of South Africa as 'exemplary and progressive …' in promoting multilingualism, but notes that English has a hegemonic status with its 'perceived and real value as an avenue to social, economic and educational opportunity' (p. 56). Roni and Athule's parents sent them to English-medium schools, despite English not being their home language.

Phonological awareness

Phonological awareness is the ability to reflect on the sounds of one's language without directly considering meaning (Stackhouse & Wells, 2001). Common phonological awareness activities include rhyming, segmenting and blending. It is widely regarded as a precursor to literacy development (Gillon, 2004; Stackhouse, Wells, Pascoe & Rees, 2002). Children with strong phonological awareness have a foundation of sound knowledge upon which phonological (sound) and orthographic (letter) representations can be mapped to enable decoding of words. This system supports generalisation and enables children to read both new and familiar words that follow the phonetic–orthographic rules of the language (Nation & Snowling, 2004). These processes need to become automatic to enable fluent reading, and reading with understanding (Wolf, 2008). Children who find 'playing around' with the sounds of their language a challenge may require further support in their phonological awareness development before they are ready to read and spell.

A paper by de Sousa, Greenop and Fry (2010) examined the phonological awareness of isiZulu-speaking children in Grade 2, learning to spell in English and with little isiZulu literacy. The children in this study were typical in that they had a solid foundation of isiZulu as their spoken language, but were learning to read and write in English. Results indicated a link between the children's isiZulu phonological awareness abilities and their spelling in both English and isiZulu. The authors suggest that this supports a language-universal hypothesis:

having a solid foundation of phonological awareness in any language may support later reading in any or all languages. However, research which has focused on the phonological awareness skills of bilingual vs. monolingual children has been inconclusive about whether bilingual children are advantaged or disadvantaged compared to monolingual peers. This may depend on the nature of the specific languages involved, the children's relative exposure and abilities in the languages and how they are taught; as well as whether they have an underlying phonologically based dyslexia/reading disability. Athule, for example, had difficulties segmenting and blending words contrasting vowel sounds /u/ and /a/ in the words 'hut' and 'hat.' His mother tongue vowel contrasts did not easily support such distinctions, but in addition his phonological deficit made it extremely difficult to develop this contrast even with letter knowledge and key word support.

Literacy

When a child enters the school system, they rely on their oral language skills as the foundation to support literacy development. In-built neural plasticity allows the child to develop reading by forming new connections between parts of the brain responsible for other functions, such as language, vision and attention (Norton & Wolf, 2012; Wolf, 2008). Difficulties in the development of oral language will have an effect on the development of written language. Ultimately this may hinder the growth of language derived from written text, e.g. vocabulary and concepts. Frith (1985) describes the development of literacy using four phases: pre-literacy, logographic, alphabetic and orthographic phases. The pre-literate child is not yet able to read or spell. Their focus is firmly on the development of oral language. At some point in the pre-school years, children will move into the logographic phase when they become explicitly aware of the particular combination of shapes, colours and symbols that consistently carry the same meaning. In the alphabetic phase children 'crack the code' and are able to match up written symbols with spoken sounds. Making these links between symbols and sounds requires formal instruction. Athule was trapped in the logographic phase as he did not have the underlying skills of phonological awareness and knowledge of letter sounds to enter into the alphabetic stage. It was only through intensive instruction, that he began to develop sufficient decoding skills and started to gain the experience and confidence needed to read.

In the orthographic phase children demonstrate knowledge that goes beyond the alphabetic – particularly important for languages such as English where spelling rules are not necessarily logical. Children need to acquire a word recognition system that contains an inventory of the irregular nature of English spelling. Although the important role of phonological awareness in the development of decoding is undeniable, skills required for word recognition are less well understood (Nation & Snowling, 2004). Norton and Wolf (2012) describe the brain's 'reading circuit' which involves the rapid integration of a number of neural systems to enable reading. This reading circuit is able to support all aspects of language (e.g. morphology, syntax, phonology, semantics and pragmatics), other relevant cognitive processes (e.g. working memory, attention, visual and motor skills), as well as higher-level language and cognition. Fluent comprehension describes

> a manner of reading in which all sublexical units, words, and connected text and all the
> perceptual, linguistic, and cognitive processes involved in each level are processed

accurately and automatically so that sufficient time and resources can be allocated to comprehension and deeper thought.

(Norton & Wolf, 2012, p. 429)

Rapid Automised Naming (RAN) has been found to tap into a number of the components of fluent comprehension (Lervåg & Hulme, 2009; Tan, Spinks, Eden, Perfetti & Spiok, 2005; Wolf, 2008). Both RAN and reading require many of the same skills (i.e. working memory, rapid eye movements, automaticity and the connection of letters to sounds). The evidence that RAN, primarily a linguistic task, is strongly predictive of reading fluency further supports the notion that oral and written language are highly integrated and interlinked (Wolf, 2008). Athule had a handful of sight words for reading and spelling, but had no ability to blend sounds to form words or decode even simple non-words. His RAN of digits was extremely weak, as was his short-term auditory sequential memory.

Innovative practice in South Africa

This section describes examples of innovative practice currently being used to support language and literacy development in South Africa. In order to make an impact on the large population with language and literacy problems, these interventions have moved beyond traditional 'pull-out' models. SLTs are key drivers of these approaches, using our detailed knowledge of language development, links between language and literacy, and therapeutic and learning principles to develop the interventions. We have realised that to make an impact on the population, we must step back and find more innovative ways to work rather than just serving the fortunate few. In this section we follow a developmental path, looking firstly at volunteer-based approaches which focus on emergent literacy in pre-literate or early readers. Then we describe the 'Virtual Reading Gym™', an online approach designed for older school-age children with literacy difficulties using peer support. Finally we briefly consider some of the work that is being done to develop literacy in adults.

Volunteer-based programmes

There are many volunteer-based programmes in South Africa run by Non-Governmental Organisations (NGOs) with a view to developing young children's literacy. These range from small, informal projects with limited funding to large, well-resourced national efforts. Acker and Klop (2015) describe some of this grassroots work in their chapter on SLTs partnering with volunteers in under-resourced communities around Cape Town. The StoryBox project was started by an SLT living on the outskirts of Cape Town near a socio-economically deprived farming community. She made links with a local school where she initially aimed to offer traditional 1:1 therapy to develop children's language and emergent literacy. Realising that this type of intervention would never change the school itself or the education of the broader community, she started to use her knowledge and skills to train parent volunteers to work with individuals, small groups, teachers and whole classes in the school. In its third year now, the project has grown to include over 20 volunteers and a range of other interventions (e.g. visual and hearing screening), and the language and literacy skills of learners within the community have increased from an average of 42% to 68% (Acker & Klop, 2015).

The StoryBox project probably owes some of its success to the specific intervention programme used with learners. The Early Literacy Programme developed by another NGO, Wordworks (www.wordworks.org.za) is the main programme used in the project. It was specifically designed to be used by volunteers working with children between the ages of five and eight who are learning to read and write. The programme is structured into comprehensive, carefully sequenced lessons, and includes assessments for evaluating outcomes. It is available in English and Afrikaans, the languages in which most children will be taught to read and write, and has been designed with explicit consideration of the fact that most children will be learning these as their second or third languages. In addition to its Early Literacy Programme, Wordworks runs other programmes in partnership with pre-schools, schools, libraries and community organisations. These include a Home–School Partnership Programme, a Grade R Teacher-Training Programme and a Home Visitors' Support Programme for children under the age of four.

Shine (www.shineliteracy.org.za) is a relatively large and structured volunteer-based literacy programme. The organisation offers language and literacy support to children in 24 primary schools in three South African provinces. Training and support are provided to volunteers, including group training to community organisations. In the Western Cape there are nine Shine Centres based in under-resourced schools where many of the children are taught in English, their second language, and are struggling with literacy. The literacy levels of all children in Grades 1–3 are assessed in these schools. Children identified as needing additional support are paired with a trained volunteer and work through a structured programme twice a week for a two-year period. The Shine programme's emphasis on assessment and monitoring of outcomes has enabled it to demonstrate effectiveness in improving literacy levels, and it is now endorsed and supported by the Western Cape Education Department.

Acker and Klop (2015) provide guidelines for setting up volunteer-based programmes and emphasise the value of having a specialist (e.g. SLT, psychologist or remedial teacher) to mentor and train volunteers. Intervention programmes should be structured, intensive and consistent, and able to be co-ordinated with classroom instruction. Much has been written about the value of volunteers and assistants, and whether, for example, they can replace an SLT (Wasik, 1998; Boyle, McCartney, O'Hare & Forbes, 2009). Findings appear contradictory, most likely because results depend on how volunteers or assistants are trained, how much support they are given and the quality of the programme which they implement. The programmes outlined in this section have been successful because the volunteers are well-trained and supported and the actual content used is theoretically sound and well-structured.

The Virtual Reading Gym™

> Reading is to the mind what exercising is to the body.
> (Richard Steele, 1709–1711)

The Virtual Reading Gym™ (www.virtualreadinggym.co.za) is an online intervention for which patent applications have been lodged. It is designed to develop reading abilities in children struggling with literacy in the Senior Primary Phase (Grades 4–7). There are many children who are not yet fluent readers by the end of the foundation phase. This has enormous implications for accessing the curriculum. Centred around carefully selected and graded paragraphs of text, the Virtual Reading Gym™ (hereafter referred to as VRG™), exposes children to meaningful, language-rich samples which include narrative, procedural and descriptive writing. Children work through on-screen activities together with the support of a peer mentor. They have multiple opportunities for developing the links between language and literacy, repetition, and supportive feedback. The activities have been designed by an SLT and aim to provide targeted, motivating, and intensive and accessible intervention for children with reading difficulties.

Targeted intervention

Children with barriers to reading do not constitute a homogenous group. Intervention must therefore target the nature of the difficulties experienced. Fast, accurate reading with fluent comprehension (Wolf, 2008) is the ultimate purpose of reading, and rate, accuracy, and/or comprehension may need to be specifically targeted. Although rate and accuracy skills are important for reading, reading comprehension relies on all components of oral language, with an essential focus on vocabulary understanding (Elliott & Grigorenko, 2014). In order to target the specific nature of an older child's reading delay, one may need to go deeper; to go beyond accuracy, rate, vocabulary and comprehension. Attention must be paid to the interplay of oral language skills, phonological awareness, executive functions and the visual system, to name a few. Working memory, one of a number of important executive functions, allows for integration of content and the ability to make predictions while reading. A rich receptive vocabulary will help with partial decoding of words, reading accuracy and therefore comprehension. A strong knowledge of both the phonology and syllable structure of words will allow access to unfamiliar words by analogy to stored letter–sound patterns. A skilled reading partner can help to mediate the reading targets for maximum benefits.

The VRG™ involves a pre-intervention assessment phase in which a child's profile of abilities and difficulties is determined. This is key for evaluating outcomes of the programme and ensuring that the intervention is appropriately targeted. The VRG™ is designed to start with reading tasks at the appropriate level and with the right balance between accuracy, rate and comprehension. It also draws heavily on readers' own errors, so that children learn exactly what is relevant to them.

The VRG™ includes training in the following areas:

- **Accuracy:** Readers' mispronounced or misread words are taught at both the syllable and phonics level with a pronunciation model and attached phonic word lists.
- **Rate:** Repeated oral reading of texts occurs with a timed element to monitor performance. Although a widely used clinical approach, Vadasy and Sanders (2008) indicate that effective fluency intervention must attend not only to repeated reading, but to all components of fluency (i.e. all skills at the single word level and semantic, orthographic and morphological targets). Readers and partners are encouraged to pause the timer to discuss the content as they read.
- **Vocabulary:** According to Wolf (2008), the more one knows about a word, the better one reads it. The programme encourages readers to actively seek out word meanings. The VRG™ aims for cumulative, repetitive learning of words based on syllable structure, orthography, semantics (definition) and syntax (use of the word in a sentence).

- **Comprehension:** Three question types are included. The first focuses on the main idea of the text; the second on the meaning of a particular word, since vocabulary skills are critical for comprehension, and often prove a particular stumbling block for second language learners (Jordaan, 2015). The third type is an inferential thinking question which goes beyond details in the text. Higher-order thinking skills become increasingly important at the senior primary stage of school.

Motivating intervention

The VRG™ is designed to be used with a reading partner or mentor – an older, better reader who encourages and guides the reader through the intervention. The reading partner could be anyone who reads well, but within the school system a peer mentoring approach may be most cost effective. Meltzer (2015) suggests an age gap of at least two years and notes that similar interests are an important consideration when selecting children for these roles. A video-based training programme is used to ensure that reading mentors know exactly how to respond to reading errors and how best to offer encouragement and suggestions for active reading. The programme also includes guided prompts on the screen to encourage the mentor to give appropriate support. Kellogg (2007) notes that to move from novice to master, specific feedback on reading performance must be received at the time of the error, and a system should be in place to score reading performance. The role of the reading partner is vital to monitor and score performance, as well as provide feedback and support.

A student's motivation or will to read is an essential factor linked to reading success (Morgan, Sideridis & Hua, 2012). Students often say, 'Reading is boring!'. This frustration may be caused by the complex interplay between the content and the language-level of the text and lack of encouragement or guidance. The VRG™ uses a game format to increase motivation. Extrinsic rewards can be useful to sustain students through more mundane tasks of phonics instruction and repeated reading. Moving beyond the use of extrinsic rewards, Meltzer (2013) stresses the need to help students, especially those with learning challenges, understand how they learn through training specific aspects of goal-directed behaviour. Her work has focused on executive functions, a number of related processes that are responsible for goal-directed behaviour such as cognitive flexibility and self-monitoring which are essential for automatic repair of reading errors. Heavily influenced by this work, the VRG™ strives to get students to be goal-directed in their reading; to critically think about *how* they read and *which aspects* of their reading process require direct training.

Intensive and accessible intervention

Intervention must be intensive in order to develop what Norton and Wolf (2012) refer to as the reading circuit. A high dosage of reading at an appropriate level will yield the best results since the ability to read fluently with good comprehension creates more connections in the language centres of the brain. As an online programme the VRG™ can be used in a range of flexible ways, with the potential for a far higher dosage than 1:1 therapy. It fits well with the literacy hour or DEAR (Drop Everything And Read) approach, which uses elements of SSR (Sustained Silent Reading, reported in Kelley & Clausen-Grace, 2006) occurring in many schools. The VRG™ is designed to be accessible to a wide audience, through the use of an online platform, which makes it available both at school and home for those with access to the technology. Even if intensive, target-specific and motivating intervention is available, it is not always accessible due to cost and transport difficulties. With its online platform, the VRG™ has the potential to reach a large number of children and make an impact on the literacy crisis.

The VRG™ was born out of a desire to make structured, language-rich, remedial reading instruction accessible and cost-effective to anyone who wishes to improve his or her reading skills. It can be used for adult literacy, students with specific language and reading disabilities and for second language learners. Readers need to have a basic level of skill: at least a Grade 1 or 2 reading ability. However, the VRG™ vision is to have greatest impact by being applied as a tool for a Response To Intervention (RTI) approach (Haager, Klingner & Vaughn, 2007) within the school system. This type of approach will involve assessment of all children in a particular grade. Children who are reading at a grade-appropriate level and respond well to the activities will need nothing further apart from continued practice and opportunity to read. Children whose reading grade is below grade level, may be given more specific and intensive VRG™ training. An even smaller group of children who respond slowly or minimally to the VRG™ may need to be considered for additional therapy in addition to the VRG™ work. The RTI approach allows scarce resources to be targeted at those who need them most, so that no child is overlooked, like Athule was, and so that all children have the opportunity to progress.

Adult literacy development

Athule's difficulties were identified late as a result of a problematic system. When a child has specific language and literacy difficulties these can be difficult to discern against a backdrop of learning multiple languages, having limited exposure to some of these languages and having teachers with limited knowledge and resources. Rose (2009) describes a dyslexic reader as having low reading accuracy due to a deficit in phonological awareness, verbal memory and verbal processing speed and who has additional weaknesses in oral language. Athule needed a highly structured and targeted language-based literacy programme in order to develop his reading. Like the VRG™, the programme needed to be cumulative and allow for intensive repetition to target phonology, letter–sound patterns, word meanings and repeated reading of texts for rate and comprehension. Athule's motivation to read was high and he was prepared to invest time and effort in improving his reading. After 86 hours of individual therapy, he had learned to segment and blend sounds in words and had sufficient grapheme–phoneme (letter–sound) knowledge to read at between a Grade 2 and an early Grade 3 level. Athule's profile of difficulties suggests reading disability beyond the challenges of learning through the medium of a second language. Whatever the reason, there are many adults in South Africa who have difficulty reading. Strengthening the education system and early identification of children with specific difficulties are urgent priorities.

In Africa, it is estimated that 38% of adults are unable to read and write. Of this number two thirds are female (UNESCO, 2014). The situation in South Africa is similar, with an estimated 32% of adults described as functionally illiterate (Aitchison & Harley, 2006). Kraut and West (2014) note that traditional adult literacy programmes may get adults reading at a very basic level, but since they are typically of short duration (less than a year) many adults do not use their newly acquired skills, and without regular use the skills are lost.

One example of innovative work with adults is in projects which use mobile phones as tools for developing adult literacy. Mobile phones are ubiquitous in South Africa (Velghe,

2014). They are cheap, widely available and even those with very few resources are likely to have access to one. Using a mobile phone requires some level of literacy, which one might suppose is a hindrance to those who are illiterate; however, research has indicated that having a mobile phone promotes literacy (Velghe, 2014). Mobile phones can provide both the means and the motivation for adults to practice literacy on an everyday basis. Kraut and West (2014) review a range of projects using the mobile phone as a means of advancing literacy and language in developing countries. They note that when mobile phones are used as part of adult literacy training, both short- and long-term gains are reinforced. Velghe (2014) details a project that focused on illiterate women living in Cape Town and their use of mobile phones to develop their literacy abilities. She saw that mobile phones were intrinsically relevant and practical for the women, and detailed the 'often laborious' but ultimately heartening results of women expanding their social networks, learning informally and finding voice, and in some cases becoming teachers of others to share their literacy skills.

Conclusion

South Africa is rich in linguistic and cultural diversity, but its education system remains weak and the large numbers of struggling children and illiterate adults testify to this. Speech and language therapists have a key contribution to make in this setting, given their knowledge of the links between language and literacy. Some relevant theories and frameworks have been presented to give an overview of what we mean by language-based literacy interventions and the premises that underlie many SLT interventions. We have provided a selective review of some examples of innovative work being undertaking in South Africa to address the literacy crisis. These examples give a sense of how interventions can move beyond traditional therapy for individuals, as they must do if we are to make any impact on the literacy crisis faced by the people of the country.

Note

1   In South Africa children enter Grade 1, the first year of formal schooling, in the year in which they turn seven.

Resources

Wordworks: http://wordworks.org.za
Shine: www.shineliteracy.org.za
The Virtual Reading Gym™: www.virtualreadinggym.co.za

References

Acker, T. & Klop, D. (2015). Partnerships with volunteers: implementing language and literacy intervention programmes in underresourced communities. In S. Moonsamy & H. Kathard (Eds). *Speech–language therapy in a school context – Principles and practices.* Van Schaik: Pretoria, pp. 237–53.
Aitchison, J.J.W. & Harley, A. (2006). South African illiteracy statistics and the case of the magically growing number of literacy and ABET learners. *Journal of Education, 39,* 89–112.
Alexander, N. (Ed.) (2005). *Mother tongue-based bilingual education in South Africa: The dynamics of education.* Cape Town: Salty Print.

Boyle, J.M., McCartney, E., O'Hare, A. & Forbes, J. (2009). Direct versus indirect and individual versus group modes of language therapy for children with primary language impairment: principal outcomes from a randomized controlled trial and economic evaluation. *International Journal of Language and Communication Disorders, 44*(6): 826–46.

Brock-Utne, B. & Skattum, I. (2009). *Language and education in Africa: A comparative and transdisciplinary analysis.* Oxford: Symposium Books.

Broom, Y. (2004). Reading English in multilingual South African primary schools. *International Journal of Bilingual Education and Bilingualism, 7*(6), 506–28.

Department of Basic Education (2011). *Report on Annual National Assessment of 2011.* Retrieved 28 April 2014 from www.education.gov.za

De Sousa, D., Greenop, K. & Fry, J. (2010). The effects of phonological awareness of Zulu-speaking children learning to spell in English: a study of cross-language transfer. *British Journal of Educational Psychology, 80,* 517–33.

Elliott, J. & Grigorenko, E. (2014). *The dyslexia debate.* Cambridge: Cambridge University Press.

Fleisch, B. (2008). *Primary education in crisis: why South African school children underachieve in reading and mathematics.* Cape Town: Juta.

Frith, U. (1985). Beneath the surface of developmental dyslexia. In Patterson, K., Marshall, J. & Coltheart, M. (Eds), *Surface dyslexia.* London: Routledge and Kegan Paul.

Gillon, G. (2004). *Phonological awareness: From research to practice.* New York: Guilford Press.

Haager, D., Klingner, J. & Vaughn, S. (Eds) (2007). *Evidence-based reading practices for response to intervention.* Baltimore, MD: Paul H. Brookes Publishing.

Heugh, K. (2009). Into the cauldron: an interplay of indigenous and globalized knowledge with strong and weak notions of language and literacy education in Ethiopia and South Africa. *Language Matters, 40*(2), 166–89.

Howie, S. (2001). *Mathematics and science performance in Grade 8 in South Africa 1998/1999.* Pretoria: HSRC Press.

Howie, S. (2004). A national assessment in mathematics within an international comparative assessment. *Perspectives in Education, 22,* 149–62.

Jordaan, H. (2011). Language teaching is no panacea: a theoretical perspective and critical evaluation of language in education within the South African context. *South African Journal of Communication Disorders, 58,* 79–85.

Jordaan, H. (2015). Multilingualism and speech–language therapy in education: theory and research. In S. Moonsamy & H. Kathard (Eds), *Speech–language therapy in a school context – Principles and practices.* Van Schaik: Pretoria, pp. 55–81.

Kathard, H., Ramma, L., Pascoe, M., Jordaan H., Moonsamy, S., Wium, A.M., du Plesssis, A., Pottas, L. & Kahn, N.B. (2011). How can speech–language therapists and audiologists enhance language and literacy outcomes in South Africa? (And why we urgently need to). *South African Journal of Communication Disorders, 58,* 59–71.

Kelley, M. & Clausen-Grace, N. (2006). R²: the sustained silent makeover that transformed readers. *The Reading Teacher, 60,* 148–56.

Kellogg, R.T. (2007). Professional writing expertise. In K.A. Ericsson, N. Charness, P.J. Feltovich & R.R. Hoffman (Eds), *The Cambridge handbook of expertise and expert performance.* New York: Cambridge University Press, pp. 389–402.

Kraut, R. & West, M. (2014). *Reading without books: 15 projects that leverage mobile technology for literacy in developing countries.* Paris, UNESCO.

Lervåg, A. & Hulme, C. (2009). Rapid automatized naming (RAN) taps a mechanism that places constraints on the development of early reading fluency. *Psychological Science, 20,* 1040–8.

Liberman, I.Y., Shankweiler, D. & Liberman, A.M. (1989). The alphabetic principle and learning to read. In D. Shankweiler & I.Y. Liberman (Eds), *Phonology and reading disability: Solving the reading puzzle.* Research Monograph Series. Ann Arbor: University of Michigan Press.

Meltzer, L. (2013). Executive function and metacognition in students with learning disabilities: new approaches to assessment and intervention. *International Journal for Research in Learning Disabilities, 1,* 2–30.

Meltzer, L. (2015). *Creating Strategic Classrooms: Empowering Students to Learn How to Learn.* IACESA conference presentation. Power point available at: www.iacesa.co.za/wp-content/uploads/2014/05/Meltzer-IACESA-Workshop-Handout-f1.pdf

Morgan, P.L., Sideridis, G. & Hua, Y. (2012). Initial and over-time effects of fluency interventions for students with or at risk for disabilities. *Journal of Special Education, 46,* 94–116.

Nation, K., Cocksey, J., Taylor, J.S.H. & Bishop, D.V.M. (2010). A longitudinal investigation of early reading and language skills in children with poor reading comprehension. *Journal of Child Psychology and Psychiatry, 51*(9), 1031–9.

Nation, K. & Snowling, M. (2004). Beyond phonological skills: broader language skills contribute to the development of reading. *Journal of Research in Reading, 27,* 342–56.

Navsaria, I., Pascoe, M. & Kathard, H. (2011). 'It's not just the learner, it's the system!' Teachers' perspectives on written language difficulties: implications for speech–language therapy. *South African Journal of Communication Disorders, 58,* 95–104.

Norton, E. & Wolf, M. (2012). Rapid automatized naming (RAN) and reading fluency: implications for understanding and treatment of reading. *Annual Review of Psychology, 63,* 427–52.

Reddy, V. (2006). *Mathematics and science achievement at South African Schools in TIMSS 2003.* Cape Town: Human Sciences Research Council.

Rose, J. (2009). *Identifying and teaching children and young people with dyslexia and literacy difficulties.* Retrieved 8 June 2014 from http://webarchive.nationalarchives.gov.uk

Snowling, M.J. & Hulme, C. (2012). Interventions for children's language and literacy difficulties. *International Journal of Language & Communication Disorders, 47*(1), 27–34.

Stackhouse, J. & Wells, B. (1997). *Children's speech and literacy difficulties I: A psycholinguistic framework.* London: Whurr Publishers.

Stackhouse, J. & Wells, B. (2001). *Children's speech and literacy difficulties II: Identification and intervention.* London: Whurr Publishers.

Stackhouse, J., Wells, B., Pascoe, M. & Rees, R. (2002). From phonological therapy to phonological awareness. *Seminars in Speech and Language, 23*(1), 27–42.

Statistics South Africa (2011). *Census 2011.* Retrieved 12 May 2014 from http://salanguages.com/stats.htm

Steele, R. (1709–1711). *Tatler,* no. 147. Retrieved 9 May 2015 from http://en.wikiquote.org/wiki/Richard_Steele

Tan, L.H., Spinks, J.A., Eden, G., Perfetti, C.A. & Siok, W.T. (2005). Reading depends on writing, in Chinese. *Proceedings of the National Academy of Science, 102,* 8781–5.

UNESCO (2014). *Literacy and non-formal education.* Retrieved 29 August 2014 from www.unesco.org/new/en/dakar

Vadasy, P.F & Sanders, E.A. (2008). Benefits of repeated reading intervention for low-achieving fourth- and fifth-grade students. *Remedial and Special Education, 29,* 235–49.

Velghe, F. (2014). '*This is almost like writing': Mobile phones, learning and literacy in a South African township.* Unpublished Doctoral Thesis, Tilburg University, Netherlands.

Walton, E., Bekker, T. & Thompson, B. (2015). South Africa: the educational context. In S. Moonsamy & H. Kathard (Eds), *Speech–language therapy in a school context – Principles and practices.* Van Schaik: Pretoria, pp. 15–37.

Wasik, B.A. (1998). *Using volunteers as reading tutors: Guidelines for successful practices. The Reading Teacher, 51,* 7, 562–70.

Webb, V.A., Lafon, M. & Pare, P. (2010). Bantu languages in education in South Africa: Ongekho akekho! The absentee owner. *Language Learning Journal, 37*(3), 273–92.

Wium, A. & Louw, B. (2013). Revisiting the roles and responsibilities of speech–language therapists in South African schools. *South African Journal of Communication Disorders,* 60, 31–7.

Wolf, M. (2008). *Proust and the squid: The story and science of the reading brain.* New York: HarperCollins Publishers.

9

FOREIGN LANGUAGE TEACHER TRAINING ON DYSLEXIA

DysTEFL resources

Joanna Nijakowska and Judit Kormos

This chapter will:

1. Discuss the importance of teacher knowledge, beliefs and attitudes in inclusive foreign language education
2. Outline the pedagogical principles of an award-winning teacher training course, the DysTEFL course
3. Provide a description of the structure and content of the teacher training resources in the DysTEFL course

Foreign language teacher training and inclusive practices

Principles of inclusive education, including foreign language education, stem from the understanding of the fact that people differ in a number of ways and they have the basic human right to equal opportunities in education. Inclusive practices aim at promoting equality in access to high-quality language education and a supportive learning environment, and at removing barriers to learning and eliminating prejudice and discrimination. Responding to and catering for the diversity of individual learning needs of all students, among whom are foreign language learners with dyslexia, should become a pursued standard in education and a defining characteristic of modern educational systems. In this chapter we will discuss the importance of teacher knowledge, beliefs and attitudes in inclusive foreign language education and outline the pedagogical principles of an award-winning teacher training course, the DysTEFL course, that assists language teachers to apply inclusive teaching practices for dyslexic language learners. This will be followed by a description of the structure and content of the teacher training resources in the DysTEFL course.

Marginalisation and exclusion from foreign language education frequently result from poor awareness of teachers of inclusive practices that can help transform mainstream language education so that it meets the needs of all learners. Certain language classroom practices might not work equally well for all students and, unless appropriate differentiation and adjustments are introduced, they can become hurdles in the way of full participation and achievement by foreign language learners with dyslexia.

Teachers' beliefs, knowledge and skills concerning inclusion strongly influence their eagerness and ability to employ inclusive practices in their classrooms (Sharma, Forlin & Loreman, 2008). While many teachers may report positive attitudes towards the idea of including all learners in mainstream classes, they tend to express considerable doubt and concern regarding their preparedness and limited training with regard to implementing inclusive instruction and catering for diversity of learning needs (Beacham & Rouse, 2012). Foreign language pre- and in-service teachers complain that they receive no or very little training about dyslexia, and ways of differentiating instruction and materials in order to provide effective schooling for those learners. They admit they lack sufficient knowledge of the nature of dyslexia and the difficulties it causes in foreign language learning. They express the need to gain a thorough understanding of effective inclusive teacher behaviour and teaching techniques to enhance the language learning processes of students with dyslexia (Nijakowska, 2014).

In fact, the pedagogy and content of the training pre-service teachers receive serve as significant predictors of their attitudes towards diversity and inclusive practices (Sharma *et al.*, 2008). Providing foreign language teachers with high-quality training which helps develop supportive attitudes towards inclusion as well as equipping them with competence to cope with the demands of inclusive education constitutes one of the major challenges foreign language teacher training institutions need to face (European Agency for Development in Special Needs Education, 2012; Florian, 2012). Appropriate training does not only impact teachers' attitudes, but also reduces their concerns, improves self-efficacy and boosts confidence in the successful implementation of inclusive teaching practices (Sharma & Sokal, 2013).

Teacher knowledge, teacher classroom practices and student achievement are tightly linked. Studies on teacher knowledge (e.g. Brady *et al.*, 2009; McCutchen & Berninger, 1999; McCutchen *et al.*, 2002a, 2002b; McCutchen, Green, Abbott & Sanders, 2009; Podhajski, Mather, Nathan & Sammons, 2009) confirm the leading role that initial teacher training schemes and continuing professional development programmes play in modifying the instructional potential of teachers and shaping the way they teach. Enhanced teacher competence and improved self-efficacy, in turn, serve as a precondition for the successful implementation of differentiated instruction targeted at accommodating the diverse learning needs of all students.

The DysTEFL course attempts to close the gap in the pre- and in-service foreign language teacher training schemes with regard to implementing inclusive practices towards learners with dyslexia by offering teachers tailor-made, targeted support. In line with the European educational priorities, it reinforces inclusive education and maximises the quality of teaching of foreign languages to learners with dyslexia and specific learning differences.

The pedagogical principles of the DysTEFL teacher training resources

In designing the teacher resources in the framework of the DysTEFL project, which won the British Council's ELTon award and was recognised with the European Language Label award, our intention was to develop a course that is built on the model of the teacher as a reflective practitioner (Tanner & Green, 1998; Wallace, 1991), who experiments with new learner-centred teaching methodologies, creatively adapts teaching methods, tasks and techniques to his/her context and then reflects on the outcomes of the learning and teaching processes. In this model, the trainer is neither a model nor a source of information, but a moderator and facilitator who helps to raise the trainees' awareness of the relevant issues, gives possible answers to questions, and provides feedback on trainees' ideas, and comments and suggestions on the work they produce.

From these underlying principles it follows that the DysTEFL course took a task-based approach to teacher development, which, as its name suggests, employs tasks to enhance learning and reflection. Therefore, the course is not a simple depository of relevant information about dyslexia and language teaching, as the team believed that such resources already exist in the form of books, journal articles and book chapters (e.g. Kormos & Smith, 2012; Nijakowska, 2010; Schneider & Crombie, 2003; Schneider & Evers, 2009; Schneider & Ganschow, 2000). Such a repository of resources would have contributed to the theoretical knowledge base of language teachers but would not have addressed teachers' attitudes, ideas and beliefs (Freeman & Johnson, 1998). Based on the outcomes of the needs analysis survey that we conducted at the outset of the project, there seemed to be a clear need for a teacher-development course that provided hands-on tasks and contributed to raising awareness of the needs of dyslexic students in foreign language classrooms. By designing a task-based resource for language teachers we aimed to develop teachers' expertise in inclusive educational practices by empowering them to be 'active users ... of theory in their own right, for their own means, and as appropriate for their own instructional contexts' (Johnson, 2006, p. 240).

Accordingly, each unit within the course follows the pattern of the reflective cycle, in which trainees first draw on their existing experiences, reflecting on their current practices, attitudes, preconceptions and the context they work in. The trainees who are in-service language teachers can draw on their previous teaching experiences in this phase. Students in pre-service teacher training programmes can recall their own language learning experiences or memories of peers or acquaintances who had learning difficulties and were learning an additional language. It is also important that trainees become consciously aware of their attitudes, beliefs and concerns at this stage. Addressing these at the beginning of each unit is crucial for effective teacher learning to take place (Waters, 2005) and for enhancing teacher's self-efficacy beliefs about inclusive practices (Guo, Piasta, Justice & Kaderavek, 2010).

This initial reflection stage is followed by an input phase during which new ideas and relevant background information are presented. Next, trainees perform a series of tasks evaluating teaching activities, materials and lesson plans. They are also asked to design new instructional tasks and teaching aids that are appropriate for their contexts. This stage requires the trainees to apply the knowledge base that they acquired in the input phase to real-world tasks that are specific to their own existing teaching environment or the future context in which they are going to work. As a final step the trainees reflect on what they learnt in the course of the unit (see Figure 9.1). This reflective stage gives them the opportunity to evaluate the feasibility, relevance and acceptability of the suggested instructional techniques and methods (Waters, 2005).

In the face-to-face and online learning versions of the course, co-operation among trainees is encouraged by means of collaborative tasks. Through these interactions trainees share their experiences, and learn about the concerns and attitudes of their colleagues. Moreover, they gain applicable knowledge and skills not only through the course materials and from the trainer but also from each other. These social interactions in the guided learning tasks help trainee teachers to co-construct knowledge (Vygotsky, 1978) and contribute to their development as teachers.

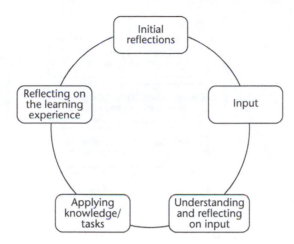

FIGURE 9.1 The reflective cycle as the basic principle of the DysTEFL teacher training course design

The structure and content of the DysTEFL teacher training resources

Based on the principles described above, three versions of the DysTEFL course have been designed. The first is a face-to-face version of the course, which can be used in language teacher education courses on site, including both pre-service and in-service teacher education provided by institutions of higher education (undergraduate and postgraduate levels), teacher-training workshops, summer schools and commercial teacher development courses (certificate- and diploma-level courses). The materials prepared for this version of the course include separate trainee's and trainer's booklets (Nijakowska *et al.*, 2013).

The second version of the course is an adapted version of the face-to-face materials made available online on a static webpage, which is freely available to interested language teachers, teacher educators, educational psychologists, special education teachers, parents and any other stakeholders (www.dystefl.eu). Finally, an accompanying interactive online version of the course was also set up using Moodle to allow for the exploitation of the course for distance education purposes and for blended learning. Even though the course exists in three different delivery formats, the same general pedagogical principles characterise all three versions. The three versions also have the same structure and use the same or highly similar tasks adapted to the nature of the learning environment.

In order to raise the awareness of language teachers of the needs of students with dyslexia when acquiring another language, to form positive attitudes to dyslexic language learners (in some contexts where negative attitudes prevail) and to facilitate the inclusion of these students, foreign language teachers need both theoretical knowledge regarding dyslexia and familiarity with practical techniques for the classroom. Successful inclusive teaching needs to be underpinned by a solid knowledge base about the nature of dyslexia and associated learning differences. Only by understanding the cognitive, emotional and social issues associated with specific learning difficulties can teachers make informed pedagogical decisions and effective adaptations in their teaching, and form positive attitudes to inclusive teaching practice.

Consequently, the course consists of four main components (see Figure 9.2). The first unit familiarises teachers with the nature of dyslexia and the associated learning difficulties such as dyspraxia, Attention Deficit and Hyperactivity Disorder (ADHD) and dyscalculia. It also aims to raise awareness of the strengths and weaknesses of individuals with learning difficulties.

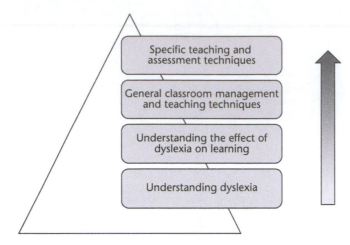

FIGURE 9.2 An overview of the content of the DysTEFL course

The second unit helps teachers understand the effects of dyslexia on the cognitive, emotional and social processes of language learning. The third unit assists teachers in developing effective teaching approaches and classroom management techniques, and the course concludes with the fourth unit on specific teaching and assessment techniques.

Just as there is no one-size-fits-all approach to teaching languages to dyslexic students, there is no such teacher development course either. Therefore, the DysTEFL resources were planned to be used in a flexible manner across a wide variety of contexts. Almost all of the units can stand alone, and there is also flexibility in the order in which the particular units of the course can be covered. Units can be omitted or taught over longer periods than one session because of the availability of additional optional tasks and resources. The original plan of the course designers was to provide a complete teacher training package that requires approximately 30 hours of instruction time. Nevertheless, the flexibility of the materials allows for it to be taught over 10 weeks in countries/institutions where a term lasts for 10 weeks but also over 15 weeks in countries/institutions where the typical academic semester consists of 15 weeks. The complete course could form the basis of a five-day summer school or teacher training course, but units can be used in shorter one- or two-day workshops as well as in half-day professional development sessions.

The ten units of the course are as follows:

1. The nature of dyslexia
2. Specific learning difficulties associated with dyslexia
3. Identification of dyslexia
4. The effect of dyslexia on foreign language learning
5. Accommodations of dyslexic learners in the foreign language classroom and overview of teaching techniques
6. Phonological and orthographic awareness in English as a foreign language
7. Techniques for teaching vocabulary and grammar
8. Techniques for teaching reading and writing
9. Techniques for teaching listening and speaking
10. The assessment of dyslexic language learners.

The first six units of the course are built on each other, and hence some familiarity with concepts and issues discussed in preceding units is necessary. Nevertheless, it is possible to leave out certain units once students have an appropriate understanding of the nature of dyslexia and its effect on learning additional languages. The last four units of the course can be taught or studied in any order. Units 6–10 can also be divided into two sessions to accommodate 15-week-long semesters.

Each unit is planned to cover a 90–120 minute long face-to-face session and should involve an additional four hours of outside-classroom study time. In the self-study version of the course students are expected to spend approximately six hours on completing a unit. The planned amount of study time reflects the requirements of credit-bearing courses in higher education in the European Union under the Bologna agreement.

In line with Figure 9.1, each unit consists of an awareness raising/reflection task, an input task, a knowledge transfer task and/or practical application task and a final reflection task. Each unit contains an *introduction* that states the aims of the unit, the kinds of tasks participants will do and an estimation of how long each task will take. *Notes for trainers* on how to organise and set up the tasks are also provided for each of the units in the trainer's booklet, which contains detailed descriptions of the course materials and tips and suggestions for the practical delivery of the course.

A large variety of tasks are used for the various phases of the unit. *Awareness raising tasks* at the beginning of each unit take the form of pair and group discussions, surveys and diary entries regarding previous experiences, attitudes, preconceptions and biases. Interview excerpts and video input also serve as means for assisting initial reflections and awareness raising.

Input tasks are brief online lectures prepared by the project team members (narrated PowerPoint presentations), existing YouTube videos of expert lecturers, freely available informational materials on academic and professional websites, book chapters and journal articles. Copyright materials such as whole book chapters and journal articles are not reproduced in the course materials, but students are referred to these sources. All the readings and lectures have a clearly stated purpose and the participants or users of the self-study materials are always set tasks that engage them with the input material. These tasks include writing summaries of the presented information, finding key points, filling in worksheets and highlighting pieces of information particularly relevant for the participants' contexts. Other tasks include checking initial reflections and preconceptions against the input.

The knowledge transfer and practical application tasks take a variety of forms including discussing, evaluating and preparing lesson plans, instructional materials and tasks. Task outcomes in this phase are individual, pair and group presentations, posters, information sheets and written reports and online forum posts. *Final reflection tasks* include writing individual diary entries, reports and engaging in pair and group discussions.

Each unit concludes with a recommended *list of resources* such as books, book chapters, journal articles and relevant internet-based material (documents, videos, etc.). A *key to activities* and model answers, where relevant, are included in the self-study materials and in the printed trainer's booklet.

What do language teachers need to know about dyslexia and specific learning differences?

As an illustration of the DysTEFL language teacher training materials and to demonstrate the educational and theoretical principles underlying these materials, we have decided to focus on the first two units of the module. These two units provide an overview of the nature of dyslexia and place it within the wider context of specific learning differences. In designing these two units, the team considered the findings of previous research that showed that teachers often lack appropriate awareness and relevant conceptual knowledge of the nature of reading, reading difficulties and learning disabilities (Moats, 1994 , 2009; Bos *et al.*, 2001; Moats & Foorman, 2003; Washburn, Joshi & Binks-Cantrell, 2011a, 2011b), and also in an EFL context (Goldfus, 2012; Nijakowska, 2014). Teacher knowledge studies (e.g. Joshi *et al.*, 2009a, 2009b; Goldfus, 2012) revealed that a likely and plausible cause of limited knowledge of basic language concepts such as phonological awareness, phonemic awareness, alphabetic principles/phonics and morphology can be attributed to insufficient and/or inadequate initial teacher training. According to Washburn *et al.* (2011a, 2011b), teacher knowledge of dyslexia cannot be separated from the knowledge of these basic language concepts.

Studies on teacher knowledge also highlight the importance of professional training in upgrading teacher knowledge, which then hopefully translates into applying appropriate instructional practices, choices and behaviours resulting in enhanced student achievement. Providing teachers with relevant theoretical knowledge that they can incorporate in their language teaching praxis is essential. Only through this can the timely and reliable identification of learning difficulties in the classroom be facilitated and an inclusive classroom environment established. Intensive specialised intervention programmes for dyslexic language learners also need to rest on evidence-based practices.

In line with our arguments above, the first unit of the DysTEFL course gives an overview of basic theories of dyslexia and helps teachers to gain awareness of the specific characteristics of dyslexic individuals. The unit starts with a brief survey that includes statements expressing common misconceptions about dyslexia (see Wadlington & Wadlington, 2005). After completing the survey, teachers are asked to watch a video lecture and read an information sheet which provide a concise summary of the nature and causes of dyslexia. Raising teachers' awareness of the common unsupported beliefs about dyslexia is instrumental in eliminating misconceptions and establishing an appropriate theoretical knowledge base. It also gives confidence to teachers in communicating relevant and accurate information to students, parents and colleagues.

In the second unit of the module on understanding dyslexia we use a different type of awareness-raising task, which allows participants to experience what it feels like to have a learning difficulty. In this task teachers have to copy a piece of text using the hand they normally do not write with and to substitute certain vowels with different signs as they write. The instructions are intentionally complex, long and presented very quickly. By completing this task, teachers can gain first-hand experience of how anxiety-provoking and frustrating certain activities can be for dyslexic language learners and how task instructions and procedures can become barriers to participation. This initial awareness raising step is also followed by video presentations and relevant readings about other learning difficulties frequently accompanying or overlapping with dyslexia.

Awareness raising at the level of how particular discourses shape thinking and expression of our thoughts is another important element of teacher education. Therefore, we also aim to familiarise teachers with the various conceptualisations of learning difficulties and dyslexia, and facilitate reflections on how terminology and language use expresses one's views and attitudes to people who have learning difficulties. Teachers are asked to read three definitions of dyslexia, two of which illustrate the bio-medical view and one the interactionist view of learning difficulties. The bio-medical definitions of dyslexia imply that disability constitutes a series of barriers in one's life and that people with disabilities show deficiencies when compared with others. This view suggests that the source of the problem is the individual and that the responsibility of the scientific community and education is to find the cause of the problem and offer a treatment for it. In this model, students are seen as having individual needs that have to be met by special education providers, schools and other educational institutions. In contrast, the environmentalist view of difficulties as a socially constructed barrier embodies the assumption that disabilities are caused by the environment and social factors (Barnes, 1996) rather than by differences across individuals. The current interactional view of disabilities exemplified by one of the definitions acknowledges the importance of both the role of the environment and that of individual differences (see e.g. Frederickson & Cline, 2002). The interactional view puts the emphasis on the intricate interplay between the educational context and individual strengths and weaknesses, and provides a framework on which successful inclusion programmes can be developed (Frederickson & Cline, 2002).

The tasks in these two units also require that teachers apply what they learned in the previous steps. In the first unit on dyslexia, participants design an information sheet about dyslexia for their colleagues. This task offers an opportunity for teachers to select relevant information, demonstrate understanding of key concepts and convey what they have learned to a specific audience. In the second unit, teachers consider the challenges specific learning differences can pose for language learners and think about possible accommodations in the classroom. They are also asked to reflect on their previous teaching experiences with students with specific learning differences and how what they learned in the first two units can be applied to assist them.

Conclusion

Teacher training schemes and teacher training materials, among other factors, directly impact the foreign language education ecosystem (Mahmoodzadeh, 2012; Tudor, 2003), and influence and shape the way both teachers and their learners function in it. Well-trained, knowledgeable, sensitive and aware teachers are better able to cater for the diverse learning needs of their students, including foreign language learners with dyslexia. These learners have a right to, and can benefit from, the mainstream schooling available to all learners, provided their teachers are able to appropriately differentiate their teaching approach in terms of materials, instruction, tasks and assignments as well as the amount of teacher support. This requires accepting difference as an asset rather than an obstacle to the learning and teaching processes, and understanding that some learners need minimal adjustments to feel comfortable in the language classroom, while others would welcome more individualised approaches.

Inclusion is an ongoing process and, for it to be successful, commitment, collaboration, rearrangements and enabling solutions introduced at the level of school management are needed (Frederickson & Cline, 2002). Support at the school and policy level, however, varies considerably across countries and educational contexts. In a large number of instructional contexts the availability, amount and quality of support offered to learners with dyslexia is regulated neither by a national nor school policy, but entirely depend on the teachers' professional skills, awareness, preparedness, and readiness to employ inclusive practices. Therefore teachers' knowledge, skills, experience and attitudes can be a key driver towards inclusion in these situations.

Teacher-knowledge studies (e.g. Brady *et al.*, 2009; McCutchen *et al.*, 2002a; Podhajski *et al.*, 2009) highlight the potential of professional training in increasing and strengthening teacher knowledge, which in turn leads to facilitating student achievement via the use of efffective instructional and classroom management practices. Our professional teacher development course on dyslexia and foreign language study – DysTEFL – seems to fully realise this potential. The course offers high-quality training for foreign language teachers on specific learning differences, inclusive classroom practices and more targeted, differentiated support for individual learners, tailored to their special educational needs, and in that way promoting the ideas of equity and social inclusion. EFL professionals have recognised, appreciated and rewarded the DysTEFL course and considered it an example of good practice, capable of exerting impact on teachers' attitudes, sentiments, self-efficacy and preparedness for applying inclusive practices towards foreign language learners with dyslexia.

The DysTEFL course was designed so that it offers a broad array of expected learning outcomes in terms of knowledge, skills and social competence. It aims to foster positive teacher attitudes towards special educational needs, specific learning differences and an inclusive approach to education. It stimulates the development of foreign language teacher knowledge – research-based content knowledge of basic linguistic concepts (e.g. constructs related to reading such as *phonological awareness* or *alphabetic principle*) and dyslexia. Teacher knowledge is not limited to understanding theoretical concepts, terms and definitions but, most importantly, involves the awareness of strategies, techniques and skills that teachers need in order to plan and conduct appropriate activities and manage the classroom efficiently. All course units address this theory-to-practice approach so that teachers' choices can be well-grounded and well-informed, and so that they know how certain theoretical concepts (e.g. *accommodation* or *differentiation*) are operationalised, and why particular teacher actions and classroom practices are reasonable, well-founded and legitimate. DysTEFL materials are meant to critically enhance teacher knowledge on the nature of dyslexia, and inclusive practices that teachers can employ to successfully identify and cater for the individual needs of foreign language learners with dyslexia across diverse learning environments and contexts.

The effectiveness of the DysTEFL course and materials has been extensively verified in the international context of both pre- and in-service foreign language teacher training with regards to different modes of delivery – both face-to-face and online. The feedback it has received has been overwhelmingly positive, course participants have stressed that the course indeed fills the gap in their training, reduces their concerns and boosts their self-efficacy – confidence, competence and capability to create appropriately differentiated and supportive learning environments for foreign language learners with dyslexia. For some teachers participation in this course has been an awareness-raising and eye-opening experience which has significantly reframed their attitudes to and beliefs about dyslexia and foreign language study, which is well reflected in the following comment: 'I can honestly say that it has been a life-changing experience. Thanks for the inspiration'.

References

Barnes, C. (1996). Theories of disability and the origins of the oppression of disabled people in Western society. In L. Barton (Ed.), *Disability and society: Emerging issues and insights* (pp. 43–60). Harlow, UK: Longman.

Beacham, N. & Rouse, M. (2012). Student teachers' attitudes and beliefs about inclusion and inclusive practice. *Journal of Research in Special Educational Needs, 12*(1), 3–11.

Bos, C., Mather, N., Dickson, S., Podhajski, B. & Chard, D. (2001). Perceptions and knowledge of preservice and inservice educators about early reading instruction. *Annals of Dyslexia, 51*, 97–120.

Brady, S., Gillis, M., Smith, T., Lavalette, M., Liss-Bronstein, L., Lowe, E., North, W., Russo E. & Wilder, T.D. (2009). First grade teachers' knowledge of phonological awareness and code concepts: Examining gains from an intensive form of professional development and corresponding teacher attitudes. *Reading and Writing: An Interdisciplinary Journal, 4*, 425–455.

European Agency for Development in Special Needs Education (2012). *Teacher education for inclusion. Profile of inclusive teachers*. Odense, Denmark: European Agency for Development in Special Needs Education. Retrieved March 18, 2015 from www.european-agency.org/sites/default/files/Profile-of-Inclusive-Teachers-EN.pdf

Florian, L. (2012). Preparing teachers to work in inclusive classrooms: Key lessons for the professional development of teacher educators from Scotland's Inclusive Practice Project. *Journal of Teacher Education, 63*(4), 275–285. doi: 10.1177/0022487112447112

Frederickson, N. & Cline, T. (2002). *Special educational needs, inclusion and diversity: A textbook*. Buckingham: Open University Press.

Freeman, D. & Johnson, K.E. (1998). Reconceptualizing the knowledge base of language teacher education. *TESOL Quarterly, 32*(3), 397–417.

Goldfus, C. (2012). Knowledge foundations for beginning reading teachers in EFL. *Annals of Dyslexia, 62*, 204–221.

Guo, Y., Piasta, S.B., Justice, L.M. & Kaderavek, J. (2010). Relations among preschool teachers' self-efficacy, classroom quality and children's language and literacy gains. *Teaching and Teacher Education, 26*, 1094–1103.

Johnson, K.E. (2006). The sociocultural turn and its challenges for second language teacher education. *TESOL Quarterly, 40*(1), 235–257.

Joshi, R.M., Binks, E., Graham, L., Dean, E., Smith, D. & Boulware-Gooden, R. (2009a). Do textbooks used in university reading education courses conform to the instructional recommendations of the National Reading Panel? *Journal of Learning Disabilities, 42*, 458–463.

Joshi, R.M., Binks, E., Hougen, M., Dahlgren, M., Dean, E. & Smith, D. (2009b). Why elementary teachers might be inadequately prepared to teach reading. *Journal of Learning Disabilities, 42*, 392–402.

Kormos, J. & Smith, A.M. (2012). *Teaching languages to learners with specific learning difficulties*. Clevedon: Multilingual Matters.

Mahmoodzadeh, M. (2012). Towards an understanding of ecological challenges of second language teaching: A critical review. *Journal of Language Teaching and Research, 3*(6), 1157–1164.

McCutchen, D. & Berninger, V.W. (1999). Those who know, teach well: Helping teachers master literacy-related subject-matter knowledge. *Learning Disabilities Research & Practice, 14*, 215–226.

McCutchen, D., Abbott, R.D., Green, L.B., Beretvas, S.N., Cox, S., Potter, N.S., Quiroga, T. & Gray, A.L. (2002a). Beginning literacy: Links among teacher knowledge, teacher practice, and student learning. *Journal of Learning Disabilities, 35*, 69–86.

McCutchen, D., Dawn R.H., Cox, S., Sidman, S., Covill, A.E. & Cunningham, A. (2002b). Reading teachers' knowledge of children's literature and English phonology. *Annals of Dyslexia, 52*, 207–228.

McCutchen, D., Green, L., Abbott, R.D. & Sanders, E.A. (2009). Further evidence for teacher knowledge: Supporting struggling readers in grades three through five. *Reading and Writing: An Interdisciplinary Journal, 22*, 401–423.

Moats, L.C. (1994). The missing foundation in teacher education: Knowledge of the structure of spoken and written language. *Annals of Dyslexia, 44*, 81–101.

Moats, L.C. (2009). Knowledge foundations for teaching reading and spelling. *Reading and Writing: An Interdisciplinary Journal, 22*, 379–399.

Moats, L.C. & Foorman, B.R. (2003). Measuring teachers' content knowledge of language and reading. *Annals of Dyslexia, 53*, 23–45.

Nijakowska, J. (2010). *Dyslexia in the foreign language classroom*. Bristol: Multilingual Matters.

Nijakowska, J. (2014). Dyslexia in the European EFL teacher training context. In M. Pawlak & L. Aronin (Eds), *Essential topics in applied linguistics and multilingualism* (pp. 129–154). Heidelberg: Springer.

Nijakowska, J., Kormos, J., Hanusova, S., Jaroszewicz, B, Kálmos, B, Imrene Sarkadi, A., Smith, A.M., Szymańska-Czaplak, E. & Vojtkova, N. (2013). *DysTEFL – Dyslexia for teachers of English as a foreign language*. Trainer's Booklet, Trainee's Booklet, CD-Rom. Cham, Germany: Druck+Verlag Ernst Vögel GmbH.

Podhajski, B., Mather, N., Nathan, J. & Sammons, J. (2009). Professional development in scientifically based reading instruction: Teacher knowledge and reading outcomes. *Journal of Learning Disabilities, 42*, 403–417.

Sharma, U., Forlin, C. & Loreman, T. (2008). Impact of training on pre-service teachers' attitudes and concerns about inclusive education and sentiments about persons with disabilities. *Disability & Society, 23*(7), 773–785.

Sharma, U. & Sokal, L. (2013). The impact of a teacher education course on pre-service teachers' beliefs about inclusion: An international comparison. *Journal of Research in Special Educational Needs*. Article first published online: 23 October 2013.

Schneider, E. & Crombie, M. (2003). *Dyslexia and foreign language learning*. London: David Fulton.

Schneider, E. & Evers, T. (2009). Linguistic intervention techniques for at-risk English language learners. *Foreign Language Annals, 42*, 55–76.

Schneider, E. & Ganschow, L. (2000). Dynamic assessment and instructional strategies for learners who struggle to learn a foreign language. *Dyslexia, 6*, 72–82.

Tanner, R. & Green, C. (1998). *Tasks for teacher education: A reflective approach*. Harlow, UK: Addison Wesley Longman Publishing.

Tudor, I. (2003). Learning to live with complexity: Towards an ecological perspective on language teaching. *System, 31*, 1–12.

Vygotsky, L.S. (1978). *Mind in society: The development of higher psychological processes*. Cambridge, MA: Harvard University Press.

Wadlington, E. & Wadlington, P. (2005). What educators really believe about dyslexia. *Reading Improvement, 42*(1), 16–33.

Wallace, M.J. (1991). *Training foreign language teachers: A reflective approach*. Cambridge: Cambridge University Press.

Washburn, E.K., Joshi, R.M. & Binks-Cantrell, E.S. (2011a). Teacher knowledge of basic language concepts and dyslexia. *Dyslexia, 17*, 165–183.

Washburn, E.K., Joshi, R.M. & Binks-Cantrell, E.S. (2011b). Are preservice teachers prepared to teach struggling readers? *Annals of Dyslexia, 61*, 21–43.

Waters, A. (2005). Expertise in teacher education: Helping teachers to learn. In K. Johnson (Ed.), *Expertise in second language learning and teaching* (pp. 210–299). Basingstoke: Palgrave Macmillan.

10

ENGLISH AS AN ADDITIONAL LANGUAGE (EAL), SPECIAL EDUCATIONAL NEEDS AND DYSLEXIA

The role of the 21st century SENCo

Abigail Gray

This chapter will:

1. Discuss the variety of new demands placed on the SENCo (Special Educational Needs Co-ordinator) in light of the 2014 UK reforms
2. Outline the need for additional specialist training for SENCos in order to successfully identify children with EAL (English as an Additional Language) and dyslexia
3. Make a case for inclusive and holistic assessment of pupils' language and literacy needs to prevent failure rather than respond to it

> Whether you can observe a thing or not depends on the theory that you use. It is the theory that decides what can be observed.
>
> (Albert Einstein)

The job description for a 21st century SENCo includes a rare combination of responsibilities: strategic, operational, educational, managerial – and of course sometimes they teach too. Few other members of a school's academic staff are expected to manifest quite such a broad range of skills – even amongst the senior team. Few other team leaders need to match a forensic command of data with an in-depth understanding of the financial underpinning of their curriculum offer and the cost of human resources. Few will find themselves faced with the task of configuring the work of their team both educationally and operationally and in direct response to pupil demand, parental input, law and legal guidance. Few school leaders become directly involved with the legal process itself, in the form of the The First-tier Tribunal (Special Educational Needs and Disability). Few will be expected to have such an informed view about effectively meeting an ever-broadening range of specific additional needs and be tasked with communicating that strategy to their colleagues and the broader community.

If you manage inclusion, it is likely that you are, or were, a SENCo. If you are not a SENCo, then I imagine that you work closely with your school SENCo, providing the strategic back-up needed to bring policy to life and to implement that strategy. Whatever your place in the management structure, my experience is that a SENCo/IM (Inclusion

Manager) is often the glue that binds SEND (Special Educational Needs and Disability) policy and practice together; tasked with identifying and enabling the most vulnerable learners in the school community; it's a tough job and getting tougher.

The impact of reform

While the new Bill (The Children and Families Act, 2014) and Code of Practice for SEND (DfE, DoH, 2015) maintain the existing legal definitions of Special Educational Needs, Learning Difficulty and Special Provision a great deal has changed for schools and SENCos. The SEND figures for 2015 (SFR, 2015) show the total number of children identified to be falling significantly; SEND, in all categories, is down 2.5%, from 17.9% to 15.4%. That's over 200,000 children who apparently no longer require SEN support. Either children have fewer needs this year or the recent SEND reforms are having a significant impact on identification.

While numbers of pupils with the highest levels of support continue to grow, a significant number of children clearly did not transition from School Action and School Action Plus to the new SEN support category. This is likely due to the fact that they lacked a 'diagnosis'. Interestingly, the recent reforms make it necessary for schools to identify the category of need in order to identify a child as 'SEN Support', requiring therefore a specific diagnostic process. It follows that if an appropriate diagnostic opportunity is not made available, is delayed, is incomplete or inappropriate the child concerned may not be identified as requiring SEN support. It's a potential chicken and egg situation that the school SENCo somehow has to resolve.

The SENCo and EAL

It is rare that I come across a SENCo who does not also have involvement in the EAL provision within a school. Having said that, in terms of SEND, it is writ large in both the 1996 Act and the new Bill that in its own right EAL does not constitute and cannot be considered a special educational need. The legal distinction between SEND and EAL is entirely necessary – avoiding the conflation of bilingualism or lack of fluency in English with the four categories of need identified in the Code of Practice. However, with a growing population of EAL pupils in the English school system, EAL and SEND pupils are likely to present in increasing numbers. In the light of the recent SEND reforms and the most recent statistics this raises a number of difficult questions about identification and diagnosis of pupils for whom language is a core issue.

Pupils with English as an additional language are growing in number in English schools. According to the figures published in the recent report by the Education Endowment Foundation (Strand, 2015) the numbers have 'doubled from 7.6% in 1997 to 16.2% in 2013'. The regional variations referred to in this report are substantial, and evident if you work in London schools, as I do. While 76% of schools have less than 5% of pupils with EAL, 8.4% or 1,681 schools have student cohorts the majority of whom have EAL, 919 of those schools are in London. It seems important to note at this point that EAL is not a measurement of language fluency but an overarching category identifying pupils as follows:

> A first language other than English should be recorded where a child was exposed to the language during early development and continues to be exposed to this language in the home or in the community. If a child was exposed to more than one language

(which may include English) during early development the language other than English should be recorded, irrespective of the child's proficiency in English.

(DCFS, 2006)

In terms of progress and attainment, Professor Strand's data shows that while EAL students begin their primary schooling with lower achievement than their First Language English (FLE) schoolmates, by age 16 the gap is very small indeed with '58.3% of EAL students achieving 5 or more A★ to C grades compared to 60.9% of FLE students'. The most significant indicator for underperformance, in respect of EAL pupils, is the group with special educational needs and disabilities whose underachievement broadly mirrored that of their FLE peers. However, on examination of the Statistical First Release from January 2015 (SFR, 2015) it appears that currently SEND is less prevalent in the EAL school population; while 16.8% of FLE pupils have an identified SEND, only 15% of their EAL classmates are similarly classified. Raising the question, why is it that EAL pupils with SEND are less likely to be identified and more specifically, do SENCos have the necessary resources available to distinguish a delay in acquiring language skills from a disorder or learning difficulty affecting literacy and language?

The diagnostic SENCo

Currently a school SENCo is not expected be a specialist practitioner in teaching students with specific learning difficulties, they are not required to study for a Certificate- or Diploma-level qualification in teaching or assessing students with specific learning difficulties. Indeed, looking closely at the construction and presentation of the much talked about 'National Award for SENCos', I could only identify one strand, from one part of four elements of study, that referred to the development of knowledge about the characteristics and impact of learning difficulties. It was under the heading 'A bit of theory first'. Which illustrates the lack of emphasis placed by our current administration on positioning specialist knowledge, research and theory about specific learning difficulties directly into schools – exacerbating the widening gap between the educational specialists and the classroom practitioners.

On page 97 of the 2014 Code of Practice the key responsibilities of the SENCos are listed. Surprisingly, it's a list taking up less than one page of A4. Brief it may be, but it is also broad. Initially, the list refers to responsibilities of co-ordination and management: oversight of the SEND policy, co-ordination and implementation of provision made in response to a 'graduated approach'. It refers specifically to the role of the SENCo in budgetary matters, the need for the SENCo to record effectively and to act as a liaison and to report to the school, parents and governors. The Code also indicates that SENCos are expected to provide 'professional guidance to colleagues'; however, there is no detail here on the extent, the nature or the parameters of that guidance.

A SENCo has to be a qualified teacher and is afforded three years to complete the National Qualification for SENCos. The National Qualification rightly underlines the important strategic role of the SENCo and the need for the SENCo to access decision-making structures. Unfortunately, it fails to include the specialist knowledge that might inform those strategic judgements and better bridge the gap between the agencies, currently external to most schools, and the practitioners within them.

While SEND pupils remain a minority in our schools it appears that the specialist knowledge required to identify, describe and support their needs is similarly marginalised.

For some time the Maintained sector has followed a 'consultative model' in terms of advice from educational psychologists and speech and language therapists. While the local educational psychologist or SENCo advisor may have the necessary experience to explain the intricacies and relevance of a full-scale IQ test – a WISC IV (Wechsler Intelligence Scale for Children), WIAT-II (Wechsler Individual Achievement Test – II) or WOND (Wechsler Objective Numerical Dimensions) – and to advise in this capacity, I have found that there is a very real knowledge gap about the nature and features of specific learning difficulties, including dyslexia, at a senior level. Members of senior teams are often unfamiliar with the bases of cognitive ability testing, including what is measured and its potential significance.

A core part of the SENCo's role is to manage a process of identifying SEND. A screening and identification system should ensure that the 'Assess' part of 'Assess, Plan, Do, Review' is timely, effective and personalised. For the dyslexic child, with EAL, this process is far from administrative. The discrepancies between attainment and underlying ability are potentially complicated by a lack of knowledge and experience in the language of assessment and instruction. To recognise, to unpick and to describe the barriers to attainment accurately requires an analytical, evidence-based approach; one which acknowledges the role of language, memory and processing in building a profile of ability. To ensure equality of educational opportunity to pupils facing challenges, in regards to a variety of additional needs, including EAL, specialist knowledge has never been more relevant or more necessary. Perhaps you need some specialist knowledge to recognise that.

As assessment and identification models begin to vary (post National Curriculum levels), and the demands on schools for accuracy and clarity in identifying additional needs increase, it seems more important than ever to be clear about how identification works. Schools need to be consistent and confident in their use of terms like 'baseline'. School leaders need to ensure that academic staff have a common appreciation of words like 'skill', 'attainment' and 'ability'; especially in regards to those who are identified as EAL, SEND or under-achieving. Confusion or a knowledge gap in this respect, at any level of seniority, can seriously influence decisions that impact a pupil's experience and opportunities. Baseline assessments obviously feed directly into mechanisms like setting and streaming. A school with a shared understanding of pupil baselines and the methodology and the principles which underpin them is a school with a great foundation for effective identification and accurate diagnosis of additional needs.

The Code of Practice 6:16 indicates that all schools should assess the skills of pupils on entry. However in 6:17 it moves straight on to looking at attainment and attainment gaps. My concern is that skills, abilities and attainments are terms often conflated by the professionals charged with describing a child's performance. Skill, ability and attainment are interrelated but certainly not the same. A child may lack a skill but have the ability to develop that skill, and in gaining the skill prove able to raise their level of attainment based on their improved access to the curriculum offer. Language is such a skill. The problem for some of our EAL pupils is that the English language is the medium of assessments of cognitive ability.

The current move away from descriptive levels to a system of assessment judgements based on subject-related, age-appropriate expectations makes the need for clarity regarding these baselining principles even more important. Teachers judge whether a child is performing below, on or above the expectations set out by the curriculum. Those judgements focus on whether the pupil's progress is adequate 'given their age and starting point'. It's all relative, 'Whether you can observe a thing or not depends on the theory that you use'. If a child has an undiagnosed learning difficulty and or EAL on entry to this system it would follow that their starting point may be lower and subsequent expectations skewed. This in turn may result in a misleading assessment of their potential and the subsequent expectations placed upon them.

While there appears to be no lack of commitment to the principles of a holistic identification process, the principles are not currently underpinned by an agreed theoretical structure or sufficient resources. While local authorities and some schools produce a range of assessment pro-formas and support materials for the assessment of children new to English, I have yet to see an integrated approach to assessment of and provision for students with EAL and SEND, whether it be dyslexia or any other specific or global difficulty.

It is surprising how often existing pupil baseline data, in terms of cognition and language, is available in school databases but not brought together for consideration. The use of a broader evidence base would provide a much more comprehensive overview on which to base a discussion about and a plan for the development of pupils' skills and attainment – placing it in the light of their underlying abilities.

More often than not specialist EAL provision in school is linked to SEND by management structure, rooming and policy but not necessarily by shared specialist knowledge. Just as additional needs registers often separate pupils by category onto separate spreadsheets – SEND on one page, EAL on another – so assessment and provision are often similarly positioned in parallel, and limited by staff designation or specialism.

My preference, in thinking about representing and recording pupil need, is more of a matrix and less of a spreadsheet. Spreadsheets compartmentalise children and their 'additional needs' into separate columns and rows. My view, illustrated in Figure 10.1, is that it is more helpful to plot how needs come together in a child. As in the case of child A, a pupil with EAL may well be a child with any number of other needs, including gifted and talented status. Looking at the range, frequency and co-morbidity of a school population would appear to me to be the place to start in formulating the best possible plan for support and the use of resources. A plan that not only identifies areas of additional need but that also cross references them and looks at priorities – building attainment in reference to ability and the development of new skills.

To be truly useful, a comprehensive and reliable cognitive baseline requires this context. To have integrity, the process of judging whether a child is doing well or should be doing

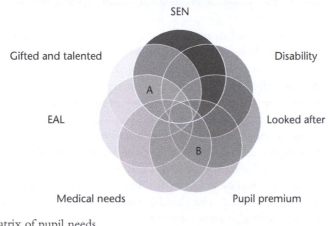

FIGURE 10.1 Matrix of pupil needs

better, should be based on a judgement that includes not only their academic attainment, individual skills and underlying ability but personal and educational history within the broader range of experience, including their status in respect of EAL.

Working with parents

The replacement of the Individual Education Plan with a Pupil Passport affords an opportunity for working with parents, as it provides SENCos with a framework for a planning process that directly involves parents and pupils, looking at the nature and effectiveness of the support offer and inviting a discussion around it. However, the document in itself is simply a prompt for the conversation to take place and a record of it. What is required to make the process effective is training for SENCos in how to run multi-agency meetings involving the parent and child. The new Code of Practice enshrines the need for greater engagement from parents and pupils with SEND. For those with SEND and EAL, additional resources are required to ensure that the barrier of language can be overcome with respect to parents as well as children. Too many schools are having to invent their own systems and find volunteers to reach out to the families of their pupils. A change on the scale outlined in Professor Strand's report (2015) surely requires a co-ordinated strategy to meet this need. In addition, schools are not obliged to create Pupil Passports for students at every stage of a graduated approach.

Achievement for All (http://afaeducation.org), 'School Improvement Programme of the Year 2014 and 2015', has at its centre, the notion of parental and child engagement and provides a model to schools for successful conversations with parents. The Achievement Coaches (of which I am one) work with school leaders, very often SENCos, to develop both infrastructure and their skills and resolve in building relationships with the most vulnerable learners by reaching out to their families. The skills that teachers learn in having 'structured conversations' ensure that time and energy is put into listening and planning with parents and children in order that they are able to articulate and define their aspirations, to ensure access to appropriate support and for the children to achieve.

Working to support teachers

The prevailing ideology of inclusion assures all parents and pupils that all teachers are teachers of pupils with SEND. The Code of Practice specifically speaks to the responsibility of classroom teachers for the progress of pupils so identified. However, this emphasis strikes me as somewhat disingenuous in that its repetition implies competency rather than obligation. The teacher in question should be competent, experienced, capable and prepared to meet the needs of their SEND pupils, but while specialist knowledge is restricted, even for the SENCo, how is this to work in practice? There is nothing in the new law or Code of Practice obliging teachers to do anything new to become more competent in this respect.

It is logical that an understanding of what legally constitutes SEND and the diagnostic process involved in identifying specific difficulties has to be relevant to everyone delivering the curriculum or managing its delivery. If all teachers are teachers of children with SEND then they need to know the basics. Can you be a successful teacher of pupils with SEND if in fact you don't know what SEND is, how it differs from a learning difficulty or how a difficulty such as dyslexia is defined? The training courses that I run have proved to me that it is yet to be common knowledge amongst teachers or teaching assistants that a diagnosis of dyslexia is made when an educational psychologist or specialist teacher recognises a characteristic pattern in a set of scores testing a child's memory and processing. Teachers and teaching assistants are still unfamiliar with the terminology describing the characteristically low scores associated with dyslexia: phonological processing, working memory and processing time. It is common in my experience, to hear practising teachers, and even SENCos describe a child as 'frustrating' because they are so good in one area and so weak in another. If all teachers were afforded the training required to fulfil the principles outlined above we would be going some way to enabling all teachers to be more effective in an inclusive classroom.

In this respect I am struck constantly by the disconnection between specialists and academics, who largely work outside of the school setting, and practitioners in school. SENCos are all too often tasked with the role of bridging this gap in its entirety. To be effective teachers of pupils with additional needs, practitioners require access to additional training. To stand any chance of keeping up with current developments and to gain traction, training about special educational needs has to fit teacher's schedules and the profiles of their current classes. The training needs to be specific, frequent, bite sized and high impact. Securing appropriate training has therefore to be linked to the nature, range and frequency of needs currently identified. Further, if the training is to inform and enhance practice, rather than be a box to tick, it has to be lead from the front by the senior team and school leaders in full support of their SENCo.

The impact of specialist knowledge

Having moved from mainstream to special education and back again I find I am constantly making comparisons, attempting to identify the common ground and the differences. As a SEND consultant in the mainstream, I am looking to translate the most advantageous and accessible aspects of special education into non-specialist settings, identifying practice that can be realistically 'scaled up'. During my time as Head of The Moat School, a small secondary school for dyslexic children, we produced outcomes that regularly confounded the predictions generated by our MidYIS (Middle Years Information System) baseline. The pupils consistently exceeded the predictions. The system providers were so intrigued by what our pupils produced year after year that they came to visit the school and as a result we had the honour of being the first school to speak at their National Conference in June 2011, on 'The use of CEM data for teachers of pupils with Specific Learning Difficulties'.

In its simplest terms what we did was to ensure that all teachers were sufficiently equipped to recognise the distinct difference between literacy and language processing, between skill and ability, and in doing so locate opportunity and build attainment. In collecting, collating and unpicking the comprehensive baseline and diagnostic data we were able to recognise both patterns and idiosyncrasy, and to allow a voice for the child and the parent in the process of generating a realistic set of motivating learning objectives.

In addition to training all teaching staff in the theory of specific difficulties, specifically but not exclusively dyslexia, the other main difference between my school and the Maintained model was our small, onsite team of therapists. The therapeutic staff were few in number and mainly part-time but long-standing and embedded members of the school staff, working inside the school community with students and with staff. They participated at every level: with parents, in a variety of teaching settings, in extracurricular life, in assemblies, in management and in ongoing training. Much of this training was in coaching teachers to recognise the assumptions they were making with regard to the fundamentals of language. They built awareness of the impact of phonological confusion, word finding difficulties and semantic confusion, and ensured teachers taught with a view to building vocabulary that could be used across the curriculum as well as in particular subject areas. They ensured we stayed awake to developments outside our walls and around the world. We were committed to being a community of teachers who were also a community of learners.

Our approach was to acknowledge that dyslexia impacts the learning process on every level while also being highly idiosyncratic. We acknowledged that dyslexic students can all too often be so overwhelmed by the classroom experience that they simply clam up while at school, and become disaffected and marginalised. We recognised that pupils could not learn if they did not understand what was expected of them and were in an environment where they felt misunderstood. We identified and worked to develop pupils' strengths and modified the curriculum proactively to include a range of literacy and non-literacy based subjects. We were always looking for opportunities to build confidence and to encourage risk taking in learning. Our success was a triangulation of specialist knowledge, ethos and resources. It was as much about attitude as it was about specialism, balancing the identification of areas of deficit with enhancing opportunities to show gifts and talents.

Learning about thinking

Currently there is some very interesting work being done in the US by the Drs Eide and Eide. They have a unique approach to looking at the cognitive function of dyslexic children. Their book (Eide and Eide, 2011) not only gives voice to the frustration that exists collectively for dyslexics in the conventional school setting but their work moves beyond that, seeking redress. Our current systems of identification focus on the deficits dyslexics often exhibit in tests of memory; most often in processing speed, phonological processing and working memory. The Eides identify a complementary model describing related strengths. After reading the book I found myself becoming increasingly excited and then frustrated in equal measure, as I realised that unless they were able to devise some kind of test to quantify and profile these strengths their ideas may not have the impact they deserve. Thankfully it would appear that this process is now underway. Their work offers a future generation of struggling learners a new opportunity to show areas of strength previously unrecognised, balancing the measurement of deficits and possible learning gaps with an accurate description of specific areas of non-verbal and verbal potential, ability and talent – talent that is often realised in adult life, but that emerges despite school rather than because of it.

If the aim is to ensure that we get the educational offer right for all learners, then we have to face the fact that we need to know more about learning and the role of language in learning. When I deliver training courses for teachers and LSAs (Learning Support Assistants) working with students with dyslexia I always do an activity in which the course members build a skills wall. Each brick names a skill or quality that may be important in delivering support to students. They are asked to build a wall prioritising those skills and qualities – the most important 'foundation' skills at the bottom the least important at the top. The 'specialist knowledge' brick is always one of the last bricks to be added. Having some specialist knowledge and understanding of a specific learning difficulty is widely seen as less important than a sense of humour.

We are not all nutritionists yet we know the constituent elements of a balanced diet. If you ask a member of the general public they will be able to tell you something about protein, carbohydrate and vitamins. Partly because it is the language of advertising and used to sell us things, partly because it is part of the school curriculum. Interestingly, we don't teach children about intelligence in the same way. We don't teach teachers about it either. There is a TV programme for every culinary process, analysing every possible aspect of our eating habits, yet I am struggling to think of one that examines how we think and process ideas and how we acquire the necessary language to do so. Why are we so allergic to thinking about thinking? Teachers are expected to meet the SEND of all learners but apparently not expected to understand how IQ was and is constructed or the role played by language. That seems like either a very big oversight, or a very effective agenda. I'm not suggesting that teachers need to become educational psychologists or speech and language therapists, but I am suggesting that all teachers should be able to read and understand a report written by one and have the opportunity to engage with specialists directly. After all, parents are expected to do this and to form opinions and make decisions about the education of their children based on this advice. This means that schools need to have very much greater access to specialist training or what is currently considered specialist training.

Conclusion

The new Code of Practice and the Children and Families Act identify the size of the SENCo's task but do not provide the tools to do the job. To meet the full range of additional needs, schools need access to EAL teachers, educational psychologists, speech and language therapists, occupational therapists and psychotherapists onsite. Without a more pre-emptive approach we are unlikely to reach all pupils; what is needed is a system that assumes the existence of additional needs rather than one which attempts to accommodate them by making exceptions. Instead of pushing back the tide by creating ever more selective structures to ration support and to restrict identification, isn't it time to invest in schools and to develop a more proactive approach? An approach that is more self-aware and more coherent, acknowledging the constructs of intelligence and cognition, an approach that identifies and explores the role of language in learning and that creates space for teachers to become both subject and learning specialists. It's time to join up the theory and the practice and to give SENCos the necessary training and support to manage the huge expectations placed upon them.

References

DCFS (2006). *Pupil Language Data: Guidance for Local Authorities on Schools' Collection and Recording of Data*. London: Department for Children, Schools and Families.

DfE, DoH (2015). *SEND Code of Practice 0–25 Years*. London: Department for Education, Department of Health.

Eide, B.L. and Eide, F.F. (2011). *The Dyslexic Advantage*. London: Hay House.

SFR (2015, 25 January). Statistical First Release, *Special Educational Needs in England*, London: Department for Education.

Strand, S. (2015). *English as an Additional Language (EAL) and Educational Achievement in England: An Analysis of the National Pupil Database*. Oxford: University of Oxford; London: Department of Education.

11

LESSONS FROM THE DYSLEXIA AND MULTILINGUALISM PROJECT

Mim Hutchings and Tilly Mortimore

This chapter will:

1. Explore the challenges posed and lessons learnt from a research project comprising a literacy intervention for vulnerable learners with English as an Additional Language (EAL)
2. Focus upon the issues and dilemmas in conceptualisation, design and implementation that challenged us throughout the project journey
3. Consider our solutions and the implications for research methodology and educational practice

Introduction

This chapter explores the challenges posed and lessons learnt from a research project comprising a literacy intervention for vulnerable learners with English as an Additional Language (EAL) – the Dyslexia and Multilingualism Project (Mortimore *et al.*, 2012). We focus upon the issues and dilemmas in conceptualisation, design and implementation that challenged us throughout the project journey, and consider our solutions and the implications for research methodology and educational practice. We fully endorse the role of research in evidence-based practice to inform choices about planning and implementation of interventions. Presenting our tentative steps towards developing a mixed methodology research practice including the voices of those involved in the project – children, teaching assistants and parents – illustrates what the project has taught us about research and future practice.

This project aimed to explore the impact of intervention upon learners' skills, incentives and interactions. Undertaken with the British Dyslexia Association (BDA) and funded by the UK Big Lottery, it investigated the possibility of identifying risk of Specific Learning Difficulties (SpLD)/dyslexia in children with EAL; developed, selected and evaluated strategies and support materials to support their literacy in English; and trained the professionals involved with the project in SpLD/dyslexia and support for bilingual learners. It was ground breaking in several ways:

- at the time (2011), few larger-scale UK studies had specifically explored interventions for children with EAL who were also potentially at risk for SpLD/dyslexia;
- also at the time, the two professional worlds of SpLD/dyslexia and bilingual learner support operated within separate silos with little interchange of expertise;
- this mixed methodology design, moving beyond the usual positivist paradigm to tap the lived experience of those involved and frame a socio-cultural perspective, was rare in SpLD/dyslexia research.

Hence the literature and previous research methodologies and findings across both worlds were examined carefully. It emerged that much research and practice tended to run in parallel with little communication between the two silos. We seemed to be encountering multiple, often dissonant, discourses and needed to find a way of working that could diminish the gaps. Solutions were sought for the pressing issues and dilemmas that emerged across the design, development and implementation of the project. This chapter explores the implications of the process for future research and practice, both for the people involved and for the development of one fundamental principle of inclusive practices – what we learn from each other when we respond to each other's views of the world.

Designing the project: Issues, dilemmas and solutions

Despite considerable variation in linguistic communities, English schools offer few bilingual programmes and English is the language of the curriculum, making it essential for children speedily to acquire fluent reading and writing in this additional majority language. Although most bilingual children succeed academically, underachievement in black and minority ethnic children had been highlighted (e.g. Ofsted, 2003). Issues emerge around creating classroom contexts that support bilingualism of linguistically diverse children. In addition the political dimension of how learners are perceived and included may fall at different points along a continuum between an additive context celebrating cultural diversity and a subtractive context privileging the monolingual culture.

Research discourses within the field of SpLD/dyslexia frequently focus on measurement, the use of valid and reliable scales rather than the voices of participants and, as a result, do not take account of children as active social agents or their right to express their views.

For this reason, and to provide a rich contextual picture, the project developed a mixed methodology approach. Statistical comparisons of literacy scores were employed to quantify the impact of the intervention programmes on the children. In addition focus groups and interviews explored the experiences of teaching assistants (TAs), children and parents.

As decisions over the design of the project progressed, a number of complex issues challenged our thinking. Firstly, school contexts in England are frequently multilingual with a rich diversity of linguistic and cultural heritages, yet the official discourse and language of the classroom is English. Secondly, focusing exclusively on *quantifying* the effects or progress would mean ignoring many contextual, qualitative aspects that influence a bilingual child's progress in literacy. These may be significant in distinguishing between literacy difficulties related to transferring to a new language, or indeed to a child's life story, and those factors that may be due to cognitive/learning differences. The identification of special educational needs in children acquiring EAL is contentious, particularly where quantitative assessment measures may be privileged over contextual and qualitative knowledge. Identifying SpLD/

dyslexia, for example, carries a high risk of misattribution of a child's difficulties to acquisition of a new language or misrecognition of a child's potential, resulting in inappropriate labelling as having Special Educational Needs (SEN) (Hall *et al.*, 2001). This in turn may result in inappropriate provision and promote endemic racism within the education system (Landon, 2000).

Hence, including qualitative aspects in the project generated opportunities for exploring some of these issues through personal stories and local experiences of the project and involved a more dialogic process that integrated the voices of participants.

A third issue was the separate strands of expertise amongst professionals. These 'silos', identified as problematic across medical, social and educational fields (Parton, 2011), emerged strongly between those professionals working with children with SEN, particularly SpLD/ dyslexia, and those working with ethnic minorities and bilingual children. The project literature review (Mortimore *et al.*, 2012) indicated that much research and practice appeared to run in parallel with little overlap between the different groups. Focus groups at the start of the project indicated that Special Educational Needs Coordinators (SENCos) and TAs were predominately experienced in areas either of SEN or of bilingualism. This was the case even in schools with significant levels of minority ethnic pupils.

These contrasting perspectives are linked to differing models and practices in research and professional approaches to learners. The complexity and risk of endemic racism in the identification of SpLD/dyslexia is associated with differing perspectives on disability, such as medical or social models. The 'medical model' of disability is rooted in an individual's biology and failure to adjust to society. The contrasting 'social model' shifts the 'problem' from the person with the impairment, locating it in social and individual attitudes and behaviours that produce physical and conceptual barriers (Barton, 1996). The inclusion agenda has been driven by the adoption of this social model framework for thinking (Booth and Ainscow, 2011). The medical model focuses predominantly on the cognitive and processing skills of a minority ethnic child, ignoring, hidden variables such as the learner's story, linguistic and cultural heritage or covert attitudes to bilingualism within the school context. The monolingual English school is frequently not an 'additive' environment, which celebrates the child's linguistic repertoire and welcomes diverse communities, but rather a 'subtractive' environment with evidence of lower levels of parental involvement, cognitive development and achievement (Cummins, 2000; Smythe and Everatt, 2004).

Traditionally, SpLD/dyslexia specialists have adopted the medical model in promoting diagnostic assessment, labelling learners and focusing support upon multi-sensory programmes for individuals delivered by experts (Turner, 1997; Ott, 2007), although the Dyslexia-Friendly Schools initiative has promoted the dismantling of barriers (McKay, 2006). The quantitative SpLD/dyslexia research discourse had predominantly followed the positivist tradition of the randomised control trial (Singleton, 2009) criticised as objectifying participants, omitting consideration of context or invisible variables and excluding the voices and cultural heritage of participants (Haslum, 2007; Wheldall and Carter, 2008). This research perspective potentially clashed with the approach of those working with ethnic minorities who have focused strongly upon the place of the learner within embedded social and cultural practices (Kelly, 2010) requiring research methodology beyond the quantitative to explore these hidden variables.

These were some of the challenges in perspective, research design and practice that influenced the project design. One solution was to explore how these differing frames of thinking could be connected and how exploring the space between these discourses might help us understand the research process. The first step was to focus on how a mixed methodology design might increase the potential for the project to inform approaches to research and to assessment and interventions in multilingual contexts. To frame our thinking we focused on how a third space (Guitterrez *et al.*, 1999; Kelly, 2010) might help us draw on multiple discourses to make sense of two differing forms of research data and the complex worlds of multilingual schools. This third space is the locus for evaluating how Space 1 (e.g. home literacy practices) and Space 2 (dominant school literacy practices) interact or compete with each other. Space 1 reflects home/family histories and religious or community links, perceptions of purpose, value and experiences of literacy, and how they influence literacy acquisition. Space 2 reflects school and all the links and funds of knowledge (Kelly, 2010) influencing perceptions and teaching of literacy. The research questioned how Spaces 1 and 2, for example, are influencing each other.

Across the project, numbers of participants, cross-cultural contexts, linguistic diversity and distance between project managers and schools demanded that we draw on competing discourses. Hence the concept of the third space worked at different levels within it – firstly to explore how different research discourses relate to each other and, secondly, the impact on those involved in the intervention.

Our literature review influenced our thinking around some less measurable dimensions of learning. Traditionally, cognition, emotion and the environment tend to be separated. Learning is a personal activity which seldom occurs in isolation and is influenced by life experiences, places of learning, the people around us and the approaches to learning encountered. Furthermore, Illeris (2009) argues it is possible to construct a view of the field of learning that includes three dimensions:

> [T]he *content* dimension of knowledge, skills, attitudes, ways of behavior – everything that can be learned – the *incentive* dimension, emotions, and motivations, and the *interaction* dimension, communication, cooperation and community – all of which are embedded in a societally-situated context.
>
> (Illeris, 2009: 46)

Our chosen design promised exploration of wider, less measurable dimensions of learning.

What did we do? Issues, dilemmas and solutions

From 2008 to 2011 percentages of children with EAL in primary schools rose from 14.4% to 16.8%. Over 300 languages were spoken and 1,700 schools contained at least 50% students with EAL. By 2013, one in six children in the system had EAL (NALDIC, 2013). Our literature review uncovered the impact of political policy on stories and life experiences, complex relationships between SpLD/dyslexia and multilingualism, social and cultural differences, and issues around literacy acquisition. The crucial time of transition from primary to secondary school with increasing pressures on literacy, alongside the changed conceptual load of the secondary curriculum, necessitates speedy change from conversational language skills (Basic Interpersonal Communication Skills – BICS) to Cognitive Academic Language Proficiency (CALP, Cummins, 2000). Our growing awareness of these issues informed the choice of intervention and materials.

As discussed, the project aimed to reconcile medical and social models, respond to contextual issues brought by participants, and provide evidence to satisfy the demands of empirical research, while privileging the voices of the children and their carers.

Some 4–10% of children in the UK may be predisposed to the risk of SpLD/dyslexia (Singleton, 2009). The Rose Review (2009) provided this definition of dyslexia as:

> A learning difficulty primarily affecting skills involved in accurate and fluent word reading and spelling. The main characteristics are difficulties in phonological processing, verbal memory and verbal processing speed. Dyslexia occurs across the range of intellectual abilities. It is best thought of as a continuum not a distinct category and there are no clear cut-off points.
>
> (Rose 2009: 11)

However, difficulties with acquiring a second language complicate identification of SpLD/dyslexia in learners with EAL, risking inappropriate provision due to their being overlooked or over-identified. Ziegler and Goswami (2005) suggest transference of both strengths and weaknesses in linguistic codes of phonology/orthography/syntax and semantics between languages. In addition, the complex, inconsistent orthography of English tests areas of dyslexic vulnerability – phonological skills, sequencing, long-/short-term memory, processing speed and listening skills (Wolf, 2008; Crombie and McColl, 2001). Hence, acquisition of literacy in English will be particularly challenging for children at risk of SpLD/dyslexia who will need specific support. The project aimed to evaluate an intervention designed for children with EAL at risk of SpLD/dyslexia.

Five issues posed dilemmas:

- identifying children potentially at risk of dyslexic-type difficulties;
- selecting materials and practices appropriate for them at transition time;
- robust and reliable evaluation of impact;
- training and supporting the TAs who would deliver the intervention;
- general project management.

Identifying the children

The dilemma was clear – mis-identification of risk of dyslexia could undermine claims made that the intervention was successful for dyslexic learners.

Our planned solution was the development of a simple system of dyslexia risk identification available for SENCos and classroom teachers. SENCos were asked to select children with adequate BICS, who had attended UK schools for over two years and whose literacy was failing to develop as quickly as their knowledge of the child might predict. Mortimore *et al.* (2012) describe the screeners selected. From the 465 children proposed, the project team used screener scores to select 215 high-risk children aged 9–11, who between them spoke 43 languages. The 55 schools covered a full range of economic contexts, urban and rural, across England.

How effective was this screening solution? Forty-four participating children underwent full assessment for dyslexia. Statistical analyses showed no significant links between full assessment and the screener outcomes (see Hansen and Mortimore, 2012). Hence, we cannot claim reliably that the literacy difficulties of all the project children were due to dyslexia.

Selecting the materials and ensuring robust and reliable impact evaluation

Dilemmas included:

- few studies had evaluated interventions for dyslexic learners with EAL;
- the need for economic viability in support time and materials throughout and beyond the project;
- the need for appropriate materials;
- the need to develop TAs' confidence and expertise in their delivery.

Our literature review covered literacy programmes for monolingual dyslexic children (e.g. Brooks, 2003; Ott, 2007); dyslexic learners acquiring a modern second language (e.g. Schneider, 2009) and EAL programme materials. A consensus prescribed a structured, reinforced, cumulative and multi-sensory programme including:

- phonological processing skills;
- verbal memory and processing speed;
- oral language development;
- explicit vocabulary teaching;
- explicit strategies to develop comprehension skills;
- morphemes.

Our practical, economically viable programme had to also provide sufficient support for the TAs and, to meet the criteria for a 'silver-standard' controlled trial (Gorard, 2001), ensure equivalent experiences for all the children. Our solution was to adopt two programmes:

- Nessy (Net Educational Systems Ltd, www.nessy.com/uk) – computer-delivered games and activities to develop phonological awareness, word patterns and spelling rules; these are dyslexia-specific materials;
- Rapid Reading (Pearson Heinemann) – learners read and discussed fiction and non-fiction texts with TAs and also used the computer reading programs.

Neither of these programmes had been developed for a specifically multi-cultural audience so appropriate items were selected.

Two children worked with each TA for 30 minutes daily for 15 weeks. Table 11.1 indicates the structure of the intervention.

Learners were divided into three groups: intervention, a paired-reading activity with a trained TA and a third waiting control group with no individual support. The 15-week Phase 2 enabled all the children to undertake the Nessy/Rapid Reading intervention and explored how far changes were sustained over time. The school SENCo tested the children's literacy skills three times. SPSS statistical analysis was undertaken to ensure reliable evaluation of the numerical data. However, the involvement of SENCos in data collection necessitated specific research training.

Training the TAs and SENCos

Mixed-method 'real life' research projects make demands upon staff time and energy – schools must see some advantage in joining and sustaining a project; school life can get in the

TABLE 11.1 The structure of the intervention

	Group 1 n=105 students	Group 2 n=47 students	Group 3 n=63 students
Pre-testing September 2010	✓	✓	✓
Phase 1: 15 weeks: October–March 30 mins per day	Nessy/Rapid Reading intervention (A)	Paired-reading (PR) (B)	Control – no intervention (C)
Interim testing February/March 2011	✓	✓	✓
Phase 2: 15 weeks February/March–July	No intervention	Nessy/Rapid Reading (A)	Nessy/Rapid Reading (A)
Final testing July 2011	✓	✓	✓

way. Our Big Lottery funding allowed us to provide participating schools with payment for TA time alongside a package of computer software, SpLD/dyslexia assessment instruments and staff training. SENCos had some management involvement and needed training to use screening and pre/post testing instruments. TAs were responsible for running the intervention. All involved needed basic knowledge of SpLD/dyslexia and dyslexia-friendly practice alongside understanding the nature of multilingualism and its implications for teaching and learning. SENCos and TAs were becoming researchers in a controlled trial so training in research ethics and practices was essential to prevent anyone from unwittingly biasing findings.

Our solution was:

- provide two days of training for both TAs and SENCos;
- booklets for all, summarising the information;
- a project activity handbook (incorporating brief record keeping) which supported the TAs' activities, developed confidence and ensured consistency;
- create links between the schools and project managers to enable support.

The training days also allowed data collection, via questionnaires and focus groups, from TAs and SENCOs concerning prior knowledge, experience and training needs. However, dilemmas around the role of the TAs within schools and tensions between their responsibilities to the research and their other duties emerged during the project and, despite all schools knowing that the funds and equipment were given in exchange for their commitment, some TAs lost time to other activities. The project demanded expertise in the TAs and confidence in their role as researchers, and we learnt much from each other.

Managing the implementation

This was a challenge for everyone. The development team contained experts bringing initially divergent opinions from both 'silos'. The mixed methodology design demanded both statistical expertise and experience with qualitative data gathering methods, alongside support for the SENCos' data gathering, support for the TAs and communication with children and carers. The geographical scope of the project, from Liverpool to South-West England, was also a huge challenge. The two project managers played a vital role.

What did we learn?

The project activities were designed to take account of the dilemmas that emerged for the research team and participants from the combination of methods, the children's needs, the parent/carer's voices, the support for the TA/SENCo researchers and the maintenance of experimental rigour. This section discusses what we learnt – in terms both of the main findings and the joys and pitfalls of the mixed methodology design. This was demanding, but permitted richer understanding of the factors contributing to the impact of the intervention and it underpins recommendations for practice. This complex project also provided practical lessons for identification of SpLD/dyslexia, programme planning and delivery.

Identifying dyslexia in children with EAL: issues for attitudes and labels

At the outset, tensions between the two silos of expertise were increased by a tendency for the SpLD/dyslexia world to seek categorisation of children by identification of SpLD/dyslexia, using a mainly quantitative cognitive assessment procedure, contentious in this context. Our major aim was to devise and test interventions for children with EAL and SpLD/dyslexia hence we had to identify a participatory group who met this criterion. The carefully researched and designed protocol failed to identify these children reliably but this was not a disaster. This confirmed existing reservations about using tests in English to identify dyslexia in multilingual children aged 9–11. One benefit that emerged for the children is the message that teachers should not wait for a 'label' of dyslexia before setting up an intervention. Data from SENCos confirmed that valuable information about the children's processing profiles obtained from the screeners could allow targeted provision. A dyslexic label is also not necessarily an advantage in many cultures (Smythe *et al.*, 2004). The intervention utilised practice confirmed as effective for both dyslexic learners and children with EAL and had a significant impact for all the children, regardless of dyslexic status.

The impact on literacy

Phase one

Mortimore *et al.* (2013) provide detailed outcomes. All three groups made progress but both intervention groups outperformed the control group particularly in single word reading and National Curriculum level (NC) writing. In areas such as spelling, phonological decoding and reading accuracy, the children who had worked with Nessy and Rapid Reading performed better than the paired-reading children. The paired-reading group made higher gains in reading fluency skills, silent reading sentence comprehension and oral receptive language. They also, surprisingly, outperformed the intervention group in NC writing levels.

Phase two

Overall, gains from Phase one were sustained across the reading skills but remained more fragile in the area of spelling and writing when intervention was discontinued. After completing the Nessy/RR intervention, the control group made significant but rather more mixed gains.

Hence the project suggests that a daily half hour, carefully structured multi-sensory intervention programme with a trained TA and two children with EAL, over a period of 15 weeks, boosts reading and spelling/writing skills effectively. These improvements are sustainable but children will need further reinforcement to automatise spelling gains.

Participants' perspectives

Including the voices of TAs, children and their carers provides insights for the future design and delivery of intervention programmes. The focus groups with children, the TAs and parents from six schools emphasised the value of all aspects of the project to the children.

TAs were positive about their involvement in the project. They valued the training and materials, indicating that they would be useful to the school in the future. They stressed the importance of time to become familiar with programmes, and establish routines and relationships with the children. Reading comprehension was a major struggle for children, and additional time was spent on activities around texts, asking comprehension questions, retelling of stories, and information and vocabulary enrichment. The interesting fiction and non-fiction texts motivated children to gain in confidence and reinvigorated their interest in reading.

The children discussed their enjoyment of the materials used. Individual children talked about their interests and preferences; remembering details of many books and aspects of the programme. Children could identify not only aspects of their reading and spelling that had improved but also how the time spent on Rapid Reading had helped them extend their vocabulary. Children know what they are interested in and have strong preferences. Materials that reflect children's interests can be an important incentive for engagement in learning. What the children appeared to value most was the challenging and interesting subject matter in the reading books and the 'fun' element of the spelling games, supporting the emphasis on the importance of context in literacy acquisition identified by Gregory (1996).

A crucial lesson, however, was how much these children valued the individual attention. TAs reported that the children's confidence and willingness to speak grew over the timescale, especially for children who were reluctant to speak initially. Children started to initiate conversation and extend discussion. Challenging, enjoyable materials combined with building supportive partnerships with children are important factors in any intervention.

Some of the narrative records kept by the TAs showed children developing critical thinking, and increasing metacognitive awareness of strengths and difficulties in reading and spelling. Over time, children talked more about their reading preferences, the nature and timing of difficulties they encountered and what helped them overcome any problems. Being able to discuss strengths, weaknesses and strategies for improvement aids children's metacognitive awareness and personal control of their learning.

In the focus groups children talked enthusiastically about languages and being bi/multilingual. Most children valued the opportunity to talk about their own and each others' languages. What emerged from these discussions was the complexity of the range of languages that children spoke or that were significant to the family. For example, Somali children arriving in the UK via Italy or the Netherlands claimed varying knowledge of Somali, Arabic and Dutch or Italian. This appeared to be a rare chance for the children to share their knowledge of languages. The focus groups became a third space where funds of knowledge from home and wider experiences (Space 1) were being utilised in school (Space 2). However, children suggested that this type of discussion was rare and in some cases that they felt they were 'not allowed' to speak home languages in school. The opportunity to draw on funds of knowledge about languages could support children's cognitive and emotional development.

Often children and parents reported use of a wider range of oral and written languages than those recorded by the schools, indicating that information essential to the establishing of children's learning profiles needs to be shared more consistently between home and school. The children's perceptions and views of the programme and multi-literacies produced an unexpected and fascinating outcome – a 'snap shot' of multilingual schools and these children as engaged global citizens, connected directly with experience of friends and family networks across the world.

Overall parents were keen to understand their children's progress in school. Parents felt the intervention had been beneficial and gave examples of changes in attitudes and behaviours such as willingness to read more and confidence in spelling. However, there were gaps in their knowledge of the precise details of their children's progress during the project. There were missed opportunities for parents and schools to work more closely together to develop a third space to enhance children's literacy across languages; for example, with paired-reading.

There are complex issues surrounding multi-literacies (Baker, 2006) with children, parents and schools valuing different types of literacy. Parents were making strategic decisions about which languages to emphasise and whether to encourage children to learn to read and write in home languages. Parents emphasised the importance of their children becoming fluent in speaking, reading and writing in English. But do schools have the capacity to support children's emotional and cognitive development through sharing knowledge about languages?

There are strong messages here for schools in terms of 'knowing your children' and how essential it is to develop knowledge of the children's stories, multi-literacies and cultural context and to ensure that this is celebrated.

Recommendations for schools

Assessment

Our failed attempt to develop robust screeners for SpLD/dyslexia confirms the need for caution in labelling children. Screeners may help to compile a profile for individualised support but should not be used as an indicator of dyslexia in bilingual learners of this age group. If a learner fails unexpectedly to become literate, schools must intervene swiftly, explore the learner's profile, hear the child's story, and develop a suitable programme regardless of 'labelling'.

Intervention

The successful project programme content included phonological processing, systematic and explicit teaching of new second-language phonemes delivered in a carefully structured multi-sensory way based on the individual's pattern of errors. It also involved explicit teaching of morphology and syllable structure, strategies for inferring meaning from context and morphology, and enrichment of vocabulary linked to the literacy intervention or contextualised.

The use of paired-reading in first language (L1), with a proficient bilingual partner, peer or adult, or in second language (specifically English) was very successful. One way forward could be to introduce paired-reading with, for example, parents/carers or older children in a variety of languages. This should include a focus on listening and reading comprehension strategies, higher-order comprehension strategies, schema work, inference work pre-reading, prediction, SQ3R (Survey, Question, Read, Recite, Review), visual and holistic approaches. The sessions also built confidence in use of language and expression and children's awareness of their own reading skills.

ICT programmes with a strong element of fun and broad interest also appeal but the ICT hardware must be reliable. Both Nessy and Rapid Reading were endorsed by the bilingual children.

Use/training of TAs

The Blatchford report (Blatchford *et al.*, 2009) questioned the effectiveness of TA support in enhancing pupils' progress. In contrast, the success of our clearly structured, TA-delivered interventions argues strongly for the deployment of trained TAs with small groups of bilingual children for daily support over a relatively short period of time. TAs reported growing specialist skills and confidence but this was not necessarily recognised or fully exploited by schools who did not always prioritise specialist TA activity over tasks demanding less skill. Schools need to recognise the trained TAs' potential to extend their provision for these learners.

Conclusion: The way forward

None of the issues and dilemmas discussed above will disappear; the intention here is to concentrate on how they might aid research and school contexts. A focus is on how the concept of a third space can inform these contexts.

Despite the challenges of the mixed methodology approach it enriched our understanding of both the quantitative and qualitative elements of the research. The full research report (Mortimore *et al.*, 2012) and sources (Hansen and Mortimore, 2012; Hutchings and Mortimore, 2014) give more detailed responses to the issues discussed in this chapter.

Adopting a mixed methodology approach which rejects notions of opposition between qualitative and quantitative research allowed for a rich dialogue about what works and why. The quantitative element affirmed the complexities of and need for caution in labelling whilst affirming what types of interventions are likely to support bilingual learners. The qualitative element emphasised the voices of participants, especially children, bringing to the fore how less-measurable dimensions of learning, emotion and environment are linked to responses to literacy. Mixed methodology has the potential to widen our understanding of what makes a difference in these rich, diverse multilingual contexts. For researchers and schools it may open doors to a deeper knowledge of how to design interventions that draw on funds of knowledge from Spaces 1 and 2 and create a third space. For teacher-researchers case studies could become a learning space for improving school practices in assessment and intervention.

The research also suggested that school responses to the identification of literacy difficulties should be holistic: acknowledging the child's story and forming links between home and school. Our findings back previous research on the value of short-term, daily, focused interventions by trained TAs (Brooks, 2003) and of enriched paired-reading (Boyle and Topping, 2012). The discussions with children, parents and TAs, especially about linguistic diversity, led us to question how future interventions could develop in a third space. This mixed methodology project has taught us the importance of aiming for a holistic perspective on what makes a difference in complex contexts.

References

Baker, C. (2006) *Foundations of Bilingual Education and Bilingualism* (4th edition). Clevedon: Multilingual Matters.

Barton, L. (Ed.) (1996) *Disability and Society: Emerging Issues and Insights*. Harlow: Addison Wesley Longman.

Blatchford, P., Bassett, P., Brown, P., Koutsoubou, M., Martin, C., Russell, A. and Webster, R., with Rubie-Davies, C. (2009) *The impact of support staff in schools*. Results from the Deployment and Impact of Support Staff project (Strand 2 Wave 2) (DCSF-RR148). London: Department for Children, Schools and Families.

Booth, T. and Ainscow, M. (2011) *Index for Inclusion: Developing Learning and Participation in Schools* (3rd edition). Bristol: Centre for Studies in Inclusive Education (CSIE).

Boyle, C. and Topping, K.J. (Eds) (2012) *What Works in Inclusion?* New York and Maidenhead: Open University.

Brooks, G. (2003) *What Works for Children with Literacy Difficulties? The Effectiveness of Intervention Schemes*. University of Sheffield and DFES Research Report No. 380.

Crombie, M. and MacColl, H. (2001) Dyslexia and the teaching of modern foreign languages. In Peer, L. and Reid, G. (Eds) *Dyslexia and Inclusion in the Secondary School*. pp. 54–63. London: David Fulton.

Cummins, J, (2000) *Language. Power and Pedagogy: Bilingual Children in the Crossfire*. Clevedon: Multilingual Matters.

Gorard, S. (2001) *Quantitative Methods in Educational Research. The Role of Numbers Made Easy*. London: Continuum.

Gregory, E. (1996) *Making Sense of a New World: Learning to Read in a Second Language*. London: Paul Chapman.

Gutierrez, K.D., Baquedano-Lopez, P. and Tejeda, C. (1999) Rethinking diversity: hybridity and hybrid language practices in the third space. *Mind, Culture and Activity*, 6(4), 286–303.

Hall, D., Griffiths, D., Haslam, L. and Wilkins Y. (2001) *Assessing the Needs of Bilingual Pupils: Living in Two Languages* (2nd edition). London: David Fulton.

Hansen, L. and Mortimore, T. (2012) 'Dyslexia and multilingualism – identification and intervention'. Insights into identifying risk of SpLD/Dyslexia in children with English as an additional language. *Patoss Autumn Bulletin*, 11–24.

Haslum, M.N. (2007) What kind of evidence do we need for evaluating therapeutic interventions? *Dyslexia*, 13(4), 234–239.

Hutchings, M. and Mortimore, T. (2014) Learning from each other. *Special edition of Transylvanian Journal of Psychology*, 147–173.

Illeris, K. (2009) A comprehensive understanding of human learning. *International Journal of Continuing Education and Lifelong Learning*, 2(1), 45–63.

Kelly, C. (2010) *Hidden Worlds: Young Children Learning Literacy in Multicultural Contexts*. Stoke-on-Trent: Trentham Books.

Landon, J. (2000) Inclusion and dyslexia – the exclusion of bilingual learners. In Peer, L. and Reid, G. (Eds) *Dyslexia – Successful Inclusion in the Secondary School*. London: David Fulton.

McKay, N. (2006) *Removing Dyslexia as a Barrier to Achievement: The Dyslexia Friendly Schools Toolkit.* Oxford: SEN Marketing.

Mortimore, T., Hansen, L., Hutchings, M., Northcote, A., Fernando, J., Horobin, L., Saunders, K. and Everatt, J. (2012) *Dyslexia and Multilingualism: Identifying and Supporting Bilingual Learners Who Might Be at Risk of Developing SpLD/Dyslexia.* www.bdadyslexia.org.uk/common/ckeditor/filemanager/userfiles/About_Us/Projects/Big_Lottery_Research_Report_Final_Version.pdf (accessed 6 June 2015).

Mortimore, T., Hutchings, M. and Northcote, A. (2013) Identifying and supporting literacy acquisition in bilingual learners potentially at risk of dyslexia: The Big Lottery Dyslexia and Multilingualism Project. In J. Everatt (Ed.) *Dyslexia, Languages and Multilingualism.* Bracknell: BDA.

NALDIC (2013) *EAL Statistics.* www.naldic.org.uk/research-and-information/eal-statistics (accessed 31 May 2012).

Ofsted (2003) The Annual Inspection Report of Her Majesty's Chief Inspector of Schools 2003–2004. www.official-documents.gov.uk/document/hc0405/hc01/0195/0195.asp (accessed 6 September 2013).

Ott, P. (2007) *Teaching Children with Dyslexia. A Practical Guide.* London: Routledge.

Parton. N. (2011) Child protection and safeguarding in England: changing and competing conceptions of risk and their implications for social work. *British Journal of Social Work*, 41(5), 854–875. doi: 10.1093/bjsw/bcq119

Rose, S.J. (2009) *Identifying and Teaching Children and Young People with Dyslexia and Literacy Difficulties. An independent report.* www.education.gov.uk/publications (accessed 12 September 2011).

Schneider, E. (2009) Dyslexia and foreign language learning. In Reid, G. (Ed.) *The Routledge Companion to Dyslexia.* London: Routledge.

Singleton, C. (2009) *Intervention for Dyslexia: No to Failure.* Hull: University of Hull.

Smythe, I., Everatt, J. and Salter, R. (2004) *International Book of Dyslexia.* Chichester: Wiley.

Turner, M. (1997) *Psychological Assessment of Dyslexia.* London: Whurr.

United Nations (1989) *Convention on the Rights of the Child.* Geneva: United Nations.

Wheldall, K. and Carter, M. (2008) A scientific approach to special education. *Australasian Journal of Special Education*, 32(1), 1–4.

Wolf, M. (2008) *Proust and the Squid. The Story and Science of the Reading Brain.* Cambridge: Icon Books.

Ziegler, J.C. and Goswami, U.C. (2005) Reading acquisition, developmental dyslexia and skilled reading across languages: a psycholinguistic grain size theory. *Psychological Bulletin*, 131(1), 3–29.

12

BILINGUALISM AND DYSLEXIA

The case of children learning English as an additional language

Linda Siegel

This chapter will:

1. Address the issue of how one can determine and evaluate dyslexia in children who are being educated in a language that is not their first language
2. Address the issue of what happens to children with dyslexia when they are being educated in a language that is not their first language
3.   Describe some evidence-supported interventions that are important for helping dyslexics learning English as a second language to acquire literacy skills

Terminology

A word about terminology is in order. In North America people who have a native language other than English are sometimes given the label English as Second Language (ESL) or English Language Learners (ELL). I believe that the British term English as an Additional Language (EAL) is more appropriate and that is the term that is used in this chapter.

Dyslexia as a language disorder

This chapter is based on the assumption that dyslexia is defined as a severe difficulty with the accuracy and/or fluency of reading words and/or pseudowords (Siegel, 1988a, 2007). Word recognition and pseudoword reading accuracy and fluency are always measured against age norms. Although there may be other difficulties, such as writing, spelling, and reading comprehension, it is important to note that decoding at the level of the individual word is the basis of dyslexia.

Dyslexia is primarily a language disorder, involving difficulties with hearing and confusing sounds within words, isolating and manipulating sounds within words, retrieving the pronunciation of letters and groups of letters quickly, relative lack of awareness of the syntax and the morphology of the language, problems with verbal working memory, and often less-developed vocabulary skills and sometimes word finding difficulties. (For reviews see Siegel, 2003, 2013; Siegel & Ryan, 1984, 1988.) It should be noted that people with dyslexia may have visual and motor difficulties but these problems are not central to the disorder of dyslexia.

Given that dyslexia is a language disorder, it is reasonable to expect that when people with dyslexia are required to learn an additional language, then they might experience difficulties. One of the purposes of this chapter is to assess the validity of this assumption. Furthermore, when people experience difficulties with reading, it may be from lack of exposure to the language (an educational problem) or a neurologically mediated difficulty such as dyslexia. One of the purposes of this chapter is to propose some methods of determining whether language minority children, in this case, children learning English as an Additional Language (EAL) have dyslexia. Obviously, the diagnosis of dyslexia in the EAL population is not a simple matter. The most important issue to be determined is whether or not they have had adequate exposure to the language. Ideally, it would also be important to determine their level of skills in their first language and to ascertain if these abilities (or lack of them) are what one would expect of a child of that age. Unfortunately, this is impossible because we have no standardized tests in most of the first languages that students in English learning environments speak. It is important to discover when they started speaking English and to whom – parents, siblings, extended family. If there are grandparents or other extended family members present in the home and if they speak a language other than English to the child this type of English language environment is important to the evaluation of reading and language skills in English. One variable that seems to make a difference is whether or not the child learning English as an additional language has older siblings. It is common in East Asian and South Asian cultures for the children in the family to play "school," with the older children acting as teachers for the younger ones. The "teachers" teach in English and this exposes their younger EAL siblings to English. We know that slightly older children make the best language models for younger children so these "school" experiences provide a linguistic advantage for children before they enter formal schooling. It is also important to understand what language experiences the EAL child has had with peers. If the child went to a preschool where many of the children and the teachers are native English speakers, then this experience provides a rich English language experience. If the child plays with native English speakers in the neighborhood, then the EAL child will learn a colloquial English and bring this experience to formal schooling.

Against this background and in order to determine whether or not the child has dyslexia, we should test the child on accuracy and fluency of reading words and pseudowords. If the child performs at the level of his or her age-matched peers, then clearly the child does not have dyslexia. If the child performs at a level with his or her age-matched EAL peers, then it is unlikely that the child has dyslexia. Of course, there are no norms for EAL speakers, and even if there were it would be important to know the first language, so this comparison is just one aspect of making a decision about dyslexia. If, on the other hand, the child's performance on reading tasks is low, then it is likely that they are dyslexic, providing that they have had sufficient exposure to reading instruction in English. An analysis of the errors that a child makes might be useful here. If the reading errors show signs of intrusion from the first language, then it may be a language problem, not a case of dyslexia. If the reading errors are similar to the ones that dyslexics of the same age make, then it is likely a case of dyslexia, assuming that there has been good teaching of reading.

Obviously, the younger the age that EAL children are exposed to English, the better that is for language learning. We do not know what in the young brain makes it easier for young children to learn languages, but it is a real phenomenon. In the future, perhaps neuroscience will provide an explanation but, at present, this critical period for language learning remains a mystery.

Children with dyslexia learning English as an additional language

For the purposes of the studies reported in this chapter, I will define dyslexia in EAL children as performance below the 25th percentile on tests of word and/or pseudoword accuracy and/ or fluency. We do not use the IQ test for reasons outlined in Fletcher *et al.* (1992); Siegel (1988b, 1989, 1992); Stuebing *et al.* (2002, 2009); and Tanaka *et al.* (2011). Furthermore, it is inappropriate, and perhaps unethical, to use the IQ test for children from a different cultural and linguistic background on whom the IQ test was not normed.

With this background in mind, I will first report on three studies of EAL children. These studies were conducted in Toronto, Ontario, Canada. One of these studies involved Canadian children who spoke Portuguese as a first language at home and knew little or no English when they came to school at age 5 (da Fontoura & Siegel, 1995). They were all from low socioeconomic backgrounds. Most of their parents were illiterate or had low levels of literacy. The second study was conducted with Canadian children who had Arabic as a first language (Abu Rabia & Siegel, 2002). The families were predominantly from low socioeconomic backgrounds. The third study was conducted with Canadian children who had Italian as their first language (D'Angiulli, Siegel & Serra, 2002). They were from predominantly middle class backgrounds. The children in all these studies were between 9 and 12 years of age. In each of these groups we defined dyslexia as a score of less than the 25th percentile (based on age norms) on a test of word recognition, the Wide Range Achievement Test (WRAT). The WRAT requires the children to read an increasingly difficult series of words, such as, "cat," "finger," "triumph," and "heinous." Children who scored above the 35th percentile were considered typical readers. In each of these three studies, we compared four groups of children. There were typical readers and children with dyslexia in the English first language group (L1). In the EAL group there were typical readers and children with dyslexia. Most of the EAL children attended what in Canada are called Heritage Language Classes in which they received instruction in reading and writing in the first language. These schools were funded by the government under the policy of multiculturalism.

Word recognition

In the case of word recognition, the Portuguese, Italian and Arabic speaking typical readers had higher scores than the English L1 typical readers. For the dyslexics, the Portuguese and Italian speaking dyslexics had significantly higher scores than the monolingual English L1 dyslexics. For the Arabic speaking children the scores of the EAL and L1 dyslexics were equivalent. Therefore in five of the six comparisons, the bilingual students had higher scores on a test of word recognition than the L1 speakers. In the case of the dyslexics in two out of the three samples the bilingual students had higher scores than the monolingual dyslexics.

Decoding

The children in the three samples were administered the Woodcock Word Attack test in which they were asked to read a series of pseudowords, pronounceable combinations of letters that are not words in the English language but can be read using decoding skills. These decoding skills involve the association between graphemes and phonemes, which presents a significant challenge for dyslexics and is at the heart of the problem for dyslexics. The Portuguese and Italian speaking typical readers had significantly higher scores on this task than the L1 typical readers. The Portuguese and Arabic speakers with dyslexia had higher scores than the L1 dyslexic children. Having an additional language seems in some cases to help dyslexics with the difficult task of learning the sounds of letters and letter combinations.

Spelling

As a spelling test the children were asked to spell an increasingly difficult series of words, such as "and," "cook," "surprise," "malfeasance." In the case of spelling, the Portuguese, Italian and Arabic speaking dyslexics had significantly higher scores than the English L1 dyslexics. The Portuguese and Italian speaking typical readers had higher scores that the L1 typical readers.

The bilingual advantage

The results from the three studies described above clearly indicate that being educated in an additional language is not a disadvantage for the dyslexics and may even reduce the reading and spelling difficulties that they experience. Many bilingual EAL typical readers have better English reading and spelling skills than typical readers who have English as a first language.

Early identification and intervention: Preventing reading difficulties in EAL and English L1 children

One of the most important issues in helping to prevent reading difficulties is how to identify children who are at risk for literacy problems. The identification of EAL children is particularly challenging, as it is difficult to determine if any language difficulties that they have are a general language problem or a result of being educated in a situation where their first language is not the language of instruction. There is also the issue that when we find children at risk we need to ascertain what is the appropriate intervention strategy. I will describe an eight-year longitudinal study in which we attempted to answer these questions.

Description of the sample

The study was conducted in North Vancouver, Canada. (See Chiappe & Siegel, 2006; Lesaux, Lipka, & Siegel, 2006; Lesaux, Rupp, & Siegel, 2007; Lesaux & Siegel, 2003; Lipka, Lesaux, & Siegel, 2006; Lipka & Siegel, 2007, 2010 a,b; Lipka, Siegel, & Vukovic, 2005; Partanen & Siegel, 2013; Siegel, 2009, 2011) for descriptions of various aspects of this study.

North Vancouver, in the Canadian province of British Columbia, is part of the greater metropolitan area of Vancouver but maintains a separate school district and other services. The community is quite varied in terms of socioeconomic levels and in the North Vancouver School District at the time of this study, 20% of the children had English as an additional language. There were a total of 30 languages in addition to English spoken by the children in this study. The most common languages were Cantonese, the language of Hong Kong and south Mainland China, and Persian, also called Farsi, spoken in Iran and neighboring areas. Chinese is a non-alphabetic language written as a morphologically based script and Persian is written in Arabic script. Approximately 1,000 children enter the school system each year. There were 30 schools in this study.

Identification of children at risk

Children in Canada enter school at age 5 in what is called their kindergarten year. At the time of this study, kindergarten was a half-day but now in some provinces it is a full school day. In some Canadian provinces, children enter school at age 4 and that is called junior kindergarten but there was no junior kindergarten in British Columbia at that time. In November and December of their kindergarten year, the children were administered a series of tests and tasks to determine the areas in which they might have difficulties. The most useful and efficient tasks involved letter and word identification from the Wide Range Achievement Test (WRAT) and phonological awareness tasks, involving phoneme identification (e.g., say the last sound in the word "cat" which is said to the children) and phoneme segmentation (e.g., say the sounds in the word "pig").

Knowing the names of the letters, as in the WRAT, is a good predictor of subsequent reading difficulties, as is phonological awareness. Of course, when we read we do not need the letter names but it is a good indicator of risk because it is an indicator of the literacy to which children have been exposed and what they remember of what they have been exposed to. We also had an oral cloze task, a measure of syntactic awareness; that is, the extent to which the child was aware of the syntax of the language. In this task sentences are read out loud to the children and they need to fill in a missing word. We say, "beep" for where the missing word is. For example, "Dad beep Bobby a letter yesterday." Understanding of the syntax of the language is important for accurate and fluent reading.

We found that 25% of the English L1 children were at risk, in that they had very low scores on these tasks. We found that 50% of the EAL children had scores on these tasks in the range that we would consider to be at risk. By comparing children to others at the same age and grade and language background, we can determine whether they have a general language problem or a problem only in their additional language.

Interventions to improve literacy

In order to improve the literacy of the children in this district, two intervention programs were used. These programs were classroom based with children sometimes being withdrawn from the classroom for special instruction. One of the programs was used in kindergarten and grade 1 and is called Firm Foundations. This program is a set of activities and games designed to teach phonological awareness, phonics, and vocabulary skills. For example, in one of the activities the children see a group of pictures and have to identify two words (e.g., book and bird) that start with the same sound. To develop their awareness of sounds they do not see print but must give their responses on the basis of pictures. This strategy is used to help them develop phonological awareness skills, that is the ability to hear and manipulate the sounds in words. Phonological awareness is an important skill that is critical for decoding print.

The intervention is a primarily whole class intervention. The children begin the day with what is called circle time. As a whole class, they work on a particular skill, for example segmenting words into syllables. The teacher says a word and they tap their arm for each syllable. They start from the wrist and work up to their nose for multi-syllable words. They also practice this skill in small groups in different centers around the classroom. The teacher organizes the children into groups informally, placing children at similar levels of skills together. Periodically, the teacher assesses the children individually to determine their mastery (or lack of it) of a specific skill.

The other intervention that the children received was called Reading 44. In the province of British Columbia, the North Vancouver School District is school district 44. It is a program designed to teach reading comprehension and vocabulary skills. It is primarily delivered to all children in the classroom.

The results of the intervention

After the intervention, 1.5% of the English L1 group had significant reading problems (dyslexia) and 1.5% of the EAL group had significant reading problems (dyslexia). Therefore, 98.5% of the children were reading at average or above average levels. The results indicated that the children in the study improved very significantly after good reading instruction. The percentage of dyslexics decreased to a small number.

When we examined the results in more detail, a number of interesting trends emerged. On the Woodcock–Johnson Word Identification test, in which the child is required to read a longer and more complicated series of words that go from easy to very difficult words, we found that the EAL children with dyslexia had *higher* scores than the L1 children with dyslexia. In order to read English words you need a combination of phonological skills and visual memory skills. Of key importance is the recognition that because of the exposure to more than one language, the EAL children may have developed an enhanced ability to hear the sounds in languages, thus increasing their phonological awareness skills. It is also possible that their exposure to other writing systems increased their visual memory for print, a skill that is particularly useful because of the lack of transparency of the English language.

It should be noted that the typical readers in both the EAL and the L1 groups had average scores at the 85th percentile, indicated that their scores were in the above average range.

Pseudoword reading

Similar results were noted on the Word Attack subtest of the Woodcock–Johnson Test. In the Word Attack subtest, the children are required to read pseudowords of increasing difficulty, beginning from very simple ones to complex multi-syllable ones. On this task, the EAL dyslexics had significantly higher scores than the L1 dyslexics. The scores of the typical readers, both the EAL and the L1 were significantly above average with means at the 84th percentile, indicating excellent knowledge of the relation between graphemes and sounds.

Reading fluency

Reading fluency was measured with a test called the Test of Word Reading Efficiency (TOWRE). In this task, to measure the fluency of reading words the child was shown a list of words or pseudowords and asked to read as many as they could as quickly as they could without skipping any. For both the word reading and pseudoword reading tests, the EAL dyslexics had significantly higher scores than the L1 dyslexics. Reading fluency is very important for efficient reading. When reading sentences or paragraphs, and in order to remember words before the next word or phrase comes in, pushing the old one out, it is important to make sure that the information goes in as quickly as possible so as not to forget it.

Word spelling

The children were administered the WRAT spelling test, in which a series of increasingly difficult words are dictated to them. The EAL children with dyslexia had significantly higher scores on this test than the L1 children with dyslexia. In addition, the EAL typical readers had significantly higher scores on this spelling test than the L1 typical readers. Therefore, bilingualism results in the development of better spelling skills in children even if they have dyslexia. There are some possible reasons for this somewhat surprising finding. For English spelling one needs at least two skills. One of these is the ability to hear sounds within words and to translate them into graphemes (letters). It is possible that children exposed to more than one language have more finely developed abilities to hear the sounds within words and thus transfer that skill to spelling. Dyslexics typically have less developed sound awareness skills but it is possible that early intensive exposure to at least one other language may improve their skills. It should be noted that the EAL children, both dyslexic and typical readers, in this study spoke one or more languages at home before they came to school and were immersed in English in a very systematic way at school.

It is also important to note that most of them received instruction in reading and writing in their "heritage language" in an after school or weekend program. For many of the children in this study, this exposure involved learning a different writing system than the English alphabet. Many of the children learned Chinese or Arabic writing. Both Chinese and Arabic script required good visual memory and visual discrimination skills. Because of the irregularity of the English language and because so many words are not written the way that they sound (for example, "said," "have," "island"), visual memory skills are important for English spelling. It is possible that the EAL children have developed excellent visual memory skills as a result of exposure to the writing system of their first language and that they transfer these skills to English. To see this positive influence of bilingualism, it is important that children receive excellent instruction in phonological awareness, phonics, vocabulary, and reading strategies.

Pseudoword spelling

Pseudoword spelling is a task in which pseudowords are dictated to children and they are required to write them down. This task is a very good measure of their phonological awareness and phonic skills. It is normally a task that is extremely difficult for people with dyslexia, as they cannot rely on their visual memory skills. English speaking dyslexics tested on this task in English always remain significantly behind typical readers. In this study, the EAL dyslexics had significantly higher scores on this task compared to the L1 dyslexics. In fact, the scores of the EAL dyslexics almost equaled those of the typical readers (the L1 and EAL typical readers did not differ on this task). In other words, the bilingual dyslexics had been able to develop their phonological and phonic skills to almost the level of non-dyslexic typical readers.

Phonological awareness skills

Phonological awareness is an important aspect of reading and spelling. It involves the ability to segment speech into syllables and phonemes. For example, "say the word *carpenter* without *pen*" (answer *carter*). This task is normally quite difficult for individuals with dyslexia. However, in this study the dyslexic EAL students had significantly higher scores on this task than the L1 dyslexic students. In addition, the scores of the EAL dyslexics were almost equal to those of the typical readers. This performance indicates that their phonological skills were well developed.

Syntactic and morphological skills

Syntactic skills refers to the awareness of the underlying grammatical structure of the language. Morphological skills in general refer to the understanding of prefixes, suffixes, and roots in a language. These skills are important in reading, as when the brain is processing text, awareness of the structure of the language and what types of words are likely to come next in the sentence is important for quick and efficient reading. Morphological skills, in this case, refers to the awareness of the grammatical functions of word endings in the English language. In general, dyslexics have poorer syntactic skills than typically developing readers. The syntactic awareness task that we used is the oral cloze task that was described earlier.

In this study, the dyslexic EAL students had much higher scores than the dyslexic L1 students on the oral cloze tasks. The scores of the dyslexic EAL students were almost equal to the scores of the typical readers. We also used a morphological task in which the children read sentences with a word missing and had to decide which of the alternative words were correct (Marinova-Todd, Siegel, & Mazabel, 2013; Siegel, 2008). An example is the following sentence: "They need to (diversionary, diversity, diversion, diversify)." The children were required to select the correct word to complete that sentence. This item required the children to understand that this sentence requires a verb at the end and that verbs in the English language often end in "ify." As in the case of the oral cloze task, the EAL dyslexics had significantly higher scores on this morphological awareness task than the L1 dyslexics.

The results of these two tasks suggest that exposure to the grammatical structure of one language can help the learning of an additional language. It as if the brain develops some metalinguistic skills that transfer to the learning of other languages.

Reading comprehension

The ultimate goal of reading is to understand what one is reading. We administered a reading comprehension task to the children in this study (Low & Siegel, 2005). Typically, EAL children, whether they are dyslexic or not, have difficulty with reading comprehension because of a variety of factors, including lack of vocabulary and cultural knowledge and difficulty processing the formal grammatical structure of the text. In this study, we found that EAL children who were dyslexic performed in a similar way to dyslexic children whose first language was English. In addition EAL typical readers performed in a similar manner to English L1 typical readers. Both of these typical reader groups had *above average* scores on these tasks. These findings are pleasantly surprising ones because it indicates that EAL status should not be a barrier to reading comprehension.

Conclusions

The results of this study indicate that children can be assessed for risk for literacy difficulties early in their schooling and can be provided with instruction that significantly reduces the incidence of reading difficulties. The interventions work well for both EAL and English L1 students.

The children who were EAL had reading, spelling, and language skills equal to (or better than) native English speakers. We found that many bilingual typical readers have better English reading, phonological, and spelling skills in their second language than children who have English as a first language.

Many dyslexics, although clearly dyslexic in English, demonstrated better reading, spelling, phonological, and syntactic awareness skills than monolingual English L1 dyslexics. It is as if exposure to a first language different from English helps dyslexic children develop advanced language skills, which then transfer to learning to read and spell in English. Perhaps their first language helps provide some protection against the potential adverse effects of their dyslexia. In certain circumstances, we conclude that bilingualism is beneficial for dyslexics. In contrast to the idea that the language problems of dyslexics may interfere with language learning in an EAL situation, we have shown that there are situations in which bilingualism may provide an advantage for dyslexics.

It is important to provide a context for this conclusion. There are several important features of this situation. First of all, the children in this district (whether EAL or English L1) received excellent literacy instruction, including phonological awareness, phonics, vocabulary, and reading strategy. In addition the EAL children were in regular classrooms, allowing them to be intensively exposed to English. Secondly, the children received instruction in literacy in their first language, allowing some aspects of their first language to provide transfer to their second language. Thirdly, the EAL children were learning English. Although it is assumed that English is a difficult language to learn to read because of the complexity and unpredictable nature of the relation between the sounds of the language and the graphemes that represent these sounds, I believe that this characteristic of English actually provides an advantage for dyslexics. There is no doubt surprise at this statement. However, I argue that because one cannot associate each letter in English with a sound as one can in more transparent language such as Italian or Spanish, people learning to read English develop additional strategies, such as paying attention to the visual or orthographic characteristics of the word that they are reading. As dyslexics have poor phonological skills but perhaps better visual memory and orthographic skills (Siegel, Share, & Geva, 1995), and reading in English encourages the development of these skills in the cases where phonological skills are inadequate, dyslexics are not at as much of a disadvantage in English. This observation does not negate the importance of phonological skills in English or any other language.

Summary and conclusion

Children at risk for dyslexia can be detected early. They can receive an intervention in an inclusive setting, which decreases the probability of subsequent reading difficulties. EAL dyslexics can develop literacy skills that are better than those of English L1 monolingual dyslexics. Bilingualism is not a barrier to acquiring good literacy skills, and in some cases it may be an advantage.

References

Abu Rabia, S., & Siegel, L.S. (2002). Reading, syntactic, orthographic and working memory skills of bilingual Arabic–English speaking children. *Journal of Psycholinguistic Research, 31*, 661–678.

Chiappe, P., & Siegel, L.S. (2006). The development of reading for Canadian children from diverse linguistic backgrounds: A longitudinal study. *Elementary School Journal, 107*, 135–152.

da Fontoura, H.A., & Siegel, L.S. (1995). Reading, syntactic, and working memory skills of bilingual Portuguese–English Canadian children. *Reading and Writing: An Interdisciplinary Journal, 7*, 139–153.

D'Angiulli, A., Siegel, L.S., & Serra, E. (2002). The development of reading in English and Italian in bilingual children. *Applied Psycholinguistics, 22*, 479–507.

Fletcher, J.M., Francis, D.J., Rourke, B.P., Shaywitz, S.E., & Shaywitz, B.A. (1992). The validity of discrepancy-based definitions of reading disability, *Journal of Learning Disabilities, 25*, 555–561.

Lesaux, N.K., Lipka, O., & Siegel, L.S. (2006). Investigating cognitive and linguistic abilities that influence the reading comprehension skills of children from diverse linguistic backgrounds. *Reading and Writing: An Interdisciplinary Journal, 19*, 99–131.

Lesaux, N.K., Rupp, A.A., & Siegel, L.S. (2007). Growth in reading skills of children from diverse linguistic backgrounds: Findings from a 5-year longitudinal study. *Journal of Educational Psychology, 99*, 4. 821–834.

Lesaux, N.K., & Siegel, L.S. (2003). The development of reading in children who speak English as a second language. *Developmental Psychology, 25*, 1005–1019.

Lipka, O., Lesaux, N.K., & Siegel, L.S. (2006). Retrospective analyses of the reading development of a group of grade 4 disabled readers: Risk status and profiles over 5 years. *Journal of Learning Disabilities, 39*, 364–378.

Lipka, O., & Siegel, L.S. (2007). The development of reading skills in children with English as a second language. *Scientific Studies of Reading, 11*, 105–131.

Lipka. O., & Siegel, L.S. (2010a). Early identification and intervention to prevent reading difficulties. In D. Aram & O. Korat (Eds), *Literacy Development and Enhancement across Orthographies and Cultures*, Literacy Studies, 101. Berlin: Springer, pp. 205–219.

Lipka, O., & Siegel, L.S. (2010b). The improvement of reading skills of L1 and ESL children using a Response to Intervention (RtI) Model. *Psicothema, 22*, 963–969.

Lipka, O., Siegel, L.S., & Vukovic, R.K. (2005). The literacy skills of English language learners in Canada. *Learning Disabilities Research and Practice, 20*, 39–49.

Low, P., & Siegel, L.S. (2005). A comparison of the cognitive processes underlying reading comprehension in native English and ESL speakers. *Written Language and Literacy, 8*, 2, 207–231.

Marinova-Todd, S., Siegel, L.S., & Mazabel, S. (2013). The association between morphological awareness and literacy in English language learners from diverse language backgrounds. *Topics in Language Disorders, 33*, 93–107.

Partanen, M., & Siegel, L.S. (2013). Long-term outcome of the early identification and intervention of reading disabilities. *Reading and Writing: An Interdisciplinary Journal, 12*, 665–684.

Siegel, L.S. (1988a). Definitional and theoretical issues and research on learning disabilities. *Journal of Learning Disabilities, 21*, 264–266.

Siegel, L.S. (1988b). Evidence that IQ scores are irrelevant to the definition and analysis of reading disability. *Canadian Journal of Psychology, 42*, 201–215.

Siegel, L.S. (1989). IQ is irrelevant to the definition of learning disabilities. *Journal of Learning Disabilities, 22*, 469–478, 486.

Siegel, L.S. (1992). An evaluation of the discrepancy definition of dyslexia. *Journal of Learning Disabilities, 25*, 618–629.

Siegel, L.S. (2003). Basic cognitive processes and reading disabilities. In H.L. Swanson, K.R. Harris, & S. Graham (Eds), *Handbook of Learning Disabilities*. New York: Guilford Press, pp. 158–181.

Siegel, L.S. (2007). Perspectives on dyslexia. *Paediatrics & Child Health, 11*, 581–588.

Siegel, L.S. (2008). Morphological awareness skills of English language learners and children with dyslexia. *Topics in Language Disorders, 28*, 1, 15–27.

Siegel, L.S. (2009). Remediation of reading difficulties in English language learning students. In K. Pugh & P. McCardle (Eds), *How Children Learn to Read*. New York: Psychology Press, pp. 275–288.

Siegel, L.S. (2011). Reducing reading difficulties in English L1 and L2: Early identification and intervention. In P. McCardle, B. Miller, J.R. Lee, & O.J.L. Tzeng (Eds), *Dyslexia Across Languages: Orthography and the Brain–Gene–Behavior Link*. Baltimore, MD: Paul H. Brookes Publishing, pp. 294–304.

Siegel, L.S. (2013). *Understanding Dyslexia and Other Learning Disabilities*. Vancouver: Pacific Educational Press.

Siegel, L.S., & Ryan, E.B. (1984). Reading disability as a language disorder. *Remedial and Special Education, 5*, 28–33.

Siegel, L.S., & Ryan, E.B. (1988). Development of grammatical sensitivity, phonological, and short-term memory skills in normally achieving and learning disabled children. *Developmental Psychology, 24*, 28–37.

Siegel, L.S., Share, D., & Geva, E. (1995). Evidence for superior orthographic skills in dyslexics. *Psychological Science, 6*, 250–254.

Stuebing, K.K., Barth, A.E., Molfese, P.J., Weiss, B., Fletcher, J.M. (2009). IQ is not strongly related to response to reading instruction: A meta-analytic interpretation. *Exceptional Children, 76*, 31–51.

Stuebing, K.K., Fletcher, J.M., LeDoux, J.M., Lyon, G.R., Shaywitz, S.E., & Shaywitz, B.A. (2002). Validity of IQ-discrepancy classification of reading disabilities: A meta-analysis. *American Educational Research Journal, 39*, 469–518.

Tanaka, H., Black, J.M., Hulme, C., Stanley, L.M., Kesler, S.R., Whitfield-Gabrieli, S. *et al.* (2011). The brain basis of the phonological deficit in dyslexia is independent of IQ. *Psychological Science, 22*, 1442–1451.

13

THEORY AND PRACTICE IN THE SUPPORT OF YOUNG PEOPLE AND ADULTS WITH ENGLISH AS AN ADDITIONAL LANGUAGE AND DYSLEXIA, IN FURTHER AND HIGHER EDUCATION

Sheena Bell and Emma Tudhope

This chapter will:

1. Help readers to understand the current context of teaching adults and young people with dyslexia and English as an Additional Language (EAL) in England
2. Explore the complex overlaps between dyslexia and EAL in the context of further and higher education
3. Share insights from supporters of students with dyslexia and EAL from further and higher education settings
4. Consider some strategies which may be applied to teaching and support programmes

Introduction

To understand the challenges of supporting young people and adults with English as an Additional Language (EAL) and dyslexia, it is crucial to consider the multi-layered, and rapidly evolving context in which educators, theorists, practitioners are working. Since the turn of the millennium, there has been a rapid increase in economic and social mobility across country and language boundaries. This has occurred, not only within the European Union, where common agreements have made it easier for both students and workers to migrate across countries, but also globally, in the context of increasingly easy mobility and internet-driven information systems. Migration of refugees due to global conflict has also increased the cultural diversity of many countries, including England. However, although much attention in terms of research and resourcing has been focussed on the support of EAL pupils in school, this has not been replicated for students in post-compulsory and vocational education. This is also mirrored in the field of dyslexia, where the majority of resources and publications has been concentrated on school-age learners rather than adults.

Although national statistics are in dispute, there is no doubt that England has become a more culturally diverse society and the demographic profile of learners and workers has changed radically. The last government's policy specifically encourages the growth of numbers of international students in Further and Higher Education (FE and HE): 'We will welcome international students to the UK, look after them while they are here and keep in touch after they have gone home' (Department for Business, Innovation and Skills, 2013, p. 60), although this may change under the current government. The last few years have also seen a steady rise in the number of economic migrants coming to England to take their place in the workforce (Office of National Statistics, 2015). Job seekers, therefore, join British students in needing to access basic, academic and vocational qualifications enabling them to enter and fulfil workplace roles. Despite current political debate and manoeuvring claiming to reflect public concern about the level of immigration, there have been, and continue to be, positive initiatives for businesses to search for candidates on an international scale both to alleviate skills shortages, and in the search for workers prepared to accept a minimum wage for less-attractive employment roles. This drive to encourage skilled workers from other countries, and train them (and their families) so that they can be productive, fully employed citizens, will continue to have an impact on how we support their ongoing education in England, and the allocation of funds to underpin this.

Alongside this, significant progress has been made in defining, assessing and supporting people with dyslexia. Dyslexia is accepted as a disability in legislation (in the Equality Act 2010). The Rose Review (Rose, 2009) made a significant contribution to raising the profile of dyslexia and encouraging the training of specialist teachers and assessors (Bell and McLean, 2011). In addition, recent changes in legislation have made it a requirement that all young people with SEN (Special Educational Needs) should be followed with a Health and Educational Care Plan, which includes transition into employment, up to the age of 25 years (Department for Education and Department of Health, 2014). Research in the field of dyslexia has also continuously emphasised the difficulty of English, with its irregular spelling patterns, inconsistent phonic structures and confusingly fickle spelling rules (Ziegler and Goswami, 2005). This language structure poses particular challenges to learners with dyslexia whose first language is English, and significant challenges to those with underlying difficulties whose first language is not English.

On another level, the English education system itself is undergoing significant changes. 'Further Education' is a college system which has traditionally combined academic and vocational training for young people towards the end of compulsory schooling (post 16 years of age), including part-time professional qualifications and apprenticeships, through to lifelong learning for adults. However, the structure of FE is now widening even further and strongly promoting partnerships with schools, universities and workplace educators. Higher education in England has been traditionally based on degree-level studies and research, but now offers academic studies alongside highly vocational studies which combine with professional, on-the-job training (for example, nursing). In addition, many English universities are now creating educational opportunities for school-age students through linked specialist colleges where vocational training takes place. Therefore, the challenge for educators is to meet the needs of an increasingly diverse student population and equip them with a much broader range of skills. Specialist practitioners, who work with students with dyslexia/EAL, will also need to respond to the challenges of supporting increasingly diverse demands on students from the widening range of courses on offer.

Transitions into employment are also crucial to students studying at FE and HE level. Employment opportunities are becoming increasingly professionalised and qualification-driven, so that workplace roles, which historically did not require literacy skills or formal qualifications, now require candidates to pass written examinations and assessments. As a result, many students with EAL/dyslexia find themselves making transitions into work roles which may be well below their capacity, because they are unable to show qualifications which map to English requirements. Consequently, this means they may need particular support to enable them to reach their potential. It is recognised that people with dyslexia, for a range of reasons, often find it challenging to make appropriate transitions from education to employment and in career progression (Bell, 2010), and this is likely to be even more of a problem for those who also have EAL. As a result, unless specialist tuition and support is put in place, students with EAL and dyslexia are unlikely to be able to demonstrate their true skills and knowledge in terms of gaining qualifications, successfully transitioning into employment, and reaching a certain income. Additionally, employers risk missing out on the range of skills such people can bring to the workplace.

The national drive for a more qualified workforce reflects government concerns with national competition in a global market. This debate also concerns the changing demands and nature of the offered employment, with the shift from labour-intensive, heavy industry, to technical and services-related work: 'In recent years there has been a marked shift in the UK economy away from manufacturing towards services – particularly knowledge intensive services' (OECD, 2015, p. 10). These new and reshaped industries require higher-level literacy skills.

Figure 13.1 summarises the shifting and multifaceted context in which the support for people with dyslexia and EAL is placed. The following section moves on to take a closer look at these learners and suggests particular challenges in assessing and providing appropriate support for them to reach their potential.

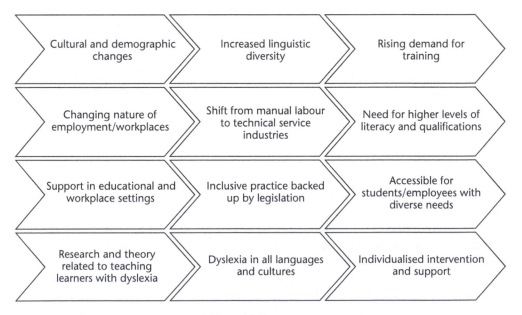

FIGURE 13.1 Current contexts – a multi-layered view

DISCUSSION POINTS

1. Institutions must adapt in order to enable people with dyslexia from diverse cultural and language backgrounds to access the knowledge and skills they need to take their place in a skilled workforce.

    Do you know how many learners with EAL there are in your classroom, institution or workplace? Has this changed in the past few years? How has your setting responded to this?

2. Inclusive practice enables all learners to reach their potential, both in terms of well-being and academic achievement. Now consider how students with special needs, such as dyslexia, are identified and supported in your context. Discuss how changes have been responded to: both at an individual and/or institutional level.

    How are educational establishments responding to these changes in order to ensure that students with dyslexia and EAL are able to fulfil their potential? What further steps could your institution take to develop or improve inclusive practice in your context?

A wide range of needs: Who are these learners?

The British Dyslexia Association states that 'Dyslexia is a hidden disability thought to affect around 10% of the population, 4% severely' (BDA, 2015). If we accept this estimate, and given that dyslexia exists in all language groups, then it is likely to affect a similar proportion of EAL students entering FE and HE in the UK. As we have seen, within English national and local contexts, colleges and higher education institutions are welcoming a diverse group of learners with both dyslexia and EAL, many of whom have complex and highly individual needs. Some learners with EAL will have spent most of their lives in England and had a long history of education using English as the language of instruction, whilst others will have newly arrived in the country. Some will have studied English as a foreign language for varying parts of their educational career, whilst others will have had no grounding in English at all. Some will be literate in their own language (just as some learners with dyslexia will have achieved very high levels of literacy), whilst others will have had extreme difficulty acquiring literacy skills, because of their dyslexia or lack of educational opportunity. Some students may not realise that they have an underlying difficulty if their first language is highly transparent, and perhaps less difficult, for a learner with dyslexia. Others may be limited in their opportunities to practise because they speak English only outside the home. Outside their studies or workplaces, many of our students speak, hear, read and access television and digital media only in their mother tongue. Nevertheless, within this diverse group there are many for whom a rapid progression in English is essential for them to be able to transition from education to employment:

> Over the years I have taught many EAL students who have arrived in the country with good qualifications and experience, such as in teaching or engineering, but have been unable to continue their career because they struggle with English and they need to retake exams in England to be able to work at the same level.

> (Dyslexia support teacher in FE)

Diversity is a strength both in educational settings and within the workforce, and has been the basis of human development; indeed, it is an essential component of an inclusive society. Harnessing this, and providing the right conditions for people to prosper and grow should be the goal of educators at all levels. In the next section we consider some of the barriers which learners with dyslexia and EAL may encounter, and how relating these to their specific differences may help us to meet their needs.

DISCUSSION POINT

A specialist EAL language tutor was working with a student who was struggling to make progress in the 1:1 tutorials. She asked for guidance from the dyslexia specialist team on whether the student may have an underlying difficulty, and how she might broach the issue with the student, as he came from a country with a lot of prejudice around disability.

In your context, when an EAL student is having difficulties, which specialist team do you refer them to? Are there issues as to how you would broach this with a student, and how would you resolve these?

Dyslexia or EAL – underlying difficulties: What is the source of the challenges facing students – and does this really matter?

Distinguishing between predicted second language difficulties, and underlying specific learning challenges such as dyslexia, is likely to be a complex task (Smith, 2010). However, in order to offer focused and appropriate support, and to encourage self-directed and confident learning, it is important for both tutors and students with EAL and dyslexia to understand their learning preferences. All full diagnostic assessment reports and exploratory, informal assessment to inform teaching programmes for students with EAL and dyslexia, need to be underpinned by a detailed background interview which explores with the student their developmental, educational and cultural history.

In England, the Rose Report (Rose, 2009) on dyslexia proposed a complex working definition of dyslexia, which acknowledges a range of difficulties, beyond purely literacy, with a strong focus on phonological/verbal processing skills. It is generally accepted that Rose's proposed dyslexic profile covers a spectrum from mild to severe, and that no two learners will have exactly the same pattern of difficulties. In England, the 'discrepancy model', which based the identification of dyslexia on the contrast between a high level of demonstrable or apparent 'intelligence', compared to unexpected difficulties in literacy, has now been widely rejected. Current educational practice is in line with Rose (2009) who stated unequivocally that 'Dyslexia exists across a range of intellectual abilities' (Rose 2009, p. 29).

However, it has been argued (Mortimore *et al.*, 2012) that Rose's focus reflects some of the difficulties that the 'monolingual English speaking population' (Mortimore *et al.*, 2012, p. 18) could face, without sufficiently taking into account some of the wider difficulties students from the bilingual dyslexic population might experience. Generally, there has been a move towards definitions of dyslexia that encompass behavioural, cognitive, biological and environmental factors (Kormos and Smith, 2012), which is useful, particularly in light of the complexity of assessing and supporting multilingual students. In this multi-dimensional model of dyslexia, difficulties with aspects of language learning may be seen to be behavioural manifestations of underlying cognitive and neurological differences, within certain environments, such as the FE or HE learning classroom, lecture theatre or workshop (Kormos and Smith, 2012).

The acknowledgement of the role that the environment can play in either enabling or creating barriers for students with dyslexia, is particularly helpful for several reasons. Firstly, it moves away from the medical model of disability, where an individual with a physical impairment or learning difference is conceptualised as having a 'problem' that needs 'treatment'. Instead, there is a move towards the social model of disability (Oliver and Barnes, 2010) where the focus is moved away from the labelled individual, to the social, cultural or learning environment and ways in which this can be adjusted or changed to remove or reduce barriers to learning (Kormos and Smith, 2012). Secondly, such a shift in focus recognises that certain environments, such as classrooms and teaching styles which do not prioritise inclusive practice, can exacerbate dyslexic-type problems. This approach acknowledges that difficulties do not necessarily need to be an inevitable part of learning for students with dyslexia. As well as helping teachers and tutors feel empowered to make changes in their teaching practice, using the social model as a lens can also encourage assessors to probe into the educational background of students who are non-native English speakers, and prioritise an appraisal of how inclusive their learning environments are, before making judgements about the nature and severity of their dyslexia.

Some crucial environmental factors faced by students with dyslexia and EAL include the effects of stress, damaged self-esteem and fear of failure: these should be added as potential overlying barriers to learning. Both dyslexia and EAL can have a negative impact on academic achievement which is so highly valued in many societies and cultures. The possible risk of such affective difficulties is recognised as a universal barrier for learners with dyslexia, and increasingly common for any student working within the current achievement-driven agenda in England (Glazzard, 2014). For EAL students, additional stress and anxiety can be caused by homesickness and the steep learning curve that comes with moving country and culture. What some of these learners have left behind should never be underestimated:

> *I was gathering information to help build a profile of a Somali student in order to plan a teaching programme. While I was asking about her family history of learning profiles, I noticed that my student had started to weep silently – she had lost her children in the war and had had to leave her country without knowing if the rest of her family were alive or dead.*
>
> (FE Specialist Teacher)

Apart from these important emotional and affective factors, there are many more underlying barriers to learning, which specialist SpLD (Specific Learning Difficulties) tutors must unpack in order to offer effective support, which the following sections summarise in relation to post-compulsory education.

A web of underlying difficulties – Finding the right thread

For specialist teachers of either dyslexic or EAL students, it may be useful to consider the overlap of underlying difficulties which cause barriers to learning at FE and HE level. The focus of teaching can then be adjusted to support the individual student. Many of the behaviours for which students seek support can be explained by either their dyslexia or EAL, but appropriate interventions rely on specialists to unpack these factors with their students.

A new [EAL] student arrived at his first tutorial concerned that he didn't fully understand his lectures or the recommended reading. He found it extremely hard to know what to write down in lectures and how to select key points in his reading, as it all seemed relevant. He had recently been identified as having difficulties with his working memory and information processing speed, which were impacting on his literacy skills.

(HE SpLD Tutor)

This HE student's story shows how dyslexic difficulties were compromising his potential to gain the maximum from the learning opportunities offered by his institution. Higher-level skills involved in studies at this level nevertheless involve literacy. The 'spiky profile', showing inconsistencies and unexpected patterns of scores in assessment tasks, which trained dyslexia specialists are accustomed to seeing in their clients, can be exacerbated, and often masked, by EAL.

The following comment by an FE support tutor shows how layers of complex needs can overlap and need careful unravelling by tutors:

On the surface, my student experiences many of the difficulties associated with dyslexia, such as problems with punctuation, spelling, grammar, pronunciation of some sounds and reading for meanings, but many of these problems are exacerbated by the fact that he is also trying to learn a new language and new subjects that are taught in that language, at college/university level.

(FE Specialist Teacher)

Reading is, predictably, an essential part of academic work. In addition, the workload of reading for all students in vocational training is increasingly high, whether in the form of online media or traditional books. Reading comprehension of relevant texts is crucial, and learners with dyslexia and EAL may find this extremely challenging, as this tutor points out:

Many students with dyslexia struggle to read for meaning, but Learner X was faced with reading many words and phrases that he had never even heard of, let alone seen.

(FE Specialist Teacher)

Thus, the challenge of learning new vocabulary, both oral and written, becomes intensified for a learner with dyslexia who is also struggling with an unfamiliar language. Table 13.1, which is by no means comprehensive, summarises how reading skills can be affected by both dyslexia and EAL, and possible causal factors.

In HE and FE, despite some measurement of practical competences such as cooking skills or styling hair, much of the current system of assessment for learning, and for demonstrating knowledge in qualifications, is predicated on the efficient use of the English writing system. Students with SpLDs and, in some cases EAL, may be eligible to receive access arrangements (special dispensations in examinations, such as extra time), if their difficulties negatively impact upon their exam performance. Increasingly, students use computers to word-process work, both in coursework and exams. Voice recognition software is now extensively used by students with dyslexia to dictate their work into written documents. However, such aids may be less accessible to learners with dyslexia and EAL because computer dictation software can struggle with non-native English accents. Table 13.2 relates some of the underlying difficulties to the challenges of study at college and university level which support tutors must take into consideration when helping writing skills.

TABLE 13.1 Challenges to efficient reading in FE/HE contexts

Dyslexia: Possible underlying causes/difficulties	Challenges in FE/HE context	EAL: Possible underlying causes/difficulties
Decoding/reading individual words Visual processing	**Word level – reading and understanding words** *(Common words, technical and specialist vocabulary)*	Unfamiliar vocabulary Unfamiliar phonics/script Lack of accents on letters (e.g. ū)
Speed of processing Working memory Decoding/reading individual words Visual processing	**Reading and understanding texts** *(Books and e-books, manuals, web-based sources)*	Unfamiliar vocabulary Unfamiliar orthographic conventions/language structure Irregularity of English phonic conventions Dealing with figurative language
Speed of processing Working memory Word level reading/decoding Visual processing	**Speed of reading** *(Dealing with high volumes of reading for assignments, exam revision)*	All of the above difficulties plus use of dictionary likely to slow reader down

TABLE 13.2 Challenges to efficient writing in FE/HE contexts

Dyslexia: Possible underlying causes/difficulties	Challenges in FE/HE context	EAL: Possible underlying causes/difficulties
Phonological awareness/processing speech sounds Visual memory Matching speech sounds to letters: phonics	**Spelling** *(Essays, reports, assignments, work logs and diaries, exams)*	Unfamiliar vocabulary Different script/letter formation Direction of writing (left to right?) Different phonic expectations/spelling conventions
Sequencing	**Sentence construction** *(Essays, reports, assignments, work logs and diaries, exams)*	Syntax/word order different in home language Unfamiliar orthographic conventions Unfamiliar grammar
Sequencing Short-term/working memory	**Planning and structuring writing at text level** *(Essays, reports, assignments, literature reviews, exams)* **Proof reading** *(All of the above)*	All of the above, plus … Different academic writing conventions
Fine motor skills Visual processing Automaticity of writing	**Handwriting** *(All of the above plus note taking)*	Use of unfamiliar script Lack of practice
Retrieval of words from long-term memory	**Speed of production of written work** *(Note taking, written assignments, work logs and diaries, exams)*	Committing to memory and retrieving new vocabulary Different grammar

For tutors of EAL students, it may seem obvious that their students will rapidly have to develop a high level of oral language skills to thrive in English educational settings and workplaces. It is also important to be aware that research has shown that a history of speech and language difficulties has been associated with the development of dyslexic-type difficulties (Hulme and Snowling, 2009). Table 13.3 explores the requirements in oral language skills in post-compulsory settings and workplaces, and suggests how specific but varying underlying reasons may contribute to barriers to success.

The nature of vocational education and training, particularly in newer universities, may now involve oral discussion and presentation skills, both as integral to study and as a form of assessment. Although this may suit many students with dyslexia, with its move away from written assignments, other stresses may occur. The style of teaching and learning in England, with a high level of independent work required and an emphasis on self-direction, may also be unfamiliar to students from other cultures, as this tutor recounts:

> *He was struggling to adapt to a very different way of being taught and assessed over here. Much of the work that we did in those initial tutorials involved helping him to navigate his way around the UK HE education system.*

> (HE SpLD Tutor)

Students arriving from education systems that are very different to that in England are likely to need specific help developing study skills within this new context (Table 13.4).

TABLE 13.3 Challenges to efficient oral skills in FE/HE contexts

Dyslexia: Possible underlying causes/difficulties	Challenges in FE/HE context	EAL: Possible underlying causes/difficulties
Speed of processing phonological information (language sounds) Inaccurate phonological processing Attention and concentration difficulties linked to dyslexia Auditory working memory Speech and language difficulties may be linked to dyslexia profiles: receptive language	**Understanding spoken English** *(Following instructions, lectures, practical classes, discussions, oral exams, communicating when on work placements)*	Unfamiliar language structure Unfamiliar vocabulary Attending to key words Distinguishing regional accents Unfamiliar delivery of learning Unfamiliar intonation/word stress/emphasis
Self-confidence in group work Speed of retrieving phonological information Auditory working memory Retrieval of words from long-term memory (rapid naming) Speech and language difficulties may be linked to dyslexia profiles: expressive language	**Producing oral English** *(Discussions, giving presentations, tutorials, oral exams, responding to questioning, communicating when on work placements)*	Self-confidence in group work Memory overload Unfamiliar language structure Unfamiliar vocabulary Unfamiliar delivery of learning Unfamiliar assessment tasks requiring oral language Unfamiliar pronunciation Cultural background

TABLE 13.4 Challenges to efficient study skills in FE/HE contexts

Dyslexia: Possible underlying causes/difficulties	Challenges in FE/HE context	EAL: Possible underlying causes/difficulties
Speed of processing Retrieval of words from long-term memory (rapid naming) Language processing overload Challenges in multi-tasking, e.g. reading, note taking and listening at the same time	**Keeping attention and focus in formal classes** *(Lectures, classes)*	Cultural differences in expectations Difficulty in decoding oral English
Working memory Sequencing	**Time management and organisation** (*remembering books and equipment*)	Cultural differences Memory overload

This section has reflected on the barriers to learning faced by students with dyslexia/EAL; in the following section we examine some successful strategies which we propose as being particularly useful for dyslexia specialists and language tutors in enabling their students to reach their potential in an FE/HE context.

DISCUSSION POINT

Consider an EAL student with additional underlying difficulties known to you. Can you relate his or her support needs to Tables 13.1–13.4?

Make a list of his or her most challenging difficulties which are barriers to learning. Now map these to the tables and suggest how understanding these can help tutors make suggestions for changing the learning environment for this student and inform an effective support programme.

Effective specialist support in FE/HE

Effective support for learners in FE/HE puts high demands on specialists to be reflective, self-evaluating practitioners. The following section draws on practical examples which professionals have suggested as being particularly useful in support at this level.

Research, albeit largely involving school-age children, has shown that regular 1:1 or small-group support sessions, to back up inclusive classroom teaching, may be necessary for pupils with dyslexia to acquire literacy skills effectively (Brooks, 2013). It may be argued that this could also be applicable to post-compulsory settings where students with EAL may well need additional individualised support in order to cope with their mainstream course. EAL learners are, effectively, acquiring literacy competence again, but in a new language. Dyslexia specialists are likely to be well-versed in the practice of multisensory teaching, which has been strongly advocated as a methodology which can be effective for both learners with dyslexia and with EAL (Tudhope, 2014; Mann, 2013). It is also important to maintain the key features of effective dyslexia support by ensuring that learners are offered a structured and cumulative programme of learning. This teacher expresses disappointment at the lack of relevant research and literature in the field:

> *I have found teaching an EAL adult with dyslexia extremely challenging. Although there is a growing body of information on how the foreign language teacher can use dyslexia teaching principles (multisensory, structured teaching) within the language classroom, there is little information on how to adapt the typical multisensory structured spelling programmes to EAL students in a 1:1 situation.*
>
> (FE Trainee Specialist Teacher)

Employing trained specialists in both dyslexia and EAL, and allowing such tutors the time to communicate, offer advice, share good practice and do their own research into specific language and cultural backgrounds, seems to be essential given the increasingly diverse backgrounds of learners in FE/HE, discussed above. This specialist teacher recounts how this close collaboration enabled her to help her student:

> *I was approached by a language tutor who wanted some specialist advice as she was working with an EAL student who was making little progress with her spelling, punctuation and grammar in their 1:1 sessions. I helped her to develop strategies and resources (such as multisensory methods, modelling, over-learning etc., with a particular emphasis on metacognition) to help the student become a more reflective learner. These strategies made a huge difference to the speed at which the student understood the language rules that she was being taught and her ability to remember them in the next session: particularly the use of colour coding to distinguish between the different elements of a sentence.*
>
> (FE Specialist Teacher)

Understanding challenges linked to language structures

For students with EAL, it is essential to adapt elements of support to meet the needs of individuals. Not only should individual strengths and weaknesses be taken into account, as is always good practice for students with dyslexia, but supporters should pay particular attention to interference, when a student's knowledge of and skills in a first language impact on the acquisition of an additional language. The following tutor explains how her developing knowledge of a student's first language helped her to adjust her teaching:

> *After the first few lessons, it became apparent that he was experiencing great difficulty pronouncing certain sounds (the consonant blends that are typically hard for Farsi speakers, such as 'r' and 'l' blends). The pace that I had set for the phonics work was way too fast for this learner, and eventually we slowed the pace right down and just chose one or two blends to work on at a time.*
>
> (FE Specialist Teacher)

Identifying first language interference, may pose challenges to dyslexia-trained professionals, who should be encouraged to liaise with colleagues trained in EAL to access appropriate resources. It may be necessary for dyslexia supporters to expand their own knowledge of general grammatical principles alongside very specific references to a learner's home language, as this practitioner suggests:

My own knowledge of the English language grammar rules is just implicit, and this meant that I had no idea what terms like 'perfect present' meant. In practice, this made it difficult for me to understand my student's first language, and the particular interference problems that he might experience in English. I eventually had to abandon some grammar teaching as I felt totally out of my depth when faced with terms like auxiliary verbs!

(FE Specialist Teacher)

Underpinning independent learning by a focus on metacognition

Working with young people and adults who are responding to the day-to-day demands of their mainstream courses always involves a certain amount of negotiation. It is crucial to maintain the balance between offering immediate responses to help with assignments, which can easily lead to providing a proofreading service, rather than promoting the acquisition of skills leading to independent learning. An important element in learning support programmes at this level is a consciously metacognitive focus: that is to say, explicitly created opportunities for 'thinking about thinking'. For learners with dyslexia and EAL, understanding and appreciating their own learning and skills profile is vital, particularly as self-confidence may be undermined by the necessity of working with, and indeed competing against, other students for whom English is a mother-tongue language.

Building on these students' confidence may involve challenging discriminatory cultural stereotypes around the notion of 'disability' that they may have been exposed to in their country of origin, as the following example shows:

We planned an initial 'Dyslexia Awareness' session for some of the EAL groups ... specifically designed to help students begin to question some of the unhelpful labels and stereotypes around the concept of disability ... Firstly, it emphasised the difference between 'specific' and 'general' learning difficulties because some of the students in the EAL classes had been used to conflating them, which was exacerbating their reluctance to be labelled as 'disabled'. Secondly, it introduced the students to positive role models of people with dyslexia, including those who had achieved academic and economic success and people in the public eye that they may be aware of.

(FE Specialist Teacher)

During support sessions, explicit and focussed discussion on an individual's most effective learning strategies are very important. This must take into account the learning profile of the learner as well as the possible underlying difficulties outlined above. Some students will come from an educational background where the teaching style is formalised and didactic, and may never have explored their own learning profile. Evaluating the student's current profile in terms of strengths and difficulties, encompassing not only literacy attainment and study skills, but also personal preferences, can enable students to capitalise on their own learning strengths, as exemplified by this tutor:

Metacognition played a central role in the teaching programme, and was particularly important for Learner X to start taking an active role in his learning. This was largely because of his history of academic failure in his own country where didactic, repetitive, auditory methods of teaching were used, which resulted in him feeling disengaged from his learning. It was vital that we built in regular reflection of how he was learning, what was working and what was not, and to modify any strategies accordingly.

(FE Specialist Teacher)

The same tutor goes on to describe how the learner used a greater understanding of his own learning style to move on with confidence:

I felt it was important to get the student to reflect on what he was already doing in order to read for meaning, before suggesting other strategies. He had never really thought of how he read before, and this was the first step in him reflecting for himself that some of his strategies were passive and weren't working for him. This, in turn, helped him to attribute some of his reading difficulties down to poor reading strategies rather than just being inherently bad at reading.

(FE Specialist Teacher)

Another tutor, at university level, described how working together to produce and apply strategies to deal with making the most of lectures was crucial:

Ilir went from feeling disenfranchised from the UK HE education system, sitting in his lectures feeling confused and overwhelmed, to starting to feel like he was in control of his learning and that he could take an active part in it.

(HE SpLD Tutor)

Using concept mapping or schemas to frame learning

Another key strategy for preparing students to thrive in mainstream education is to develop their ability to create their own 'schemas' or 'concept maps' (Deponio *et al.*, 2000, p. 58). Schemas can be used to help students to relate new information to established knowledge, but also to organise information in a way that is meaningful to them. In many establishments lecture notes are provided in advance, and if this is not done systematically it can be requested for students with disabilities such as dyslexia. Tutors can then work with students to develop strategies for enhancing understanding in the lectures and other teaching sessions:

We started to work on strategies to develop his comprehension of his lectures, in advance, through developing very simple 'schemas', or concept maps to help him organise the information into meaningful groups, rather than relying on a linear note-taking system.

(HE SpLD Tutor)

The tutor goes on to describe in detail how she used this approach in a highly individualised way to build up learning strategies:

I explained that the lecture objectives are supposed to be a guide to help you know what you need to learn and the level, or depth you need to learn it. In the instances where the lecturer hadn't included objectives, we looked through the slides and surmised our own. These objectives then formed the basis for the design of our schema. For example, the objectives for one lecture indicated that there would be two key stages: a section on the possible causes of a health problem, and a comparison of different treatments/solutions. We created a schema with a chart so that Ilir could easily map out these comparisons according to theme and then add information from the slides before the lecture, in the lecture and then from his subsequent reading.

(HE SpLD Tutor)

It can be extremely useful to engage the learner in conceptualising information by relating the contents of their studies to pre-existing knowledge, either from previous qualifications in another language, or workplace experience. The following example shows how this can be applied in practice:

I encouraged him to reflect on this material and draw upon his previous experience as a medical practitioner in Kosovo in order to evaluate it: Which of the treatments did he think were the most effective and why? If there were any unfamiliar concepts/words, he looked them up using a dictionary application, and would use a pronunciation application if he needed to rehearse this.

(HE SpLD Tutor)

Finally, this tutor relates how this approach transformed the student's learning experience:

Although Ilir initially struggled to create these schemas independently, he went to his lecture knowing what was going to be covered, how it was going to be structured and he had a system for putting pieces of information into meaningful categories. As we had also discussed some of the content verbally prior to the lecture and related it to his previous experience, he also felt more engaged in his learning: sometimes feeling passionate about a particular view or theory. It was much easier for him to select key points in his reading for lectures, because if it didn't relate directly to the lecture objective, he didn't need to note it down. Because of his pre-lecture preparation, he was familiar with the key vocabulary and the key concepts used, leading to an increase in his comprehension.

(HE SpLD Tutor)

Conclusion: Moving forward

- In the context of increasing cultural diversity, FE/HE institutions should be aware of the needs of students with both dyslexia and EAL, and ensure that resources are in place to support them.
- Many of the practical difficulties and barriers to learning which these students may experience can be linked to both dyslexia and EAL characteristics and underlying difficulties. Both mainstream and specialist tutors, and the students themselves, can benefit from understanding these multi-dimensional learning preferences.
- Communication between EAL and specialist SpLD tutors/teachers is needed to access specialist skills and knowledge.
- Joint training opportunities for tutors from both EAL and dyslexia communities and backgrounds are needed.
- Further research focussing on young people and adults with dyslexia/EAL in post-compulsory education is needed to expand a body of literature highlighting evidence-based good practice in FE/HE.

Acknowledgements

With thanks to the following students and teachers who have generously shared their stories and experiences with us: Jo Coley, Kate Connery, Dr Alan Dunbar, Julie Holmes, Mark Hurdus, Dr Alice Lawrence, Victoria Mann, Jean Matthews, Mehrdad Siahpoush and Christine Webb.

Further reading

Everatt, J. (2012) *Dyslexia, languages and multilingualism*. Bracknell: British Dyslexia Association.
   This short book contains some useful chapters outlining the particular challenges that the English language can pose to EAL learners with dyslexia. Professor Ian Smyth has also written a chapter on how assistive and adaptive technology can be used effectively with this group of learners.

Kormos, J. and Smith, A.M. (2012) *Teaching languages to students with specific learning differences*. Bristol: Multilingual Matters.
   Although not specifically written for HE/FE practitioners, this is a fantastic guide to understanding some of the key principles involved in effectively identifying and supporting students with EAL and dyslexia.

Pavey, B., Meehan, M. and Waugh, A. (2010) *Dyslexia-friendly further and higher education*. London: Sage.
   A practical and useful guide for professionals working in FE and HE environments.

Swan, M. and Smith, B. (2001) *Learner English: A teacher's guide to interference and other problems* (2nd ed.). Cambridge: Cambridge University Press.
   An invaluable resource for practitioners who are interested in distinguishing between expected and unexpected literacy difficulties of learners from particular language backgrounds learning English.

Useful websites

British Dyslexia Association (BDA): www.bdadyslexia.org.uk
National Association for Language Development in the Curriculum (NALDIC): www.naldic.org.uk

References

BDA (British Dyslexia Association) (2015) *What are specific learning difficulties?* Available online: www.bdadyslexia.org.uk/educator/what-are-specific-learning-difficulties (accessed 24 April 2015).

Bell, S. (2010) Inclusion for adults with dyslexia: examining the transition periods of a group of adults in England: 'Clever is when you have come to a brick wall and you have got to get over it without a ladder'. *Journal of Research into Special Educational Needs* 10(3) 216–226.

Bell, S. and McLean, B. (2011) Good practice in training specialist teachers and assessors for people with dyslexia. In Peer, L and Reid, G. (eds) *Special educational needs: A guide for inclusive practice*. London: Sage Publications, pp. 127–140.

Brooks, G. (2013) *What works for children and young people with literacy difficulties? The effectiveness of intervention schemes* (4th ed.). London: SpLD Trust.

Department for Business, Innovation and Skills (2013) *International education: Global growth and prosperity*. London: HM Government.

Department for Education and Department of Health (2014) *Special educational needs and disability code of practice: 0 to 25 years*. London: DfE.

Deponio, P., Landon, J., Mullin, K. and Reid, G. (2000) Dyslexia and bilingualism – implications for assessment, teaching and learning. In Peer, L. and Reid, G. (Eds) *Multilingualism, literacy and dyslexia: A challenge for educators*. London: David Fulton Publishers. pp. 52–69.

Glazzard, J. (2014) The standards agenda: reflections of a special educational needs co-ordinator. *Support for Learning* 29(1) 39–53.

Hulme, C. and Snowling, M.J. (2009) *Developmental disorders of language learning and cognition.* Chichester: Wiley-Blackwell.

Kormos, J. and Smith, A.M. (2012) *Teaching languages to students with specific learning differences.* Bristol: Multilingual Matters.

Mann, V. (2013) Dyslexia and international students: supporting international students with dyslexia in English for academic purposes. *Inform* 11, 9–11.

Mortimore, T., Hansen, L., Hutchings, M., Northcote, A., Fernando, J., Horobin, L., Saunders, K. and Everatt, J. (2012) *Dyslexia and multilingualism: Identifying and supporting bilingual learners who might be at risk of developing SpLD/dyslexia.* British Dyslexia Association and the Lottery Fund.

OECD (2015) Policy context for employment and skills in England. *Employment and skills strategies in England.* OECD Publishing. doi: 10.1787/9789264228078-en

Office of National Statistics (2015) Migration Statistics Quarterly Report, February 2015. Available online: www.ons.gov.uk/ons/rel/migration1/migration-statistics-quarterly-report/february-2015/stb-msqr-feb-2015.html#tab-1--Net-migration-to-the-UK (accessed 3 April 2015).

Oliver, M. and Barnes, C. (2010) Disability studies, disabled people and the struggle for inclusion. *British Journal of Sociology of Education* 31(5) 547–560.

Rose, J. (2009) *Identifying and teaching children and young people with dyslexia and literacy difficulties.* London, Department for Children, Schools and Families.

Smith, A.M. (2010) Adapting assessment procedures for learners with different first languages. *PATOSS Bulletin* 23 37–42.

Tudhope, E. (2014) How can dyslexia negatively impact upon acquiring English as an additional language and what can dyslexia/SpLD tutors do to address these issues? *PATOSS Bulletin* 27 9–12.

Ziegler, J.C. and Goswami, U. (2005) Reading acquisition, developmental dyslexia and skilled reading across languages: A psycholinguistic grain size theory. *Psychological Bulletin* 131(1) 3–29.

14

TWO BILINGUAL CASE STUDIES FROM A SPECIALIST DYSLEXIA PRACTITIONER'S PERSPECTIVE

Working in Germany

Maya Jakubowicz

This chapter will:

1. Provide the reader with examples of some of the difficulties bi/multilingual dyslexic learners face in the classroom
2. Look at the emotional needs of such learners
3. Identify some of the issues that need considering within schools as to how such learners are appropriately supported

Context

As a trilingual dyslexia specialist practitioner and trained TEFL (Teaching English as a Foreign Language) teacher working in English within the independent international sector in Germany, I have frequently observed the academic, social, emotional and often cultural challenges that many dyslexic children and adolescents face. I find that specific background difficulties in learning and curriculum access regularly relate to issues such as slow processing, weak phonological skills and working memory, delayed early language development and weak higher-order language skills, as well as cultural differences. Another problem is that there is a dearth of dyslexia trained and qualified educators working in English.

I am further aware of a lack of understanding of the concept of dyslexia by some educators and parents – as well as the concern voiced by certain parents that if dyslexia is diagnosed, some may believe that their child is of low cognitive ability and 'give up' on them. Having lived in Germany for seven years, my experience is that dyslexia may not be as well understood or accepted here as it is in the UK or USA – especially within the independent sector.

The German vs English language

German has a 'semi-transparent orthography'; such languages are characterised somewhere between shallow and deep orthographies. English has a somewhat more complex and less predictable set of rules, which contributes to the challenges experienced by German dyslexic learners studying in English as an additional/foreign language. I have also observed that it can be a significant struggle for more severely dyslexic native English speaking learners when trying to acquire and effectively use the German language. The overload on working memory and processing in dyslexic learners is significant – perhaps more so in bi/multilinguals than in monolinguals.

Special needs in Germany

Germany forbids discrimination on the basis of physical or mental disability. The German Social Welfare Code IX (SGBIX) (2001) is based upon the premise of equal opportunity and participation.

Germany's education system is decentralised and as a result each federal state manages children with special needs in slightly different ways. Since 2000, federal states have applied a joint definition of special educational needs (SEN), with a distinction between permanent disability and temporary learning difficulties (e.g. slow learners or those with literacy difficulties). However, due to a federal harmonisation agreement on SEN, the principles of support for children experiencing difficulties during the learning process and of integration with mainstream education wherever possible are the same nationally.

Dyslexia – State primary schools are required to employ one specially trained teacher to recognise and support children with dyslexia; that teacher works closely with school psychologists. In some cases a specialist learning programme may be designed; examination provisions may be made available for those with more severe needs. This structure is not necessarily the same within the independent sector.

Case studies

I set out two case studies below written from a practitioner's perspective. The children's names and schools have been changed.

Case 1 – Tobias

Tobias was aged 8 years 7 months at his first assessment and 9 years 5 months at his review. He was referred for assessment and specialist teaching by his class teacher who had observed his ongoing challenges within the mainstream English speaking classroom.

Background

Tobias is a German born bilingual German/English student; his mother tongue is German. His parents report a family history of challenge related to literacy learning.

Medical history

Tobias was a full-term baby; no problems were evident during the pregnancy or at birth. He wears glasses for both close and distance work throughout the school day. There is no history of difficulties related to ear infections or to loss of hearing. He eats and sleeps well and is considered to be healthy.

Language of learning

Tobias attends an English speaking school where no instruction is given in any language other than English – with the exception of German language lessons. The majority of his classmates speak English, some more fluently than others. His school has a large proportion of native German speaking students learning English as a Second or Foreign Language; there are a lesser number of British or American native English speakers who are required to learn German as an additional language. All students are required to partake in German lessons irrespective of their mother tongue.

He has been regularly exposed to both written and spoken German and does not struggle as much in German lessons as he does in all other lessons conducted in English. Although he reads better and more accurately in German than he does in English, his spelling is only marginally better in German.

Reasons for referral

Tobias was referred for assessment and specialist dyslexia teaching by his new classroom teacher some six weeks into the beginning of the academic year. The teacher observed that he was struggling to grasp what was being taught, could not recall information and struggled to follow class routines. The significance of his lack of academic progress quickly became evident to her when she reviewed his written work, tests and tasks – most of which were poor and incomplete. Furthermore, she observed that he was easily distracted by other students and had difficulty maintaining focus. He had been struggling academically for at least two years.

He had received no specialist tutoring either in or out of school prior to my intervention. His class teacher requested guidance on the type of support she could give him across the curriculum, pointing out that she was willing to make changes in classroom management in order to meet his needs.

Observations in class

In German language lessons, Tobias struggled less with word pronunciation and had a larger vocabulary from which to work than he did in English lessons. Simplified spoken English enabled him to cope better, as it helped avoid a vast amount of auditory information being missed, especially as he was too embarrassed to ask questions. It was noticeable that he struggled to start pieces of work.

During my initial observation it quickly became clear that copying from the board was a serious struggle for Tobias; he spent much time staring at the board and the wall doing very little work. He was unable to copy at any speed without constantly looking up and down between the board and his page, copying no more than three letters at once; he often lost his place, as a result of which he copied the wrong letters making his work incomprehensible.

A right-handed boy, he held the pen tightly and wrote in an awkward manner. He pressed down hard on the paper adding pressure to his hand; he shook it often to release the tension. He frequently erased his work, appearing very concerned about being seen to make mistakes.

When the teacher set tasks he kept moving on his chair and looking around the room; maintaining focus was a further compounding problem. I noted that one task, due to take no more than 10 minutes, took him 25 minutes – and then he gave up. He had managed to write only a small amount with so many spelling errors that it was difficult to understand.

Additional to this already challenging task was the fact that he was not familiar with much of the English language vocabulary with which he was presented. Compounded by his second language learning difficulties, this dyslexic child faced increased pressure upon his language skills, visual perceptual skills, working memory and processing skills.

Following on from the observation, a formal specialist teacher assessment was undertaken. Additionally, interviews with staff were conducted and a thorough review of information from home and from school was undertaken.

Classroom recommendations were initially made in relation to classroom management, visual perception, repetition, simplification of language, instruction with the use of visuals and the provision of fiddle toys. However, it soon became evident that these modifications alone were insufficient to meet his needs. At the end of the assessment process, an individual multisensory and cumulative programme was prepared, comprising both short- and long-term plans, as well as further and more individualised specific guidance for the class teacher who was the one who would be with him for the majority of his time at school.

Initial formal testing

Spelling

The Graded Word Spelling Test indicated that his spelling age was more than three years below his chronological age. When writing the alphabet sequence, the letter 'j' was written as 'y' – possibly German–English letter–sound confusion. Letters were clearly written; and 'b', 'd' and 'z' were correctly sounded when spoken, however they were written in reverse. Tobias additionally displayed sequencing and organisational difficulties.

Phonological skills

Tobias's phonological awareness was tested using the Phonological Awareness Skills Test. Weak skills were evident in rhyme production, phoneme isolation of final sounds, phoneme blending, phoneme deletion of the first sound in consonant blends, and phoneme deletion of initial sounds in consonant blends. However, concepts of the spoken word, rhyme recognition, syllable blending, syllable segmentation, syllable deletion, phoneme isolation of initial sound, phoneme segmentation, phoneme deletion of final sounds and phoneme substitution proved to be better.

He scored at a low level in the Rapid Naming section of the Comprehensive Test of Phonological Awareness. Like in many other dyslexic students, a relationship existed between poor rapid naming ability and reading difficulties, which in his case was compounded by the need to learn in a second language. His phonological awareness weaknesses were likely to have been impacted by sequential and working memory difficulties. These in turn will have impacted upon his grammatical and vocabulary development.

Reading

The Alpha to Omega reading placement test had to be discontinued as he was working at such a low level. Tobias attempted to decode and guess at letters and words when he was unsure. Letter pronunciation weaknesses caused him further difficulties, making the process of decoding and word building harder for him, causing him more stress. Scores indicated that teaching of reading would need to be preceded by the basic prerequisites for learning and development of oral language skills in English.

Writing

A timed free writing exercise was set. His script was laboured and slow, and he struggled to commit his thoughts to paper. Mistakes were again made with the letters 'j' and 'y' – possibly a German–English letter–sound confusion. Tobias's written words per minute count was low, indicating that he should be given extra time both in classroom tests and examinations, to allow him to undertake the task more successfully.

Organisational skills

Tobias showed visible signs of distress when he could not find his books on the initial day I observed him in class. I was informed that this difficulty extended to items such as his pencil case, slippers, flask, etc. He apparently became very upset when his bag was hidden behind the other children's school bags. He liked his things labelled so that he knew they were his; he enjoyed making labels for his possessions in school.

I was informed that any break from his daily routine was so distressing that 'he can remain upset for hours'. On the couple of occasions when our 1:1 lessons had to be moved, he was so distraught that he did not manage to function effectively in school for the following two lessons. Familiar and consistent sequences in events were essential for him. He struggled to cope with general classroom routines, as they seemed to place him outside his comfort zone.

Recalling information was a challenge made even more difficult by having to complete tasks and respond in a language that did not come naturally to him. Tobias was clearly challenged by dyslexia – and other possible emerging learning difficulties. This was made harder for him by being placed within a bilingual learning environment.

Intervention plan

There were many gaps in his knowledge which needed closing and he did not have a secure foundation on which to build; without a strong foundation he seemed unable to progress. As Schneider and Crombie (2003) noted, 'Without explicit instruction, the student will likely remain unsuccessful. However, being shown and given plenty of opportunities to practice he will be able to utilise the given strategies successfully'.

He was provided with twice-weekly 50 minute withdrawal lessons on a 1:1 basis for the academic year. Work was initially carried out to develop basic verbal vocabulary and grammar in English; this gave him confidence. The written language programme taught was structured, cumulative and multisensory and targeted the development of reading, reading comprehension, spelling and writing. We worked on decoding strategies for reading, sound awareness skills and sight word recognition as well as single syllable words and the importance of the closed syllable/short vowel, open syllable/long vowel. Recognition of beginning and ending sounds, working memory, listening comprehension skills, fine motor skills, sequential and organisational skills were all targeted. Even when he began to make progress, it was observed that his slow writing speed was affecting his learning, as he was physically unable to keep up with written work in class.

Providing opportunities for overlearning and repetition were essential for Tobias's ability to learn and progress. Having used this methodology continuously has helped him learn, and additionally boosted his self-confidence when approaching new work.

Although ways to help him academically were needed, it soon became evident that emotionally he needed support too. He was very aware of his challenges and frustrations when despite his best efforts he knew that he was significantly underachieving. He assumed that he was 'stupid'. Significant amounts of work were carried out to help raise his self-esteem, confidence and resilience, as well as motivation.

I liaised with the class teacher to ensure that strategies used in 1:1 sessions were reinforced within the classroom. As well as a high level of differentiated work, we went as far as working together to ensure that only the spelling rules taught in his 1:1 sessions were the ones corrected across the curriculum; this served to aid reinforcement of his work and his self-esteem. Study skills were essential for Tobias as they are for other dyslexic children – particularly for a dyslexic child trying to cope with studying in a second language.

Tobias always completed work set for him, both at school and at home. His parents and I met on a couple of occasions in order to discuss homework strategies and learning games, e.g. breaking work down into smaller more manageable chunks, paired reading, games to train his memory and writing tasks. His parents complied completely with the programme prepared for them, including supporting holiday work. He enjoyed our lessons greatly and made significant progress.

He was authorised test and examination provisions so that he had the chance to best present what he knew. Teachers were encouraged to help him take leadership roles and compliment him on the work he did well. A personal log was kept in order to demonstrate progress. Careful monitoring of progress in all aspects of academic, social and emotional functioning was organised.

Conclusions

When I first met Tobias he did not believe in himself; this extreme lack of self-confidence affected him emotionally, socially and academically. Shortly after we began working together he started to feel more confident and positive, as with each step of progress he felt a sense of achievement. This resulted in a significant change in emotional wellbeing and attitude towards learning, both in his 1:1 lessons and in the mainstream classroom. His extreme fear of failure slowly dissipated until he became more receptive to new challenges and was willing to take chances.

He now makes good use of capital letters and his handwriting has become clearer. Writing tasks can still challenge him as he finds it hard to get his ideas onto paper and his performance is still slow. When he now reads his work out loud, he notices that he has omitted some words and is often able to self-correct. He can now verbally explain his work well in English which pleases him.

Although a disparity of ability still exists between his spoken and written language, after a few months of 1:1 lessons, his classroom teacher commented that not only had he managed to complete tasks successfully (albeit with extra time) but he had been able to read back and discuss his work. She and he were both overjoyed!

We all worked as one unit to support Tobias – parents, school, specialist teacher and of course Tobias himself. It was essential that he learned to see his strengths and not focus upon his weaknesses in language and learning; he learned that he could capitalise upon his strengths. As his confidence and skills improved, so his ability to succeed increased.

Referrals

Tobias made good progress but it was relatively slow, and the gap between him and his peers continued to widen.

- He was referred to an educational psychologist for an in-depth assessment of his wide range of academic, social and emotional needs.
- He was referred to an occupational therapist to investigate his motor skills and visual perceptual needs as well as to investigate his sensory needs.
- Referral to a paediatrician was also discussed with his family.

Case 2 – Andrew

Background

Andrew is a 10-year-old native English speaker whose father is German. There is dyslexia in the family. At the time the initial tests were carried out, he was 9 years 1 month old; he was then assessed by an educational psychologist. Although he has been exposed to German since birth as one parent is German, he has little ability to use that language. He studies in a mainstream classroom; no special provisions have been implemented and prior to my intervention, he had received no additional tuition.

Medical history

Andrew was a full-term baby; no problems were evident during the pregnancy or at the birth. Although he suffers from allergies, he is considered to be healthy. He has a history of ongoing ear infections and had glue ear as a young child; bilateral grommets were inserted. Fluctuating hearing in his early years caused difficulties with the development of spoken language. He wears glasses; without them he cannot read at either close or long distance.

Reasons for referral

Andrew was referred to me as he had been lagging in class academically and socially. It was reported by his teachers that he often struggled during lesson times and had not made as much progress as expected. His German language tutor noted that German was taught as Andrew's additional language. He had been held back in the German Beginner's class at school with younger children for two years with no possibility of being moved up into the Intermediate class, due to lack of progress. His class teachers observed that he was struggling with all of writing, spelling and languages.

There was no specialist dyslexia teacher at his school prior to my arrival. No previous referral had been made, despite significant concerns. He was not able to cope with being taught a second language. When I first met him, he told me that he was beginning to hate school and almost everything was getting too hard.

Observation – German medium

In German language lessons, Andrew struggled with all that was presented to him. He was unable to retrieve spoken words successfully and was not able to participate in the written tasks, as he did not understand what was expected of him. He could not hold a basic conversation in German. Pronunciation was also difficult for him.

During my initial observation it quickly became clear that copying from the board was a serious effort for him; he was unable to copy at any speed. He struggled to both decipher and remember the written word and retain it for a sufficient length of time to allow him to commit the information correctly into his book.

He generally had little understanding of what was expected of him. Andrew began to disrupt classes and became argumentative with his teacher a few minutes into lessons. He was clearly distressed, likely due to his lack of familiarity with the German language. He was fully aware that he could not fulfil expectations. He had a far greater vocabulary in English than in German and in that language could verbally present his thoughts well. He was teased by his classmates when he could not keep up.

Observation – English medium

Andrew tried hard and clearly enjoyed the creative part of the lesson. He was required to draw, which he did precisely and with absolute clarity; his drawing was creative and detailed, and at a higher level than that of the other children in his group of four.

He was quiet and accepted encouragement by the three girls in his group. He verbally expressed his thoughts well but could not do so in writing. A left-handed boy, he held the pen awkwardly and pressed very hard on the paper. He regularly tried to hide his work from his peers. During a task, whilst using a personal white board he wrote and then wiped off all his work whilst the rest of the group kept theirs on the table face upwards so that they could see each other's answers; he seemed embarrassed to show his work.

Andrew wore glasses and placed his face very close to the paper when writing and drawing; his posture was awkward. He was unable to sit still and often leaned on the table to play with his pen during set tasks. One task related to a story on which the class had been working; he seemed to have forgotten the discussion point set and required regular prompting. It appeared that he could neither remember nor cope with the work. At 15 minutes into the lesson, Andrew had lost all focus and interest and sat playing with a sponge.

Formal testing

Following on from the observations, a formal specialist teacher assessment was carried out. Additionally interviews with staff were conducted and a thorough review of information from home and from school was undertaken.

Spelling

The Graded Word Spelling Test indicated that Andrew's spelling age was two years six months below his chronological age. He attempted to write words according to the sounds he was familiar with, but found this challenging. His phonological awareness skills were weak. Andrew was confused by the 'j' and 'y' sounds, and 'sh' in English was written 'sch' as in German. The different sounds 'apt' and 'ept' (as in the word 'except') were confused when he wrote. The use of the 'silent h' was unknown to him (e.g. 'honest'). His knowledge of the short and long vowels was insecure and he did not understand that, e.g., the same vowel sound can be represented by different letters. Although German and English have some similarities, dyslexic learners find lengthy words and sentence structures very challenging.

Phonological skills

Andrew's phonological awareness was tested using the Comprehensive Test of Phonological Processing (CTOPP – 2). Results indicated that Andrew's phonological awareness skills were poor. He scored at a particularly low level in the Rapid Naming section. Dyslexics often have poor working memory; this can heavily impact upon phonics acquisition; this can also be related to the former presence of glue ear (Peer, 2005). This weakness will affect both spelling and reading and so will affect the student's performance at school.

Reading

An assessment of basic literacy skills was undertaken using the Neale Analysis of Reading Ability, 2nd Revised edition (NARA–II). He scored at a level which was between two and three years behind his chronological age for comprehension and accuracy. Speed of reading was also slow. The Alpha to Omega placement test indicated that Andrew should begin at stage one in order to cement grammatical structures and basic literacy skills.

Free writing

Andrew was given five minutes to write about a topic of his choice; he asked if he could continue once the time was up as he wanted to finish his sentence. He omitted and confused a great number of words, and when reading back he realised that what he had written was not matching what he was telling me.

He could not decipher the difference between the sounds 'b', 'd' and 'g' clearly and therefore had a problem spelling words which included these sounds. This may well be the result of a previous fluctuating hearing problem such as glue ear; processing and working memory appeared to be affected too.

Social skills

Andrew experienced difficulties in the playground. He found it hard to play with the other children as he could not follow and remember the rules of games. As time went on, he was invited to play with them less and less, both at school and at home; this led to greater isolation from his peers.

Organisational skills

He was very particular about the order in which his pens and pencils were kept in his pencil case. He became anxious if each pen was not inserted correctly into its 'right place'. He struggled to recall his school timetable and bring the right books to class. He was forgetful and had been perceived by staff as 'lazy' and 'disinterested'. As many teachers do not have knowledge of dyslexia, frequently these children are unfairly treated as their difficulties are misunderstood. The more stressed and disorganised he was the angrier he became; this often led to screaming and shouting at home and temper tantrums both at home and school. The frustration level felt by many dyslexic learners in school is high.

He tried hard to follow the general classroom routines but struggled to recall them all which caused him added anxiety. When he did successfully recall a routine, he looked visibly pleased with himself.

Andrew was clearly challenged not only by the difficulties of dyslexia and other possible comorbid difficulties, but even more so by learning within a bilingual environment. Recalling information was already a challenge due to his dyslexia, made even more difficult by having to carry things out and respond in a language that did not come naturally to him.

He also struggled to understand and cope with the emotions he faced, which were further affected by bullying and isolation which further knocked his confidence; this placed further strain on his already weak ability to maintain friendships.

Intervention plan

Many gaps needed filling as so much of his knowledge was insecure. He needed opportunities for overlearning alongside visual input so that information could move into long-term memory; repetition and revision were essential for successful outcomes. Work was done on spoken language to develop his basic knowledge and skills; this also gave him confidence.

Andrew did not have the benefit of early intervention. He was provided with twice-weekly 50 minute withdrawal lessons on a 1:1 basis for the academic year. The programme taught was structured, cumulative and multisensory and targeted the development of reading, reading comprehension, spelling and writing. Opportunities for overlearning and repetition were essential to Andrew's ability to learn, progress and increase his confidence when approaching new work or working further in-depth on existing work. It was important to also work on manual dexterity, fine motor skills and sequencing, auditory and visual memory, sound segmentation, omission and reversals of letters, pronunciation of letters and words. Emotional wellbeing and social interaction were high on the school's agenda. Ongoing support was provided to try and improve confidence, self-esteem and resiliency.

Conclusion

Andrew recognised that he had been failing since he started school. It was evident when I met him that he lacked self-confidence. Lack of self-esteem impacted upon him emotionally, socially and educationally. He had few coping strategies which led to frequent anger and tears at home and at school. He had been excluded by many of his peers; some of whom bullied him.

Initially, on a few occasions when he forgot to bring his homework he would tell me that it had never been set. It transpired that many arguments at home had taken place over misplaced books and incomplete schoolwork. When we looked through the homework book together, it was often the case that he had done it but then erased it as he believed it was wrong. When I told him he had done a great job he would retrace/write over his work and smile with relief. The constant erasing greatly subsided after we had worked together for a few weeks.

Andrew enjoyed our work together and soon began to feel more confident and positive, as with each lesson he felt a sense of achievement. This was reflected within the mainstream classroom too.

His handwriting became clearer and more precise, although he still found it hard to complete a written task; he was eventually able to read back what he had written with more clarity. He has learnt to better express his ideas. Writing tasks can still challenge him as he finds it hard to get his ideas onto paper; his performance is still slow. When he now reads his work out loud, he does so with more confidence; he takes pride in his work. He still gets very upset if he has misunderstood what has been asked of him, but his responses have become less extreme. Although a disparity of ability still exists between his spoken and written language, after a few months of 1:1 lessons, his classroom teacher commented that he had become less aggressive and withdrawn.

Andrew was so distressed, sad, fed up and confused when we first met; he had no understanding of himself at that time. Parents and staff worked together with him to help him overcome many of his difficulties related to language and learning. It was essential that all staff who came into contact with him understood his difficulties and adapted to meet his needs. As his confidence improved, his ability to succeed increased.

The lack of early intervention following early glue ear and loss of hearing had a significant negative impact upon his schooling until specialist help was received and better understanding was in place.

Referrals

- Andrew was referred to an educational psychologist who confirmed dyslexia and set out his strengths and weaknesses as well as a plan of action.
- A further hearing test was recommended because of sound confusion.
- Andrew's emotional needs were such that he needed some sessions with a psychologist; referral was made.
- Occupational therapy was recommended due to difficulties with the physical side of handwriting.

Conclusion

In bi/multilingual dyslexic children, academic, social, emotional and cultural factors all need to be considered. The impact of being bilingual, studying in a second language and attempting to cope with dyslexia is hefty. Often these children have not been identified before I see them, and they arrive in my room with their 'baggage' of low expectation, frustration and sometimes anger. They certainly do not understand themselves.

The challenges of learning in a bilingual environment and being dyslexic are great – even with additional 1:1 specialist teaching sessions. The day to day learning problems that dyslexic learners face are countless, and if appropriate intervention is not made, the student is highly likely to significantly underachieve. Early intervention is the key to success. This requires schools to ensure that teachers are informed, trained and have key people to whom to turn. Classroom teachers need more training to support these children within mainstream classrooms, both when they are receiving specialist teaching and when they are not.

The children I have worked with have all struggled to varying degrees with a lack of confidence and poor self-esteem. It is essential to care for the emotional wellbeing of a child with dyslexia, as they are vulnerable; a child who does not believe in himself will not succeed. The emotional impact will bear upon educational and social functioning too. The earlier the intervention, the better the outcomes are likely to be. Teachers, specialists, parents and the child ideally should work together.

It is essential that teachers are aware of the potential negative impact the classroom can have on a bi/multilingual child with dyslexia if they are not handled with skill and understanding. There must be sensitivity in how comments are phrased and demands made. Often, many such learners are requested to carry out tasks they could not possibly fulfil in their mother tongue, let alone in a second or third language. A child's strengths should be given much praise and the focus should be shifted away from the areas of difficulties, whilst specialists develop these skills. Feelings of failure easily spiral upward, and unless dealt with, may have a negative impact for life.

If school policies were encouraging of appropriate early intervention, fewer students would suffer, behaviour would be better and achievement would be greater. Likewise, if teachers received more support, they too would be able to make a bigger difference in the classroom for the struggling student. If a school does not have a specialist dyslexia teacher on site, then consideration should be given to training current staff.

When class teachers have a clearer understanding of the difficulties a dyslexic child faces daily in the classroom, less focus is placed upon the child's behaviour so that much stress and misunderstanding is avoided. With increased understanding of these difficulties, a more positive, calm and accepting environment is created which will help the dyslexic child feel less vulnerable and more successful. A teacher who understands the ongoing challenges faced as a result of dyslexia can create 'dyslexia friendly' classrooms. On a 1:1 basis, multisensory, cumulative, structured and targeted teaching and language development is most helpful for dyslexic learners.

We still have a lot to learn with regards to bilingual and dyslexia education. We should remember the now well-known quotation from Dr Harry Chasty (former Director of the Dyslexia Institute, UK, and psychologist) who said, 'If this child doesn't learn the way we teach, can we teach him the way he learns, and, can we then extend his range of learning options?'.

Bibliography

Alexander-Passe, N. (2013) Researching the emotional side to dyslexia: Dyslexia and self-esteem. www.dyslexia-research.com/page28.html

Berninger, V.W., Abbott, R.D., Swanson, H.L., Lovitt, D., Trevadi, P., Lin, S.J., *et al.* (2010) Relationship of word- and sentence-level working memory to reading and writing in second, fourth, and sixth grade. *Language, Speech, and Hearing Services in Schools*, 41, 179–193.

British Dyslexia Association. *Identifying and supporting bilingual learners with SpLD*. www.bdadyslexia.org. uk/common/ckeditor/filemanager/userfiles/About_Us/Projects/Big_Lottery_Research_Report_ Final_Version.pdf

Brooks, G. (2002) *What Works for Children with Literacy Difficulties? The effectiveness of intervention schemes*. DfES Research Report RR380.

Chasty, H. (1997) Meeting the challenges of specific learning difficulties, in *Children's Difficulties in Reading, Spelling and Writing*, Pumfrey, P. and Elliott, C. (Eds). London: Falmer, p. 269.

Crombie M. (1999) *Foreign Language Learning and Dyslexia*. www.languageswithoutlimits.co.uk/resources/Dxa1.pdf

Crumpler, M., Vernon, P. and McCarthy, C. (2006) *Graded Word Spelling Test*, 3rd edition, London: Hodder Education.

Csizér, K., Kormos, J. and Sarkadi, Á. (2010) The dynamics of language learning attitudes and motivation: lessons from an interview study of dyslexic language learners. *The Modern Language Journal*, 94, 470–487.

Cummins, J. (1984) *Bilingualism and Special Education*. Clevedon: Multilingual Matters.

Dowrick, P.W., and Yuen, J.W.L. (2006) Literacy for the community, by the community. *Journal of Prevention and Intervention in the Community*, 32, 81–96.

Draffan, E.A. (Ed.) (2012) *Dyslexia and Useful Technology*. Bracknell: British Dyslexia Association.

Edwards, L. (2003) Writing instruction in kindergarten: examining an emerging area of research for children with writing and reading difficulties. *Journal of Learning Disabilities*, 36, 12, 136–149.

German Social Welfare Code IX (SGBIX) (2001).

International Dyslexia Association's fact sheet on at-risk students and the study of foreign language at school. www.interdys.org/ewebeditpro5/upload/AtRiskStudentsForeignLanguage2012.pdf

Kormos, J. and Smith, A.M. (2012) *Teaching Languages to Learners with Specific Learning Difficulties*. Clevedon: Multilingual Matters (Chapters 4, 6 and 7).

Martin, D. (2011) 'Dyslexia and literacy difficulties in multilingual contexts', NALDIC Conference 19. www.naldic.org.uk/Resources/NALDIC/Professional%20Development/Documents/NC19_Martin_Dyslexia_in_multilingual_contexts.pdf

McColl, H. (2000) Can all children benefit from foreign language learning? Extract from *Modern Languages for All*. David Fulton Publishers: London, pp. 5–10. www.languageswithoutlimits.co.uk/resources/Extract1.pdf

Meltzer, L. (2010) *Promoting Executive Function in the Classroom: What Works for Special Needs Learners*. New York: Guilford Press.

Moats, L.C. (2000) *Speech to Print: Language Essentials for Teachers*. Baltimore, MD: Paul H. Brookes Publishing.

Martin, D. *Dyslexia and Multilingualism*. www.naldic.org.uk/Resources/NALDIC/Professional%20Development/Documents/NC19_Martin_Dyslexia_in_multilingual_contexts.pdf

Peer, L. (2005) *Glue Ear: An Essential Guide for Teachers, Parents and Health Professionals*. London: David Fulton.

Peer, L. and Reid, G. (Eds) (2000) *Multilingualism, Literacy and Dyslexia: A Challenge for Educators*. London: David Fulton.

Peer, L. and Reid, G. (Eds) (2012) *Special Educational Needs: A Guide for Inclusive Practice*. London: Sage.

Reid, G. *Dyslexia: Teaching Approaches*. www.drgavinreid.com/free-resources/dyslexia-teaching-approaches

Reid, G. and Green, S. (2011) *100+ Ideas for Supporting Children with Dyslexia*. New York: Continuum.

Reraki, M. 'Classroom-based interventions for achieving "dyslexia-friendly" classrooms in language education', International Conference: The Future of Education. http://conference.pixel-online.net/FOE/files/foe/ed0004/FP/0578-SOE388-FP-FOE4.pdf

Schneider, E. and Crombie, M. (2003) *Dyslexia and Foreign Language Learning*. London: David Fulton.

Programmes for testing and teaching

Cooke, A. (2002) *Tackling Dyslexia*, 2nd edition, London and Philadelphia: Whurr Publishers. (Teaching strategies, lesson plans, methods of instruction are given. A programme is provided catering for varied levels.)

Cryer, L. (2004) *Eye Track*. Manchester: SEMREC in association with David Fulton.

Cryer, L. (2004) *Phoneme Track*. Manchester: SEMREC in association with David Fulton.

Frederickson, N., Frith, U. and Reason, R. (1997) *PHAB (Phonological Assessment Battery)*. Berkshire: NFER-Nelson. (This is also good for ESL pupils.)

Hornsby, B., Shear, F. and Pool, J. (2006) *Alpha to Omega Teacher's Handbook*, 6th edition. Oxford; Heinemann Publishers. (A teacher's book for instruction and a student book for reading and self-correction. *Alpha to Omega* has a CD with printable worksheets for the whole programme.)

Neale, M.D. (1997) *Neale Analysis of Reading Ability*, 2nd edition (NARA–II). Windsor: NFER-Nelson.

Further useful resources

Some useful resources for ESL/EFL teachers working with dyslexic learners:

www.tefl.net/esl-articles/dyslexia.htm

http://dystefl.eu/uploads/media/DysTEFL_Booklet_Trainer.pdf

http://stickyball.net/templates/allrusty-fjt/images/logo.png

http://jollylearning.co.uk/overview-about-jolly-phonics/

www.youtube.com/watch?v=Djz82FBYiug

www.youtube.com/watch?v=X2YAqhzaheE

www.gamzuk.com/swap_fix.htm

www.readsuccessfully.com/trugs-for-schools

www.readsuccessfully.com

http://spellasaurus.com

www.nessy.com

www.dyslexiaactionshop.co.uk/stiledyslexia.html#.VgBGuTYVjIU

www.crossboweducation.com/shop-now/phonics-teaching-resources/phonics-teaching-resources-games/Alpha-To-Omega-Pelmanism-Games

www.semerc.com (Granada Learning/SEMERC Granada Television)

www.ncld.org

Other useful websites

http://berlin.angloinfo.com/information/family/schooling-education/special-needs-education

www.nhs.uk/Conditions/Dyslexia/Pages/Treatment.aspx

www.dgspj.de

www.gesetze-im-internet.de/sgb_9

www.thedyslexia-spldtrust.org.uk

www.inclusive.co.uk/software/dyslexia-software

www.gophonics.com/dyslexia.htm

www.interdys.org/ewebeditpro5/upload/AccommodatingStudentsWithDyslexiaInAllClassroomSettings10-02.pdf

www.cambridgeenglish.org/help/special-requirements

www.ldonline.org/article/5885

www.dyslexiaaction.org.uk/files/dyslexiaaction/stress_survey.pdf

www.beingdyslexic.co.uk/pages/information/teachers/teaching-tips/confidence-building-in-dyslexic-children.php

conference.pixel-online.net/FOE/files/foe/ed0004/FP/0578-SOE388-FP-FOE4.pdf

15

CONTRADICTIONS/DILEMMAS AROUND DIFFERENTIATION OF HOMEWORK FOR STUDENTS WITH DYSLEXIA STUDYING ENGLISH AS A FOREIGN LANGUAGE

Maria Rontou

This chapter will:

1. Analyse the contradictions that emerge around the issue of differentiation of homework for students with dyslexia by an English as a Foreign Language (EFL) teacher
2. Show that contradictions are created by the unclear school and Ministry of Education policy in Greece on the differentiation of homework for students with dyslexia
3. Suggest the necessity of redesigning the Ministry's and school policy on the differentiation of homework

Introduction

This chapter discusses the issue of differentiation for students with dyslexia in English as a Foreign Language (EFL) classes. The data included in the analysis come from EFL classes in Greece but the issues raised around differentiation for students with dyslexia have implications for other foreign language learning contexts around the world.

Dyslexia is also referred to as 'specific learning difficulties'. 'The nature and relationship of both concepts and their relationship remains controversial'. What is referred to as dyslexia could be considered as 'a variety of dyslexias' which could be included under the term specific learning difficulties (Pumfrey and Reason, 1991). The term 'dyslexia' is used in this chapter as it is 'embedded in popular language' (Reason, 2002).

A Greek policy document from the Ministry of Education on the issue of assessing students with dyslexia mentions that they have 'normal intelligence' but manifest specific difficulties in learning, especially in reading, writing and spelling and they often manifest 'attention deficit' (MNER, 2006).

Greek and English spelling and reading processes

Greek is an orthographically transparent language with irregular spelling, especially for vowels, which may pose difficulties in spelling for children with reading disability. Protopapas and Skaloumbakas (2007) found that Greek 7th grade children with reading disability have spelling accuracy difficulties but also reading and reading speed difficulties.

On the other hand, Spencer (2000) argues that there is considerable deviation in the one-to-one mapping of phonemes to graphemes in English while the Greek language deviates only a little, as Greek phoneme–grapheme correspondence is straightforward in reading but not in writing (Miles, 2000). Therefore, the Greek alphabetic system is more transparent than the English (Goswami et al., 1997). Spencer (2000) argues that this lack of transparency in English causes problems in reading and spelling. In fact, Seymour et al.'s (2003) research has shown that reading accuracy in transparent languages like Greek can be very high while reading performance in English was only 34%. Therefore, one may hypothesise that Greek students with dyslexia might face more difficulty in reading English than Greek because of the opacity of the English language.

Differentiation

Differentiation is important for all students with special needs in order to access the learning of EFL. The needs and abilities of students with dyslexia as well as all students with specific or general learning difficulties should be considered by EFL teachers. The focus of this chapter is on the needs of Greek students with dyslexia learning EFL because, as discussed previously, they may face difficulties in reading and spelling English because of the opacity of the English language as opposed to the transparency of the Greek language (Spencer, 2000).

Differentiation is a means of curriculum access and should be a part of a specialised programme for individual students with dyslexia (Reid, 2009). As Reid (2009) suggests, it is important that differentiation is seen as a way of supporting all students, and that the stigma felt by students who receive a different type of programme from the others in the class is minimised.

Differentiation enables students to demonstrate what they can achieve and to experience satisfaction in their learning. Teachers can differentiate the teaching material, the texts (Wearmouth et al., 2003), the class organisation or the teaching strategies (Karava and Zouganeli, 2013) and they can accept different kinds of response according to the abilities of students (Crombie, 2000). For example, differentiating material by task in a listening exercise may involve some students writing their responses, while some students draw them, and other students put them on audiotape (Crombie, 2000). Differentiated texts that are more readable for students with dyslexia because of sentence length, complexity and presentation can also be part of a differentiated approach (Wearmouth et al., 2003).

Extra time

Crombie's study (1997) with 25 11–16-year-old Scottish students with dyslexia learning French showed that students with dyslexia performed poorly in reading and writing but also in speaking and listening, and they required more time than the control students to complete the tasks of reading in both English and French. This finding has implications for teachers: they need to allow students with dyslexia extra time for processing information. Crombie and McColl (2001) also suggest that teachers of modern foreign languages should be prepared to allow students extra time to answer questions and to complete work, because students with dyslexia tend to be slower in responding to incoming information. The issue of extra time was also mentioned in Nijakowska's (2000) study, which found that 66% of teachers allowed their students with dyslexia more time to complete a task.

Research has shown that students with dyslexia ask for extra time in class. The adolescents with dyslexia in Thompson and Chinn's study (2001) mentioned being given more time as important for their learning. Johnson (2004) reports a survey study including 67 useable questionnaires from students with dyslexia in secondary schools. Among other elements, the students said being given time to think and write was important. In this chapter the issue of extra time to complete homework is investigated.

Different or less homework

Mackay (2004) refers to differentiated homework as a dyslexia-friendly strategy. This means giving students different tasks to do at home, and not just less work as mentioned in Lappas (1997) and Arapogianni (2003). Both students and parents in Lappas (1997) complained about the amount of homework, while in Arapogianni's (2003) study teachers gave less homework to students with dyslexia in order to support them. Pollock and Waller (2003) also argue that the amount and type of homework that teachers give to students with dyslexia should be carefully considered because these students are more tired by the end of the day than their peers, as everything requires more thought and takes them longer. In my study I investigated the issue of less homework for students with dyslexia as well as extra time for homework.

Research questions

The research questions that this study aimed to investigate were:

1. What differentiation do students with dyslexia need and are offered regarding homework when they learn EFL in Greek state secondary schools?
2. Do Greek EFL teachers give Greek students with dyslexia extra time for homework or less homework?
3. What contradictions emerge when students and teachers try to meet their objects and goals regarding differentiation of homework?

Theoretical framework

A theoretical framework was needed for this study that explores human learning within organisational systems in a collective way. Activity theory and the work of Engeström (2001) provided one such framework. Socio-cultural activity theory was initiated by Vygotsky (1978, 1987) when he tried to explain the learning process by arguing that learning enables people to think or do something beyond their capability, and that this is done in a historical, cultural and social context, with one or more people. Vygotsky believed that human activity happens when the subjects, those whose actions are analysed, resolve a shared problem, an 'object', by using 'tools' to achieve a goal (Martin, 2008). Engeström (2001) describes how the current understanding of activity theory has evolved through three generations of research. The first generation contributed to activity theory the idea of 'mediation' which was represented in Vygotsky's (1987) triangular model (Figure 15.1) linking the subject and the object through mediating artefacts (Engeström, 2001).

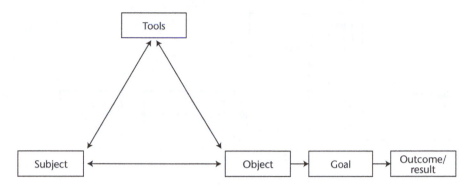

FIGURE 15.1 The principal relationship in an activity system

In the second generation, which was developed from Leont'ev's writing, (Leont'ev, 1978, 1981; Engeström, 2001) Engeström expanded the triangular representation of an activity system to enable the examination of activity systems at an organisational level as opposed to a focus on the individual actors operating with tools (Daniels, 2004). This expansion of the Vygotskian triangle represents the social or organisational elements in an activity system through the addition of the elements of community, rules and division of labour (see Figure 15.2).

Activity theory was chosen as a theoretical framework for the data collection and analysis of this study because it allowed the inclusion of different groups of participants and the investigation of the relationship between them. The second principle of activity theory, multi-voicedness was useful for this study as it enabled the investigation of multiple points of view on the same issue, those of the EFL teachers, the students, the parents and the Ministry of Education (Engeström, 2001).

Therefore, the subjects of learning of the activity system in School 2 (the school where the study took place) are EFL Teacher 2 and two students with dyslexia, Stathis and Thodoris (see Figure 15.2). A possible object of learning, that is, what the subjects are working on, is differentiated homework or extra time for homework (Daniels, 2004). The goal in an activity system is the result of the 'creative effort' that can be achieved when the problems are resolved (Davydov, 1999). A possible goal in this study is inclusion of students with dyslexia.

The community representing the wider socio-cultural influences includes the context of the activity, that is, the people who are concerned with the same object: the headteacher of the school, the other students and teachers, the Local Education Authority (LEA) and the Ministry of Education (Leadbetter, 2004; Daniels, 2004). Therefore, the activity is a collective one and not an individual action of the teacher only or the students only (Engeström, 2001).

The division of labour in this study refers to the division of tasks between the EFL teacher, the headteacher and students. The rules are the principles regulating the actions of the participants and they can be both written and unwritten – for example, the national policies on dyslexia and their interpretations by the headteacher of the school (Daniels, 2004) as well as the routines and professional practices of the teachers.

Since activity theory is deeply contextual and studies specific local practices it is often linked with the use of case studies (e.g. Engeström, 1999a, 1999b, 2001) that take context and its details into account (Denscombe, 2003). An appropriate design for this study using activity theory as a theoretical framework was a case study. This was appropriate because it aimed to go into sufficient detail and explore the complexities of dyslexia provision, and multiple sources were necessary for the collection of data (Denscombe, 2003).

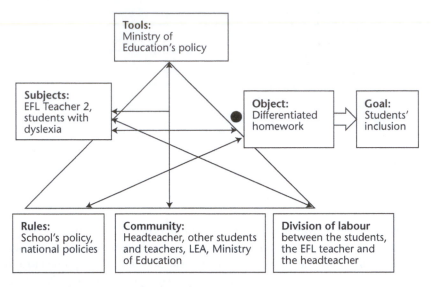

FIGURE 15.2 Second generation of activity theory

Methodology

Methods

The study included multiple methods for triangulation purposes, which is a characteristic of case studies (Robson, 2002): semi-structured and unstructured ethnographic interviews with an EFL teacher and two students and lesson observation with field notes and digital audio recording of EFL lessons. The wider study included interviews with the mothers of four students, two fathers and three more teachers, and collection of documents.

The interviews with participants were conducted in the Greek language and they were transcribed and translated into English. This process involved construction of meaning and interpretations by the transcriber and translator (Marshall and Rossman, 2006). One problem was that the interviews in spoken form were transcribed in the Greek language, which had to be translated in written form into the English language. This created a problem of equivalence.

The case studies in this chapter are ethnographic because this study had a longitudinal element as it involved contact with participants in a setting over a prolonged period of time (Brewer, 2000). The researcher spent 16 weeks collecting data with School 2 participants. The researcher also kept contact with EFL Teacher 2 and attended seminars with her the year after the study.

The data were analysed using activity theory in order to investigate the perspectives of the different groups of participants and the relationship between them, as well as the relationship between the participants and the tools, the rules, the community and the division of labour, and how these influence the achievement of participants' goals. Patterns in teachers', students' and parents' needs became the focus of the analysis as well as the contradictions in the achievement of the participants' goals. Contradictions are tensions or dilemmas that arise from the processes within and between the elements of the activity system and become the object of collaborative learning (Martin, 2008). Therefore, the analysis aims to identify the contradictions that arise when the teachers, students and parents try to work on their objects as well as the factors that caused these contradictions. Contradictions between elements of the activity system are indicated in Figures 15.2 and 15.3 by lightning-shaped arrows (Engeström *et al.*, 1999).

Context and participants

The data for this study come from a state secondary school in Athens which is referred to as School 2 because in the wider study there is School 1, although there are no data from School 1 on the issues that this chapter deals with. School 2 was a lower secondary school. The data used in this chapter from School 2 involved two 12–13-year-old boys and their EFL teacher. Stathis and Thodoris attended the low-ability EFL class at school. Stathis attended EFL lessons at a language school for C class. Thodoris, who had an IQ of 119, attended EFL lessons at a language school for B class. The diagnostic report was the same for both of them: they both had normal IQ and faced difficulties in spelling, handwriting and dyscalculia according to their diagnostic reports.[1] EFL Teacher 2 had 19 years of teaching experience, eight of which were in the state sector.

The selection of schools was guided by convenience, that is, the accessibility of schools and the availability of individuals in them due to professional contacts (Cohen *et al.*, 2007; Fine and Shulman, 2009). The headteacher had also given the researcher the information that there were students with dyslexia in the school. The EFL teacher selected was the one who had students with dyslexia in her classes and who agreed to participate in the study after being informed about its aims and procedure.

The criterion for choosing students was a dyslexia diagnosis and their parents' informed consent to participate in the study. In order not to identify the school and the participants, pseudonyms were used for the students and the teachers' names were replaced with codes like EFL Teacher 2, Headteacher 2 (Delamont, 2002).

The researcher was not a teacher at the schools in which the research was conducted but was a teacher permanently employed by the Greek Ministry of Education working in another LEA. Although an outsider to the two schools, the researcher was part of the same culture, had passed through the same educational system, had grown up and gone to school in the same area as the first school, and had lived in the area of the second school.

Findings

Accommodation for homework

Students from School 2 said they needed extra time for homework or less homework. In this section I investigate the issue of extra time for homework from the perspective of the two students and EFL Teacher 2.

Students' perspectives

Thodoris would like to have less work to do at home for EFL:

M You would like to … have less studying to do at home for English.

Th Yes, because … apart from English there are other subjects.

(Interview with Thodoris)

Thodoris thinks EFL Teacher 2 gives the class too many exercises for homework. He said she gives the class around seven exercises out of the ten that the book includes as well as vocabulary to learn:

Th When Miss gives us [homework], for example, if the book has ten exercises, we do three in class and [the remaining] seven are for homework … she gives us vocabulary as well though …

(Interview with Thodoris)

Later in the same interview Thodoris said he wants the EFL teacher to give them less exercises for homework: 'to give less exercises generally'.

Thodoris also suggested that the teacher should give more time to the whole class to do the exercises she gives for homework. He wants to have five days or a week to do the exercises:

Th She can … give us in a paper 20 exercises … and she should give them to us on Monday for example and they should be due for Friday or they should be for the following Monday.

(Interview with Thodoris)

Thodoris agreed with me that he needs more time to write essays at home and do homework than other students (lines 11–13). Therefore, some differentiation regarding homework would be useful for him (lines 6–10):

6   M   There can be an arrangement about this [homework]
7   Th Yes
8   M   about what you will bring at least, she can say that you will do two out
9   of the three, to do this differentiation.
10 Th Yes.
11 M   Considering that in order for you to write an essay you may need more
12   time than another student
13 Th Yes
    M   Who doesn't make mistakes
15 Th Yes, of course.

(Interview with Thodoris)

Stathis also said he needs more time than other students to write homework because of his dyslexia. Therefore, since he has not got this time, sometimes he does not do all the exercises:

St sometimes … I don't have time to do many things and maybe because of this problem …, because of dyslexia … I need more time and because there isn't more time
M Mmm

St I don't do the exercises. I try to do the exercises though, it doesn't happen all the time, it's only once in a while that I don't bring exercises …

(Interview with Stathis)

EFL Teacher 2's perspective

EFL Teacher 2 told me that she does not mind if students with dyslexia do not do all exercises (lines 3, 5). Instead, she claims that she encouraged the whole class to do half of the exercises if they do not have enough time as long as they are correct (lines 14–15).

1	M	Sometimes Stathis said he does two out of the three exercises for
2		example
3	T2	I don't have a problem with that.
4	M	Because he finds it hard, it takes him more time to write them and
5	T2	I don't have a problem with that, you saw that today I told them 'do
6		half …'
11	T2	I generally have told everybody because you saw there are more weak
12		students in class, it is not only Stathis
13	M	Mmm
14	T2	I have told them that if you don't have time to do all of them, do half
15		but do them right.

(Interview with EFL Teacher 2)

She also said she gives extra time to students who do not manage to finish homework on time. She tells them to do it during the weekend:

T2 I have told them I don't mind, they can come and tell me that 'I didn't have time to do all of them because I couldn't'. That's it, s/he will do them at the weekend, it is not obligatory to do them from one day to the next.

(Interview with EFL Teacher 2)

EFL Teacher 2 said she does not reprimand students with dyslexia for not doing homework because she does not want to embarrass them:

T2 You cannot reprimand them [concerning homework in class]. S/he may be embarrassed.

(Interview with EFL Teacher 2)

At the same time she wants to treat all students in the same way, both the 'good ones' and the 'weak ones' in order not to be accused of being unfair. For this reason, she notes down everybody who has not brought the homework:

M so that they don't say that you treat someone unfairly.

T2 Oh I don't I don't. Let me tell you something, I think that this is the only thing that they won't say because I try to behave in the same way with everybody.

M Yes.

T2 Both to excellent students and to not good students.

M Mmm

T2 And I am strict to everybody, that is there is no way, … you saw that let's say, I made a note of all those that hadn't brought homework, all of them …

(Interview with EFL Teacher 2)

EFL Teacher 2 also said she is more lenient with students with dyslexia than with other students: 'I am definitely more lenient' (Interview with EFL Teacher 2). However, in the beginning of my study, I observed her reprimanding Stathis for not doing the homework, which means that she is not always lenient with students with dyslexia and she does not give them extra time for homework from the outset:

> Stathis didn't have a book for the second time and hadn't done the homework twice and she shouted at him. She said if they don't bring their book three times she will deduct one grade.

(Field notes)

In Figure 15.3 Thodoris', Stathis' and EFL Teacher 2's object of giving more time to students with dyslexia to complete the homework is partially met. This happens because EFL Teacher 2 contradicts herself, probably because she wants to support students with dyslexia and weak students by giving them extra time but at the same time she tries to be fair and treat all students in the same way. Therefore, she has to note down they have not brought the homework. The teacher may not differentiate the homework for students with dyslexia because there is no school policy on how much homework to give to these students or on how much time to give them to complete the homework. If there is such a policy then the EFL teacher will not be accused of being unfair to any of the students in the class. There is a systemic contradiction in the lack of a school policy on homework (rules) which means that the subjects' goal should be to create such a policy.

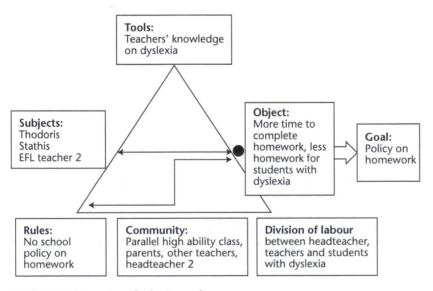

FIGURE 15.3 More time for homework

Discussion and conclusion

In this chapter I have shown that Thodoris and Stathis would like to have fewer exercises to do for homework in EFL or to be given more time to do them. EFL Teacher 2 claims that she tries to be more lenient to students with dyslexia by not reprimanding them as much as other students for not doing their homework, and she may give them extra time for homework. However, she cannot clearly differentiate the homework for them as there is no school policy on making accommodation for homework and the teacher does not want to be accused of being unfair. This finding indicates a need for the Ministry of Education or headteachers to design a policy on homework and how to differentiate it for students with dyslexia.

Teachers in Nijakowska's (2000) and Arapogianni's studies (2003) gave less homework to students with dyslexia, which is what Thodoris and Stathis said they wanted. Students with specific learning difficulties and their parents in Lappas' (1997) study also complained about the amount of homework. My study differs from other studies in its reference to school policy as a rule that created a contradiction in the activity system, and thus in the identification of a solution to the problem of giving extra time in class and for homework. It also investigates the issue from the perspective of teachers as well and students, that has not been done by other researchers.

Activity theory allowed the inclusion of different groups of participants in the study that has not been done by other researchers. It allowed the creation of new knowledge on dyslexia provision in Greek urban schools and the identification of what is problematic about it and where change can start. However, the subjects in this study try to manage the situation by individual solutions and not collaborative learning (Virkkunen and Kuutti, 2000). Other studies on dyslexia provision could be conducted using a Developmental Work Research methodology, in which teachers, students and parents are brought together in workshops where they can discuss their objects and goals and the contradictions emerging when they try to achieve their goals. They can then collectively decide on solutions to their problems, and their implementation can be investigated by the researchers.

Note

1   Diagnoses that Greek state schools accept are produced in state diagnostic centres that give an IQ test to students and tests that assess students' reading, writing, spelling, reading comprehension, maths, phonological skills, speech etc. The reports produced by the same diagnostic centre are usually similar.

References

Arapogianni, A. (2003). *Investigating the approaches that teachers in Greece use to meet the needs of children with dyslexia in secondary schools*. MA thesis, University of Birmingham.

Brewer, J.D. (2000). *Ethnography*. Buckingham: Open University Press.

Cohen, L., Manion, L. and Morrison, M. (2007). *Research methods in education*. London: Routledge.

Crombie, M.A. (1997). The effects of specific learning difficulties (dyslexia) on the learning of a foreign language in school. *Dyslexia, 3*, 27–47.

Crombie, M.A. (2000). Dyslexia and the learning of a foreign language in school: Where are we going? *Dyslexia, 6*, 112–123.

Crombie, M. and McColl, H. (2001). Dyslexia and the teaching of modern foreign languages. In L. Peer and G. Reid. (Eds), *Dyslexia: Successful inclusion in the secondary school*. London: David Fulton Publishers.

Daniels, H. (2004). Activity theory, discourse and Bernstein. *Educational Review, 56*(2), 121–132.

Davydov, V.V. (1999). The content and unsolved problems of activity theory. In Y. Engeström, R. Miettinen and R.L. Punamaki (Eds), *Perspectives on activity theory* (pp. 39–51). Cambridge: Cambridge University Press.

Delamont, S. (2002). *Fieldwork in educational settings: Methods, pitfalls and perspectives*. London: Routledge.

Denscombe, M. (2003). *The good research guide for small-scale social research projects* (2nd ed.). Maidenhead: Open University Press.

Engeström, Y. (1999a). Activity theory and individual and social transformation. In Y. Engeström, R. Miettinen and R.L. Punamaki (Eds), *Perspectives on activity theory* (pp. 19–38). Cambridge: Cambridge University Press.

Engeström, Y. (1999b). Innovative learning in work teams: Analysing cycles of knowledge creation in practice. In Y. Engeström, R. Miettinen and R.L. Punamaki (Eds), *Perspectives on activity theory* (pp. 377–404). Cambridge: Cambridge University Press.

Engeström, Y. (2001). Expansive learning at work: Toward an activity theoretical reconceptualization. *Journal of Education and Work, 14*(1), 133–156.

Engeström, Y., Engeström, R. and Vahaaho, T. (1999). When the centre does not hold: The importance of knotworking. In S. Chaiklin, M. Hedegaard and U. Jensen (Eds), *Activity theory and social practice*. Aarhus: Aarhus University Press.

Fine, G.A. and Shulman, D. (2009). Lies from the field: Ethical issues in organizational ethnography. In S. Ybema, D. Yanow, H. Wells and F. Kamsteeg (Eds), *Organizational ethnography: Studying the complexities of everyday life* (pp. 177–195). London: Sage.

Goswami, U., Porpodas, C. and Wheelwright, S. (1997). Children's orthographic representations in English and Greek. *European Journal of Psychology of Education, 12*(3), 273–292.

Johnson, M. (2004). Dyslexia-friendly schools – Policy and practice. In G. Reid and A. Fawcett (Eds), *Dyslexia in context: Research, policy and practice*. London: Whurr.

Karava, E. and Zouganeli, K. (2013). Educational approaches of the program of studies of foreign languages. In V. Dendrinou and E. Karava (Eds), *Foreign language education for the promotion of multilingualism in Greece today: Approaches and teaching practices*. Athens: University of Athens.

Lappas, N. (1997). *Specific learning difficulties in Scotland and Greece: Perceptions and provision*. Unpublished PhD thesis, University of Stirling, Stirling.

Leadbetter, J. (2004). The role of mediating artefacts in the work of educational psychologists during consultative conversations in schools. *Educational Review, 56*(2), 133–145.

Leont'ev, A.N. (1978). *Activity, consciousness, and personality*. Englewood Cliffs: Prentice-Hall.

Leont'ev, A.N. (1981). *Problems of the development of the mind*. Moscow: Progress.

Mackay, N. (2004). The case for dyslexia-friendly schools. In G. Reid. and A. Fawcett (Eds), *Dyslexia in context: Research, policy and practice*. London: Whurr.

Marshall, C. and Rossman, G.B. (2006). *Designing qualitative research*. London: Sage.

Martin, D. (2008). A new paradigm to inform inter-professional learning for integrating speech and language provision into secondary schools: A socio-cultural activity theory approach. *Child Language Teaching and Therapy, 24*(2), 173–192.

Miles, E. (2000). Dyslexia may show a different face in different languages. *Dyslexia, 6*, 193–201.

MNER (2006). Examination of physically disabled candidates. Athens: Ministry of National Education and Religious Affairs.

Nijakowska, J. (2000). Dyslexia – Does it mean anything to a foreign language teacher? In L. Peer and G. Reid. (Eds), *Multilingualism, literacy and dyslexia: A challenge for educators* (pp. 248–256). London: David Fulton Publishers.

Pollock, J. and Waller, E. (2003). *Day-to-day dyslexia in the classroom*. London: Routledge.

Protopapas, A. and Skaloumbakas, C. (2007). Traditional and computer-based screening and diagnosis of reading disabilities in Greek. *Journal of Learning Disabilities, 40*(1), 15–37.

Pumfrey, P.D. and Reason, R. (1991). *Specific learning difficulties (dyslexia): Challenges and responses.* London: NFER–Routledge.

Reason, R. (2002). From assessment to intervention: The educational psychology perspective. In G. Reid and J. Wearmouth (Eds), *Dyslexia and literacy: Theory and practice* (pp. 187–200). Chichester: John Wiley & Sons.

Reid, G. (2009). *Dyslexia: A practitioner's handbook* (4th ed.). West Sussex: John Wiley & Sons.

Robson, C. (2002). *Real world research: A resource for social scientists and practitioner–researchers* (2nd ed.). Oxford: Blackwell.

Seymour, P.H.K., Aro, M. and Erskine, J.M. (2003). Foundation literacy acquisition in European orthographies. *British Journal of Psychology, 94,* 143–174.

Spencer, K. (2000). Is English a dyslexic language? *Dyslexia, 6,* 152–162.

Thomson, M. and Chinn, S. (2001). Good practice in the secondary school. In A.J. Fawcett (Ed.), *Dyslexia: Theory and good practice.* London: Whurr.

Virkkunen, J. and Kuutti, K. (2000). Understanding organizational learning by focusing on 'activity systems'. *Accounting Management and Information Technologies, 10,* 291–319.

Vygotsky, L.S. (1978). *Mind in society: The development of higher psychological processes.* Cambridge, MA: Harvard University Press.

Vygotsky, L.S. (1987). *Thought and language.* Cambridge, MA: MIT Press.

Wearmouth, J., Soler, J. and Reid, G. (2003). *Meeting difficulties in literacy development: Research, policy and practice.* London: Routledge Falmer.

16

APPROACHING DYSLEXIA AND MULTIPLE LANGUAGES

Gilda Palti

This chapter will:

1. Review dyslexia in first and other languages
2. Review specific cognitive and linguistic advantages of bilingualism or multilingualism
3. Suggest introduction of these cognitive advantages in the educational provision for dyslexic pupils

Overview

Dyslexia involves the accumulation and interaction of multiple cognitive risks. Bilingualism has been considered to be an additional risk factor for dyslexic pupils. Research has shown that the same cognitive inefficiencies count for, or help identify, dyslexia in the first and other languages. Among these are deficiencies in phonological awareness and processing, fluency and retrieval speeds, and short-term and working memory skills. Given that similar cognitive processes apply across languages, the provision for supporting dyslexic pupils in the main language could also be applied to the other languages, as knowledge is transferable between the languages. Some specific cognitive and linguistic advantages that are found in bilingual or multilingual pupils could be used to facilitate support for dyslexic pupils in other languages. These include: cognitive control and supervisory attentional system, problem solving and creative thinking, metalinguistic awareness, and conceptual transfer (Bialystok, 2001). The environmental experience of using multiple languages provides significant practice in the attention and inhibition centres and promotes their development. These cognitive skills can facilitate the learning process for dyslexic pupils in other languages.

Identifying dyslexia in other languages

Dyslexia, according to the British Dyslexia Association (BDA), is

> a learning difficulty that primarily affects the skills involved in accurate and fluent word reading and spelling. Characteristic features of dyslexia are problems with phonological

awareness, verbal memory and verbal processing speed. Co-occurring difficulties may be seen in aspects of language, motor co-ordination, mental calculations, concentration and personal organisation.

In addition, dyslexic individuals have visual and auditory processing difficulties. Dyslexic pupils have difficulty in acquiring literacy skills using the "conventional" teaching methods. There is a general notion that their difficulties are exacerbated when they have to develop competence in literacy in an additional language.

With the rise in family migration, there is an increase in the number of bilingual or multilingual pupils attending schools. Thus, the issue of learning another language, and bilingualism in general, adds further challenge for the educational professionals trying to identify and support dyslexic pupils.

As suggested by the definition, dyslexia is a syndrome manifesting a constellation of many characteristics. It is difficult, therefore, to assess and diagnose dyslexia based on one characteristic, and the addition of another language complicates diagnosis. As a result, teachers in multi-ethnic classrooms tend to withhold judgment about students using an additional language who may show similar warning signs to those noted in pupils with dyslexia in the first language, because they tend to attribute these difficulties to lack of sufficient language skills (Geva, 2006).

There are often reports of confusion, as those struggling with learning an additional language may be categorised as having learning difficulties, while those having genuine learning difficulties may be missed because their problems are attributed to lack of proficiency in the other language. It is important, therefore, to develop strategies to guide teachers and educators in distinguishing literacy difficulties that are due to the learning process of an additional language, and those that are due to specific learning difficulties, like dyslexia. This will help in minimising over- or under-diagnosis of specific learning difficulties. The available research suggests that it is possible to diagnose dyslexia in the additional language.

Research on the acquisition of the second language among pupils with no specific learning difficulties reports that problems at the level of vocabulary, phonological awareness and grammar are the best predictors of general difficulties in the learning of the second language (Purpura, 1997). There is no evidence in research to suggest that a pupil's performance in school will be affected solely by being bilingual. Similarly, there is no evidence to suggest that pupils become confused, lag behind or have behavioural problems as a result of their bilingualism. The fact that the pupil is bilingual does not have an effect on the chances of the pupil experiencing a specific learning difficulty. Therefore, a pupil struggling to acquire literacy skills in the additional language, despite appropriate support, may present some learning problems that require further investigation.

Assessing specific learning difficulties

When assessing for specific learning difficulties, in general, phonological awareness and processing speeds are found to be some of the most common indicators of dyslexia. Everatt and co-workers (Everatt et al., 2002; Everatt and Reid, 2010) noted that pupils with dyslexia performed worse than individuals with English as a second language on measures of phonological processing, suggesting that such measures could identify underlying deficits associated specifically with dyslexia.

In another research project (Everatt *et al.*, 2000), a series of measures used in a number of dyslexia screening tests were administered to groups of 7–8 year old English monolinguals and Sylheti/English bilinguals. The screening measures assessed phonological skills, rapid naming, the ability to recite or repeat sequences of verbal and non-verbal stimuli, and visual and motor skills. Within these groups, a subgroup of pupils was distinguished by poor spelling and reading, in the absence of general ability, sensory, emotional or behavioural problems, i.e. specific literacy difficulties. The results suggest that phonological tests were useful measures in differentiating bilinguals with specific learning difficulty from their peers with no specific learning difficulty. Inefficiencies in phonological measures, in particular, were found consistently across bilingual and monolingual groupings of pupils with specific learning difficulties.

Transfer between languages

Transfer between languages, was noted by Geva (2006), who suggested that in general terms, pupils who have decoding and spelling problems in their first language, have difficulties in their second language as well. Phonological awareness, rapid naming, and to some extent verbal working memory are sources of individual differences that are associated with reading development and difficulties, in both languages, regardless of whether these skills are measured in children in their first or second language, and whether the language is alphabetic or non-alphabetic. The suggestion is that the same underlying cognitive and linguistic component skills that are crucial for learning of literacy skills in monolingual pupils (for example, phonemic awareness, speed of processing, visual processes), contribute across diverse languages and writing systems. This also means that these skills influence the development of literacy skills in other languages. Therefore (Geva, 2006), one can expect positive transfer if the same underlying processing factors facilitate the acquisition of literacy skills in the second language, in the way they do in the first language. Another outcome is that performance in these processing factors in one language would be related to literacy skills in the other language. The transfer notion was earlier suggested by Gillon (2004), who found that phonological awareness skills in a native alphabetic language can be transferred to the learning of a second language.

It is important, however, to be aware that phonological problems may differ in their intensity in different languages. For example, Snowling (2013) suggested that, of the alphabetic languages, English is the most difficult to learn, and phonological problems will lead to serious delays in learning to read. By contrast, other languages like Italian and Finnish have far simpler letter-to-sound encoding rules, and the consequences of a phonological deficit will be less apparent. In some cases, caution must be exercised as tests of phonological awareness and processing may not always identify these difficulties. There is evidence (Snowling, 2013) that if children have good language skills, they may be able to compensate for phonological problems.

On another dimension, Connie Suk-Han Ho and Kin-Man Fong (2005) have shown that the script of the language has not been proven to affect learning of a second language. A study that examined whether Chinese dyslexic children having difficulties learning English as a second language was due to a different script, suggests that the pupils were generally weak in phonological processing in both languages. This finding reinforces other comparative surveys of reading literacy that suggest that the orthographic structure of the language does not impact on the acquisition of reading in a second language.

Similarly to bilingualism, Mark Seidenberg (2013) suggested that the dialect of the language spoken is also an emerging risk factor. For children who speak different dialects at school and at home, learning to read is going to be much harder. They may appear to misread words at school when they are actually pronouncing them in the way that is correct at home.

Although testing phonological awareness and processing speeds are found to be essential in identifying specific learning difficulties, it is important to look at other indicators as well. For example, in languages with shallow orthographies such as German and Dutch, speed of naming, rather than phonemic awareness is a stronger predictor of reading success or failure (Givon, cited in Geva, 2006).

To ensure that pupils are not being missed, it is important, based on the above findings, to assess bilinguals who may be at risk of specific learning difficulties, in as many of the areas known to be related to learning difficulties as possible. It is essential also to consider the family's cultural and linguistic background, and parental attributions about their children's academic difficulties, using cultural informants to gather information and place it in context (Givon, cited in Geva, 2006).

Thus, the professional investigating the reasons for difficulties in learning literacy in an additional language, should also look into the following issues in the first/main language:

- family history of specific learning difficulties;
- early speech development in mother tongue (delayed?);
- difficulties that the pupil has experienced in the first language (review school reports, and interview parents and the pupils themselves);
- unusual patterns of strengths and weaknesses;
- inconsistencies between oral and written abilities;
- phonological development and processing speed;
- working memory;
- difficulty in responding to appropriate intervention in class;
- the kinds of errors made in reading and spelling, as the errors made by dyslexic pupils differ in quantity and quality from those made by non-dyslexic pupils (these include reversals and changing sequence of letters, confusion between different vowels and consonants, confusion of syllables);
- progress and learning over time – persistent language and reading difficulties in spite of adequate instruction should not be ignored.

Very often, the factors affecting the learning of the first language, also affect the learning of the additional language.

Challenging issues

The issues that are most challenging to dyslexic pupils when learning an additional language are found to be:

- phonological awareness – discriminating between vowel sounds, understanding and using rhymes, matching sounds to letters;
- understanding/knowing the unstressed morphemes, such as possessives, plurals, past tense ('-ed'), and other suffixes and prefixes;

- grammatically correct word order;
- building a wide-ranging vocabulary repertoire;
- speed of retrieving words/vocabulary;
- identifying keywords in a text for skim reading.

As dyslexia is often diagnosed using standardised tests, this may cause a misinterpretation of the pupil's profile, particularly when assessed in the additional language. The extent to which norm-referenced assessments can be used to classify children accurately, has been questioned in the field of educational psychology (Elliott, 2003; Haywood and Lidz, 2007). One suggestion is to use a dynamic assessment when assessing bilingual or multilingual pupils. Bridges and Catts (2011) showed that the dynamic screening measure of phonological awareness uniquely predicted end-of-year reading achievement and outcomes. Educators may be able to determine more accurately the sources of difficulty in children performing poorly on assessments, the prognosis for their achievement, and as a consequence – devise appropriate interventions.

Error analysis is another useful source of information when trying to identify specific learning difficulties among bilingual pupils. It is important to consider the transfer of specific skills from the first language. One should consider whether errors occur across the board or are limited to specific differences, such as those related to writing systems. Errors across the board are more suggestive of a disability than errors that are typical of learners from a given linguistic background, and that disappear over time (Geva, 2006).

As a general rule, cognitive inefficiencies that are found to affect learning in the first language, such as working memory, phonological awareness and processing, phonological fluency and retrieval, and speeds of processing, have been found to identify specific learning difficulties in the additional language. Background information on the first language development, and familial and cultural knowledge should be sought. Error analysis and dynamic assessment may be used as additional sources of diagnosis. Persistent language difficulties in spite of adequate educational support should not be ignored.

Cognitive advantages of bilingualism

Learning additional languages has been generally believed to be another barrier for dyslexic pupils to overcome. Some parents and school staff have opted to drop the learning of an additional language, to allow the dyslexic pupils to concentrate on the main language used in the educational institution. However, research suggests that bilingualism, and exposure to additional languages, can offer a number of cognitive and linguistic advantages that can be applied to facilitate the teaching of bilingual dyslexic pupils. Among the advantages identified are: cognitive control, problem solving and creative thinking, metalinguistic awareness, and conceptual transfer (Bialystok, 2001).

Bialystok (2001) suggested that bilingual children have an enhanced inhibitory control in ignoring certain perceptual information, i.e. they are good at selectively attending to important information and ignoring misleading cues (cognitive control). Bilingual children are constantly sorting and filtering out extra perceptual information since, for every object or action, bilingual children assign two words, or labels, one in each language that they speak (Bialystok and Martin, 2004). They have to develop the ability to choose the appropriate label. Thus, they nurture their capacity to focus on relevant and appropriate information and restrict their attention to information unrelated to the context. Bilingual pupils were found to be significantly faster than monolinguals in identifying the target in the more difficult conjunction search, providing evidence for better control of visual attention (Friesen *et al.*, 2014).

Pupils who develop bilingually typically outperform monolinguals on tests of executive functions. Executive functions consist of various cognitive skills that help the individual act on information handled, helping with planning, organising, attentiveness, transferring and generalising information. Bilingualism may "train the brain", enabling improved performance under conditions of competitive information selection during information transfer (Stocco *et al.*, 2014).

In her study, Swathi Kandru (2011) examined working memory, attention and novel word learning skills of early sequential bilinguals. The participants were Hindi–English bilinguals and native-English monolinguals. The results showed that bilingual students performed more effectively than monolinguals on tasks placing demands on working memory and response inhibition. The bilingual advantage was also observed on a visual–verbal paired associate learning task. Bilingual individuals learned novel words in a new language (Spanish) faster and recalled them better than monolinguals. The suggestion is that early bilingualism leads to better executive functioning, which in turn aids with the efficient learning of novel words. The study confirms previous studies that a better-developed executive functioning is to be found among bilingual pupils. These include cognitive control and the supervisory attentional system, i.e. management of cognitive processes, including working memory, reasoning, task flexibility and problem solving, as well as planning and execution.

Bialystok and Codd (1997) found that bilingual children were more advanced in performing a series of number tasks, particularly those requiring high levels of selective attention. It is said that the metalinguistic skills, the ability to use knowledge about language, of the bilingual children enabled them to perform better because of their ability to self-correct.

Bilingual children performed significantly better on both verbal and non-verbal measures, specifically on those tasks that required mental and symbolic flexibility and concept formation (Peal and Lambert, 1962). They have stronger analogical reasoning ability, particularly in non-verbal skills.

The ability to use knowledge about language, metacognition – word awareness (Bialystok, 1988); syntactic awareness (Galombos and Hakuta, 1988); richness of word definitions (Lauchlan and Carrigan, 2013); and phonological awareness (Campbell and Sais, 1995), has been shown to be better amongst bilingual children. The advantages of bilingualism for metalinguistic awareness, including the enhancement of highly developed skills in pragmatic competence, communicative sensitivity and flexibility, as well as skills in translation and the acquisition of further languages, have been described by Jessner (2008). Transfer of language occurs when bilingual pupils use the understanding they have of a concept in another language. For example, Lemberger (2002) has shown that Russian–English bilinguals were able to learn scientific concepts more rapidly than monolingual peers. This transfer between languages suggests that bilingual children may find it easier to learn further languages, when compared to monolinguals.

Many of the studies with positive results have investigated transfer of learning between similar languages such as Spanish and English (e.g. Durgunoglu *et al.*, 1993). However, transfer of some skills and knowledge has been shown to occur even where the two languages have quite different writing systems such as Japanese and English (Cummins, 1991) or Chinese and English (Bialystok, 1997). The cognitive processes underlying successful transfer of learning between languages, the conditions that enhance positive transfer from one language to the other, and the differences between individuals who manage the transfer between languages successfully and those who do not, is a complicated process that is not yet fully understood, or transferred to applicable format.

Although there are clearly some cognitive advantages in being bilingual, inevitably there are also some disadvantages. One such disadvantage is found to be in a slower speed of vocabulary retrieval (Kaushanskaya *et al.*, 2011, p. 421), which may affect the performance of the bilingual pupils on timed tasks.

The educational provision provided to dyslexic pupils, in general, is based on the multi-sensory structured language approach, teaching letter–sound knowledge and increasing phoneme awareness. Since the underlying cognitive inefficiencies of specific learning difficulties are similar across languages, the same type of educational intervention could be applied when supporting bilingual pupils.

Regarding practical measures, based on the reviewed literature, the suggestion is that the key to working with dyslexic bilingual pupils, similar to with monolingual dyslexic pupils, is to use a structured multi-sensory language approach, embedding the development of phonological processing and fluency, while bringing to awareness the cognitive advantages found in the milieu of bilingualism. These include: enhanced inhibitory control, better executive functioning, improved analogical reasoning and enhanced metacognition.

Multi-sensory educational provision – key points

In practice, a multi-sensory educational provision programme may include:

- using the enhanced cognitive control by helping the pupil focus on relevant and appropriate information, and ignore irrelevant information;
- using the advantage of better-developed analogical reasoning ability to transfer concepts between languages;
- introducing a complicated idea/concept in a structured and manageable way, i.e. introduce an easy part and then add to that other parts until the concept is understood, and apply it to different languages;
- emphasising the differences and the similarities of rules across the languages (metacognition);
- explaining grammatical rules and comparing them across the languages;
- spiralling back over concepts, and comparing overlapping and similar concepts in other languages.

Conclusion: Approaching dyslexia and multiple languages

Dyslexia involves the accumulation and interaction of multiple cognitive risks, and learning a new language has been considered to be an additional cognitive risk factor for dyslexic individuals. However, there is no evidence to suggest that a pupil's performance in school will be affected solely by being bilingual. Research has shown that the same cognitive inefficiencies account for, or help identify, dyslexia across languages. Among these are problems related to:

phonological awareness and processing, fluency and retrieval speeds, and short-term and working memory skills. Thus, as knowledge is transferable between languages, the provision for supporting bilingual dyslexic pupils across languages should be similar. To facilitate support for dyslexic bilingual pupils, some specific cognitive and linguistic advantages found in non-dyslexic bilingual pupils could be embedded in the programme. These include strengths with regard to: cognitive control, problem solving and creative thinking, metalinguistic awareness, executive functions, and conceptual transfer (Bialystok, 2001). Studies confirm that the associations between complex mechanisms in the bilingual brain may have important implications for early bilingual education. Specifically, they suggest that it could be easier for educators to support bilingual dyslexic pupils than monolingual dyslexic pupils.

Any provision should take into account the variety of bilingual students. There are those who use one language at home (a minority language), and another language at school or in the outside world (majority language). This is complicated by different dialects or pronunciations of words used at home and in school. It can also be that monolingual dyslexic pupils receive more majority-language support at home than their multilingual dyslexic peers who speak a minority language at home. The latter may be affected by the slower local language acquisition of the migrating parents.

When children experience specific learning difficulties, many parents and educators are encouraged to concentrate on one language when initially learning literacy skills. The choice of the language can be an additional stress factor for the family already experiencing stress because of migration. They may need to choose between the paternal or maternal native language; minority or majority languages; or a local language and a language spoken by both parents that is not necessarily either one's mother tongue. However, research supports the argument that there are advantages in the use of multiple languages in children's development and education. The studies highlighting the cognitive benefits of bilingualism, such as enhanced executive functioning, better metacognition, enhanced inhibitory control and analogical reasoning, support this notion. Use of multiple languages is not only a benefit for the children's education and cognitive development, but also for their emotional wellbeing. Using the multiple languages they are exposed to, has a positive effect on their self-identity, and on the family's integrity. They do not have to choose one language and ignore another, a choice that may have an emotional impact on a parent or both parents. There is also the added benefit of helping the child in communication with the extended family in the country of origin.

As Cummins (1991) suggests, it is very important that pupils are encouraged to continue their native language development. The pupil should have the opportunity to read, and discuss academic issues and social issues in their native language. Conceptual knowledge in one language can be transferred to another language, as, if the child already understands a concept in the native language, then the only thing left is acquiring the label for the term in the other language. It is much harder to acquire both the concept and the label in the other language.

Multilingual pupils should be shown that their native language and culture are just as important as the newly learned language and culture. Schools can generate activities that incorporate the different cultural backgrounds, to increase the confidence and the success of their pupils.

With increased knowledge about the learning processes in general and for dyslexic pupils in particular, and about the cognitive advantages of the use of multiple languages in education, more guidance is now available to educators and parents. The cognitive advantages that research has found, and their application in educational provision, can affect the social and emotional wellbeing of pupils and their families. This is important, because any learning situation should take into consideration all the factors – cognitive, emotional and social for a successful intervention. It is evident that more research is needed to reveal the advantages of learning multiple languages, and to develop methods for their practical application in the education of dyslexic individuals.

References

Bialystok, E., 1988. Levels of bilingualism and levels of linguistic awareness. *Developmental Psychology*, 24, 560–567.

Bialystok, E., 2001. *Bilingualism in development: language, literacy and cognition*. New York: Cambridge University Press.

Bialystok, E. and Codd, J., 1997. Cardinal limits: Evidence from language awareness and bilingualism for developing concepts of number. *Cognitive Development*, 12, 85–106.

Bialystok, E. and Martin, M.M., 2004. Attention and inhibition in bilingual children: Evidence from the dimensional change card sort task. *Developmental Science*, 7, 325–339.

Bridges, M.S. and Catts, H.W., 2011. The use of a dynamic screening of phonological awareness to predict risk for reading disabilities in kindergarten children. *Journal of Learning Disabilities*, 44(4), 330–338.

Campbell, R. and Sais, E., 1995. Accelerated metalinguistic (phonological) awareness in bilingual children. *British Journal of Developmental Psychology*, 13, 61–68.

Connie Suk-Han Ho and Kin-Man Fong, 2005. Do Chinese dyslexic children have difficulties learning English as a second language? *Journal of Psycholinguistic Research*, 34(6), 603–618.

Cummins, J., 1991. In *Language processing in bilingual children*. Cambridge: Cambridge University Press.

Durgunoglu, A.Y., Nagy, W.E. and Hancin-Vhatt, B.J., 1993. Cross-language transfer of phonological awareness. *Journal of Educational Psychology*, 85(3), 453–465.

Elliott, J., 2003. Dynamic assessment in educational settings: Realising potential. *Educational Review*, 55(1), 15–32.

Everatt, J. and Reid, G., 2010. Motivating children with dyslexia. In J. Fletcher, F. Parkhill and G. Gillon (Eds) *Motivating literacy learners in today's world*. Wellington: NZCER Press.

Everatt, J., Smythe, I., Adams, E. and Ocampo, D., 2000. *Dyslexia*, 6(1), 42–56.

Everatt, J., Smythe, I., Ocampo, D. and Veii, K., 2002. Dyslexia assessment of the bi-scriptal reader. *Topics in Language Disorder*, 22, 32–45.

Friesen, D.C., Latman, V., Calvo, A. and Bialystok, E., 2014. Attention during visual search: The benefit of bilingualism. *International Journal of Bilingualism*. doi: 10.1177/1367006914534331

Galombos, S.J. and Hakuta K., 1988. Subject-specific and task specific characteristics of metalinguistic awareness in bilingual children. *Applied Psycholinguistics*, 9, 141–162.

Geva, E., 2006. Learning to read in a second language: Research, implications, and recommendations for services. In R.E. Tremblay, R.G. Barr and R. De V. Peters (Eds) *Encyclopedia on Early Childhood Development* [online]. Montreal, Quebec: Centre of Excellence for Early Childhood Development, pp. 1–12.

Gillon, G.T., 2004. *Phonological awareness: From research to practice*. New York: Guilford Press.

Haywood, H.C. and Lidz, C.S., 2007. *Dynamic assessment in practice: Clinical and educational applications*. New York: Cambridge University Press.

Jessner, U., 2008. A DST model of multilingualism and the role of metalinguistic awareness. *The Modern Language Journal*, 92, 270–283.

Kandru, S., 2014. University of York: MSc in Reading, Language and Cognition. Thesis titled: *Novel word learning and executive functioning in Hindi–English speakers: A bilingual advantage*.

Kaushanskaya, M., Blumenfeld, H.K. and Marian, V., 2011. The relationship between vocabulary and short-term memory measures in monolingual and bilingual speakers. *International Journal of Bilingualism*, 15(4), 408–425.

Lauchlan, F. and Carrigan, D., 2013. *Improving learning through dynamic assessment: A practical classroom resource*. London: Jessica Kingsley Publishers.

Lemberger, N., 2002. Russian bilingual science learning: Perspectives from secondary students. *International Journal of Bilingual Education and Bilingualism*, 5(1), 58–71.

Peal, E. and Lambert, W., 1962. The relation of bilingualism to intelligence. *Psychological Monographs*, 76, 1–23.

Purpura, J.E., 1997. An analysis of the relationships between test takers' cognitive and metacognitive strategy use and second language test performance. *Language Learning*, 47(2), 289–325.

Seidenberg, M.S., 2013. The science of reading and its educational implications. *Language Learning and Development*, 9(4), 331–360.

Snowling, M., 2013. Untangling dyslexia. *The Psychologist*, 26(11), 788.

Stocco A., Yamasaki B., Natalenko R. and Prat C., 2014. Bilingual brain training: A neurobiological framework of how bilingual experience improves executive function. *International Journal of Bilingualism*, 18(1), 67–92.

17

READING SKILLS IN CHILDREN PROVIDED SIMULTANEOUS INSTRUCTION IN TWO DISTINCT WRITING SYSTEMS

Insights from behaviour and neuroimaging

Nandini C. Singh, Sarika Cherodath, T.A. Sumathi, Rozzel Kosera, Kate Currawala, Bhoomika Kar and Geet Oberoi

This chapter will:

1. Describe the phenomenon of biliteracy
2. Discuss phonological and reading profiles along with neural reading circuitry in children provided simultaneous biliterate instruction
3. Highlight the role of orthographic depth and the hippocampus in such biliterate acquisition

Introduction

In modern-day societies, there is vast variation in the cultural environment in which literacy is acquired. One such environment is biliteracy, which is the acquisition of literacy skills in two or more distinct languages. Populations in such milieus have to learn to read a non-native language in addition to their native language. Consequently, the relationship between the two languages as well as the writing systems they use is an important factor for facilitation of biliteracy.

The writing system that a language uses affects acquisition of literacy because each system is based on a different set of symbolic relations and requires different cognitive skills (Coulmas, 1989). The smallest identifiable unit of language is a grapheme. A writing system embodies a language by segregating it into a sequence of these graphemes. For instance, the English writing system is phonemic, Chinese is morpho-syllabic where each syllable can correspond to several different morphemes or meaningful units of language, while Hindi is alpha syllabic, that is, each letter represents a consonant with an inherent vowel called *akshara*, which can be modified using vowel diacritics (called *maatra*).

Orthography, on the other hand, defines the set of rules vis-à-vis how to use the symbols belonging to a certain script. The orthography of a script reflects the pronunciation of the language. Different languages differ in their orthographic depth. English, for example, is orthographically deep wherein the same set of letters can be pronounced differently. In the words 'cow' and 'low', /ow/ is pronounced differently. Conversely, languages such as Spanish and Italian, which have the same Roman script as English, have a simple one-to-one sound-mapping system that makes them orthographically transparent. These orthographically consistent languages may rely more on grapheme–phoneme recoding strategies because grapheme–phoneme correspondences are relatively constant, whereas in English, irregularity is found to be much higher for smaller grapheme units than for larger units (Treiman, Mullennix, Bijeljac-Babic & Richmond-Welty, 1995). Consequently, for English, a variety of tactics augmenting grapheme–phoneme conversion strategies have to be used to aid reading.

The 'grain size' hypothesis proposed by Goswami and Ziegler (Goswami, Ziegler, Dalton & Schneider, 2003; Ziegler & Goswami, 2005) concerns the size of a processing unit in reading. Languages which vary in grain size vary in their use of phonological units represented in print. Alphabetic languages use phonemes whereas syllabic languages employ larger sound units – syllables. This brings to the fore two variables that might affect biliteracy acquisition, namely (1) grain size and (2) orthographic consistency/transparency. Research investigating grain size has suggested that awareness of larger grain sizes develops faster in children in comparison to awareness of smaller ones (Ziegler & Goswami, 2005), and therefore reading development differs in languages according to their grain size. Additionally, writing systems vary in their consistency in mapping of sounds onto units of print, also known as orthographic depth (Katz & Frost, 1992). If languages were to be arranged based on orthographic depth, Spanish, with near univalent spelling-to-sound mapping would occupy one end of a continuum and opaque orthographies such as English would fall on the other end (Seymour, Aro & Erskine, 2003). Behavioural studies also suggest that reading development proceeds slowly in deep orthographies as compared to transparent ones (Ziegler & Goswami, 2005). That differences in sound–letter mapping are reflected in differences in neural reading circuitry has also been reported. Cortical reading networks for transparent and opaque orthographies in monolinguals weigh activations in different regions of the brain and impose different cognitive demands (Bolger, Perfetti & Schneider, 2005; Paulesu et al., 2000). Adult monoliterate readers of transparent writing systems employ phonological assembly for reading (Carreiras, Mechelli, Estévez & Price, 2007), whereas readers of opaque writing systems rely more on lexical strategies (Paulesu et al., 2000). Consequently an interesting question is – how does orthographic depth of a writing system modulate reading pathways in biliterate readers who read one transparent and another opaque orthography? A crucial factor for determining the challenges of such a situation is the relationship between the two writing systems. A review of the neuroimaging literature indicates functional plasticity in reading networks in skilled biliterate readers. One of the first studies in such a population, was conducted by Das and co-workers (Das, Padakannaya, Pugh & Singh, 2011) in proficient Hindi–English biliterates. While Hindi is a transparent orthography, English is deep, and the behavioural and neuroimaging evidence from such adults demonstrated orthography-dependent reading strategies. This study found that reading low-frequency words in the transparent orthography – Hindi – was executed by a dorsal route via the inferior parietal lobule implicated in phonological processing, whereas reading low-frequency English words was accomplished via the inferior temporal region involved in lexical recall. Similar results were also reported in adult Spanish–English readers (Das et al., 2011; Jamal, Piche, Napoliello,

Perfetti & Eden, 2012). Adult Spanish–English readers demonstrated involvement of semantic processing through the left middle temporal gyrus while reading Spanish, and activation in the frontal regions for English, indicating increased phonological processing demands.

However, there is precious little known about how orthographic depth shapes reading networks in biliterate children. Therefore, a natural question which arises is – what are the patterns of reading acquisition in an educational environment where children are required to learn to read two languages that vary in orthographic depth but speak only one of them?

In recent years, the phenomenon of simultaneous reading instruction in the native and a second language is becoming an increasingly common feature of language learning environments across the globe, wherein non-native language learning parallels reading acquisition (Ranguelov, De Coster, Norani & Paolini, 2012; Saiegh-Haddad & Geva, 2010; Silver, Hu & Iino, 2002; Q. Wang, 2007). This is particularly true of some South-east Asian countries, where educational policies dictate learning English along with the native language in school (Deterding & Kirkpatrick, 2006). In this case, however, the native language seldom shares the writing system with English. Such biliterate educational settings have two main features which distinguish them from typical biliterate settings:

1. Learning distinct writing systems.
2. Absence of spoken language exposure in the second language prior to reading acquisition.

Past work in the field of biliteracy has focused on sequential biliteracy and has suggested that languages written in the same writing system (English and Spanish, as compared to English and Chinese, for instance) provides children with the prospect of transferring reading principles across the languages, enabling them to transfer the strategies and skills that they build up in one of the languages. Hence, languages based on the same principles, allow children to enjoy an added advantage of being able to apply the principles learnt in one language to the other, aiding their passage into literacy (Bialystok, Luk & Kwan, 2005).

We discuss in this chapter, behavioural and reading profiles of a unique population of children provided simultaneous biliterate instruction in two languages that vary in script and in orthographic depth. Located in the Indian subcontinent, the population discussed represents a classic example of biliteracy, in which the language pairs differ in grain size as well as transparency, which, as discussed above, are known to impact reading strategies. The population described had simultaneous literacy instruction in their native language, Hindi, and a second unfamiliar language, English. Thus, while the phonology of Hindi is familiar, that of English is unfamiliar. We describe here, the writing systems of the two languages investigated, in an attempt to highlight the cognitive challenge in reading faced by Hindi–English biliterate children. Hindi, written in *Devanagari* script has a near transparent orthography with almost univalent mapping of sounds onto the basic written units, also called *aksharas*. It is an alpha syllabary with a blend of alphabetic and syllabic properties – it has distinct consonants and vowels akin to alphabetic scripts, but each grapheme or visual unit corresponds to a syllable as seen in syllabic scripts. Each *akshara* can represent a vowel in full form (अ) or a consonant with an embedded vowel (ख) or vowel diacritic above it, below it or on either of its sides (e.g. diacritic above – खे, below – खु, on either side – खा, खि) (Das *et al.*, 2011). Thus, *Devanagari* has a complex visual organisation, where consonants are arranged left-to-right, but vowels are placed on the sides, above or below the consonant which demands additional visual processing (Vaid & Gupta, 2002). In contrast, English uses an alphabetic Roman script with a visually simple left-to-right arrangement of letters but has an inconsistent sound-to-letter mapping. Thus, the one fundamental factor that is common to both writing systems is the alphabetic principle, namely that letters/alphabet names represent sounds. In addition to variation in writing systems, Hindi–English biliterate children also face the cognitive challenge of learning to read a second language in which they have no prior exposure to spoken language.

Models of reading acquisition proposed in the past have suggested a role for knowledge of phonology in learning to read. According to a model proposed by Ehri (1998), at the beginning stages of reading acquisition, called the pre-alphabetic stage, children use visual features of print to identify words. When they progress to the partial alphabetic stage they begin to associate letters with sounds but are not yet adept at it. In the fully alphabetic stage, they learn to appreciate the systematic regularities in mapping of print to speech sounds and eventually when they reach the consolidated alphabetic stage, they are able to recognise words instantly by sight. The strategy at the fully alphabetic stage is economical in a scenario where they possess knowledge of the spoken language. Other hypotheses suggest that in situations where children lack prior exposure to the spoken language, they may use rote memorisation to store associations between visual attributes of print and the words' pronunciations or meanings (Frith, 1985; Gough & Hillinger, 1980) similar to a pre-alphabetic stage in monolingual children. However, such effects of unfamiliarity of phonology of second language, have not been systematically and specifically investigated in reading tasks. Our sample population provides an ideal setting to explore this effect on neural networks of reading.

The participants in this study were children between the ages of 8 and 10 years, who had received simultaneous reading instruction in Hindi and English since the age of 6. In the light of the simultaneous reading instruction and similarity in alphabetic principles across the two writing systems (Hindi and English) we hypothesised:

1. Matched phonological skills across the two languages.
2. Similar accuracies in reading words.
3. Differences in non-word reading accuracies reflecting variation in orthographic depth.
4. A different reading strategy for English since the phonology of English was unfamiliar.

We proposed that reading in English, but not Hindi would rely on rote memorisation

Materials and methods

Study 1 – Phonological and reading profiles in children provided simultaneous biliterate instruction

Participants and task descriptions

Fifty-three typically developing, in the age group 8–10 years (mean age 9.3 years, SD = 0.65), Hindi–English biliterate children from schools in New Delhi and Allahabad, cities of Northern India, participated in the behavioural study. The participants belonged to two groups, 20 children belonged to the age group 8–9 years (mean age 8.6 years), and 33 children belonged to the age group 9–10 years (mean age 9.6 years). The native language for all participants was Hindi, while English was acquired primarily through schooling. At school, children simultaneously learnt to read both Hindi and English (from 5 years onwards), with English being the medium of instruction and within-classroom communication, whereas Hindi was primarily spoken at home. All participants had normal intelligence as tested on Coloured Progressive Matrices (CPM) (Raven, Raven & Court, 1962).

Behavioural tasks

PHONOLOGICAL AWARENESS TASKS

Tasks for testing English phonological skills included rhyming and phoneme replacement. While those for Hindi included rhyming and syllable replacement.

RHYMING TASK

The rhyming task in English included of sets of three single-syllable words (e.g. "kite" – "bite" – "park"), of which the child had to identify the two words with matching or rhyming sounds ("kite" and "bite"). The test contained 12 items.

The rhyming task in Hindi (तुकांतपरीक्षा) made use of sets of three words consisting of either one (e.g., नाम – काम – नील) or two syllables (e.g., हाथी – होली – साथी). The test contained eight sets of single-syllable words and four sets of two-syllable words, making a total of 12 items.

PHONEME REPLACEMENT TASK

In the phoneme replacement task, the child was asked to replace the initial phoneme, that is, the first sound of a given word with a new sound which was provided (e.g. "map" with a /k/ makes "cap"). The child was required to make ten new words by substituting initial sounds.

The syllable replacement task in Hindi required the child to replace the initial syllable, that is, the first segment of a given word with a new segment which was provided, thus forming a new word.

Example: 'नीला' में <नी> की जगह <ता> देता है 'ताला'

WORD AND NON-WORD READING TASK

WORD READING

For word reading in both Hindi and English, the child was required to read aloud a list of 50 standardised words that were all taken from the textbooks of Classes 3, 4 and 5, and arranged in order of increasing difficulty.

NON-WORD READING

Non-word reading tasks comprised three practice items, followed by 30 test items. The 30 test items were constructed by replacing two or more letters from real English/Hindi words that were chosen from textbooks of Classes 3, 4 and 5.

Accuracy data were recorded for both word and non-word reading.

Study 2 – Neuroimaging profiles of children provided simultaneous biliterate instruction

Participants, stimuli and methods

A separate set of 34 Hindi–English biliterate children (23 males) (mean age 9.21 years, SD = 0.69) participated in the neuroimaging study approved by the Human Ethics Committee of the institute. Similar to the children in the behavioural study, the participants in the neuroimaging study were also tested on phonological and reading tasks (see Cherodath & Singh, 2015 for details).

Brain activity was recorded while children read aloud words and non-words in English and Hindi that appeared on a screen, and while they fixated on the symbol strings displayed in between without any oral response. The reading task in each language had alternating word and non-word reading blocks interspersed with baseline blocks with symbol string fixation. Each rest block had a symbol string presented for 20 seconds while the task block had ten words/ non-words, each presented for a brief duration of two seconds. Sixty words and 60 non-words were presented in a randomised fashion from a list of 80 high-frequency words and 80 non-words. In each language participants performed two runs of the fMRI task, with six task blocks and six rest blocks. The total duration of the reading task was 16 minutes. The stimuli were presented using E-Prime 1.0 software (E-Prime Psychology Software Tools Inc., Pittsburgh, USA) on a computer, from where it was projected onto the screen on the head-mounted apparatus inside the scanner. The children's vocal responses were captured using a noise-cancelling, optical microphone (FOMRI II Dual Channel, version 1.1, Optoacoustics Ltd, Or-Yehuda, Israel) to monitor task performance. Functional imaging data was processed with SPM8 software (Wellcome Department of Cognitive Neurology, UK). Details of the image acquisition parameters and data analysis are published elsewhere (Cherodath & Singh, 2015).

Diffusion tensor magnetic resonance imaging (DTI) image analysis was performed using FSL toolbox (www.fmrib.ox.au.uk/fsl/fslwiki). Eddy current compensation was performed in preprocessing steps, and the DTIFIT tool was used to create diffusion tensor models at each voxel. The tensors were fitted onto the raw diffusion data and the Brain Extraction Tool (BET) was used to extract images after removing noise. Individual FA (fractional anisotropy) maps were created and fitted into standard MNI space using affine transformation and non-linear registration and then averaged to create a mean Fractional Anisotrophy (FA) map. The mean FA map was then skeletonised and used at a threshold of 0.2. The Tract Based Spatial Statistics (TBSS) tool was used to extract FA measures. FA values are known to reflect integrity of white matter microstructure (Le Bihan *et al.*, 2001) and have been demonstrated to show variations which mirror differences in cognitive abilities in typical individuals (Klingberg *et al.*, 2000; Olson *et al.*, 2009; Penke *et al.*, 2010).

Results

Results from study 1

Behavioural study

The mean scores for both age groups of phonological and reading tasks collected for the behavioural study are summarised in Table 17.1. Analysis of cross-linguistic correlations,

TABLE 17.1 The mean percent scores and standard deviations for various behavioural measures in Hindi and English and CPM scores for the participants in the behavioural study. p-values for cross-linguistic comparisons of measures are also given. Significant results are marked with asterisks

	Age group 8–9 years, n=20 (mean age = 8.6 years, SD = 0.4 years)					Age group 9–10 years, n=33 (mean age = 9.6, SD = 0.4years)				
CPM Standard score	Mean 108.50		SD 8.50			Mean 108.90		SD 9.70		
	English		Hindi		p-value	English		Hindi		p-value
	Mean	SD	Mean	SD		Mean	SD	Mean	SD	
Rhyming	90.8	10.1	87.9	13.1	0.43	94.9	6.9	91.9	7.9	0.10
Syllable replacement	–	–	93.0	9.2	0.26	–	–	95.9	10.6	0.13
Phoneme replacement	88.0	17.0	–	–		92.1	8.6	–	–	
Word reading	90.9	5.9	89.1	7.0	0.38	92.4	6.5	92.3	6.3	0.94
Non-word reading	79.8	16.8	82.7	17.3	0.60	79.4	15.5	88.2	10.0	0.01*

revealed significant correlations between rhyming scores ($r = 0.32$, $p < 0.01$). Similarly, phoneme replacement in English and syllable replacement in Hindi was also significantly correlated ($r = 0.35$, $p < 0.01$). Thus, all phonological measures were found to be strongly correlated between the two languages. Cross-language comparisons of reading scores showed no significant differences between languages for word reading. However, non-word reading accuracy was significantly greater in Hindi as compared to English ($p < 0.01$).

A three-way ANOVA of reading scores with age (8–9, 9–10 years), language (English, Hindi) and stimulus type (words, non-words) was performed. The results of the analysis are given in Table 17.2. We did not observe any main effects of age or language, indicating absence of developmental effects or language differences in reading scores. However, a main effect of stimulus type was observed, with non-word reading scores being consistently lower than word reading scores. A significant interaction was found between language and stimulus type, with a larger difference between reading accuracies for words and non-words in English rather than Hindi. The interaction effect suggested an effect of orthographic depth, with the transparent language – Hindi – being more facilitative in decoding non-words than English (Figure 17.1).

TABLE 17.2 Results from three-way ANOVA of reading scores for words and non-words. Significant results are marked with asterisks.

Effect	F	Sig.
Main effect of age	1.486	.224
Main effect of language	1.783	.183
Main effect of stimulus type	29.841	.000★
Age × language	1.035	.310
Age × stimulus type	.006	.937
Language × stimulus type	4.529	.034★
Age × language × stimulus type	.494	.483

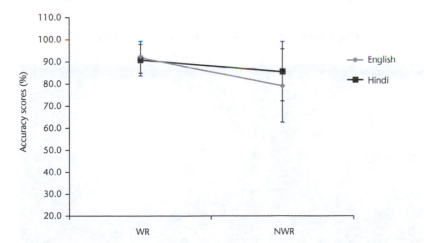

FIGURE 17.1 The effect of orthographic depth across the two languages in behavioural scores of reading. Word (WR) and non-word reading (NWR) percent accuracies are shown for English (blue diamonds) and Hindi (red squares). While no differences are seen in word reading scores across Hindi and English, significantly higher non-word reading scores are seen for Hindi as compared to English.

Results from study 2

Similar to the participants in study 1, the participants in study 2 also showed matched performances in phonological processing and reading, in that significant differences in non-word reading were seen only in English.

Imaging results

Figure 17.2 shows a rendering of activation patterns while reading English and Hindi. A shared network for reading both languages was observed, which consisted of bilateral precentral and postcentral gyri (BA 3/4), middle and inferior occipital gyri (BA 18/19), the hippocampus and the cerebellum.

To examine differences in orthographic depth, word and non-word activations patterns were investigated for both Hindi and English. As seen in Figure 17.3, differences in word and non-word activation patterns were seen in English. Similar significant differences were not seen for Hindi.

In order to explore effects of familiarity of second language on activation patterns, we performed a whole brain correlation of participant age with activation patterns for non-words and words in each language. A cluster in the right hippocampus showed a significant negative correlation of activity (cluster level FWE corrected, $p = 0.008$) with age in years (corrected to one decimal place) for English non-words after small volume correction with a sphere of radius 6 mm (Figure 17.4).

DTI results

Previous reports suggest that hippocampal connectivity with the posterior cingulate cortex determines performance in memory tasks in typical individuals (L. Wang *et al.*, 2010) and disorders impairing memory affect this connectivity through the hippocampal division of the cingulum bundle (Nir *et al.*, 2013). In the light of these, we further investigated the role of

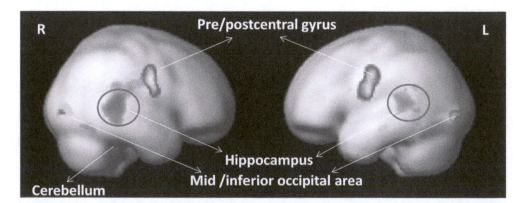

FIGURE 17.2 Shared reading network (yellow) for reading English (in red) and Hindi (in green), which consisted of bilateral precentral and postcentral regions, visual cortices, the hippocampus and the cerebellum. Circled in red are clusters activated in the bilateral hippocampus during reading.

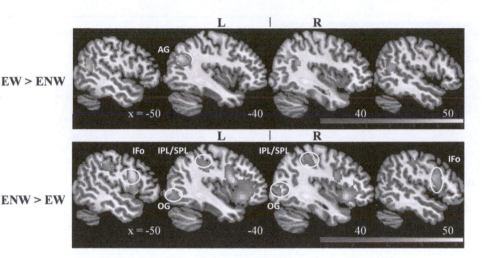

FIGURE 17.3 Sagittal slices demonstrating subtractions across word and non-word reading conditions in English (FDR corrected, $p < 0.05$, $k > 10$). The top panel shows regions activated while reading English words in comparison to non-words (EW > ENW) (T = 3.10) and the bottom panel shows regions exhibiting higher activity while reading English non-words in comparison to words (ENW > EW) (T = 2.85). English words showed higher activity in the left angular gyrus (AG) whereas English non-words showed higher activity in the bilateral inferior frontal operculum (IFo), parietal lobules (IPL/SPL) and the occipital region (OG).

Adapted from S. Cherodath and N.C. Singh, *Brain and Language*, 2015

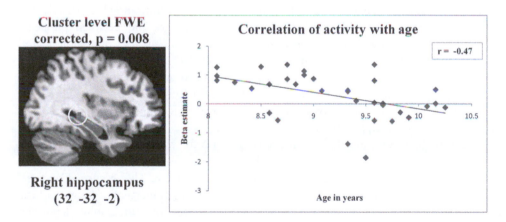

FIGURE 17.4 Results from whole brain correlation analyses of activity with age, showing correlation plots of activity in English non-word reading condition with age, from a cluster in the right hippocampus (red).

the hippocampus in second language reading by examining FA values of the hippocampal portion of cingulum tract. Preliminary data from five participants show significantly higher FA in the right as compared to the left cingulum bundle leading to the hippocampus, indicating higher myelination in the right hemisphere tracts (Figure 17.5). This trend suggests a key role of the right hippocampus in reading in biliterate readers of a foreign second language.

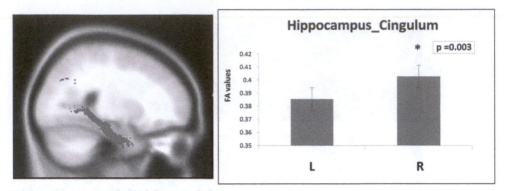

Hippocampus subdivision – right cingulum bundle

FIGURE 17.5 Results from FA analysis of a hippocampal section of the cingulum bundle on the left and right, showing higher mean FA in the right cingulum bundle (red).

Discussion

Our population of biliterate children described here are unusual in that they acquired literacy simultaneously in languages that vary in grain size and orthographic depth, and the results presented here add new knowledge to the understanding of bilingual biliteracy. As described earlier Hindi–*Devanagari* and English orthographic systems share a fundamental principle in that they both are alphabetic in nature and involve mapping letters to sounds. Our results showed that despite different grain sizes for Hindi and English, significantly high correlations were seen between both rhyming skills in the two languages and between phoneme replacement in English and syllable replacement in Hindi. This suggests that phonological skills for the two languages are correlated with each other. Consequently, we anticipate that good phonological skills in the native language will lead to good phonological skills in a second language. Similar results have also been reported for Korean–English in children (M. Wang, Park & Lee, 2006) and we therefore propose that there is cross-language phonological transfer across different alphabetic languages.

Results of the three-way ANOVA for reading scores for words and non-words (Table 17.1) suggested an effect of orthographic depth. Non-word reading was found to be more accurate in the transparent language, Hindi, as compared to English. The absence of language effects indicated that this was not due to the native language advantage, but because of the transparency of Hindi. These findings point towards an effect of orthographic depth and reveal an advantage in decoding during reading in a transparent language in biliterate children which is in line with Ziegler and Goswami's theory of reading acquisition (Ziegler & Goswami, 2005), which proposes novel word reading to be easier in a transparent orthography as compared to a deep one.

The matched proficiencies in word and non-word reading seen in the behavioural data were reflected in a shared cortical network for reading in both English and Hindi (Cherodath & Singh, 2015). This network is comprised of components in the bilateral motor cortex, visual regions, hippocampus and cerebellum. Postcentral gyri and the cerebellum are believed to carry out somatosensory feedback during speech (Price, 2010), while precentral gyri have been suggested to be part of a phonological network mediating sound–letter mapping while reading (Vigneau *et al.*, 2006). Activity in the superior temporal gyri, was observed at lower thresholds ($p < 0.001$, uncorrected) indicating that phonological mechanisms via superior temporal gyri were recruited, but to a lesser extent. We propose that as reading skills mature, superior temporal cortices begin to be actively engaged. The recruitment of a shared circuitry for reading languages, despite differences in writing systems, clearly indicates that the developing biliterate brain with simultaneous reading instruction recruits a largely common neural mechanism for reading.

In our previous study, the orthographic differences between the two languages were also investigated via subtraction analysis between word and non-word stimuli separately (Cherodath & Singh, 2015). As shown in Figure 17.4, English words preferentially engaged the left angular gyrus which is a salient feature reported in other word reading studies known to carry out lexical processing at whole-word level (Joubert *et al.*, 2004). English non-words on the other hand activated the left inferior frontal region (BA 44) and inferior parietal region (BA 40) associated with phonological processing (Burton, 2001; Fiez, 1997; Fiez & Petersen, 1998) and print-to-sound conversion in assembled reading respectively (Booth *et al.*, 2002; Cao *et al.*, 2006; Chen, Fu, Iversen, Smith & Matthews, 2002). The engagement of bilateral superior parietal lobules (BA 7) observed during English non-word reading, has also been associated with processing untrained/unfamiliar words (Bitan, Manor, Morocz & Karni, 2005). No such differences were observed for Hindi and a subtraction analysis of the word and non-word reading networks (and vice-versa) for Hindi yielded no significant activations.

The subtraction effects indicated that for English, word reading relies on neural substrates mediating lexical processing, whereas non-words rely on neural substrates implicated in grapheme-to-phoneme conversion. Unlike English, Hindi showed no significant differences in responses to words and non-words in the subtraction analysis, implying use of similar reading strategies across these categories. The converging evidence from behaviour and neuroimaging in our study points towards dual reading strategies in the relatively opaque language, English, but not in Hindi, indicated an orthographic depth effect. Evidence for such orthographic depth effects have been found in English monolinguals (Fiebach, Friederici, Müller & Von Cramon, 2002) as well as Hindi–English biliterate adults (Das *et al.*, 2011) and suggests that mechanisms for reading in populations receiving simultaneous biliterate instruction, are indeed shaped by the orthographic features of the underlying writing system. That such flexibility in reading is also demonstrated by children only reiterates the plasticity of the developing brain.

A novel and interesting finding was bilateral activation of the hippocampus across all reading conditions, not prominently documented in earlier studies on reading in children. The decreased reliance with increase in age for decoding non-words in the second language, English, demonstrates additional cognitive demands placed on the developing biliterate brain for learning to read an unfamiliar language. Further, preliminary results from diffusion imaging indicated increased FA in the right hemisphere tracts leading to the hippocampus, further confirming a special role for the right hippocampus in biliterates reading a foreign second language.

Involvement of the right hippocampus has been previously observed in recall of learnt words (Schacter *et al.*, 1996). The reduced engagement of the hippocampus with learning or increase in stimulus familiarity has also been previously documented (Breitenstein *et al.*, 2005; Opitz & Friederici, 2003; Strange *et al.*, 1999). Theories on reading acquisition have also highlighted the importance of memory in early stages of reading, for retrieval of newly learnt associations between letters and sounds (Ehri & Wilce, 1985). In the light of this collective evidence, we attribute the recruitment of the right hippocampus to the formation of robust form–sound association processes, which mediate reading in the unfamiliar second language. This process probably achieves automaticity with age with increased familiarity of the language, and might be important in reading acquisition in biliterate children in culturally diverse language environments where second language learning accompanies reading acquisition.

Our findings have important implications for biliterate education. In the light of cross-linguistic phonological transfer, language teachers should focus on building strong language skills in the native language and recognise that strong native language skills can be transferred to the second language. The results presented here also highlight the fact that biliterate children at risk for dyslexia need to be assessed in both languages. To the best of our knowledge, this is not the case. This is primarily because of the absence of assessment batteries in native languages. In India, this is particularly true and is urgently needed. Only when systematic evaluations of both phonological and orthographic skills are carried out in both languages will we begin to truly understand dyslexia in biliterate populations.

Acknowledgements

The authors would like to acknowledge the Cognitive Science Initiative of the Department of Science and Technology, Government of India for financial support and the National Brain Research Centre, India for intramural funding.

References

Bialystok, E., Luk, G., & Kwan, E. (2005). Bilingualism, biliteracy, and learning to read: Interactions among languages and writing systems. *Scientific studies of reading*, 9(1), 43–61.

Bitan, T., Manor, D., Morocz, I.A., & Karni, A. (2005). Effects of alphabeticality, practice and type of instruction on reading an artificial script: An fMRI study. *Cognitive Brain Research*, 25(1), 90–106.

Bolger, D.J., Perfetti, C.A., & Schneider, W. (2005). Cross-cultural effect on the brain revisited: Universal structures plus writing system variation. *Human brain mapping*, 25(1), 92–104.

Booth, J.R., Burman, D.D., Meyer, J.R., Gitelman, D.R., Parrish, T.B., & Mesulam, M. (2002). Functional anatomy of intra- and cross-modal lexical tasks. *Neuroimage*, 16(1), 7–22.

Breitenstein, C., Jansen, A., Deppe, M., Foerster, A.-F., Sommer, J., Wolbers, T., *et al.* (2005). Hippocampus activity differentiates good from poor learners of a novel lexicon. *Neuroimage*, 25(3), 958–968.

Burton, M.W. (2001). The role of inferior frontal cortex in phonological processing. *Cognitive Science*, 25(5), 695–709.

Cao, F., Bitan, T., Chou, T.L., Burman, D.D., & Booth, J.R. (2006). Deficient orthographic and phonological representations in children with dyslexia revealed by brain activation patterns. *Journal of Child Psychology and Psychiatry*, 47(10), 1041–1050.

Carreiras, M., Mechelli, A., Estévez, A., & Price, C.J. (2007). Brain activation for lexical decision and reading aloud: Two sides of the same coin? *Journal of Cognitive Neuroscience*, 19(3), 433–444.

Chen, Y., Fu, S., Iversen, S.D., Smith, S.M., & Matthews, P.M. (2002). Testing for dual brain processing routes in reading: A direct contrast of Chinese character and pinyin reading using fMRI. *Journal of Cognitive Neuroscience*, 14(7), 1088–1098.

Cherodath, S., & Singh, N. (2015). The influence of orthographic depth on reading networks in simultaneous biliterate children. *Brain and Language*, 143, 42–51.

Coulmas, F. (1989). *The writing systems of the world*. Oxford: Blackwell.

Das, T., Padakannaya, P., Pugh, K., & Singh, N. (2011). Neuroimaging reveals dual routes to reading in simultaneous proficient readers of two orthographies. *Neuroimage*, 54(2), 1476–1487.

Deterding, D., & Kirkpatrick, A. (2006). Emerging South-East Asian Englishes and intelligibility. *World Englishes*, 25(3–4), 391–409.

Ehri, L.C. (1998). Grapheme–phoneme knowledge is essential for learning to read words in English. In L. Metsala & L.C. Ehri (Eds) *Word recognition in beginning literacy*. Hillsdale, NJ: Erlbaum, pp. 3–40.

Ehri, L.C., & Wilce, L.S. (1985). Movement into reading: Is the first stage of printed word learning visual or phonetic? *Reading Research Quarterly*, 20, 163–179.

Fiebach, C.J., Friederici, A.D., Müller, K., & Von Cramon, D.Y. (2002). fMRI evidence for dual routes to the mental lexicon in visual word recognition. *Journal of Cognitive Neuroscience*, 14(1), 11–23.

Fiez, J.A. (1997). Phonology, semantics, and the role of the left inferior prefrontal cortex. *Human Brain Mapping*, 5(2), 79–83.

Fiez, J.A., & Petersen, S.E. (1998). Neuroimaging studies of word reading. *Proceedings of the National Academy of Sciences*, 95(3), 914–921.

Frith, U. (1985). Beneath the surface of developmental dyslexia. In K. Patterson, J. Marshall & M. Coltheart (Eds) *Surface dyslexia, neuropsychological and cognitive studies of phonological reading*. London: Erlbaum, pp. 301–330.

Goswami, U., Ziegler, J.C., Dalton, L., & Schneider, W. (2003). Nonword reading across orthographies: How flexible is the choice of reading units? *Applied Psycholinguistics*, 24(2), 235–247.

Gough, P.B., & Hillinger, M.L. (1980). Learning to read: An unnatural act. *Annals of Dyslexia*, 30(1), 179–196.

Jamal, N.I., Piche, A.W., Napoliello, E.M., Perfetti, C.A., & Eden, G.F. (2012). Neural basis of single-word reading in Spanish–English bilinguals. *Human Brain Mapping*, 33(1), 235–245.

Joubert, S., Beauregard, M., Walter, N., Bourgouin, P., Beaudoin, G., Leroux, J.-M., et al. (2004). Neural correlates of lexical and sublexical processes in reading. *Brain and Language*, 89(1), 9–20.

Katz, L., & Frost, R. (1992). The reading process is different for different orthographies: The orthographic depth hypothesis. In R. Frost & L. Katz (Eds) *Orthography, phonology, morphology, and meaning. Advances in psychology*. Amsterdam: Elsevier, p. 67.

Klingberg, T., Hedehus, M., Temple, E., Salz, T., Gabrieli, J.D., Moseley, M.E., et al. (2000). Microstructure of temporo-parietal white matter as a basis for reading ability: Evidence from diffusion tensor magnetic resonance imaging. *Neuron*, 25(2), 493–500.

Le Bihan, D., Mangin, J.F., Poupon, C., Clark, C.A., Pappata, S., Molko, N., et al. (2001). Diffusion tensor imaging: Concepts and applications. *Journal of Magnetic Resonance Imaging*, 13(4), 534–546.

Nir, T.M., Jahanshad, N., Villalon-Reina, J.E., Toga, A.W., Jack, C.R., Weiner, M.W., et al. (2013). Effectiveness of regional DTI measures in distinguishing Alzheimer's disease, MCI, and normal aging. *NeuroImage: Clinical*, 3, 180–195.

Olson, E.A., Collins, P.F., Hooper, C.J., Muetzel, R., Lim, K.O., & Luciana, M. (2009). White matter integrity predicts delay discounting behavior in 9- to 23-year-olds: A diffusion tensor imaging study. *Journal of Cognitive Neuroscience*, 21(7), 1406–1421.

Opitz, B., & Friederici, A.D. (2003). Interactions of the hippocampal system and the prefrontal cortex in learning language-like rules. *Neuroimage*, 19(4), 1730–1737.

Paulesu, E., McCrory, E., Fazio, F., Menoncello, L., Brunswick, N., Cappa, S.F., et al. (2000). A cultural effect on brain function. *Nature Neuroscience*, 3(1), 91–96.

Penke, L., Maniega, S.M., Murray, C., Gow, A.J., Hernández, M.C.V., Clayden, J.D., et al. (2010). A general factor of brain white matter integrity predicts information processing speed in healthy older people. *The Journal of Neuroscience*, 30(22), 7569–7574.

Price, C.J. (2010). The anatomy of language: A review of 100 fMRI studies published in 2009. *Annals of the New York Academy of Sciences*, 1191(1), 62–88.

Ranguelov, S., De Coster, I., Norani, S., & Paolini, G. (2012). *Key data on education in Europe 2012*. Education, Audiovisual and Culture Executive Agency, European Commission.

Raven, J.C., Raven, J., & Court, J. (1962). *Coloured progressive matrices*. London: H.K. Lewis.

Saiegh-Haddad, E., & Geva, E. (2010). Acquiring reading in two languages: An introduction to the special issue. *Reading and Writing*, 23(3), 263–267.

Schacter, D.L., Alpert, N.M., Savage, C.R., Rauch, S.L., & Albert, M.S. (1996). Conscious recollection and the human hippocampal formation: Evidence from positron emission tomography. *Proceedings of the National Academy of Sciences*, 93(1), 321–325.

Seymour, P.H., Aro, M., & Erskine, J.M. (2003). Foundation literacy acquisition in European orthographies. *British Journal of Psychology*, 94(2), 143–174.

Silver, R., Hu, G., & Iino, M. (2002). *English language education in China, Japan, and Singapore*. Singapore: National Institute of Education.

Strange, B., Fletcher, P., Henson, R., Friston, K., & Dolan, R. (1999). Segregating the functions of human hippocampus. *Proceedings of the National Academy of Sciences*, 96(7), 4034–4039.

Treiman, R., Mullennix, J., Bijeljac-Babic, R., & Richmond-Welty, E.D. (1995). The special role of rimes in the description, use, and acquisition of English orthography. *Journal of Experimental Psychology: General*, 124(2), 107–136.

Vaid, J., & Gupta, A. (2002). Exploring word recognition in a semi-alphabetic script: The case of *Devanagari*. *Brain and Language*, 81(1), 679–690.

Vigneau, M., Beaucousin, V., Herve, P.-Y., Duffau, H., Crivello, F., Houde, O., *et al.* (2006). Meta-analyzing left hemisphere language areas: Phonology, semantics, and sentence processing. *Neuroimage*, 30(4), 1414–1432.

Wang, L., LaViolette, P., O'Keefe, K., Putcha, D., Bakkour, A., Van Dijk, K.R., *et al.* (2010). Intrinsic connectivity between the hippocampus and posteromedial cortex predicts memory performance in cognitively intact older individuals. *Neuroimage*, 51(2), 910–917.

Wang, M., Park, Y., & Lee, K.R. (2006). Korean–English biliteracy acquisition: Cross-language phonological and orthographic transfer. *Journal of Educational Psychology*, 98(1), 148–158.

Wang, Q. (2007). The national curriculum changes and their effects on English language teaching in the People's Republic of China. In J. Cummins and C. Davison (Eds) *International handbook of English language teaching*. Berlin: Springer, pp. 87–105.

Ziegler, J.C., & Goswami, U. (2005). Reading acquisition, developmental dyslexia, and skilled reading across languages: A psycholinguistic grain size theory. *Psychological Bulletin*, 131(1), 3–29.

18

THE EMOTIONAL AND MENTAL HEALTH CHALLENGES OF ACCULTURATION, MULTILINGUAL STRESS AND MIGRATION

Richard Soppitt

This chapter will:

1. Address the emotional and mental health aspects of migration for children and adolescents
2. Discuss the challenges of cultural integration for young people's mental health
3. Explore educational and cognitive aspects of multilingualism

Immigrant youth: Acculturation, identity and adaptation

The psychology of intercultural adaptation was first discussed by Plato. In the fourth century BC in his Laws, Plato identified the tendencies in human beings to travel and to imitate strangers but argued against this as it risked losing in his view the superiority of the Greek culture.

International migration is a global phenomenon that is growing in scope, complexity and impact. Migration is both a cause and effect of broader development processes and an intrinsic feature of our ever globalising world. While no substitute for development, migration can be a positive force for development when supported by the right set of policies. The rise in global mobility, the growing complexity of migratory patterns and its impact on countries, migrants, families and communities have all contributed to international migration becoming a priority for the international community (UN Population Report, 2014).

Migration has been viewed as a source of both crisis and opportunity for individuals and societies. The psychology of those factors that contribute to making the process a positive, rather than a negative, factor in personal and societal development has been studied.

Acculturation is the process of cultural and psychological change that follows intercultural contact (Berry, Phinney, Sam & Vedder, 2006). Cultural changes, affecting a group's customs, and their economic and political life combine with psychological changes, such as individuals' attitudes toward the acculturation process, their cultural identities and their social behaviours in relation to the groups in contact.

The end point of the adaptations also have a core psychological purpose, supporting a person's well-being and social skills.

Considerable research has been devoted to the understanding of immigration, acculturation and adaptation of adults, but much less among youth. A key issue is whether the findings from research with adult immigrants can apply to youth.

Data from a large international study of immigrant youth in 13 immigrant-receiving countries (Berry et al., 2006) helps the understanding of how immigrant youth live within and between two cultures, namely those of their immigrant parents, families and communities on the one hand, and those of their peers and the larger society on the other hand. It also considers the patterns of relationships between engagement with intercultural relations and successful adaptation.

Early research had assumed that immigrants would inevitably be absorbed into the receiving society, in a unidirectional process. However, others (Berry, 1980) proposed that there are two independent dimensions underlying the process of acculturation: individuals' links to their cultures of origin and to their societies of settlement. Such links include affinity for involvement in the two cultures (acculturation attitudes), and in the behaviours that they engage in (e.g. their language knowledge and use, including written language and social relationships). Phinney (1990), supported a bidirectional approach and argued that immigration is the systemic experience of acculturation by groups; individuals may have independent identities with respect to their cultures of origin and to their societies of settlement.

Such theories have led to the proposing of four acculturation states:

1. Assimilation is when there is little interest in cultural maintenance combined with a strong affinity for interacting with the larger society.
2. Separation occurs when cultural maintenance is sought while involvement with others is avoided.
3. Marginalisation exists when neither cultural maintenance nor interaction with others is sought.
4. Integration occurs when both cultural maintenance and involvement with the larger society are sought.

The view developed by Ward (1996) is that there are two distinct ways of adapting to acculturation. Psychological adaptation relates to personal well-being and good mental health. Sociocultural adaptation relates to individuals' social competence in managing their daily life in the intercultural setting.

Studies have shown that perceived discrimination is negatively related to immigrant adaptation. Acculturation is a process over time, and with longer residence, youths would be more likely to be integrated into their country of residence.

Age, gender, religion and the socioeconomic status of the family have all been identified as possible sources of variation, as has the ethnic composition of the immediate neighbourhood.

Berry et al. (2006) found that religious preference was related to youth acculturation in 13 broadly Judeo-Christian societies of settlement. Integration predominated for the Judeo-Christian immigrant youth; however, this was also the case for those with Eastern religions.

Adaptation varied according to gender; boys had slightly better psychological adaptation than girls, but had poorer sociocultural adaptation. Females may be more at psychological risk for acculturation problems than males. Research supports the notion that a combination of a strong ethnic and a strong national orientation is conducive to immigrant youths' positive adaptation.

Research indicates that cultural maintenance should be supported by the immigrant community, and permitted by the society as a whole. Moreover, participation and inclusion in the life of the larger society should be sought by the immigrants, and permitted and supported by the larger society. Educational inclusion is a key determinant for young people's healthy acculturation.

If public policy and institutional change work toward the acceptance of diversity and equality, then discrimination might decrease in the long term. Adolescents who are confident in their own ethnicity and proud of their ethnic group may be better able to deal constructively with discrimination, by taking proactive steps to combat it. Teachers, therapists and parents can all profit from knowing that the integrative way of acculturating is likely to lead these young people to more satisfactory and successful transitions to adulthood in their culturally diverse societies.

A foundational principle of multiculturalism is the emphasis on cultural diversity. However, the value of this is perceived differently by majority and minority group members reflecting their competing interests and implications. Berry and Kalin (1995) argue that groups are more in favour of multiculturalism when they see gains of multiculturalism for themselves. Mainstream groups often view the desire of migrant groups to maintain their culture as a threat to the majority culture and the unity of the society (Van Oudenhoven, Prins & Buunk, 1998). Moreover, acceptance of cultural diversity is seen as a threat to their superior cultural and social status. In contrast, migrants are more supportive of the ideal of multiculturalism since it offers many advantages to them, such as maintaining their own culture and obtaining higher social status in society. The psychological benefits to the migrants in maintaining their cultural identity and therefore having greater productivity and fewer mental health issues are not always appreciated by mainstream culture. Empirical studies need to focus more on mutual views of majority and minority group members, as the realisation of a multicultural society depends substantially on their reciprocal attitudes and behaviours (Arends-Tóth & Van De Vijver, 2003).

Mental health implications of migration

Stansfeld *et al.* (2004) addressed the prevalence of psychological distress in different ethnic groups amongst adolescents. They found that rates of psychological distress were similar to rates in UK national samples in boys and girls. Bangladeshi pupils, although highly socially disadvantaged, had a lower risk of psychological distress. Non-UK White girls had higher rates of depressive symptoms which may be related to recent migration. Low rates of psychological distress in Bangladeshi pupils in this sample relative to White pupils, despite socio-economic disadvantage, could be associated with cultural protective factors, such as social cohesion.

Does cultural integration explain a mental health advantage for adolescents?

Bhui, Lenguerrand, Maynard, Stansfeld and Harding (2012) looked at the issue of whether cultural integration measured by cross-cultural friendships explains a mental health advantage for adolescents. A prospective cohort of over 6,000 adolescents was recruited from 51 secondary schools in 10 London boroughs. Cultural identity was assessed by friendship choices within and across ethnic groups. Cultural integration is one of four categories of cultural identity. Using gender-specific linear-mixed models the authors tested whether cultural integration explained a mental health advantage, and whether gender and age were influential. Demographic and other relevant factors, such as ethnic group, socio-economic status, family structure, parenting styles and perceived racism were also measured and entered into the models. Mental health was measured by the Strengths and Difficulties Questionnaire as a 'total difficulties score' and by classification as a 'probable clinical case'.

Overall mental health improved with age, more so in male than female students. Cultural integration (friendships with own and other ethnic groups) was associated with the lowest levels of mental health problems especially among male students. This effect was sustained irrespective of age, ethnicity and other potential explanatory variables. There was a mental health advantage among specific ethnic groups: Black Caribbean and Black African male students (Nigerian/Ghanaian origin) and female Indian students. This was not fully explained by cultural integration, although cultural integration was independently associated with better mental health.

Cultural integration was associated with better mental health, independent of the mental health advantage found among specific ethnic groups: Black Caribbean and some Black African male students and female Indian students.

During adolescence, integrated peer relationships and dress preference may be proxy measures for cultural identity. Bhui *et al.* (2008a) investigated the influence of different proxy measures for cultural identities on the risk of common mental disorders among Bangladeshi and White British pupils. Cultural identity, expressed by clothing preferences, influenced mental health; but the effects differed by gender and ethnic group. Bangladeshi girls who preferred traditional clothes from their own cultural group were less likely to have mental health problems than Bangladeshi girls showing an equal preference for clothing from their own and other cultures.

Refugee children

Measham *et al.* (2014) found that refugee children are at risk for mental health disorders including post-traumatic stress disorder (PTSD) and depression, emotional and behavioural issues, disturbed sleep, nightmares, grief reactions, inattention, social withdrawal, and medically unexplained symptoms. Children may also express distress in ways that do not fit within prevailing diagnostic paradigms, and the identification and management of their difficulties may be complicated by selective mutism, speech or learning disorders, or other constitutional issues. Particularly vulnerable groups are children and women who have suffered sexual and physical abuse (Lorek *et al.*, 2009).

Refugee children are prone to severe stressors during the pre-migratory, migratory and post-migratory periods. In their home countries, children may witness or experience war atrocities, be deprived of food and water, and be separated from family members, predisposing them to PTSD and severe adjustment disorders. They can experience other hardships including significant disruption of their daily lives, separation from key attachment figures and disruption of schooling leading to an additional need for catch up in their future education. Specific learning impairments are likely to be missed until later, when the additional stress of learning a new language will further add to the complexities of identification and remediation.

Throughout migration, they may become separated from caregivers and suffer from exposure to violence and harsh living conditions, poor nutrition and uncertainty about the future. From a Maslow's hierarchy of needs perspective, physical safety, especially for children in refugee camps, who may be exposed to infectious disease, malnutrition, food insecurity, domestic abuse and sexual violence will take priority over education.

Upon arrival in a new host country, children may experience stress related to their family's adaptation and acculturation, family conflict, difficulties with education in a new language, and experiences of social exclusion and discrimination.

In summary, child refugees are at risk for a variety of mental health problems, particularly when pre- and post-trauma risks are present. They have the capacity for resilience and post-traumatic growth, especially when protective factors are enhanced or supported in a holistic manner. The stigma around mental health services, which may be accentuated by cultural and religious perspectives, and because distressed refugee children may present with non-specific physical symptoms of distress as markers of mental health disorder, means that primary care providers have a key role in detecting, assessing and proposing treatment to vulnerable children.

Issues around multilingualism and cognitive and language development

Bialystok, Craik, Green and Gollan (2009) cover the psychology of bilingualism and note that the regular use of two languages by bilingual individuals has been shown to have a broad impact on language and cognitive functioning.

Four areas of interest were discussed.

a) The differences between monolinguals and bilinguals in children's acquisition of language
Children learning two languages from birth follow the same milestones for language acquisition as monolinguals do (e.g. first words, first use of grammar) possibly using different strategies for language acquisition; they generally have a smaller vocabulary in each language than do monolingual children. Adult bilinguals typically take longer to retrieve individual words than monolinguals do, and generate fewer words on verbal fluency/in-category naming tests.

b) Cognitive processing in both children and adults
There is enhancement of executive control functions in bilinguals. On tasks that require inhibition of distracting information, switching between tasks, or holding information in mind while performing a task, bilinguals of all ages outperform comparable monolinguals.

It is postulated that bilinguals recruit control processes to manage linguistic performance and that these become enhanced for other unrelated aspects of cognitive processing. Preliminary evidence also suggests that the executive control advantage may even postpone Alzheimer's and other dementias by up to five years.

c) Brain networks responsible for language processing in bilinguals
Neuroimaging research identifies the networks used for various nonverbal executive control tasks and shows that bilinguals manage attention to their two language systems using the same networks that are used by monolinguals performing nonverbal tasks.

d) Special circumstances that surround the referral of bilingual children (e.g. language delays) for clinical intervention
Bialystok *et al.* (2009) make the valid point that such referrals are typically based on standardised assessments using normative data from monolingual populations, e.g. vocabulary size and lexical retrieval. Such measures are often different for bilinguals, both for children and adults.

The authors concluded that extending this pattern to education, it would be reasonable to assume that there is a cumulative effect of learning language that, at least in the intense environment of immersion programmes, confers some cognitive advantages on children even if they do not become highly fluent speakers.

Acculturation and psychological well-being among immigrant adolescents in Finland was studied by Liebkind and Jasinskaja-Lahti (2000) in a comparative study of adolescents from different cultural backgrounds.

This study investigated the effects of acculturation on the psychological well-being of nearly 600 immigrant adolescents. The respondents were 11 to 20 years old, originally from the former Soviet Union, Turkey, Somalia and Vietnam, and now living in Finland. To gain an understanding of the complexity and specificity of the relationship between acculturation and psychological well-being, a large range of existing psychological well-being scales measuring acculturative stress, behavioural problems, self-esteem, life satisfaction and sense of mastery were used as dependent variables. Most indices of psychological well-being were clearly and negatively related to perceived discrimination, and some of them were also positively related to second-language proficiency. In addition, the adolescents' experiences of parental support and adherence to traditional family-related values promoted their psychological well-being.

The majority of newcomers face the challenge of mastering the mainstream host country's language while also adjusting to a new school and gaining academic skills. Academic language proficiency is highly predictive of academic success. While oral proficiency can be developed within a couple of years, students will take, on average, four to seven years under optimal conditions to acquire the level of language skills necessary to be competitive with native-born peers in the classroom. Language fluency is also a significant predictor of positive academic adjustment in studies of first- and second-generation immigrant students.

Many immigrant students face the singular challenge of acquiring a new language. Struggles in language are evident in a review by Suárez-Orozco, Bang and Onaga (2010), where only 7% of a studied sample had developed academic English skills comparable to those of their native-born English-speaking peers after an average of seven years in the United States. When English learners are not able to participate and compete in mainstream classrooms, they often read more slowly than native speakers, do not understand double-entendres, and are not exposed to the same words and cultural information as their native-born middle-class peers. Their academic language skills may also prevent them from sustaining engagement or performing well on assessments designed for native English speakers.

Mental health implications of immigration and multiculturism

Immigrant children and youth suffer anxiety disorders, depression, and post-traumatic stress disorders, which can significantly impair functioning (such as academic functioning) for these children. Factors such as parental well-being and peer relationships can moderate or exacerbate the symptomatic and functional impact of such disorders. Second-generation children have been found to be at higher risk of more behavioural conditions, such as substance abuse, conduct disturbance and eating disorders, than the first generation of immigrant youth. This may be a result of this group facing the chronic stresses created by poverty, marginalisation, stigma or discrimination without the secure identity and traditional values of their parents, while not yet having a secure integrated cultural identity and skills.

Second-generation youths, who tended to hang out with friends, were more exposed to the media, and spent less time with their families and in religious activities, have been found to have a significantly higher risk of substance abuse and suicidality than more traditional Mexican-born youth in US studies. Various studies have shown greater risk for eating disorders in more acculturated immigrant youth both in the United States and in Europe (Miller & Pumariega, 2001).

Specific conditions

Psychosis

In general, studies of the prevalence of schizophrenia have focused on adults, and have shown that members of the African-Caribbean population have consistently been identified as 3–12 times more likely to receive a diagnosis of schizophrenia than their White English counterparts. Laurens, West, Murray and Hodgins (2007) examined the associations of ethnicity and migrant status with a triad of antecedents for at-risk mental states leading to schizophrenia in a UK community sample of children aged 9–12. Their research concluded that the prevalence of the antecedents of schizophrenia was greater among children of African-Caribbean origin residing in the UK compared with White British children. This mirrors the increased incidence and prevalence of schizophrenia spectrum disorders or psychosis among adults of African-Caribbean ethnicity.

These findings of a higher prevalence of schizophrenia in UK ethnic minority groups parallel the exceptionally high incidence rate of schizophrenia and other psychoses in immigrant and ethnic minority groups in Western Europe generally (Singh & Burns, 2006) and have significant implications for service provision in areas with larger migrant communities. At-risk mental states in young people whereby there are a constellation of quasi-psychotic symptoms, such as hearing voices addressing the young person, illusions and visual hallucinations, need to be taken seriously and referred to Early Intervention in Psychosis teams which generally operate for the age range of 14–35 nationally. Development of appropriate Youth Mental Health Services which have expertise in the transcultural aspects of psychiatry is also desirable.

A number of transcultural psychiatry authors stress the importance of institutional racism and the social construction of psychiatric categories in understanding these findings. For example, Sashi Sashidharan, a Birmingham-based psychiatrist (2001, p. 244) noted the salience of institutional racism in ethnic minority care and warned that

> until we begin to address racism within psychiatry, in its knowledge base, its historical and cultural roots and within its practices and procedures, we are unlikely to achieve significant progress in improving services for minority ethnic groups.

Frederick Hickling a psychiatrist from Jamaica correlates the elevated Black incidence rate of schizophrenia with social alienation and racism experienced by Black people in the UK, and misdiagnosis by White British mental health professionals (Hickling, 2005).

Other common mental disorders (CMD)

Studies of adolescents have shown lower rates of psychiatric disorders among Nigerian and Ghanaian boys, and Indian girls (Maynard & Harding, 2010a) and Bangladeshi young people (Stansfeld *et al.*, 2004) as compared with White British youth; results which may be explained by different parenting styles (Maynard & Harding, 2010b), or cultural identity (Bhui *et al.*, 2005), but more work is required.

In conclusion, the findings of studies on the mental health of immigrant and refugee populations (Pumariega, Rothe & Pumariega, 2005) can be summarised as follows:

1. Proximity to traumatic events, duration of exposure and intensity of the traumatic experience may affect psychological response. Vulnerability to people trafficking and sexual exploitation are particular risks in this population.
2. Children and adolescents are influenced by the response of others (family, peers, community and cultural environment) to such trauma during and after the traumatic experience.
3. Immigrant adolescents are less symptomatic and demonstrate better social functioning than their adult counterparts. This finding may point to a relative resilience conferred by this particular developmental stage.
4. There may be increased risks for second-generation children and youth (the children of immigrants), who may face more chronic stressors and have less protective factors from their parents' culture.
5. Mental health factors, most of which go unrecognised by teachers and untreated, can adversely affect the immigrant's successful adaptation and functioning after immigration. Religious coping factors can help to ameliorate the stress of transitions and life events (Bhui, King, Dein & O'Connor, 2008b).
6. Older adults have the highest risk for mental health problems resulting from immigration, with the possible exception of traumatised immigrants. Lack of cultural flexibility, isolation from family members and the community, and health risk factors contribute to this increased risk. This is especially relevant if this leads to the immigrant youths becoming young carers for older relatives alongside their other challenges.

Accessing support for mental health issues related to specific learning difficulties

Mental health disorders associated with specific learning difficulties include anxiety, depression, Attention Deficit Hyperactivity Disorder (ADHD) and other neurodevelopmental issues such as Autism Spectrum Disorder (ASD). Margari *et al.* (2013) found comorbidity in 62.2% of their total sample of those with specific learning difficulties: ADHD was present in 33%, anxiety disorder in 29%, developmental coordination disorder in 18%, language disorder in 11% and mood disorder in 9%.

Maughan and colleagues in their paper 'Reading problems and depressed mood' (2003) found robust links between severe, persistent reading problems and increased risk for depressed mood in a community sample of boys aged 7–10 years old. In a paper on literacy and mental disorders, Maughan and Carroll (2006) found increased rates of both generalised anxiety and separation anxiety disorder among 9–15 year olds with reading difficulties, but no excess of specific phobias. These were reflected in both concerns about school and social anxiety. Education-related stressors are considered to play a key role. With regards to anxiety and depressed mood, a bidirectional relationship between anxiety, depression and academic achievement has been suggested, and this makes empirical and intuitive sense (Margari *et al.*, 2013). What is effective treatment in one area does not necessarily improve the other, so remediation has to be directed to each of the problem areas (Maughan and Langton, 2008).

Barriers to seeking help from mental health services include discrimination, stigma, poverty, the power differential in therapeutic relationships, and a lack of optimism. Gateways into care include the accommodation of personal narratives in a care plan, a highly trained and competent workforce, and awareness of cultural issues and acculturation stresses for families as well as the life cycle stressors facing families in general. In this way cultural psychiatry research has led to positive changes in theory and practice in mainstream psychiatry, health care and beyond.

At present, mental health services in many countries are facing difficulties due to unprecedented demand and shrinking commissioning budgets. Early intervention for those who have low self-esteem due to difficulties in keeping up with their peers in schools, or who have been targeted for bullying due to standing out as different due to dyslexia is vital.

School counselling services have been cut back in recent years. There are many good mental health resources, such as the Solihull Approach (www.solihullapproachparenting. com/our-range-of-courses), available to school nurses, teachers and those working in schools, as well as to parents. Increasing awareness of professionals of the need to be alert for anxiety disorders, low mood and somatic complaints which can be markers of depression, and in older children the presence of self-harm as coping strategies can lead to earlier support from mental health services.

Interventions using workshops that reduce the stigma of mental illness have been shown to be effective when delivered in school settings (Pinfold *et al.*, 2003). This in turn will increase help-seeking behaviour. Culturally sensitive psychoeducation about mental illness especially for those in high-risk situations, including presenting with specific learning difficulties, is needed.

Education and mental health integration will be advanced when the goal of mental health includes effective schooling, and the goals of effective schools include the healthy functioning of students (Atkins, Hoagwood, Kutash & Seidman, 2010).

Psychological therapies are usually indicated before pharmacotherapy. Medication can be usefully employed as part of a holistic strategy. Other interventions such as mindfulness, relaxation techniques and sensory diet interventions can all help reduce anxiety and help focus. Adequate remediation of specific learning difficulties combined with appropriate community Child and Adolescent Mental Health Services (CAMHS)/school counselling, and a recognition that challenging behaviour developing from the age of seven onwards can relate to unremediated dyslexia, are all areas that schools should be addressing in partnership with local CAMHS and commissioning groups.

The independent review of dyslexia for the Department for Children, Schools and Families in England by Sir Jim Rose (2009) advises teachers to identify children who are failing to learn to read or write early, and urges educators to take account of co-occurring difficulties, such as social communication and attentional problems and emotional disorders.

The Children and Young People's Improving Access to Psychological Therapies (CYP IAPT) programme, included in the Department of Health's *Talking Therapies: A four year plan of action*, is a four year service transformation project which began in 2011 working with existing specialist CAMHS.

The conclusions of a recent review (Cooper, 2013) into school-based counselling in UK secondary schools are that commissioners should give consideration to developing school-based mental health provisions; and that school-based counsellors – working with colleagues in the field of child and adolescent mental health – have the potential to contribute to an increasingly comprehensive, integrated and 'young person-centred' system of mental health care.

Additional key action points were to ensure that young people from BME (Black, Mixed and Ethnic minority) backgrounds have equity of access to school-based counselling and CAMHS interventions; and to further consider how school-based provision, including counselling, can assist the whole school to build resilience and improve behaviour, attainment and psychological well-being. These are fitting aspirations upon which to end this chapter.

Discussion points

1. Given there is over-representation of children from BME backgrounds in the care system and the growing multilingual population in the UK, what are the implications for planning effective joined-up services for children?
2. How can services better consider the neglect and loss of home/first language of multilingual children and the potential impact on their developmental trajectories, cultural identities and mental health?
3. What are the benefits for individuals, families and societies which the multilingual outlook brings?
4. There appears to be a rise in nationalism in current political narratives, how might this play out positively or negatively in relation to promoting appropriate services for multilingual children and their families?

Website resources

- www.solihullapproachparenting.com/our-range-of-courses
  Good examples of interventions in primary care to support mental health, and information for parents and young people.
- www.mothertongue.org.uk
  Promoting training, interpreters and resources for mental health in a multicultural context.
- www.rcpsych.ac.uk/healthadvice/translations.aspx
  Mental health information in a range of languages from the Royal College of Psychiatrists.

References

Arends-Tóth, J., & Van De Vijver, F.J. (2003). Multiculturalism and acculturation: views of Dutch and Turkish–Dutch. *European Journal of Social Psychology*, 33(2), 249–266.

Atkins, M.S., Hoagwood, K.E., Kutash, K., & Seidman, E. (2010). Toward the integration of education and mental health in schools. *Administration and Policy in Mental Health and Mental Health Services Research*, 37(1–2), 40–47.

Berry, J.W. (1980). Acculturation as varieties of adaptation. In A. Padilla (Ed.), *Acculturation: Theory, models and some new findings* (pp. 9–25). Boulder: Westview Press.

Berry, J.W., & Kalin, R. (1995). Multicultural and ethnic attitudes in Canada: An overview of the 1991 national survey. *Canadian Journal of Behavioural Science*, 27, 301–320.

Berry, J.W., Phinney, J.S., Sam, D.L., & Vedder, P. (2006). Immigrant youth: Acculturation, identity, and adaptation. *Applied Psychology*, 55(3), 303–332.

Bhui, K., Khatib, Y., Viner, R., Klineberg, E., Clark, C., Head, J., … Stansfeld, S. (2008a). Cultural identity, clothing and common mental disorder: A prospective school-based study of White British and Bangladeshi adolescents. *Journal of Epidemiology and Community Health*, 62(5), 435–441.

Bhui, K., King, M., Dein, S., & O'Connor, W. (2008b). Ethnicity and religious coping with mental distress. *Journal of Mental Health*, 17(2), 141–151.

Bhui, K.S., Lenguerrand, E., Maynard, M.J., Stansfeld, S.A., & Harding, S. (2012). Does cultural integration explain a mental health advantage for adolescents? *International Journal of Epidemiology*, 41(3), 791–802.

Bhui, K., Stansfeld, S., Head, J., Haines, M., Hillier, S., Taylor Hillier, S., … Booy, R. (2005). Cultural identity, acculturation, and mental health among adolescents in East London's multiethnic community. *Journal of Epidemiology and Community Health*, 59, 296–302.

Bialystok, E., Craik, F.I., Green, D.W., & Gollan, T.H. (2009). Bilingual minds. *Psychological Science in the Public Interest*, 10(3), 89–129.

Cooper, M. (2013) *School-based counselling in UK Secondary Schools: A review and critical evaluation.* Glasgow: University of Strathclyde.

Hickling, F.W. (2005). The epidemiology of schizophrenia and other common mental health disorders in the English-speaking Caribbean. *Revista Panamericana de Salud Pública*, 18(4–5), 256–262.

Laurens, K.R., West, S.A., Murray, R.M., & Hodgins, S. (2007). Psychotic-like experiences and other antecedents of schizophrenia in children aged 9–12 years: A comparison of ethnic and migrant groups in the United Kingdom. *Psychological Medicine*, 38(8), 1–9.

Liebkind, K., & Jasinskaja-Lahti, I. (2000). Acculturation and psychological well-being among immigrant adolescents in Finland: A comparative study of adolescents from different cultural backgrounds. *Journal of Adolescent Research*, 15(4), 446–469.

Lorek, A., Ehntholt, K., Nesbitt, A., Wey, E., Githinji, C., Rossor, E., … Wickramasinghe, R. (2009). The mental and physical health difficulties of children held within a British immigration detention centre: A pilot study. *Child Abuse & Neglect*, 33(9), 573–585.

Margari, L., Buttiglione, M., Craig, F., Cristella, A., de Giambattista, C., Matera, E., … Simone, N. (2013). Neuropsychopathological comorbidities in learning disorders. *BMC Neurology*, 13(1), 198.

Maughan, B., & Carroll, J. (2006). Literacy and mental disorders. *Current Opinion in Psychiatry*, 19(4), 350–354.

Maughan, B., & Langton, E.G. (2008). Leseferdighet og psykiske vansker [Literacy and emotional difficulties, in Norwegian]. In F.E. Tønnessen, E. Bru & E. Heiervang (Eds), *Lesevansker Og Livsvansker – Om Dysleksi Og Psykisk Helse* (pp. 111–20). Stavanger, Norway: Hertervig Akadmisk.

Maughan, B., Rowe, R., Loeber, R., & Stouthamer-Loeber, M. (2003). Reading problems and depressed mood. *Journal of Abnormal Child Psychology*, 31(2), 219–229.

Maynard, M.J., & Harding, S. (2010a). Ethnic differences in psychological well-being in adolescence in the context of time spent in family activities. *Social Psychiatry and Psychiatric Epidemiology*, 45(1), 115–123.

Maynard, M.J., & Harding, S. (2010b). Perceived parenting and psychological well-being in UK ethnic minority adolescents. *Child Care, Health and Development*, 36(5), 630–638.

Measham, T., Guzder, J., Rousseau, C., Pacione, L., Blais-McPherson, M., & Nadeau, L. (2014). Refugee children and their families: Supporting psychological well-being and positive adaptation following migration. *Current Problems in Pediatric and Adolescent Health Care*, 44(7), 208–215.

Miller, M.N., & Pumariega, A.J. (2001). Culture and eating disorders: A historical and cross-cultural review. *Psychiatry*, 64(2), 93–110.

Phinney, J. (1990). Ethnic identity in adolescents and adults: A review of research. *Psychological Bulletin*, 108, 499–514.

Pinfold, V., Toulmin, H., Thornicroft, G., Huxley, P., Farmer, P., & Graham, T. (2003). Reducing psychiatric stigma and discrimination: Evaluation of educational interventions in UK secondary schools. *The British Journal of Psychiatry*, 182(4), 342–346.

Pumariega, A.J., Rothe, E., & Pumariega, J.B. (2005). Mental health of immigrants and refugees. *Community Mental Health Journal*, 41(5), 581–597.

Rose, J. (2009). *Identifying and teaching children and young people with dyslexia and literacy difficulties: An independent report*. London: Department for Children, Schools and Families.

Sashidharan, S.P. (2001). Institutional racism in British psychiatry. *Psychiatric Bulletin*, 25(7), 244–247.

Singh, S.P., & Burns, T. (2006). Race and mental health: There is more to race than racism. *British Medical Journal*, 333, 648–651.

Stansfeld, S.A., Haines, M.M., Head, J.A., Bhui, K., Viner, R., Taylor Hillier, S.… Booy, R. (2004). Ethnicity, social deprivation and psychological distress in adolescents: School-based epidemiological study in East London. *British Journal of Psychiatry*, 185, 233–238.

Suárez-Orozco, C., Bang, H.J., & Onaga, M. (2010). Contributions to variations in academic trajectories amongst recent immigrant youth. *International Journal of Behavioral Development*, 34, 500–510.

UN Population Report (2014). www.un.org/en/development/desa/population/theme/international-migration/index.shtml

Van Oudenhoven, J.P., Prins, K.S., & Buunk, B.P. (1998). Attitudes of minority and majority members towards adaptation of immigrants. *European Journal of Social Psychology*, 28, 995–1013.

Ward, C. (1996). Acculturation. In D. Landis & R. Bhagat (Eds), *Handbook of intercultural training* (2nd ed.; pp. 124–147). Thousand Oaks, CA: Sage.

19

POLICY CONSIDERATIONS IN ADDRESSING THE NEEDS OF L2[1] LEARNERS WHO MAY HAVE DYSLEXIA

Esther Geva and Yueming Xi

This chapter will:

1. Present a critical review of diagnostic assessment of dyslexia among students who speak more than one language
2. Provide a brief overview of dyslexia-related policies in five countries: the US, Canada, Mainland China, Taiwan and Hong Kong
3. Propose a list of policy implications pertaining to assessment and instruction for dyslexic children who are also L2 learners

The problem

Tao is a native Chinese-speaking student who moved from Beijing to Toronto with his parents three years ago when he was 12. Prior to his move, Tao's poor performance in Chinese and English was attributed by his family and teachers to laziness and lack of motivation. He also felt socially and emotionally isolated from his peers. After moving to Toronto, he was placed in an English Language Learners (ELLs) classroom and his academic skills in Chinese were not assessed. However, Tao's performance in decoding, reading fluency and reading comprehension in English have not improved much in comparison to other students with a similar background, in spite of intensive ELL support and extensive exposure to English language and literacy. His language status (i.e., ELL) was taken as the reason for his academic difficulties, and his delay in developing reading skills was largely ignored.

As you read this chapter, think about whether Tao might be assessed in each of the countries we discuss below or perhaps in your country. If yes, what criteria and procedures would be used? What policies are in place to ensure that his educational needs are met fairly? What policies might impact options for unbiased assessment, intervention and accommodation made available to him? What policies might impact the quality of the intervention he may receive and the follow-up/tracking procedures available?

Tao is only one of 622,300 students with Learning Disabilities (LD) aged 15 or older in Canada (Statistics Canada, 2012), but there is no estimate of allophones (i.e., people in

Canada whose mother tongue is neither English nor French) in the LD population. Population mobility has accelerated markedly under global integration, not only in Canada but in all countries. These global trends impose significant pressure on schools to respond to the needs of a body of students that is Culturally and Linguistically Diverse (CLD).

The overall objective of this chapter is to investigate and compare educational policies formulated for LD populations in five different countries with a special focus on CLD students who may have LD, in particular dyslexia, and to examine how recent research trends are reflected in the legislation in different countries. It is important to point out at the outset that the definition of LD is not stable or consistent across jurisdictions. These fluctuations reflect revisions as a function of new knowledge gained through research and various local policies and legislation, and sometimes of ideological beliefs.

The chapter is divided into three sections. In the first section, we briefly review research on language development among dyslexic students who also speak more than one language (L2 learners), and present some critical challenges to assessment of dyslexia among ELL/L2 students. In the second section we examine briefly dyslexia-related policies in five countries and districts. We begin with the US and Canada. English is the societal language in the first and English and French are the societal languages in the second, and both countries absorb a large number of immigrants each year. We then shift to three countries where Chinese is the societal language – China, Taiwan and Hong Kong. In the final section, we propose a list of policy recommendations pertaining to assessment and instruction for L2 learners who may also have dyslexia.

Issues in the assessment of L2 learners who may have dyslexia

All countries and districts reviewed in this chapter have large minority and/or L2 populations. Canada and the US are major immigrant receiving countries. In mainland China, there are 55 minority ethnic groups, and 60 million people come from a minority language background (State Council Information Office, 2009). In Taiwan, half a million indigenous residents from 16 minority ethnic groups speak around 10 different languages (Council of Indigenous Peoples, 2015; Hong, 2002). Chinese and English are both taught as academic subjects in China, Hong Kong and Taiwan, and in Hong Kong both Chinese and English are used as the language of instruction in mainstream classrooms. Given these demographic facts it is evident that explicit policies are needed to address diagnostic and instructional needs of ELLs/L2 learners with LD in each of these countries.[2]

A focus on consistent and well-informed diagnosis in each country is important because a careful diagnosis should lead to timely and appropriate intervention and the application of appropriate instructional accommodations. According to Johnson, Humphrey, Mellard, Woods and Swanson (2010), diagnosis has two functions: classification and explanation. Classification involves having a set of behavioral criteria and characteristics that clinicians can use to determine whether an individual has an LD. In relation to LD, behaviors that raise concerns are observations of below average academic achievement in reading, writing and mathematics. These observations are typically assessed by individually administered standardized achievement tests. Assessment of academic achievement is a central aspect of all of the commonly used definitions of LD. However, there is a general consensus among experts in the field of LD that low academic achievement is not sufficient to diagnose an LD (Hale *et al.*, 2010; Tannock, 2013). The situation becomes more complex when the reading difficulties of ELLs/L2 learners are at stake. As is the case with monolingual learners, some L2 learners may have an LD such as dyslexia (i.e., have difficulties in developing accurate and fluent word reading and spelling skills) and they require program accommodations and interventions to minimize the effects of reading disabilities on academic achievement. Therefore, there is an urgent need to examine LD-related legislation and policies across nations to better address the growing need for the provision of special education services to CLD students who have LD. Tao's ELL status coupled with his LD symptoms raises three issues. First, why were his dyslexic symptoms largely ignored by related stakeholders in both China and Canada? Second, how can CLD students with LD best be served? Third, how can the rights of these individuals to receive adequate instruction and/or accommodation be legally protected? In this chapter we address these three issues.

The notion of LD was introduced by Kirk in 1963, and dyslexia is considered as a Specific category of LD (SLD). Historically, the diagnosis of dyslexia was largely based on exclusive criteria of symptoms, meaning that diagnostic criteria were based on what dyslexia is *not* instead of what dyslexia *is*. Having difficulties, together with a considerable discrepancy between performance on intelligence tests and academic achievement were often required in the diagnosis. The underlying rationale was that among typically developing children there should be a positive correlation between performance on intelligence tests and achievement tests, and that when there is a meaningful gap between intelligence and achievement tests this may be a clue to the existence of LD. A more detailed account of the historical and theoretical underpinnings of this approach is beyond the scope of this chapter. Yet, it is important to note that a growing body of research has suggested that intelligence is irrelevant for diagnosing dyslexia (e.g., Algozzine & Ysseldyke, 1983; Catts, 1989; Das, Mishra & Kirby, 1994; Fletcher, 1992; Lyon, 1995; Rack, Snowling & Olson, 1992; Scarborough, 1998; Siegel, 1989; Stanovich, 1986; Vellutino, Fletcher, Snowling & Scanlon, 2004). Much has been written about issues in the assessment of intelligence in ELLs/L2 learners. Due to space limitations we will not review these issues here, except to point out that in the case of ELLs/L2 learners it may be difficult to establish discrepancies because it may be more difficult to obtain a "true" estimate of cognitive abilities of ELLs/L2 learners, leading to a lower likelihood that ELLs/L2 learners who have LD will actually be identified as such (Geva & Wiener, 2015).

Children with dyslexia face difficulties with word reading and spelling skills, including the ability to recognize words and decode/spell new words. A key underlying characteristic of monolingual children and ELLs with dyslexia is their difficulty with phonological awareness (e.g., National Reading Panel, 2000). Research has shown that L1 and L2 readers who have dyslexia have similar cognitive and word reading profiles in spite of the fact that by the definition they are less proficient in the second language (Geva & Herbert, 2012; Geva, Yaghoub-Zadeh & Schuster, 2000). Some ELLs/L2 learners may have poor decoding and phonological processing skills that are not explained in terms of having poor English language proficiency, but rather in terms of poor underlying cognitive skills associated with dyslexia.[3]

Approaches to assessment undertaken by clinicians to diagnose LD include Response To Intervention (RTI) (Fletcher & Vaughn, 2009) and the assessment of cognitive processing deficits that are associated with achievement difficulties (for example, phonological awareness and working memory). Examining a family history of LD and excluding factors not typically considered to be associated with LD such as poor instruction, poverty, inconsistent schooling, and cultural and linguistic differences are other essential components.

When it comes to ELLs/L2 learners one notices both over-identification of ELLs as having LD when they do not (Cummins, 1984; Harry & Anderson, 1994; Paton, 1998) and under-identification of L2 learners who actually have dyslexia but have not been diagnosed as such (Limbos & Geva, 2001; Solari, Petscher & Folsom, 2012; Zehler, Fleischman, Hopstock, Pendzick & Stephenson, 2003). Over-identification occurs when children from certain ethnic and linguistic minorities are diagnosed as having LD due to lack of sufficient information, lack of careful consideration of their linguistic and educational experiences, injudicious interpretation of performance on normed tests, bias and low expectations (McCardle, Mele-McCarthy, Cutting, Leos & D'Emilio, 2005). Thanks to warnings about these practices in many jurisdictions, recent immigrant students are often not screened and assessed for dyslexia for a number of years, as there is a prevailing belief in school systems that dyslexia can only be disentangled from English language proficiency after five to seven years when students have had ample opportunities to learn English (Cummins, 1984). This well-intentioned approach has led to the adoption of a "wait-and-see" approach in school systems. The under-identification problem is noted when persistent ELL/L2 difficulties with learning to read are attributed to their L2 status coupled with a belief that as they will improve their oral language skills, their reading skills will improve as well, and in some cases lower expectations of certain CLD groups (McCardle *et al.*, 2005; Solari *et al.*, 2012). In principle, the prevalence of LD should not vary among different groups, and both over- and under-identification are problematic.

Geva and Wiener (2015) also caution against questionable reliance on test norms developed for more homogenous populations when interpreting performance. Instead they recommend that the performance and progress of ELLs/L2 learners suspected of having dyslexia or other types of LD be compared to that of a more relevant reference group. If the majority of ELLs/L2 learners from a given CLD group progress appropriately for given skills, it is difficult to justify the attribution of difficulties that a small number of children have in learning to decode to their L2 status.

It is important to bear in mind that the underlying causes of reading difficulties experienced by children who have a language and reading impairment are dimensional and not dichotomous. That is, someone may be severely dyslexic, or mildly dyslexic, or have difficulties on specific aspects of word reading even though the symptoms are not severe enough to qualify for a diagnosis of LD. Moderate to severe LD can be expected to impact performance throughout the lifespan (National Association of School Psychologists, 2007). Yet, jurisdictions vary in the definition of cut-offs below which children and adolescents can qualify for a diagnosis of having an LD.

Learning disability policies in five countries

A comparison of documents and policies points to an interesting phenomenon concerning the definition and legislation pertinent to LD/dyslexia among the countries reviewed below. Legislation, non-legislative policies and regulations, and practice regarding LD vary among provinces in Canada and states in the US. Additionally, the widely accepted traditional IQ–achievement discrepancy method in diagnosing students with LD (dyslexic students in particular) has gradually been withdrawn in the US and Hong Kong, but it is still practiced in Canada and Taiwan. It is important to note though that with the publication of the DSM-V in 2013, which contra-indicates this approach, various bodies continue to grapple with the question of how important it is to consider average intelligence as a component of identifying LD (e.g., Ontario Ministry of Education, 2014). In Mainland China, this debate has been absent so far, as public awareness and relevant legislative proposals to protect the rights of students with LD to receive systematic assessment and instruction have emerged only recently, thanks to the joint efforts of researchers, parents and educational practitioners.

United States

LD is the largest category of disabilities accounting for 42% of the total population of school-age disabled students served by special education in the US (Cortiella & Horowitz, 2014), and 4.7% of the total public school enrollment (National Center for Education Statistics, 2015). In the US the prevalence of dyslexia, a category of SLD, is 10% to 15% of the total school enrollment.

While laws ensuring equal access to education for dyslexic children are formulated at the federal level, there are significant intra-state discrepancies in legislation, non-legislative policies and regulations, and practice. At the federal level, equal rights for the provision of free and appropriate public education for dyslexics are protected under the Individuals with Disabilities Education Act (IDEA) 2004, Section 504 of the Rehabilitation Act of 1973, and the Americans with Disabilities Act 1990 (Cortiella & Horowitz, 2014). Most states have not developed laws for dyslexics, and practice varies considerably as some states have a much more comprehensive screening, placement and accommodation system designed for dyslexic children (e.g., Texas) than others (e.g., Alabama). Youman and Mather (2012) point out that

> As of July of 2012, 22 states had statewide dyslexia laws, three of which provide a dyslexia handbook to inform parents and educators about the proper procedures for students in public and private educational settings. An additional three states have drafted a dyslexia handbook to provide resources and guide school personnel and parents in both identification and intervention for children with dyslexia. Of the remaining states, six have laws making their way through the legislature, and two have tried to increase dyslexia awareness through creation of a dyslexia week and dyslexia month.
>
> (p. 2)

States are making significant progress toward a more specified legal system where the right to receive equal educational opportunities is statutorily protected. States vary in the age at which screening and assessment take place, and the scope of screening that is mandated (e.g. Ohio and Texas) (Youman & Mather, 2012). Identified students under the IDEA 2004 are placed under Individualized Education Programs (IEPs) where targeted instruction is provided. It is also important to mention that the IDEA 2004 provides explicit guidelines for assessing ELLs who may have dyslexia, and stipulates that students from linguistic minority backgrounds must be assessed in their most proficient language (Youman & Mather, 2012).[4]

In line with the bulk of research evidence, the IDEA 2004 gradually withdrew the IQ–achievement discrepancy approach while highlighting the importance of the RTI system and the use of research-based methods when screening students who may be dyslexic. When the IQ–achievement discrepancy approach is used, supplementary assessment such as a behavior checklist must be employed as part of the identification process (Youman & Mather, 2012).

This implies that instead of excluding students who have expected low reading levels (i.e. both reading performance and IQ are below the age average), the US is embracing a more inclusive support system to accommodate the needs of all students who have one or more types of LD.

Nevertheless, concern about the inadequacy of intervention, accommodation and teacher training has been voiced (Cunningham, Zibulsky, Stanovich & Stanovich, 2009; Moats, 2009; Spencer, Schuele, Guillot & Lee, 2008). Complying with the IDEA 2004 and the recently revised DSM-V, SLD is usually used as an umbrella term in school settings with dyslexia fitting under it. One of the consequences is that in states that identify SLD students in a non-categorical manner, special education specialists may be less able to provide dyslexic students with focused instruction that is tailored to their learning needs. Furthermore, Youman and Mather (2012) point out that most states do not make accommodation for dyslexic students in statewide high-stakes testing. In those that do, students identified with SLD, not dyslexia specifically, will be given accommodation according to their IEP plan that may not fully satisfy their special needs. Also, teachers in states lacking related teacher preparation laws (e.g., Alabama, Delaware and Indiana) are not equipped with the skills to cope with the demands of students with reading difficulties. In those that do, they are often trained to work with students with SLD in general, but lack the skills needed for instruction in specific areas of difficulty such as dyslexia and understanding the needs of ELLs who may also have SLD.

Canada

As is the case in the US, LD is the largest category of disabilities in Canada, accounting for 81% of the total population requiring special education services (Kohen, Uppal, Khan & Visentin, 2006). The Canadian Provinces and Territories vary in the proportion of children with LD out of all children with disabilities who require special education services, ranging from 69% in British Columbia to 89% in Prince Edward Island (Kohen, Uppal, Khan & Visentin, 2006).

Canada does not have a federal law specifically drafted for students with LD, and educational policies and instruction are mainly dealt with at the provincial jurisdiction level (Siegel & Ladyman, 2000; Wiener & Siegel, 1992). At the same time, the Canadian Charter overrides all provincial laws and provides students with LD with the right to receive appropriate education if provincial regulation is absent (Wiener & Siegel, 1992). Wiener and Siegel (1992) stated that "As no Charter cases applying to children with LD have yet reached Supreme Court, there is considerable debate about how the Charter will be interpreted" (p. 344). The answer came in 2012 when the Canadian Supreme Court overturned a decision made by British Columbia Supreme Court regarding a dyslexic citizen, Jeffrey Moore. He had filed a legal case against a school district in British Columbia for closing the special education program in his school with the excuse of funding shortages, thereby denying him the right as a student to receive education commensurate with his disability. This decision of the Supreme Court is likely to have far-reaching impact as the Canadian Supreme Court explicitly stated that "There is no dispute that J's dyslexia is a disability" (Canadian Supreme Court, 2012).

At the provincial and territorial level, we examined local School Acts (in Alberta, British Columbia, Manitoba, Newfoundland and Labrador, and Prince Edward Island) and Education Acts (in New Brunswick, Nova Scotia, Ontario, Québec, Saskatchewan, Nunavut, Yukon) and found that as of 2015, only Ontario and Québec refer explicitly to LD in their legislation. This has remained unchanged since 2008 when Kozey and Siegel published their policy paper. All provinces have LD-related non-legislative policies and regulations formulated for students with LD.

The IQ–achievement discrepancy approach remains the major diagnostic criterion across provinces. For example, *Policy/Program Memorandum No. 8* released by the Ontario Ministry of Education (2014) explicitly defines LD as "academic underachievement that is inconsistent with the intellectual abilities of the student (which are at least in the average range)" (p. 2). In addition, the definition of LD stipulated by the Learning Disabilities Association of Canada (LDAC) has guided policy-making in eight provinces (Manitoba, British Columbia, Alberta, Ontario, Nova Scotia, New Brunswick, Newfoundland and Labrador, and Saskatchewan), all of which adopted an IQ–achievement discrepancy approach (Klassen, 2002; Kozey & Siegel, 2008). Of the remaining two provinces, Québec categorizes LD students as at-risk and Prince Edward Island defines LD in a non-categorical manner, without mentioning the need to establish discrepancy in the diagnostic process (Kozey & Siegel, 2008).

Provinces also differ in articulating how large a discrepancy should be to qualify for a diagnosis of LD. For example, a gap of at least two standard deviations between measured learning potential and academic achievement is required to be identified as having LD in British Columbia, while at least one standard deviation is required in Saskatchewan (Organization for Economic Co-operation and Development, 2004). Such inconsistency poses significant practical problems for students who move between provinces as they may be identified as having LD and thus be provided with academic support and accommodation before moving, yet lose their LD status after moving to another province.

Similar to the US, problems of accommodation and inadequate teacher preparation for this population are prevalent. Most schools and districts adopt a "wait-and-see" approach when assessing students from minority backgrounds. Students are often under-diagnosed because their limited language proficiency cannot be easily disentangled from their LD symptoms and over-diagnosed for the same reason (Geva & Herbert, 2012). Tao's case is characteristic of an immigrant student not being provided with appropriate accommodation due to under-diagnosis. Additionally, teachers (especially those in bilingual day schools and French and Chinese immersion programs) are not given adequate training to work with LD students, to distinguish between difficulties related to LD or their L2 status, or to adapt instruction to the needs of L2 students who have LD. On the whole, while LD-related legislation and policies tend to respond to research advances, policies pertaining to L2 learners who may also have LD are complex, at times contradictory, and do not address adequately the best interests of these students.

China

In China, 2.46 million children aged 6 to 14 have a disability in one or more of the following categories: vision, hearing, language (speaking problems), physical, mental health and intelligence (National Statistical Bureau of People's Republic of China, 2007). Until recently LD has not been recognized as a type of disability. If students are not able to read, it is typically attributed to a lack of motivation or sluggishness (Meng & Shu, 1999).

Contrary to the long-held belief that native Chinese-speaking students are not prone to dyslexia because of the unique orthographic writing system of Chinese, research emerging in the past two decades has identified several subtypes of dyslexia among Chinese-speaking students. The dual language processing pathways model is now widely accepted in dyslexia research when studying Chinese-speaking children (e.g., Yin & Weekes, 2003). In essence the model acknowledges that multi-deficits in visuospatial and phonological processes underlie dyslexia in this population. Related studies (e.g., Chan & Siegel, 2001; Ho & Bryant, 1997) have also showed that phonological awareness is important in reading Chinese.

Despite the growing body of research in the area of dyslexia, there is still a dearth of policy papers in general. Wang and Yu (2007) located only 83 empirical studies (i.e., experimental studies, surveys and questionnaires, case studies and interviews) on developmental dyslexia in Chinese from 1996 to 2006, and these studies include academic articles as well as unpublished Master's and Doctoral theses. While one can find a literal translation of the term LD in Chinese, the meaning attributed to this term in Chinese does not map onto definitions used in other countries, and is often seen as an equivalent to intellectual disability. Likewise, equivalent terms to dyslexia and reading disability do not exist and their meaning has to be explained. We searched in the China National Knowledge Infrastructure, the largest and most authoritative integrated knowledge resources database in China, but were unable to locate any nation-wide or district-wide regulations regarding diagnostic procedures, screening batteries, assessment and intervention, or placement options for students with LD.

At the same time, there has been a growing awareness of the terms LD and dyslexia in China in recent years. In 2013, the Assistant Dean of the Management School of Tsinghua University in China submitted a legislative proposal on *Enhancing Accommodation for Dyslexic Students and Implementing Educational Equality* to the First Annual Session of the 12th National Committee of the Chinese People's Political Consultative Conference. In collaboration with local government and research institutes, special centers for dyslexic students have emerged in Beijing, Guangdong, Shenzhen and Anhui (Su & Shu, 2014). It is likely that such joint efforts will bring the topic of dyslexia-related research and regulation to the forefront of the education reform movement in China in the near future. Given the recency of the emergence of such awareness of dyslexia in China, it is not surprising that to date little discussion or research (Zuo, Li, Gu, Jiao & Zhang, 2014) have been directed towards the educational needs of dyslexic children from minority language backgrounds, or mainstream children whose home language is Chinese but who attend bilingual English–Chinese programs. So far, studies in relation to minority students with dyslexia are mainly conducted in Xinjiang province with Uyghur children. Furthermore, not much attention has been allocated to the training of teachers who can help monolingual and L2 children with dyslexia improve their reading skills, and to make the necessary accommodations.

Taiwan

In Taiwan, students with LD account for 23.46% of the total school enrollment (Ministry of Education, 2012). Among the non-Indigenous population, students with LD account for 25.6% of the total student population with disabilities (as cited in Wang, 2006). This number is substantially higher for Indigenous students, who account for 32.98% of the total population with disabilities (as cited in Wang, 2006).

The definition of dyslexia in Taiwan's legislation also adopts an IQ–achievement discrepancy approach. In the most recent official definition delimited in the Amended Bill of Assessment Criteria for Disabled and Gifted Children (Ministry of Education, 2013), LD is defined as a type of cognitive disability in listening, speaking, reading, writing or calculation, caused by central nervous system dysfunction intrinsic to individuals rather than by intelligence, emotional and sensory problems, or environmental factors such as inappropriate education or lack of cultural stimuli. This definition echoes the National Joint Committee on Learning Disabilities definition (1990) in that it is characterized by an emphasis on central nervous system dysfunction, indicating that dyslexia is a persistent neurobiological problem intrinsic to individuals.

Aligned with the development of LD laws in Western countries, Taiwan also experienced an expansion of the coverage of special education services from deaf and blind people to other categories. The first special education law, the Special Education Implementation Act was enacted in 1970, but it was not until 1977 that an amendment to this act was published and LD children were included as a category of students with disabilities. This population was first entitled to equal access to educational opportunities in 1984 based on the Special Education Act 1984, yet at that time in Taiwan, there was no consensus as to what LD was. Relatedly, the right to receive equal educational opportunities is protected under The Constitution of The Republic of China (Taiwan) 1947, as well as the revised Special Education Act (Ministry of Education, 2014). Detailed requirements for the identification, accommodation and re-accommodation, and intervention provided to children with LD are stipulated under the Special Education Act 2014.

In Taiwan, the funding allocated for special education in 2001 comprised 3.72% of the total education budget, and increased to 4.3% by 2006 (Ministry of Education, 2007). Resources are offered and shared by counties and cities and not restricted to school districts. According to the regulations, students with a diagnosed LD should be placed in the least restricted environment commensurate with their developmental level, and the law states that appropriateness of placement should be re-evaluated each year by local education administrative authorities (Ministry of Education, 2014). Both the budgetary commitment and the requirement to re-evaluate student progress are important components of a policy that acknowledges the changing needs of students with LD.

There is a notable shortage of qualified teachers who specialize in LD and dyslexia in Taiwan. According to item 7 of the Special Education Act 2014, people who have acquired three credits or above in special education subjects (the type of college is not mentioned) qualify for teacher or related leadership positions in special education schools or general education schools with special education classrooms. Moreover, special education teachers are not specialized in working with children with specific types of disability; they are trained to work with all students with special needs but not students with dyslexia in particular. Importantly, to date there has not been much attention to the special education needs of Indigenous children (e.g., Wang, 2006) nor to students in English–Chinese bilingual programs. Therefore, policies are needed to develop effective instructional approaches, and more intensive training is needed to prepare highly qualified teachers to work with students with dyslexia, whether they are mainstream, CLD and/or L2 learners.

Hong Kong

In Hong Kong, students who have dyslexia account for 10% of the total enrollment (Chan, 2008), a prevalence that is comparable to the international level. Among all students with dyslexia, prevalence rates vary depending on the severity of cases: 9.7 to 12.6% mild cases,

2.2 to 2.3% moderate cases, and 1.3 to 1.6% severe cases (The Hong Kong Society of Child Neurology and Developmental Paediatrics, 2008).

In Hong Kong there is no relevant legislation concerning LD. The Code of Practice on Education 2001 enacted under the Disability Discrimination Ordinance 1995 protects all students with special needs. Yet in this code, LD was not recognized as a type of disability, although it used a dyslexic student as an example. It was not until 2007 when the Rehabilitation Program Plan was published that LD was included as a type of disability (Tsui, Li-Tsang & Lung, 2012).

Hong Kong has a comprehensive system designed for dyslexic students that includes identification, intervention and accommodation. Students suspected by parents or teachers of having LD are referred for psychoeducational assessments conducted by educational psychologists located in a school-based assessment center, the Education Bureau, the Department of Health or private agencies (Tsui *et al.*, 2012). Diagnostic tools include the Chinese Handwriting Assessment Tool, the Hong Kong Specific Learning Difficulties Behaviour Checklist and the Hong Kong Test of Specific Learning Difficulties in Reading and Writing. Interestingly, behavior checklists serve as the major screening tool in Hong Kong whereas literacy measures are the main ones in the US (Lu & Zheng, 2009).

In terms of intervention and accommodation, Hong Kong employs a three-tier intervention model to support students with special needs in mainstream classrooms, and funding is allocated to schools according to the number of students involved in each tier. The Education Bureau developed the New Funding Model plan in 2003/2004 and revised it in 2008/2009. Under the current New Funding Model, schools can be allocated HK$10,000 annually for each student with special educational needs (LD included) who needs tier-2 support, HK$120,000 for the first one to six students who need tier-3 support, and HK$20,000 for each additionally admitted student who needs tier-3 support (The Hong Kong Institute of Education, 2012). Funding is used to design courses, and for training programs and after-school activities based on students' needs. Accommodation for testing is also made. Students with special needs taking the Hong Kong Certificate of Education Examination or Hong Kong Advanced Level Examination can apply for examination accommodation (Tsui *et al.*, 2012).

Recognition of the need for high-quality teachers to work with students with LD has been explicitly placed on Hong Kong's educational agenda. Due to a lack of in-depth knowledge of dyslexia among teachers, the Education Bureau launched a five-year professional training plan in 2007/2008, in which at least one Chinese language teacher and one English language teacher from each general education school are expected to complete an in-depth course on how to adapt teaching to the needs of SLD (The Hong Kong Institute of Education, 2012). As with the recommendation made for China, we suggest that there is an urgent need to formulate school policies to protect the equal education rights of students with LD including those attending bilingual programs.

Recommendations

Based on the above research and review of policies, in this section we make the following general recommendations:

1. Evidence of persistent failure on various reading components in spite of high-quality teaching should be accepted as sufficient to qualify students to receive necessary accommodation and intervention mandated by policies and legislature. Attempts to establish IQ–achievement discrepancies are contra-indicated in the case of ELLs/L2 learners – they are irrelevant at best, and negatively biased, at worst.

2. Early identification and intervention targeting deficits in phonological processing skills, orthographic processes, and morphological skills are effective in alleviating severe subsequent reading failure in L1 learners and ELLs/L2 learners. "Wait-and-see" policies should be replaced with evidence-based policies and practices.

3. Policies are needed that foster the training of highly qualified personnel to diagnose and teach ELLs/L2 learners having LD on the basis of complementary, research-supported, techniques.

4. When assessing ELLs/L2 learners, performance should be compared to the reference group and caution should be exercised in interpreting performance on standardized measures on the basis of inappropriate norms.

5. Valuable information for disentangling dyslexia from L2 status can be obtained by observing learning over time and the application of response to intervention techniques. These techniques should be promoted.

6. Regardless of students' language status (i.e., monolingual or ELLs/L2 learners), it is important to remember that dyslexia is a lifelong yet constantly changing learning deficit. Therefore, instruction should encompass components of decoding, reading fluency, language and reading comprehension, and continue to be provided on an ongoing basis using evidence-based techniques and access to assistive technology.

7. Funding should be allocated based on individual needs of children with decoding difficulties, not on arbitrary cut-off levels based on budgetary considerations.

8. A joint effort from all stakeholders is needed to create the least restrictive environment for all students with LD. Schools should not withhold access to support services on the basis of arbitrary and often discriminatory definitions of entitlement.

9. Dyslexia-related legislation should be informed by research and be consistent across jurisdictions to ensure that students receive equitable educational support.

10. Policies should encourage researchers to conduct evaluation studies that examine the effectiveness of L2-based assessment, accommodations, and intervention approaches with different groups of learners.

11. Professional training should prepare qualified teachers to work with students with LD, including those who are ELLs or L2 learners.

12. Mechanisms for enabling collaboration between policy-makers, leaders, reading specialists, speech–language pathologists, teachers and parents should be fostered through various knowledge-mobilization strategies.

13. Policies that allow for alternative approaches that de-emphasize identification and labelling and promote approaches such as RTI can help identify early strengths and weaknesses so that all students, including struggling ELLs/L2 learners, can receive relevant and timely intervention and accommodations and be monitored regularly.

Conclusion

In this chapter, we have examined dyslexia policies in the US, Canada, China, Taiwan and Hong Kong. While the US and Hong Kong are adopting RTI in the diagnosis of dyslexia, the IQ–achievement discrepancy approach is still widely used in Canada and Taiwan. The US, Canada and Hong Kong have comprehensive support systems to protect equal educational opportunities for dyslexics including identification, classification, instruction and accommodation. Hong Kong has a more developed diagnostic and support system than Taiwan, but the legal rights of students with LD to receive appropriate education are not fully acknowledged in Hong Kong's laws. There has been general progress in the area of dyslexia research in Mainland China in the past two decades, yet legislation is glaringly absent.

The situation is more complex where ELLs/L2 learners who may have dyslexia or another LD are concerned. Researchers are faced with two major challenges in this regard. First, there are no consistent identification criteria across states/provinces and countries, resulting in difficulty in providing consistent services to ELLs/L2 learners. Second, at-risk ELLs cannot be easily distinguished from dyslexics in the early years, though approaches for disentangling reading difficulties related to LD from reading difficulties associated with L2 status have emerged in recent years.

Notes

1 L2 = Second language
2 For the sake of simplicity we refer to these as L2 learners when we discuss cultural and linguistic minorities or children in bilingual programs in China, Hong Kong and Taiwan, and ELLs when we refer to cultural and linguistic minorities in Canada and the US.
3 It is important to acknowledge that while this chapter focuses on dyslexia, there are other types of reading-related LDs that are associated with persistent language difficulties such as language impairment and difficulties with fluent reading. Recent research has shown that it is possible to identify among ELLs students who exhibit these profiles (e.g., Geva & Massey-Garrison, 2013; Farnia & Geva, 2013).
4 See Geva and Wiener (2015) for a more recent discussion of this well-intentioned but complex provision.

References

Algozzine, B., & Ysseldyke, J. (1983). Learning disabilities as a subset of school failure: The over-sophistication of a concept. *Exceptional Children, 50*, 242–246. doi: 10.1177/001440298305000307

Canadian Supreme Court. (2012). *Moore v. British Columbia (Education), 2012 SCC 61, [2012] 3 S.C.R. 360*. Retrieved from https://scc-csc.lexum.com/scc-csc/scc-csc/en/item/12680/index.do

Catts, H.W. (1989). Defining dyslexia as a developmental language disorder. *Annals of Dyslexia, 39*(1), 50–64. doi: 10.1007/BF02656900

Chan, C.W. (2008). Overview of specific learning disabilities (SLD)/dyslexia developments over the last decades in Hong Kong. *Hong Kong Journal of Paediatrics, 13*, 196–202.

Chan, C.K.K., & Siegel, L.S. (2001). Phonological processing in reading Chinese among normally achieving and poor readers. *Journal of Experimental Child Psychology, 80*, 23–43. doi:10.1006/jecp.2000.2622

Cortiella, C., & Horowitz, S.H. (2014). *The state of learning disabilities: Facts, trends and emerging issues*. New York: National Center for Learning Disabilities.

Council of Indigenous Peoples. (2015). *Yuanzhumin fenbu [Distribution of indigenous peoples]*. Retrieved from www.apc.gov.tw/portal/docList.html?CID=6726E5B80C8822F9

Cummins, J. (1984). *Bilingualism and special education: Issues in assessment and pedagogy*. Cleveland, UK: Multilingual Matters.

Cunningham, A.E., Zibulsky, J., Stanovich, K.E., & Stanovich, P.J. (2009). How teachers would spend their time teaching language arts: The mismatch between self-reported and best practices. *Journal of Learning Disabilities, 42*, 418–430. doi: 10.1177/0022219409339063

Das, J.P., Mishra, R.K., & Kirby, J.R. (1994). Cognitive patterns of children with dyslexia: A comparison between groups with high and average nonverbal intelligence. *Journal of Learning Disabilities, 27*, 235–242. doi: 10.1177/002221949402700405

Farnia, F., & Geva, E. (2013). Growth and predictors of change in English language learners' reading comprehension. *Journal of Research in Reading, 36*(4), 389–421. doi: 10.1111/jrir.12003

Fletcher, J.M. (1992). The validity of distinguishing children with language and learning disabilities according to discrepancies with IQ: Introduction to the special series. *Journal of Learning Disabilities, 25*(9), 546–548. doi: 10.1177/002221949202500901

Fletcher, J.M., & Vaughn, S. (2009). Response to intervention: Preventing and remediating academic difficulties. *Child Development Perspectives, 3*, 30–37. doi: 10.1111/j.1750-8606.2008.00072.x

Geva, E., & Herbert, K. (2012). Assessment and interventions in English language learners with LD. In B. Wong & D. Butler (Eds), *Learning about learning disabilities* (4th ed., pp. 271–298). San Diego, CA: Elsevier.

Geva, E., & Massey-Garrison, A. (2012). A comparison of the language skills of ELLs and monolinguals who are poor decoders, poor comprehenders, or normal readers. *Journal of Learning Disabilities, 46*(5), 387–401. doi: 10.1177/0022219412466651

Geva, E., & Wiener, J. (2015). *Psychological assessment and intervention with culturally and linguistically diverse children and adolescents*. New York: Springer.

Geva, E., Yaghoub-Zadeh, Z., & Schuster, B. (2000). Understanding individual differences in word recognition skills of ESL children. *Annals of Dyslexia, 50*(1), 121–154. doi: 10.1007/s11881-000-0020-8

Hale, J., Alfonso, V., Berninger, V., Bracken, B., Christo, C., Clark, E., ... Yalof, J. (2010). Critical issues in response-to-intervention, comprehensive evaluation, and specific learning disabilities identification and intervention: An expert white paper consensus. *Learning Disability Quarterly, 33*(3), 223–236. doi: 10.1177/073194871003300310

Harry, B., & Anderson, M.G. (1994). The disproportionate placement of African American males in special education programs: A critique of the process. *Journal of Negro Education, 63*, 602–619. doi: 10.2307/2967298

Ho, C.S.-H., & Bryant, P.E. (1997). Phonological skills are important in learning to read Chinese. *Developmental Psychology, 33*(3), 946–951. doi: 10.1037/0012-1649.33.6.946

Hong, W.R. (2002). *Taiwan de yuyan zhengce hequhecong [The direction of Taiwan's language policy]*. Retrieved from http://mail.tku.edu.tw/cfshih/ln/paper18.htm

Johnson, E.S., Humphrey, M., Mellard, D.F., Woods, K., & Swanson, H.L. (2010). Cognitive processing deficits and students with specific learning disabilities: A selective meta-analysis of the literature. *Learning Disability Quarterly, 33*, 3–18. doi: 10.1177/073194871003300101

Kirk, S. (1963). *Behavioral diagnosis and remediation of learning disabilities*. Paper presented at the Conference on the Exploration into the Problems of the Perceptually Handicapped Child. Evanston, IL: Fund for the Perceptually Handicapped Child.

Klassen, R. (2002). The changing landscape of learning disabilities in Canada: Definitions and practice from 1989–2000. *School Psychology International, 23*(2), 199–219. doi: 10.1177/0143034302023002915

Kohen, D., Uppal, S., Khan, S., & Visentin, V. (2006). *Access and barriers to educational services for Canadian children with disabilities*. Ottawa, ON: Canadian Council on Learning.

Kozey, M., & Siegel, L.S. (2008). Definitions of learning disabilities in Canadian provinces and territories. *Canadian Psychology, 49*, 162–171. doi: 10.1037/0708-5591.49.2.162

Limbos, M., & Geva, E. (2001). Accuracy of teacher assessments of second-language students at-risk for reading disability. *Journal of Learning Disabilities, 34*, 136–151. doi: 10.1177/002221940103400204

Lu, X.X., & Zheng, P.Y. (2009). Yingyong "sanceng zhiyuan moshi" bangzhu you teshu xuexi kunnan de xuesheng: Linian yu shijian [Using "three-tier supporting model" to help students with learning disabilities: Ideology and Practice]. *Journal of Basic Education, 18*(2), 87–103. Retrieved from http://hkier.fed.cuhk.edu.hk/journal/wp-content/uploads/2010/08/jbe_v18n2_87-103.pdf

Lyon, G.R. (1995). Toward a definition of dyslexia. *Annals of Dyslexia, 45*, 3–27. doi: 10.1007/BF02648210

McCardle, P., Mele-McCarthy, J., Cutting, L., Leos, K., & D'Emilio, T. (2005). Learning disabilities in English language learners: Identifying the issues. *Learning Disabilities: Research & Practice, 20*(1), 1–5. doi: 10.1111/j.1540-5826.2005.00114.x

Meng, X.Z., & Shu, H. (1999). Hanyu ertong yuedu zhangai yanjiu [Research on dyslexia among Chinese-speaking children]. *Psychological Development and Education, 4*, 54–57.

Ministry of Education. (2007). *Teshu jiaoyu fazhan baogaoshu [Report on the development of special education].* Taipei, Taiwan: Ministry of Education.

Ministry of Education. (2012). *101 Niandu teshujiaoyu tongji baogao [Year 101 annual of statistics of special education].* Taipei, Taiwan: Ministry of Education.

Ministry of Education. (2013). *"Shenxin zhangai ji zifu youyi xuesheng jianding jizhun" xiuzheng caoan zongshuoming [An explanation to the Amended Bill of Assessment Criteria for Disabled and Gifted Children].* Taipei, Taiwan: Ministry of Education.

Ministry of Education. (2014). *Special Education Act.* Retrieved from http://edu.law.moe.gov.tw/LawContentDetails.aspx?id=FL009136

Moats, L. (2009). Still wanted: Teachers with knowledge of language. *Journal of Learning Disabilities, 42*, 387–391. doi: 10.1177/0022219409338735

National Association of School Psychologists. (2007). *NASP position statement on identification of students with specific learning disabilities.* Retrieved from www.nasponline.org/assets/Documents/Research%20and%20Policy/Position%20Statements/Identification_of_SLD.pdf

National Center for Education Statistics. (2015). *Digest of education statistics: 2013.* US Department of Education. Retrieved from https://nces.ed.gov/programs/digest/d13/ch_2.asp

National Joint Committee on Learning Disabilities. (1990). *Definition of learning disabilities.* Retrieved from www.ldonline.org/about/partners/njcld/archives

National Reading Panel. (2000). *Teaching children to read: An evidence-based assessment of the scientific research literature on reading and its implications for reading instruction.* Bethesda, MD: National Institute of Child Health and Human Development.

National Statistical Bureau of People's Republic of China. (2007). *2006 Nian dierci quanguo canjiren chouyang diaocha zhuyao shuju gongbao (dier hao) [2006 The second national census on disabled population (No. 2)].* Retrieved from www.stats.gov.cn/tjsj/ndsj/shehui/2006/html/fu3.htm

Ontario Ministry of Education. (2014). *Policy/Program Memorandum No. 8: Identification of and program planning for students with learning disabilities.* Retrieved from www.edu.gov.on.ca/extra/eng/ppm/ppm.html

Organization for Economic Co-operation and Development. (2004). *Equity in education: Students with disabilities, learning difficulties, and disadvantages.* Paris, France: OECD Publications Service.

Patton, J.M. (1998). The disproportionate representation of African Americans in special education: Looking behind the curtain for understanding and solutions. *The Journal of Special Education, 32*, 25–31. doi: 10.1177/002246699803200104

Rack, J.P., Snowling, M.J., & Olson, R.K. (1992). The nonword reading deficit in developmental dyslexia: A review. *Reading Research Quarterly, 27*, 29–53. doi: 10.2307/747832

Scarborough, H.S. (1998). Predicting the future achievement of second graders with reading disabilities: Contributions of phonemic awareness, verbal memory, rapid naming, and IQ. *Annals of Dyslexia, 48*(1), 115–136. doi: 10.1007/s11881-998-0006-5

Siegel, L.S. (1989). IQ is irrelevant to the definition of learning disabilities. *Journal of Learning Disabilities, 22*(8), 469–486. doi: 10.1177/002221948902200803

Siegel, L.S., & Ladyman, S. (2000). *A review of special education in British Columbia.* Victoria, BC: British Columbia Ministry of Education.

Solari, E.J., Petscher, Y., & Folsom, P.S. (2012). Differentiating literacy growth of ELL students with LD from other high-risk groups and general education peers: Evidence from Grade 3 to 10. *Journal of Learning Disabilities, 47*(4), 329–348. doi: 10.1177/0022219412463435

Spencer, E.J., Schuele, C.M., Guilot, K.M., & Lee, M.W. (2008). Phonemic awareness skill of speech–language pathologists and other educators. *Language, Speech, and Hearing Services in Schools, 39*, 512–520. doi: 10.1044/0161-1461

Stanovich, K.E. (1986). Matthew effects in reading: Some consequences of individual differences in the acquisition of literacy. *Reading Research Quarterly, 21*, 360–407. doi: 10.1598/RRQ.21.4.1

State Council Information Office. (2009). *Zhongguo de minzu zhengce yu geminzu gongtong fanrong fazhan [China's ethnic policy and common prosperity and development of all ethnic groups]*. Retrieved from www.lawinfochina.com/display.aspx?lib=dbref&id=82

Statistics Canada. (2012). *Learning disabilities among Canadians aged 15 years and older*. Retrieved from www.statcan.gc.ca/pub/89-654-x/89-654-x2014003-eng.htm

Su, L.P., & Shu, M. (2014). Yazhou bufen diqu "yuedu zhangaizheng" qunti fuwu yanjiu [Research on services to dyslexia groups in Asia]. *Library and Information Service, 58*(12), 56–63. doi: 10.13266/j.issn.0252-3116.2014.12.009

Tannock, R. (2013). Rethinking ADHD and LD in DSM-5: Proposed changes in diagnostic criteria. *Journal of Learning Disabilities, 46*, 5–25. doi: 10.1177/0022219412464341

The Hong Kong Institute of Education. (2012). *Study on equal learning opportunities for students with disabilities under the integrated education system*. Retrieved from www.eoc.org.hk/EOC/Upload/ResearchReport/IE_eReport.pdf

The Hong Kong Society of Child Neurology and Developmental Paediatrics. (2008). *Special issue on specific learning disabilities*. Hong Kong: Printhouse Production Centre Limited.

Tsui, C.M., Li-Tsang, C.W.P., & Lung, P.Y.G. (2012). Dyslexia in Hong Kong: Challenges and Opportunities. In W. Sittiprapaporn (Ed.), *Learning disabilities* (pp. 31–48). Retrieved from www.intechopen.com/books/learning-disabilities/dylexia-in-hong-kong-challenges-opportunities

Vellutino, F.R., Fletcher, J.M., Snowling, M.J., & Scanlon, D.M. (2004). Specific reading disability (dyslexia): What have we learned in the past four decades? *Journal of Child Psychology and Psychiatry, 45*(1), 2–40. doi: 10.1046/j.0021-9630.2003.00305.x

Wang, S.H. (2006). Guoxiao yuanzhumin xuexizhangai ertong yu feiyuanzhumin xuexizhangai ertong zai weishi ertong zhili liangbiao de biaoxian fenxi [A comparative study on the performance on WISC-III between indigenous and non-indigenous students with LD]. *Dongtaiwan Teshujiaoyu Xuebao, 8*, 191–214. Retrieved from www.cse.ndhu.edu.tw/ezfiles/75/1075/img/237/east8-9.pdf

Wang, Y.B., & Yu, L. (2007). Woguo jinshinianlai hanyu yueduzhangai yanjiu huigu yu zhanwang [The review and prospect of Chinese developmental dyslexia study in the recent decade]. *Advances in Psychological Science, 15*(4), 596–604. doi: 10.3969/j.issn.1671-3710.2007.04.003

Wiener, J., & Siegel, L. (1992). A Canadian perspective on learning disabilities. *Journal of Learning Disabilities, 25*, 340–350. doi: 10.1177/002221949202500602

Yin, W.G., & Weekes, B.S. (2003). Dyslexia in Chinese: Clues from cognitive neuropsychology. *Annals of Dyslexia, 53*, 255–279. doi: 10.1007/s11881-003-0012-6

Youman, M., & Mather, N. (2012). Dyslexia laws in the USA. *Annals of Dyslexia, 63*(2), 133–153. doi: 10.1007/s11881-012-0076-2

Zehler, A.M., Fleischman, H.L., Hopstock, P.J., Pendzick, M.L., & Stephenson, T.G. (2003). *Descriptive study of services to LEP students and LEP students with disabilities* (No. 4). Arlington, VA: US Department of Education, Office of English Language Acquisition.

Zuo, P.X., Li, Z.T., Gu, Q., Jiao, P.P., & Zhang, M. (2014). Xinjiang hanzu yu wewuerzu yuedu zhangai ertong yuedu tezheng de bijiao yanjiu [Comparative study of reading characteristics between Han and Uyghur children with dyslexia]. *Chinese Journal of Child Health Care, 22*, 18–20. Retrieved from http://118.145.16.237/zgetbjzz/CN/abstract/abstract505.shtml

20

NEIGHBOR LANGUAGES IN SCANDINAVIA IN A MULTILINGUAL WORLD

Michael Dal

This chapter will:

1. Discuss why the ability to understand neighbor languages – Swedish, Danish and Norwegian – in Scandinavia has become poorer during the last 30 years
2. Identify a number of language problems concerning linguistic domain loss in Scandinavia
3. Discuss the necessity of developing a communicative, context-related and content-based pedagogy for learning neighbor languages in Scandinavia

Overview

In some areas of Europe, e.g. Scandinavia, the languages are so close that people from countries in these areas understand each other when speaking and writing in their mother tongue. However, research shows that the ability to understand a neighbor language in, for example Scandinavia, is getting poorer and English is gaining the position of being some kind of "lingua franca". This chapter addresses the problem of linguistic domain loss in Scandinavia, explains research on how well or poorly young people can understand neighbor languages, and describes the necessity of implementing a contemporary, active and context-related language pedagogy when teaching neighbor languages in a multilingual world.

Introduction

The origin of languages has always been a central question for linguistics. New findings can help change the way we understand ourselves and the language we use. In 2012 professors of linguistics Jan Terje Faarlund and Embley Edmonds announced that they believed they could prove that English is in reality a Scandinavian language (Nickelsen, 2012). The popular belief had until then been that English descends directly from Old English or Anglo Saxon. However, new findings suggest that the British did not just borrow words and concepts from the Vikings and their descendants. What we today call English is actually a form of Scandinavian. The essential idea behind Faarlund and Edmond's argument is that many words in English initially belonged to Norwegian and/or Danish and the syntactic structures in modern English are Scandinavian rather than West Germanic (Faarlund & Edmonds, 2014). The findings of Faarlund and Edmonds can be and are widely discussed in linguistics but their controversial conclusions can perhaps help us better to understand the foundation of the cultural connections among inhabitants in the whole North Atlantic area.

The similarities among the Nordic languages have been studied for many years. In all the Nordic countries (except for Finland, which has its own eponymous Finnish language family) a lot of words are more or less the same even though they are written and pronounced differently. An example of this is the word for "meat", which is "kød" in Danish, "kött" in Swedish, "kjött" in Norwegian and "kjöt" in Icelandic and Faroese. This word probably has roots all the way back from the Old Norse language where it is supposed to be found as "kettwu" (Karker, 1983). The similarities are especially clear when it comes to the three Scandinavian languages (Danish, Norwegian and Swedish). For decades or even centuries people from these three neighboring countries have been able to understand and communicate with each other in their mother tongue, which is considered to be quite unique.

Research states that the Scandinavian languages since the 15th–16th centuries have undergone similar development. All three languages have taken in loans from German, and around the Protestant Reformation they were influenced by French. In the 20th century the three languages were strongly influenced by English, especially in the latter half of the century.

In the mid-1930s a Danish lawyer and writer, Sven Clausen, started an initiative to coordinate the Scandinavian languages. Clausen was against the German influence on the Scandinavian languages and from his point of view the three languages (Danish, Norwegian and Swedish) were moving away from each other (Lund, 2003, 2006). During and after the Second World War there arose a need to further define the Nordic community and in 1952 the Nordic Council was established. It is the official inter-parliamentary body of the Nordic Region. The Council has members from all the Nordic countries as well as from the Faroe Islands, Greenland and the Åland Islands. Ten years after its foundation, in 1962, the Nordic member countries signed the Helsinki Treaty which has been the basis for cooperation since then. The treaty secures among other things legal, social, economic, environmental and cultural cooperation between the governments of Denmark, Finland, Iceland, Norway and Sweden. In article 8 of the treaty it is explained that "educational provision in the schools of each of the Nordic countries shall include an appropriate measure of instruction in the languages, cultures and general social conditions in the other Nordic countries".

In 1981 the Nordic governments signed the Nordic Language Convention which is a convention between Denmark, Finland, Iceland, Norway and Sweden on the right of Nordic nationals to use their mother tongue in the Nordic Countries and in 2006 the governments signed the Language Declaration. This declaration focuses on teaching the Scandinavian languages as neighbor languages in Denmark, Sweden and Norway and as foreign languages in the other Nordic countries. Also, the declaration focuses on parallel use of English and the main Nordic languages, the multilingual society and multilingual citizens, and the language used by official agencies. Thus, today neighbor languages are a compulsory element in the school curriculum in all of Scandinavia. In addition Danish and Swedish are taught as a foreign language in primary and secondary school in Iceland and Finland.

The ability to understand the native languages among Scandinavians seems today to be declining, especially among young people. Instead, English appears to be the preferred lingua franca, in particular in spoken language. It is for example obvious when conferences are held within the Nordic community and when young Scandinavians meet across borders. In these situations there often is a need to define which language should be the official language of the activity. In more and more cases English is chosen as the official language for the activity in question.

Linguistic domain loss in Scandinavia

About 20 years ago the term "domain" was an unknown word outside a narrow sociolinguistic circle. However, today the term has become much more common and all journalists concerned with language policy in Scandinavia use the term without reflecting on the meaning of the word. It has become a household word used in many contexts.

The concern about the pressure from the English language on Scandinavian languages resulted in linguists around 1990 starting to use the concept in order to further explain the development of the Scandinavian languages. The condition has been described as the Scandinavian languages losing domains to English – particularly Danish and Norwegian.

The concept of linguistic domains originates from the German linguist Schmidt-Rohr in the 1930s and was revived in the 1970s and credited to the American sociolinguist Joshua Fishman (Fishman, 1972a, 1972b). The notion of domain was initially used to sort out different areas of language use in multilingual societies where language choice is relevant. Fishman argues that language choice within multilingual groups is far from random. He defines language domains as a language activity, which is determined by time, place, topics and relationships – also referred to as *classes of interlocutors* (Fishman, 1972a: 437). Furthermore, he divides the language domains into five areas covering, family, friendship, religion, work and education. He states that bilingual language users have a language choice and this choice can be dependent on the situation, e.g. a choice between formal or informal use of language. This means, for example, that a person in one domain can speak and use one language but changes to another language when entering another domain.

Later researchers added that age, gender, education and occupation widely influence the choice of language. Also elements such as interlocutors' language skills, vocabulary, family relations, topic, situation and the purpose of the interaction (for example, if the communication has a purpose of invoking authority, giving instructions or orders, or excluding someone from the conversation) can have an impact on the choice of language (Gal, 1979; Grosjean, 1982).

Pia Jarvad (2001) discusses how there is a possible domain loss in Danish and a shift to English. One can point out that there is a problem using the theory of domain loss in Scandinavia because the theory presupposes a multilingual society. Even though English is widely regarded as a global language, Scandinavia does not belong to the first inner circle where English is the first language (as it is, e.g., in England, New Zealand and the US). Nor does Scandinavia belong to the second circle where English is a second language (e.g. India and Singapore). On the contrary, Scandinavia belongs to the growing surrounding third circle where English is a foreign language (Crystal, 1997; Kachru, 1992). Thus, English in most cases does not in the Scandinavian countries have a position as a possible mother tongue, which is the case for other languages brought in by refugees and migrants from other parts of the world (e.g. Turkish, Persian, etc.). In those instances we have a clear example of multilingualism, where language users have the choice to shift between their original mother tongue and their new "mother tongue" or second language, e.g. Danish, Norwegian or Swedish.

However, it makes sense to compare the use of English and the use of Scandinavian languages, although the main question is not what makes a language user choose between their mother tongue and their second language (e.g. Turkish as opposed to Danish) in different scenarios? The question is rather what motivates the language users to give up using their own language – their mother tongue – in favor of a foreign language?

Jarvad examined the use of English in six domains in Denmark, in business, culture, administration and EU policy, consumption, science and education. The main results are, among other things, that in many businesses the working language is English particularly in those concerns that work in an international market. In the cultural arena, television and film have a leading role. Jarvad found that in 1993 about 80% of the programs on one of the private TV stations consisted of movies in a foreign language with subtitles in Danish. According to a study by Henrik Gottlieb (1994) foreign television programs with Danish subtitles are the most watched material in Denmark. About 85% of this material originates from English-speaking countries. When it comes to the use of English in administration and EU policy it seems that since the beginning of the 1990s use of Danish has been declining in favor of English, and politicians and officials are more or less forced to use English as a working language to have their opinions noticed. In the area of consumption and advertisements English is becoming increasingly visible. For example, more than 40% of the advertisements on television use English words and language, in many cases without translations or subtitles. In science English is an important language. Jarvad reports that back in 1990 31% of the scientific articles written at the theological, humanistic and sociological faculties at the University of Copenhagen were written in English. A look at natural science and medicine in the same year reveals that 82–84% of scientific articles were written in English. One can say conclusively that in 2001 English was already very obvious in different domains, and in some domains (e.g. in natural science and medicine) it even seems to some extent to have replaced Danish.

Jarvad's results were remarkable and also indicative of the situation in the two other Scandinavian countries. Newer research implies that English is still becoming more and more visible and gradually more used in all of Scandinavia. The digital revolution also seems to have had a major influence. Jónsson, Laurén, Myking & Picht (2013) have studied how professional communication is practiced in the Nordic countries. Like Jarvad they also conclude that English is increasingly used as a lingua franca especially in research and teaching at university level. In their study they also examine the use of the terms domain/domain loss and parallel language. Scandinavian professionals can write and communicate in English but will always have some limitations because English is not their mother tongue or second language. Also, it is noteworthy that it seems as if writers of international research literature never or seldom quote and refer to non-English literature. This indicates that if a researcher in, for example, Scandinavia wants his/her work to have an impact professionally he/she needs to communicate in English. The study by Jónsson *et al.* is organized around an analysis of documents concerning the language policies in the Nordic countries and the conclusions are, among other things, that it is necessary to implement an active language policy which aims to defend the domains; that is, to oppose and prevent a domain loss, especially in research and teaching (p. 171).

It is important to remember that though English is a dominant language today, other languages have during history vigorously influenced the Scandinavian languages. The vocabulary in the Scandinavian languages is today dominated by words from different languages though we today experience them as Scandinavian. In other words it is not a new thing that languages outside the Scandinavian area influence the Scandinavian languages. In fact it is a natural development.

At the beginning of the 20th century it was common and more or less required that Scandinavian academics could read and write in German and preferably also in French. English was rarely used as a transnational language, though known and used by some academics. The change in the situation today is that since the 1990s the requirements of internationalization/globalization in education have been satisfied by only using one language – English – which is a living first language in a large part of the world. That means that globalization is linked to the use of one – and only one – language (Haberland, 2009). One can claim that this has developed into a general discourse. Perhaps this is one of the reasons why young people choose to speak English when meeting peers from other Scandinavian countries. Speaking another language than English would – so to speak – be understood as a violation of the code of the general discourse.

An important question is also to what degree young people in Scandinavia understand the other Scandinavian languages? Do young people choose to use English because they do not understand the other Scandinavian languages?

Young people's understanding of Scandinavian languages

In 1976 Øivind Maurud conducted research on how young Scandinavian men understood the Scandinavian languages. Soldiers in Denmark, Norway and Sweden were exposed to spoken and written texts in the two other Scandinavian languages. The participants were tested by being asked questions about the contents of the texts. Also, they were asked to translate certain words in the texts into their own language. The results of the research were that Norwegians seemed to significantly better understand neighboring spoken languages than the Swedish and Danish participants, and the Danish participants were more capable of understanding the neighboring languages than their Swedish counterparts (Maurud, 1976).

Maurud's research has been criticized for having a skewed gender focus by not including females. As part of a common Nordic initiative "Inter Nordic Language Comprehension" Lars-Olof Delsing and Katarina Lundin Åkesson (2005) conducted research among young people in Scandinavia in 2002, this time including both male and female participants. The aim of the research was to find out how high school students in Scandinavia understood neighbor languages. Another purpose was to find out how well immigrants in Scandinavia understood the other Scandinavian languages. In addition, the research had a purpose of finding out how well young people living outside Scandinavia (that is young people in Finland, Iceland, Greenland and the Faroe Islands), understood the Scandinavian languages (Delsing & Åkesson, 2005).

Each participant was tested in the two Scandinavian languages that he/she did not speak. The participants all resided in one of the Scandinavian capitals, Copenhagen, Oslo or Stockholm. However, because of their geographical location, inhabitants of Copenhagen supposedly have a closer relationship to neighbor languages than for example inhabitants of Stockholm. To avoid biased results participants were also chosen from one other city in each of the Scandinavian countries, Århus in Denmark, Bergen in Norway and Malmö in Sweden. The test material included two sequences of listening comprehension and one sequence of reading comprehension. The test materials were all prefabricated texts and not texts arising in a communication situation.

The results of the study are in many ways the same as Maurud's. Young people in Norway seemed still to better understand their neighbors than their peers in Sweden and Denmark. They had an average score of 6.14 points out of 10, while young people in Sweden and Denmark had an average score of 4.38 and 3.87. Delsing and Åkesson's study also includes data from the other Nordic countries and it seems as if the young people in the Faroe Islands were best able to understand Danish, Swedish and Norwegian as they on average scored 7 points out of 10. Young people in Finland seemed to have most difficulties understanding the Scandinavian languages as they scored 2.14 points out of 10 (see Table 20.1).

Delsing and Åkesson also tested the participants' knowledge of English, though the test was less wide-ranging than the test of knowledge of neighbor languages (see Table 20.2). The results indicate that all participants understood English better than a neighbor language. However, the Norwegians seemed to understand Swedish better than English. The Norwegians and the Swedish participants seemed to understand English on an equal level, and the Danes seemed to understand it least.

The study concludes that most of the young people in Scandinavia were not especially good at understanding neighbor languages. The study also included a test of the participants' parents and it seems as if that generation was significantly better at understanding neighbor languages. Immigrants to Scandinavia did not manage to understand the neighbor languages as well as the native Scandinavians. Scandinavian high school students seemed to be capable of understanding English and almost all informants achieved a higher score for their knowledge of English than for their knowledge of neighbor languages.

The study was organized around different types of texts and not, for example, a communication situation. It would be interesting to know what language young people use when they have to solve a task over a longer time period, e.g. in a joint school project.

TABLE 20.1 The main results of the study by Delsing and Åkesson (2005)

Country	Test language: Danish	Test language: Norwegian	Test language: Swedish	Neighbor language (average)
Denmark	–	4.15	3.59	3.87
Sweden	3.80	4.97	–	4.38
Norway	6.07	–	6.21	6.14
Finland	1.54	1.63	3.24	2.14
Faroe Islands	8.28	7.00	5.75	7.00
Iceland	5.36	3.40	3.34	4.03
Greenland	6.61	3.73	2.23	4.19

TABLE 20.2 The results for knowledge of English (Delsing & Åkesson, 2005)

Country	Average knowledge of English	Country	Average knowledge of English
Denmark	5.7	Finland	6.02
Sweden	7.08	Faroe Islands	7.60
Norway	7.09	Iceland	7.17

Scandinavian languages in practice

In the last 10–15 years many Scandinavian teachers have taken part in joint projects involving schools and young people all over Scandinavia. Every year the Nordic Council supports different exchange and joint projects. An example of this is from 2014 where 69 high school students from Norway (23), Sweden (25) and Denmark (21) took part in a project that involved collaboration over the internet, two visits to partner schools and solving a joint project. All the students were 17 years old. The aim of the project was to research, compare and discuss how news is communicated in the three Scandinavian countries. The project was linked to courses in their mother tongue and sociology. Six teachers, two from each country, participated in the project. The project lasted eight months.

The students were interviewed in groups during and after they had finished the project.

The students first met in Norway where their initial assignment was to establish a digital communication platform. For that they used Skype, e-mail and established a joint private website hosted at the Norwegian partner school. The teachers reported that in the beginning the students started to communicate in English. All the assignments, however, were presented in one of the Scandinavian languages (Danish, Swedish and Norwegian) and it was expected that the students would submit their projects in the Scandinavian languages. According to the teachers it only took about one day before the students decided by themselves to speak in their mother tongues.

Throughout the project the students communicated by e-mail and Skype. Almost all digital communication was done in Scandinavian languages. English was rarely used and then only to explain words and concepts if some major misunderstandings arose.

When the students met face-to-face in the partner schools their work and social language was the three Scandinavian languages and not English except at the very beginning. Altogether, the students and their teachers met face-to-face three times, that is once in each participating school. The purpose of the meetings was to develop parts of the project and carry out certain tasks. All tasks were presented in one of the Scandinavian languages and all teachers' and students' presentations were done in the Scandinavian language.

During the project the students, among other things, were asked how well they communicated with each other. A majority or 98% of the participants stated that they preferred to speak in their own mother tongue when communicating with the students from the other Scandinavian countries. Also, they explained that they had little difficulty in understanding each other. The participants were asked whether they had more difficulty in understanding spoken language than written language. About 60% of the participants said that in some cases they better understood written language and that they better understood one language rather than another. Generally, the Danish students and the Swedish students seemed to understand better the Norwegian students' spoken language, whereas the Norwegian students better understood spoken Danish. When the Danish and the Swedish students spoke with each other it seemed as if in some cases they needed to make an extra effort. However, the students pointed out that as the project progressed the understanding of spoken language in all three Scandinavian languages got significantly better.

After the project the students were asked about their experience of using their own mother tongue to communicate with peers from the two other Scandinavian countries. All agreed that they had had a very good experience and that in future they probably would not communicate in English with people from the other Scandinavian countries. Many of the interviewed students agreed that "it's much easier and better to communicate in your own language instead of using a foreign language because then you can be much clearer and express your opinions on your own premises". Also, almost all the students stated that they had learned to be more open towards the Scandinavian languages. They said that it is only a question of better articulating, having patience and asking if you don't understand what is said the first time.

Almost all of the students and their teachers were very satisfied with the professional outcome of the project. Many students even claimed that if the project had been submitted in English the results would probably have been a little poorer. At least, they felt that it was easier to deal with and present the results of their work in Scandinavian languages. A group of students stated that using the Scandinavian languages made their final product more balanced, and they even experienced their approach as more well-thought-out.

Discussion and conclusion

Research and different kinds of data indicate that English is an increasingly dominant language in all of Scandinavia and that English is today an important foreign language. The results of testing young people, as for example Delsing and Åkesson (2005) did, indicate that even though young people understood some of the text materials in the two other neighbor languages presented to them in a test, their understanding was far from 100%. In fact, it seems as if the young people better understood text materials in English. However, it also seems that young people are willing to use and better understand neighbor languages, when they are part of communication and have an authentic purpose. Taking part in joint Scandinavian projects it looks as if the students both understand written and spoken language in a context where they are urged to, and the setting enforces the use of the Scandinavian languages. In most cases the students perceived it as a very positive experience. Many teachers express the same positive attitude when they report on joint exchange projects. Margareta Sihlberg and Peter Hobel (2005) for example describe a joint project between a high school in Stockholm and a high school in Copenhagen as being very successful. The students discovered that it was fairly easy to read texts in Swedish and Danish and to understand spoken Swedish and Danish. The students needed to make an effort but as soon as the code was broken, they found it easy to understand each other. The authors point out the fact that it was "motivating for the students to know that their own written products were a part of an authentic communication" (p. 210). In other words, when language learning and language use take place in an active setting and when it is context related, students feel much more motivated to use and learn another language. This insight is not new and has in fact been known in foreign language acquisition since the mid-1970s. Different pedagogies within foreign language learning have since then been developed to emphasize the use of language in an active, cooperative and collaborative context.

In Scandinavia, neighbor languages have been an obligatory part of the school curriculum. For many years this part of the curriculum was fulfilled by reading a text or two in the neighbor languages when learning the mother tongue. This is not a very active way of learning and understanding another language, because emphasis is first of all on translation and not on the use of language and the context the text or language appears in. The method is similar to the ancient grammar and translation method inherited from the teaching of Latin.

In the last 10–15 years teachers of neighbor languages have been more aware of developing a contemporary, active and context-based pedagogy, a pedagogy where collaboration, cooperation and task-based learning are keywords. Instead of only reading and translating texts in neighbor languages the purpose today is to activate all language skills (e.g. listening, reading, writing and talking) by letting the students work with different kinds of authentic, modern materials in order to communicate about them. The website "The Nordic countries in schools" (Norden i skolen: http://nordeniskolen.org/da) is a good example of teaching material using a more contemporary didactic. It is sponsored by the Nordic Council, free to use and consists of authentic texts, films, videos, audios and games organized in different themes. With each text and theme one can find different tasks of different complexity. On the website there is also a dictionary with audio, so students can hear the words; and classes (students and teachers) can through one part of the website find peers to collaborate with in the other Scandinavian countries. Almost 10,000 individuals are today registered users of the website. An initiative like this can be understood as an interesting and effective way to make young people aware of the necessity of conserving the uniqueness of the Scandinavian languages in a school context.

English is today an important language to learn – in Scandinavia as elsewhere. There is no doubt about that, but the question is whether English should be the preferred lingua franca in all contexts. There is today no reason to believe that the Scandinavian languages will die out although worldwide they are considered to be minor languages. The Scandinavian languages have through history been capable of taking in loans and changes without destroying their essence. The Scandinavian languages are constantly developing as are all other languages. But because Scandinavian languages are considered to be minor languages one needs to be aware of the direction in which the languages develop. It is necessary to outline a language policy as Jónsson *et al.* (2013) suggest in order to shape an overall framework for future development. Each country in Scandinavia has since the 1980s developed a reasonably clear policy in the field, but policies, laws and regulations do not guarantee viable development. Language develops due to practice – not because of a policy. When it comes to inter-Scandinavian language understanding it is of great importance that all Scandinavians – and perhaps especially the younger generation – understand why it is of great importance to conserve the ability to be able to understand and speak to each other in their own mother tongue. That is certainly a unique circumstance in a globalized and multilingual world.

References

Crystal, D. (1997). *English as a global language*. Cambridge: Cambridge University Press.

Delsing, L.-O., & Åkesson, K.L. (2005). *Håller språket ihop Norden?* (Vol. 573). Kbh.: Nordisk Ministerråd.

Faarlund, J.T., & Edmonds, E. (2014). *The language of the vikings* (Vol. 3). Olomouc: Palacký University.

Fishman, J.A. (1972a). Domains and the relationship between micro- and macrosociolinguistics. In J. Gumperz & D. Hymes (Eds), *Directions in sociolinguistics. The ethnography of speaking.* (pp. 407–434). New York: Holt, Rinehart and Winston.

Fishman, J.A. (1972b). *Language in sociocultural change: essays*. Stanford, CA: Stanford University Press.

Gal, S. (1979). *Language shift: social determinants of linguistic change in bilingual Austria*. New York: Academic Press.

Gottlieb, H. (1994). *Tekstning: synkron billedmedieoversættelse*. Kbh.: Center for Oversættelse, København Universitet.

Grosjean, F. (1982). *Life with two languages: an introduction to bilingualism* (5th printing. ed.). Cambridge, MA: Harvard University Press.

Haberland, H. (2009). English – the language of globalism? *Rask. Internationalt tidsskrift for sprog og kommunikation,* 17–45.

Jarvad, P. (2001). *Det danske sprogs status i 1990'erne med særlig henblik på domænetabe.* University of Copenhagen: Dansk sprognævn.

Jónsson, S., Laurén, J., Myking, J., & Picht, H. (2013). *Parallellspråk og domene: nordisk språkplanlegging på 2000-tallet.* Oslo: Novus forlag.

Kachru, B.B. (1992). *The other tongue: English across cultures* (2nd ed.). Urbana: University of Illinois Press.

Karker, A. (1983). Otte sprog i Norden. In A. Karker & B. Molde (Eds), *Sprogene i Norden* (pp. 1–7). Copenhagen: Gyldendal.

Lund, J. (2003). *Den sproglige dagsorden. Udfordringer til dansk sprog [The language agenda. Challenges for the Danish language].* Copenhagen: Gyldendal.

Lund, J. (2006). Norden, de nordiske sprog – og nordisk sprogpolitik. In L. Madsen (Ed.), *Nabosprogsdidaktik* (pp. 19–39). Copenhagen: Dansklærerforeningen.

Maurud, Ø. (1976). *Nabospråksforståelse i Skandinavia: en undersøkelse om gjensidig forstaelse av tale- og skriftspråk i Danmark, Norge og Sverige.* Stockholm: Nordiska rådet.

Nickelsen, T. (2012). English is a Scandinavian language. *Apollon.* http://sciencenordic.com/english-scandinavian-language

Sihlberg, M., & Hobel, P. (2005). Når elever mødes, og nabosprog bliver talt – nabosprogsundervisning i gymnasiet. In L. Madsen (Ed.), *Nabosprogsdidaktit* (pp. 199–216). Copenhagen: Dansklærerforeningen.

POSTSCRIPT

Lindsay Peer and Gavin Reid

This book we hope continues the pioneering work established through the British Dyslexia Association's 1st International Conference on Multilingualism in 1999, and we are delighted by the follow-up initiatives that have taken place. The contents of this book are evidence that – although we all agree there is much to be done still – there is without doubt vigorous research and insightful classroom practices taking place. We are also indebted to those contributors who have identified the wider social and cultural issues that are so important for individuals and families. This book therefore has not only educational implications but implications for policy, communities and society.

We do wish to identify three key points to take this debate forward as a postscript to this book:

1. **International collaboration** – there has been evidence of this in the book and it is crucial that this must continue – all countries can learn from each other.
2. **Multidimensional research** – we need to continue to focus not only on the classroom and literacy angle but on the implications of this for successful learning, and particularly the impact of this on young people with dyslexia.
3. **Positive appreciation** – when children are faced with difficulties, and demands on teachers increase, it is all too easy to focus on the challenges and unwittingly portray a negative perspective. It is important that this is turned on its head and that the positive aspects of bi/multilingualism – which have been covered in this book – are highlighted and gain prominence.

Once again we wish to thank all the contributors and the publishing team at Routledge for supporting us in this endeavour.

INDEX